6/18

Oliver!

Oliver!
A Dickensian Musical

Marc Napolitano

OXFORD
UNIVERSITY PRESS

OXFORD
UNIVERSITY PRESS

Oxford University Press is a department of the University of
Oxford. It furthers the University's objective of excellence in research,
scholarship, and education by publishing worldwide.

Oxford New York

Auckland Cape Town Dar es Salaam Hong Kong Karachi
Kuala Lumpur Madrid Melbourne Mexico City Nairobi
New Delhi Shanghai Taipei Toronto

With offices in

Argentina Austria Brazil Chile Czech Republic France Greece
Guatemala Hungary Italy Japan Poland Portugal Singapore
South Korea Switzerland Thailand Turkey Ukraine Vietnam

Oxford is a registered trademark of Oxford University Press
in the UK and certain other countries.

Published in the United States of America by
Oxford University Press
198 Madison Avenue, New York, NY 10016

© Oxford University Press 2014

Library of Congress Cataloging-in-Publication Data
Napolitano, Marc.
Oliver! : a Dickensian musical / Marc Napolitano.
pages cm
Includes bibliographical references and index.
ISBN 978-0-19-936482-4 (hardcover : alk. paper)
1. Bart, Lionel. Oliver! 2. Musicals—History and criticism. I. Title.
ML410.B2587N36 2014
782.1'4—dc23
2014003286

3 5 7 9 8 6 4 2
Printed in the United States of America
on acid-free paper

With love and gratitude to my first and greatest teachers,
my mother and father.

CONTENTS

PREFACE AND ACKNOWLEDGMENTS

Like Charles Dickens, my fondness for the theater emerged at an early age. Although my elementary school did not have a drama program, a team of long-suffering soccer moms unfailingly arranged an annual musical revue. The shows were hardly master-pieces, and our parents seemed more interested in photographing us in our costumes than paying attention to what exactly we were attempting to enact, but I remember the palpable sense of excitement that everyone felt when the yearly set of musical numbers was revealed.

In the fifth grade, the revue was set to include numbers from a show called *Oliver!* At the urging of my father, I rented the film version, and from the moment that the workhouse orphans descended the dilapidated staircases to sing "Food, Glorious Food," I was enthralled. I wept for Oliver, delighted at the antics of the Artful Dodger, cowered in the presence of Bill Sikes, fell in love with Nancy, and was instantly cap-tivated by Fagin, so much so that I could actually see myself joining the ranks of the pintsized pickpockets who made up his gang. Even more captivating was the film's musical score; Lionel Bart's enchanting melodies embedded themselves in my memory forever. As a result of watching this film, my excitement about participat-ing in the revue increased exponentially, and I was delighted at the thought of step-ping into the role of a cockney urchin and crooning "Consider Yourself" alongside my classmates.

If someone had told me then that I would one day be a Dickensian whose research would focus primarily on musical adaptations of Boz's works, I probably would not have believed him. Nevertheless, my fondness for *Oliver!* has brought things full circle, for it was *Oliver!* that served as my introduction to Dickens. True, I had previ-ously read *A Christmas Carol*, and I had watched several film versions of that immortal novella, but Dickensian London did not truly come alive for me until I experienced *Oliver!* Though I was in store for some unpleasant surprises a few years later when I actually took up *Oliver Twist* for the first time (the very thought of Fagin as an evil villain was shocking to me), watching *Oliver!* marked the beginning of what would become a lifelong fascination with Dickens's stories and characters.

I doubt that many academics are given the chance to work on projects that involve their studying the two subjects that they most love—in my case, Dickens and musical theater. I am deeply indebted to Oxford University Press for granting me the oppor-tunity to do so, and to Norm Hirschy for his unwavering belief in the project and his unceasing interest and encouragement throughout its evolution. I am likewise grateful to Lisbeth Redfield for her guidance and patience, and to my reviewers, whose advice has proved indispensable in refining my manuscript.

Over the course of my research, I have received a significant amount of assistance from a wide variety of people. I would like to thank the numerous archivists, librarians, producers, and theater managers who have aided me in my attempts to untangle the convoluted and contradictory history of *Oliver!* especially Rosy Runciman of the Cameron Mackintosh Archives and Brenda Evans of the Lionel Bart Foundation. Without their tireless assistance, this project would never have come to fruition. I am likewise indebted to Sir Cameron Mackintosh, Lady Nobuko Albery, Derek Dawson, John Cohen, Ian Albery, Chelsea Weathers and Helen Baer of the Harry Ransom Center, Kristy Davis of the Mander and Mitchenson Collection, the fantastic staff at the Victoria and Albert Museum's Theatre Collection, the librarians at the University of Bristol Theatre Collection, the personnel at the BFI Archives, and the research librarians at the University of North Carolina at Chapel Hill, especially Tommy Nixon. I am equally grateful to the various parties who shared their personal reflections on *Oliver!* and the life and career of Lionel Bart; my fondest thanks to Tsai Chin, Alastair Davidson, Edna Doré, Julian Glover, Jack Grossman, Roger Hardwick, Harry Landis, Carmen Munroe, Donald Pippin, Trevor Ray, and Tony Robinson.

I would like to offer my most sincere gratitude to Allan Life, Tim Carter, Laurie Langbauer, Beverly Taylor, Tom Reinert, Jeanne Moskal, Joe Viscomi, Deborah Thomas, Crystal Lucky, Lauren Shohet, Heather Hicks, Sterling Delano, Robert Wilkinson, Kate Matthews, and Tom Arduini. I am also incredibly grateful to my colleagues at West Point for their collegiality and support, most especially to Scott Krawczyk, Elizabeth Samet, Sean Cleveland, Peter Molin, Nicholas Utzig, Tony McGowan, and Robert Mcloughlin for their guidance and counsel.

Information and text in this book appeared previously in my article "Can a Fellow Be a Villain All His Life?: Fagin, Jewishness, and Musical Performance" as published in *Ecumenica: Journal of Theatre and Performance* 6.1 (Spring 2013). My thanks to *Ecumenica*'s editorial board and to Carolyn Roark. I would like to thank the various parties who granted permission for the use of the photos and illustrations featured in this book. Every effort has been made to trace and contact copyright holders.

No expression of gratitude would be complete without acknowledging my family, whose faith has sustained me throughout the rigors of academia, and whose love I am thankful for every day of my life. I am particularly grateful to my mother, Joann, for her tireless aid and encouragement. Mom, you are, and always shall be, my hero— thank you for believing in me. I am likewise thankful to my father, Ralph, whose passion for education has been an inspiration to me from my childhood onward. Thanks also to my brother, Scott, my sister, Christa, and my brother-in-law, Chris, for never growing tired of my incessant talk of Charles Dickens. To my Nanna, and also to my Nonno, who sadly did not live to see this publication, I will always strive toward your wisdom, your courage, and your character.

COMPANION WEBSITE FOR
OLIVER!: A DICKENSIAN MUSICAL

www.oup.com/us/oliver

Oxford has created a website to accompany *Oliver!: A Dickensian Musical.* The reader is encouraged to consult this resource, which presents several appendices containing information regarding *Oliver!*'s production history. Appendix A offers a summary of Bart's musical, while Appendix B presents a summary of Dickens's original text for the point of comparison; of note is Bart's omission of Monks, which eliminates the inheritance plot that drives the second half of Dickens's novel. Appendix C recounts the backstage "feud" between Ron Moody and Georgia Brown during the initial West End production and presents specific details regarding the onstage improvisations that so frustrated both parties. Finally, Appendix D offers a listing of major West End and Broadway productions of *Oliver!*, while Appendix E presents a discography of various recordings of the musical score.

Oliver!

Introduction

This text is a "biography" of Lionel Bart's *Oliver!*, the most popular and success-ful English musical from the golden age of Broadway. The previous sentence is admittedly paradoxical, for it defines *Oliver!* as English while simultaneously fram-ing its historical popularity in the context of an American theatrical institution. This paradox connects to the more general and enduring contradiction posed by the term *English musical*, for, as Sheridan Morley once quipped, during the aforemen-tioned golden age "the descriptive 'musical' barely needed the modifying 'Broadway' or 'American', so closely were the terms allied."[1] Morley had previously noted that "the British stage musical has never achieved on its home territory the dominance that its American counterpart has had on Broadway: the musical is without any doubt America's greatest achievement in the live theatre in this century."[2] The overt "Englishness" of Bart's musical is therefore all the more significant when set against the historical American dominance of the stage musical as a theatrical genre.

Oliver!'s Englishness is an inescapable part of its legacy. For many English crit-ics and theatergoers, this trait was the defining characteristic of Bart's musical. As such, I briefly considered calling this text *Oliver!: An English Musical*. The designation seems fair. After all, *Oliver!* was written by an Englishman. It premiered in London. It embraced several English traditions (both theatrical and musical). It was adapted from a canonical English novel. This final quality alludes to my revised title, which purposefully draws attention to the literary roots of Bart's masterpiece, though my labeling *Oliver!* a "Dickensian musical" as opposed to an "English musical" may seem like hair-splitting given Dickens's remarkable status as the most conspicuously English novelist of his—or any—age. Malcolm Andrews observed that

> [i]n his own day Dickens was recognised as a master of the knowledge of English life: 'he is so thoroughly English, and is now part and parcel of that mighty aggre-gate of national fame which we feel bound to defend on all points against attack.' This review appeared in 1850, soon after *David Copperfield* had come to an end, when Dickens was on the crest of his career. Even a century and a quarter later, it is hard to think of any other English writer whose imaginative world remains so fully assimilated into the national identity.[3]

The fact that Bart based his musical on a Dickens novel reinforced his piece's Englishness in a way that perhaps no other source could.

Nevertheless, calling *Oliver!* a Dickensian musical carries its own semantic burdens. These burdens do not necessarily relate to the musical's fidelity (or lack thereof) to its textual source; just because *Oliver!* takes tremendous liberties with Dickens's story, characters, and themes does not preclude its being "Dickensian." Adhering to now out-moded theories of adaptation, one might describe *Oliver!* as being "true to the spirit" of Dickens, and many critics did precisely that. Furthermore, Bart found the ideal means of reinforcing *Oliver!*'s English identity and Dickensian pedigree through his approach to the musical score. Though *Oliver!*'s musical narrative is organized according to the tenets of the American book musical, many of its songs are steeped in the traditions of the English music hall. In this framework, Bart's achievement in creating *Oliver!* seems fairly straightforward: in spite of his writing in the American tradition of the postwar Broadway musical, he created an unmistakably English musical through his creative merging of two English cultural institutions: Dickens and music hall.

Such an interpretation is a broad oversimplification of a more complex cultural relationship, as dictated by the abstractness and ambiguity surrounding the afore-mentioned terms and institutions. This abstractness seems inescapable when dis-cussing *Oliver!*'s Englishness, for the vague *idea* of *Oliver!* as an English musical was essential to its popularity in the United Kingdom; countless reviewers drew atten-tion to this characteristic and promoted *Oliver!* with something bordering on nation-alistic excitement. But was *Oliver!* English simply because it seemed a direct counter-offensive to the American shows that had invaded the West End and dominated the musical genre up to that point? That position is complicated by the fact that Bart bor-rowed heavily from the American musical tradition. Still, this reality presented yet another opportunity for the English press to tout the show as an English triumph. Through *Oliver!*, the English had allegedly beaten the Americans at their own game.

The "internal" components of *Oliver!* that highlighted its English roots—namely, its Dickensian pedigree and its music-hall score—were likewise associated with dis-courses on Englishness and English community. Indeed, the English public's cultiva-tion of a sense of English community around *Oliver!* was ironically evocative of these two components. In his own era, Dickens constantly promoted the notion of his read-ership as a large and diverse community, noting in the first issue of *Household Words*, "[w]e hope to be the comrade and friend of many thousands of people, of both sexes, and of all ages and conditions, on whose faces we may never look. [. . .] In the bosoms of the young and old, of the well-to-do and of the poor, we would tenderly cher-ish that light of Fancy which is inherent in the human breast."[4] The latter sentence hints that Dickens ambitiously sought to build a community of humanity as opposed to a community of Englishmen (and women); still, the English circulation and the intrinsically English concerns of *Household Words*, as chronicled by Sabine Clemm in her outstanding text, resulted in the construction of a distinctly English community founded on the notion of the journal (and of Dickens himself) as a distinctly English institution. The transition from author to institution may have reduced Dickens to an abstraction, but it likewise made his popularity all the more transcendent. Just as the concept of *Oliver!*'s Englishness, as supplemented by its Dickensian roots, was vital to its fame and acclaim, Juliet John has noted that "[t]he idea of Dickens was integral to the popularity of his writings."[5]

The other uniquely English component of Bart's adaptation—the music-hall-influenced score—evokes similar examples of communities built around abstract *ideas* of Englishness. The romanticized image of East Enders congregating in taverns to sing comical cockney ballads has become part of the lore surrounding the music hall, and it remained a vital concept even as music hall evolved into a more regimented and mainstream form of entertainment. Truthfully, the image gained further dominance *after* this evolution as traditionalists lamented the loss of "authentic" working-class intimacy for the sake of mass entertainment; still, that evolution likewise resulted in the building of a significantly larger, interclass English community (yet another link to Dickens, as John has written that "Dickens must have been the first novelist to consciously cultivate the idea of a cross-class 'intimate public' in order to bond a mass readership"[6]). Though these images, and the laments that they eventually inspired, rested on broad generalizations, their mutual effect was to promote the same communal and popular notions described above: music hall, like Dickens, became synonymous with Englishness, and more specifically, with "cross-class" English community.

In the context of Benedict Anderson's discussion of nationalism and the nation, this phenomenon is all the more fitting, for "regardless of the actual inequality and exploitation that may prevail in each, the nation is always conceived as a deep, horizontal comradeship."[7] The belief that everyone in Victorian England was reading Dickens, or that everyone in England knew the songs of the music halls, was essential to the growth and sustainment of these communities and the larger Englishness that they represented. In all of the aforementioned cases, however, the emphasis on community can be regarded with a certain skepticism, though that same skepticism may very well apply to the notion of the English national community as a whole. Anderson famously used the term "imagined communities" when discussing nationalism, noting that "the members of even the smallest nation will never know most of their fellow-members, meet them, or even hear of them, yet in the minds of each lives the image of their communion."[8] Granted, actual communion can in fact exist within the preceding examples: friends might congregate to read Dickens (or to hear his works read aloud), people might visit the music hall together, and certainly, an audience of theatergoers experiencing *Oliver!* briefly shared a communal experience for those two and a half hours. Nevertheless, part of the draw of these cultural activities was the notion that, by participating, one was establishing oneself as part of a much larger community made up of thousands of people whom one would never meet face to face, as Dickens himself notes in the previously quoted passage from *Household Words*: the imagined community of Dickens's readership, the imagined community of the music hall, and the imagined community of *Oliver!*—each one a microcosm of the imagined community of England.

In keeping with this discussion of imagined communities and manufactured national identities, it is important to consider that the two most overtly English components of *Oliver!*—its Dickensian background and its music-hall score—are similarly ambiguous and imprecise. As noted, the Dickensian component of *Oliver!* is nebulous, relating more to ideas, impressions, and images that we popularly associate with Dickens and with *Oliver Twist* itself as opposed to concrete realities regarding the writer, his narrative, and his social vision as documented in his text. There is a basic distinction between Dickens and Dickensian, even though Dickens himself sought to weaken that distinction in the hope of transforming himself from an English author into an English cultural phenomenon. Similarly, Peter Bailey has noted that the term "music hall" is an abstraction that "mobilises a limited but still resonant set of associations that fall into place in a familiar collage of names and images."[9] In light of these ambiguities, it is not surprising that the notion of *Oliver!* as an English musical (or as a Dickensian musical) is vague and complex...like the notion of Englishness itself.

It is here, however, that the historical significance of *Oliver!* becomes most apparent, for *Oliver!*'s Englishness reflects the concerns of a distinct period and context, namely, the postwar era. Certainly, the cultural tumult and general fragmentation of this period necessitated new definitions of Englishness, and the very concept of Englishness now seemed threatened by the collapse of the empire, the final failure of Victorianism, and perhaps more significantly, by a globalized Western culture dominated by the United States. John ironically notes that Dickens himself may have anticipated such a usurpation despite his living in an era defined by English global supremacy: "Seeing America for the first time, Dickens realized that the future of what he saw as mass culture might be American as opposed to Dickensian."[10] The American musical's dominance over the West End musical theater at the time of *Oliver!*'s debut was just one example of this larger cultural trend, and the nationalistic notion that *Oliver!* allowed the English to break the American monopoly on modern musical theater is vital to understanding its enduring power.

Moreover, *Oliver!*, with its reliance on Dickensian tropes and music-hall songs, was infused with an old-fashioned Englishness; still, to say that *Oliver!*'s popularity was attributable to a nostalgia for Victorian Englishness, for Dickensian domesticity, or for the empire seems false in light of the musical's dynamic, contemporary energy and subversive spirit—after all, the true heart of *Oliver!*'s narrative lies with Fagin and his gang as opposed to lying with the respectable Victorian gentleman, Mr. Brownlow. Hence, *Oliver!*'s Englishness is steeped in a more general longing for a sense of English community, as embodied by Dickens and the music hall. However artificial these two institutions—and their imagined communities—may have been, their centrality to the discourse surrounding Englishness was unquestionable, even in the postwar age...especially in the postwar age. Building off Antony Easthope's theories of contemporary Englishness, Clemm astutely notes that there is a sharp contrast between an imagined community and an imaginary community, for the "act of imagination exists side by side with the material manifestations of nationhood in a mutually dependent symbiosis."[11] As Easthope points out, national cultures are created "through institutions, practices and traditions" but also "through narratives and discourses."[12] Certainly, the "narratives and discourses" surrounding *Oliver!* were laden with references to the show's national identity, as "epitomized" by its Dickensian roots and music-hall score, and the triumph of *Oliver!* as an English musical represented the larger triumph of the cultural narratives surrounding Dickens and music hall as embodiments of Englishness: the communal Englishness associated with these two cultural institutions was central to the public's understanding of *Oliver!*'s own Englishness, and thus, to *Oliver!*'s nationalistic success. However artificial or constructed the Dickensian components of *Oliver!* (or the very notion of Dickensian-ness) may be, *Oliver!*'s success is therefore evocative of Dickens's own view regarding the ability of popular art and mass entertainment to facilitate a sense of English community in the face of modernity; John writes that

> Dickens strives to project utopian, sometimes nostalgic visions of cultural unity and community which are the salve to anxieties arising from his instinctive cultural modernity. As we have seen, certain popular cultural forms offered Dickens a model in this respect. Modern 'mass' culture, at its best, would for Dickens enable a larger 'imagined community' to replace lost or passing forms of communal and cultural activity.[13]

Notably, the central theme of *Oliver!* is community, and Oliver himself temporarily achieves the "utopian, nostalgic vision" described above when he becomes part of the thieves' den; though the world of the thieves revolves heavily around the idea of imagination (as a conniving old thief becomes a benevolent and tuneful patriarch, picking pockets becomes a music-hall routine, and a decrepit den becomes a joyous world of music and laughter) this is not an imagined community but an interactive community made up of the most cohesive and musical collection of characters in the piece. It is also the group that most directly embodies the Englishness of Dickens and music hall.

In calling *Oliver!* a Dickensian musical, I should likewise acknowledge that *Oliver!* is arguably the most popular version of Dickens's *Oliver Twist* ever created—no small achievement given the multitude of stage and screen versions of this particular novel. Indeed, *Oliver!* may be the most popular and widely known adaptation of *any* Dickensian text not featuring the words *Christmas* or *carol* in the title. The general public's familiarity with the story of the orphan who dared to ask for more gruel (and with Dickensian waifs in general) seems inextricably connected to their familiarity with Bart's memorable and infinitely singable musical score. Literary purists may object to this phenomenon in light of Bart's deviations from his source, yet Bart's creative liberties in writing *Oliver!* seem strangely inconsequential in this context, for his adaptation—whatever its infidelities—is partly responsible for the unceasing cultural resonance of Dickens's text and characters. In fact, the purist argument becomes somewhat absurd in light of the aforementioned ambiguities surrounding the very word *Dickensian*. As noted, Dickens does not simply exist in the concrete words of his texts, but also in our abstract popular memory, and the cultural memory of *Oliver Twist* has invariably been shaped by the popularity of *Oliver!*

That same popularity, and the popularity of the stage musical as a theatrical genre, has previously inhibited serious scholarly engagement and analysis, though fittingly, this was once true of Dickens. The line between *Oliver Twist* and *Oliver!* has become blurred, but Dickens himself blurred lines between serious literature and popular reading.[14] He also blurred the lines between the man and the authorial persona, between the object and the image.

Oliver! built on and contributed to the traditional mass appeal of Dickens. It also anticipated a new tradition of English musical theater that would fully embrace the possibilities of mass culture. Andrew Lloyd Webber has described Lionel Bart as "the father of the modern British musical"[15]—high praise, particularly coming from someone of Lloyd Webber's prominence. Still, Lloyd Webber's description complicates the assessment of *Oliver!* as an English musical, in part because Lloyd Webber's own musicals, though English in origin, seem to be defined by their global dominance as opposed to a specific Englishness (or even a specific Britishness). Nevertheless, following its West End debut, *Oliver!* achieved a level of global success that was unprecedented in the history of English musical theater. Bart did everything in his power to encourage this global popularity; he likewise met his fair share of suspicion and resentment from American critics on first sending *Oliver!* to Broadway. In this and many other respects, *Oliver!* anticipated the "megamusical"[16] movement, and the fact that a musical inspired by a Dickens novel exerted such influence on the foundations of contemporary English musical theater is yet another example of the Victorian author's unique legacy in the realms of English culture and global mass culture.

I began this introduction by acknowledging the paradoxical nature of the text's subtitle and transitioning to the more general paradoxes surrounding *Oliver!* as an "English musical," but as Jay Clayton notes, such paradoxes have come to define Dickens's place in contemporary culture: "Incongruity, contradiction, the juxtaposition of mismatched signifiers and ill-assorted values—these are the tokens by which Dickens travels today."[17] If Dickens is, as Clayton suggests "perhaps the most 'postmodern' Victorian writer,"[18] *Oliver!* is perhaps the most significant example of Dickens's postmodern incongruities. In view of these cultural concerns, the purpose of this text is not strictly archival, though the story of *Oliver!*'s development, debut, and legacy is essential. However, the text also analyzes *Oliver!* in relation to Dickens while avoiding the trappings of traditional fidelity criticism. As the previous pages have hinted, to measure *Oliver!* solely in relation to *Oliver Twist* is to ignore the larger theoretical and cultural issues surrounding the popular legacy of this adaptation.

Chapter 1 traces the various and distinctive historical narratives that shaped the development of *Oliver!*, including the story of *Oliver Twist*'s adaptive afterlives, the evolution of the postwar English theater, the development of English pop music, and the emergence of Lionel Bart as a dominant force in both of these aforementioned postwar cultural institutions. Bart's success in adapting Dickens's novel was due in large part to the sense of theatrical and musical experimentation that defined the era in which he wrote. The rebellious youth culture of the postwar era, the "fashionable" working-class culture of the 1950s, and the theatrical experimentalism that helped transition the West End from drawing-room comedies to kitchen-sink dramas all coalesced to facilitate Bart's theatrical education, allowing him to showcase his skills as a songwriter whose lyrics and melodies were shaped by the cockney culture of the East End.

Chapters 2 and 3 chronicle *Oliver!*'s development, as Bart and his creative team spent months writing and rewriting the musical. Bart's initial efforts to frame the adaptation as a Tommy Steele vehicle underscore his "poperetta" approach to adapting Dickens. Nevertheless, Bart's main collaborators, notably set designer Sean Kenny and director Peter Coe, helped to ground the project more fully in the Dickensian source, adding the necessary "grit" to balance out the "glitz" that defined Bart's initial conception. While Chapter 2 traces Coe's revisions to the libretto, Chapter 3 gives particular attention to Kenny's contributions, as his groundbreaking scenery helped to define both the narrative and the tone of Bart's adaptation. Kenny's massive and revolutionary set, now regarded as being decades ahead of its time, is yet another indication of *Oliver!*'s influence upon the megamusicals of the 1980s.

In spite of its tumultuous developmental period, *Oliver!* proved an immediate triumph in the West End. Chapter 4 documents the positive reception of the piece by English audiences and critics, who, somewhat strikingly, chose to ignore the musical's infidelity to its literary forebear. Instead, English theatergoers and reviewers rejoiced in the creation of what they considered to be a distinctly English musical, honing in on the Dickensian narrative and the music-hall-influenced score as representative of this Englishness. Though this understanding of the show oversimplified the complex cultural legacies of these institutions, the fact that these components proved vital to the idea of *Oliver!*'s Englishness reinforces their significance to discussions (and constructions) of Englishness.

Chapter 5 presents a reading of the musical and documents how Bart used music to compensate for the loss of Dickens's verbose narrator, to accentuate the emotional highpoints of Dickens's novel, and to develop the personalities of Dickens's characters. Bart centered his adaptation on the question of "Where Is Love?" tracing Oliver's journey from desolate isolation to joyful camaraderie. However, he also complicated that journey through the musical and cultural contrasts between Oliver's hidden middle-class pedigree and his friendship with the thieves; the disparity between the working-class communal ethos of "Consider Yourself" and the middle-class competitive ethos of "Who Will Buy?" epitomizes this complication. Bart's redemption of Fagin, another subversive challenge to the Victorian conservatism of the original text, likewise complicates Oliver's progression by presenting the old man as a potentially more desirable guardian than the middle-class Mr. Brownlow. The chapter also addresses the complexity of Nancy, whose tragic storyline served as a poignant indication of Bart's determination to "raise the stakes" of the postwar English musical libretto.

Chapter 6 recounts the global reception of *Oliver!* as the show proved to be one of the first English postwar musicals to achieve significant acclaim abroad. The 1963 Broadway production of *Oliver!* proved a rousing success, temporarily reversing the direction of the one-way traffic between Broadway and the West End. The popularity of international productions of *Oliver!* established a viable global market for the big-budget 1968 film adaptation, as discussed in Chapter 7. Highly decorated and widely popular, the film version reinforced the work's influence on the general perception of *Oliver Twist*, significantly molding the cultural perception of the original novel and creating an even larger global community for Bart's revised vision of Dickens's social polemic. Notably, the film would likewise influence subsequent revivals of the stage property, as the conventions of the contemporary megamusical facilitated the adaptation of Bart's music-hall show into a "poperetta" steeped in cinematic grandeur. Chapter 7 concludes with an analysis of the reinvention of this musical, as conducted under the watchful eye of the English impresario Sir Cameron Mackintosh.

In attempting to write *Oliver!*'s biography, I have had to face the unfortunate reality that the paper trail is woefully insufficient. Key drafts of the libretto and musical score have been lost to posterity, and much of what remains is incomplete or undated, thus negating any hope of a precise chronology. Furthermore, there are conflicting accounts of various aspects of the show's development. These inconsistencies revealed themselves early on in the musical's existence, and even the show's producer, Sir Donald Albery, felt as though it was impossible to create an exact account of the musical's gestation.[19] In regard to the numerous periodicals cited throughout this text, I have frequently had to rely on archival scrapbooks, several of which have lacked complete or accurate citation information. I have endeavored to overcome these deficiencies to the best of my ability; what follows is a logical approximation of how *Oliver!* evolved from a vague concept inspired by an immortal (and highly marketable) image to a set of incredibly memorable songs, to a full-scale Dickensian adaptation, to a revolutionary and enduring English musical.

CHAPTER 1

⌒

Setting the Stage: *Oliver Twist*, Lionel Bart, and Cultural Contexts

One of the innumerable challenges presented by *Oliver!* is the inclination to view it in a vacuum as the only enduring English musical from the pre–Lloyd Webber era. Doing so certainly adds to its distinctiveness (and simultaneously, to the significance of Lionel Bart's achievement), and the general dearth of "canonical" English musicals from the postwar era through the 1970s implies that there is a basic reality to this oversimplification. However, given the sheer multiplicity of texts and contexts that influenced the development of *Oliver!*, such generalizations are ultimately antithetical to developing an authentic understanding of Bart's Dickensian musical as a product of its period. Moreover, although *Oliver!*'s Englishness is arguably its most important and enduring quality, the abstract nature of Englishness, coupled with the fact that traditional definitions of this trait were in a state of flux at the time Bart was writing, requires that *Oliver!*'s biography be contextualized in relation to larger cultural movements. Before proceeding with a discussion of how Bart's theatrical and musical background shaped his approach to conceptualizing *Oliver!*, this chapter will explore four of the most noteworthy cultural trends to influence his musical: (1) the evolution of *Oliver Twist* from text to "culture text"; (2) the postwar English theater's reflections of (and contributions to) general English cultural shifts; (3) the emphasis on pop and rock music in postwar English youth culture and the gradual development of English pop; and (4) the stagnation of the English musical in the wake of the integrated American musical's apotheosis.

THE *TWISTIAN* CULTURE TEXT

Oliver Twist remains one of Dickens's most well-known works thanks largely to its afterlife in various media. In her sourcebook on the novel, Juliet John asserts that it "has become, in Paul Davis' phrase, a 'culture text',"[1] borrowing the term that Davis coined to characterize *A Christmas Carol*: "We remember the *Carol* as a cluster of phrases, images, and ideas. The images of Tim riding on Bob Cratchit's shoulder or of Scrooge huddled behind his desk while Bob shivers on his high stool are etched on our consciousness; 'Bah! Humbug!' and 'God bless us, every one!' echo in our minds."[2] Many of Davis's points are immediately applicable to *Oliver Twist*: the images of Oliver standing before the copper with his bowl or of Fagin standing over the fireplace with his toasting fork are etched on our consciousness; Oliver's "Please, sir, I want some more" and Fagin's raspy "my dears" echo in our minds. The immortal scene in which the title character asks for a second helping, a scene which Paul Schlicke describes as "mythically evocative," is "perhaps the most widely known image Dickens ever created."[3] In fact, the only Dickensian text to eclipse *Oliver Twist* in the realm of popular adaptations is the "mythical" *Christmas Carol*. As in the case of *A Christmas Carol*, the basic appeal of *Oliver Twist* is elemental—equivalent in many ways to the primordial power of fairy tales.

The development of the *Twist*ian culture text reinforces the power of adaptations, and it also underscores the marketability of the story. The very existence of a culture text implies that a story has been retold so many times in popular media it has ingrained itself in the cultural consciousness of a population, a feat that can only be achieved in contemporary society if the story is commercially viable. According to Mary Cross, some advertisers believe that "[a]ds are mere mirrors, just reflecting culture, not creating it."[4] Similarly, it is possible to view adaptations of *Oliver Twist* as historical artifacts that reflect the cultural values of the period in which they were produced. However, Cross counters this argument by pointing out that "some of the

Figure 1.1: Oliver Twist asking for more: arguably the most enduring and powerful image in the entire Dickens canon.
Source: Production of *Oliver!* at Theatre Royal, Drury Lane. Photograph by Catherine Ashmore. Copyright Oliver Productions Ltd. & Oliver Promotions Ltd.

first words we speak are brand names; some of the first rhymes we remember and first tunes we hum are straight out of commercials. [...] [W]e learn to shop, participating in the system by choosing and consuming products."[5] The notion of advertisements creating and shaping culture rather than simply echoing it is analogous to the notion that adaptations create and shape the public understanding of their source texts. Though *Oliver!* obviously *reflects* the values of the 1950s and early 1960s, its true significance lies in its *defining* the popular perception of *Oliver Twist*.

The power of *Twist* adaptations to influence the general perception of Dickens's text dates all the way back to the Victorian era. H. Philip Bolton's archival text *Dickens Dramatized* indicates that, in the nineteenth century, *Twist* was the most regularly adapted of Dickens's novels. Hack playwrights repeatedly pirated *Twist* in the hope of crafting a marketable melodrama, and many of these nineteenth-century adaptations read like virtual duplications of their predecessors. The regular recurrence of certain scenes reinforces the idea that the theatrical versions of *Oliver Twist* staged in this era were actually adaptations of adaptations, as opposed to their being adaptations of Dickens's novel, a fact that is essential to understanding the concept of *Twist* as a culture text.[6] This trend has continued up to the present day: recent adaptations of *Oliver Twist* have clearly been influenced by *Oliver!*, while *Oliver!* is heavily patterned on the 1948 David Lean film.

The general tendencies in Victorian adaptations of *Oliver Twist* were initiated by the very first stage version, an unfortunate "burletta in two acts" written before Dickens had completed his text.[7] More successful early stage adaptations, including C. Z. Barnett's version, first staged in May 1838, and George Almar's version, first staged in November of that same year, dramatize many of the same chapters and emphasize similar emotional highpoints. Table 1.1 breaks down the original novel in terms of essential events in the plot, documenting which of these episodes were included in various adaptations produced in the mid-Victorian era and the early twentieth century.[8]

Several of the patterns are obvious: the workhouse is omitted, the Maylie scenes are significantly condensed or eliminated entirely, comic scenes involving the Bumbles are always included (and frequently open up the play), and heavy emphasis is placed on Nancy's scenes, particularly her confrontations with Sikes and her clandestine meetings with Rose and Brownlow.

If Edwardian stage versions of *Oliver Twist* were defined largely by the melodramatic tastes and tendencies of the Victorian period, the turn of the century likewise created new opportunities for adaptors to reshape the cultural perception of the novel through the innovative medium of film. The first decade of the twentieth century witnessed the production of numerous film versions of *Oliver Twist*. Given the early prominence of cinema in America, the initial film versions of Dickens's novels were presented not only in a new medium but likewise, in a different cultural context—one that eventually revolved heavily around the marketing of cute kid actors to receptive American audiences.

Fresh off from his impressive debut in Charles Chaplin's Dickensian masterpiece *The Kid*, Jackie Coogan evolved into America's foremost child star and transitioned from playing a *Twist*ian character in the Chaplin film to playing Oliver Twist

Table 1.1. EPISODES FROM *OLIVER TWIST* INCLUDED IN SELECT VICTORIAN AND EDWARDIAN STAGE ADAPTATIONS

Novel Episode	James Elphinstone & Frederick Neale (1855)	John Oxenford (1868)	Cyril Searle (1878)	J. Comyns Carr (1905)	Arthur Williams (1912)	Bransby Williams (1928)
Oliver's birth; workhouse satire						
Mrs. Mann and Mr. Bumble introduction						
Oliver asks for more						
Oliver is almost apprenticed to Gamfield						
Sowerberry becomes Oliver's master	✓					
Oliver meets Noah	✓					
Oliver learns the trade	✓	✓				
Oliver beats Noah and is punished	✓					
Oliver escapes to London and meets the Dodger	✓	✓	✓			✓
Oliver meets Fagin	✓	✓	✓		✓	✓
Fagin counts up his treasures	✓	✓	✓		✓	✓
The Dodger and Charley turn over their pickings	✓		✓	✓	✓	
Oliver learns to play the "game"			✓			
Mr. Brownlow's pocket is picked; Oliver is arrested	✓	✓	✓		✓	✓ (off-stage)
Mr. Fang's courtroom	✓	✓	✓		✓	
Oliver is taken in by Brownlow	✓				✓	✓
Sikes and Fagin plot to recapture Oliver	✓		✓		✓	✓

Scene					
Recovery at Brownlow's house; Oliver's errand	✓	✓		✓	✓
Oliver's abduction by Sikes and Nancy	✓	✓	✓ (off-stage)	✓	✓ (off-stage)
Fagin robs and abuses Oliver; Nancy intervenes	✓	✓	✓	✓	✓
Bumble bullies Dick	✓	✓			
Bumble slanders Oliver before Brownlow	✓	✓	✓	✓	✓
Fagin, Dodger, and Bates lecture Oliver					
Fagin and Sikes plot; Sikes threatens Oliver	✓	✓	✓	✓	✓
Botched robbery of the Maylie house	✓	✓	✓	✓	✓
Bumble courts Mrs. Corney	✓				
Death of Old Sally		✓	✓	✓ (off-stage)	✓
Fagin plots with Monks					
Introduction of the Maylie household					
Losberne questions Oliver; Blathers and Duff arrive					
Oliver recovers under the Maylies' care		✓			
Rose Maylie's illness					
Harry and Rose's courtship	✓	✓	✓	✓	
Domestic problems of the Bumbles	✓				

(Continued)

Table 1.2. CONTINUED

Novel Episode	James Elphinstone & Frederick Neale (1855)	John Oxenford (1868)	Cyril Searle (1878)	J. Comyns Carr (1905)	Arthur Williams (1912)	Bransby Williams (1928)
Monks bribes the Bumbles	✓	✓	✓			✓
Nancy tends to Sikes	✓	✓	✓	✓		✓
Nancy meets Rose	✓	✓	✓	✓	✓	✓
Oliver reunites with Brownlow						
Noah and Charlotte join Fagin's gang	✓					
Trial of the Dodger	✓ (off-stage)					
Sikes prevents Nancy from leaving the house			✓			
Nancy meets Brownlow and Rose at the bridge	✓	✓	✓	✓	✓	✓
Fagin sends Sikes after Nancy	✓	✓	✓	✓	✓	✓
The murder of Nancy by Sikes	✓	✓	✓	✓	✓	✓
Sikes attempts to flee London						
Brownlow captures and interrogates Monks	✓			✓	✓	✓
The death of Sikes	✓	✓			✓	
Revelation of Oliver's parentage	✓					
Downfall of Monks and the Bumbles						✓
Fagin's last night alive	✓			✓	✓	✓

himself in Frank Lloyd's 1922 adaptation. Coogan's depiction of the title character is best defined as "Chaplinesque" in its delightful yet delicate balance of comicality and pathos. The young actor's performance is so lively and engaging that there are moments where one wonders if the film was truly conceived of as a Dickensian adaptation, or rather, as a vehicle for its star; as a *New York Times* reviewer noted, it was difficult to determine "whether it is Mr. Dickens or little Jackie Coogan that is drawing [audiences]."[9] Marketing the film around Coogan seems to imply the sort of usurpation of meaning that Cross associates with advertising campaigns; Coogan's popularity thus helped to reshape the culture text of *Twist* during this period, as his incarnation of the character prefigured several of the film adaptations that would follow, notably, the first "talkie" version. This 1933 *Oliver Twist* takes the American elements of the earlier movie even further, as Dickie Moore embraces the "Our Gang" style of acting in the hope of charming his audience; watching the film, one would half-expect him to exclaim "gee whiz!" or "hot dog!" Equally unsettling is how the film exploited its source, as studio distributors were advised to design marketing campaigns around Dickens's characters.[10]

Recalling Schlicke's claim about the mythical scene in which the protagonist holds aloft his bowl, it is not surprising that the product placement plan crafted for the film revolved around the image of Oliver asking for more; in yet another description that calls to mind the usurpation of the Dickens text on the part of the culture text, Martin Green notes that advertisers consistently appropriate myths, allowing advertising to become its own mythical system as "products displace the world of the spirit."[11] Oliver's "mythic" request for more gruel is thus easily transformed into a commercial image, and his words are easily transformed into a slogan. This trait would affect the development of the global *Twist*ian culture text long before Bart began work on his musical, though it would eventually prove a unique and critical factor in the conception of *Oliver!* (see Chapter 2).

Whatever its value as an example of marketing, the 1933 adaptation of *Oliver Twist* is a poor film *and* a poor adaptation, one that completely dismisses the English roots of Dickens. The next major film version of the novel would mark a tremendous departure from the trends started by the Americans, as a gifted British director sought to reclaim *Twist* for the English. David Lean's 1948 film version of *Oliver Twist* is one of the greatest Dickensian films of all time. It is also the single most important adaptation of the novel leading up to *Oliver!* Many critics perceived an anti-Semitic agenda lurking beneath the surface of the Lean adaptation, but the director's central purpose was actually grounded in his determination to restore the Englishness of the Dickens text. In fact, Lean's effort was just one facet of a larger attempt on the part of the English film industry to retake control of English cultural properties that had previously been claimed by Hollywood. As a *New York Times* article on the development of Lean's *Oliver Twist* noted:

> The British motion picture people seem to be serious about this matter of England owning London in general and the London of Dickens in particular. They staked out their claim most emphatically in 'Great Expectations' and now they plan to put on the finishing touches of ownership in 'Oliver Twist' which the Cineguild group of the

J. Arthur Rank Organization is currently filming at Pinewood studios. Surprisingly enough the British encountered some difficulty in wresting the title 'Oliver Twist' away from America. The picture people here discovered that at least two American companies had put in prior claims to the title. The claims had lain dormant for ages but with the sudden Dickensian renaissance after 'Great Expectations' the claims began showing signs of life.[12]

In the same article, a Cineguild official opined that "[s]omehow or other we feel that London belongs to us [...] and while we recognize that Hollywood can do amazing things we still think we can do Dickens better."[13] This "competition" between American and British film producers over the "proper" way in which to produce Dickens foreshadows several of the cultural negotiations that Lionel Bart would face in writing *Oliver!*

Here, the culture text of *Oliver Twist* began to shift from the cheery and sentimental tone of the early American films toward the stark austerity of postwar England. Lean had previously captured this same severity in his celebrated adaptation of *Great Expectations*, specifically in the depiction of Satis House; nevertheless, he memorably ended the film on a bright and redemptive note by having Pip tear down the curtains and escort Estella into the sunlight of a promising future. Though Lean ends his *Oliver Twist* on a similarly optimistic note, it is a more subdued optimism. Oliver finds comfort in the embrace of Mrs. Bedwin, but he has endured tremendous suffering up to this point.

Lean's use of Pip and Oliver as representatives of enduring Englishness in the face of trauma and deprivation is a prime example of Dickens's own enduring power as an English institution; the high cultural stakes of the previously discussed battle over English authors as cinematic properties therefore becomes all the more understandable. Granted, Lean's respect for Dickens did not translate to an unwavering fidelity to the letter of the literary text. The filmmaker was meticulous in streamlining Dickens's *Oliver Twist* for the screen in the hope of creating a dynamic cinematic narrative. However, the Lean adaptation's cultural legacy is grounded less in the deletions and more in two significant additions. The opening scene, which depicts the beleaguered and pregnant Agnes limping her way to the parish workhouse in the midst of a thunderstorm, presents a haunting image that would resonate with subsequent adaptors. Even more significantly, the finale to the Lean adaptation has eclipsed Dickens's own finale in the popular memory of the story; the climax atop the roof of Fagin's lair is breathtaking.[14]

Great Expectations will likely remain the favorite of the two Lean adaptations. However, *Oliver Twist*—with its darker tone, its harsher violence, and its more horrific depiction of suffering—is ultimately the more effective representation of Dickens's cultural relevance in the postwar English cinema. It is yet another example of Dickens's paradoxical postmodern status that cinematic adaptations of his works could serve to underscore the sense of dispossession pervading postwar England while simultaneously reminding the English of their proud national heritage (as epitomized by Dickens, their "national author").

But what of the most controversial element of Lean's film, Alec Guinness's portrayal of Fagin? Here, artistic vision clearly surpassed political correctness, as John points out "that Lean did more for the reputation of film in 1948 than for harmonious race relations."[15] Up until the point that Lean began work on his *Oliver Twist*, the 1933 adaptation starring Dickie Moore was the only "talkie" version in existence. Lean was keenly aware of the flaws in the earlier film, though the poor performances and low production values were likely of less concern than the Americanized tone of the adaptation. Dickens scholar Joss Marsh bemoans the insensitivity of Lean's depiction of Fagin, but she concludes that the director was willing to incorporate such a distasteful element out of a basic determination "to reclaim a British text from its American usurpers, by all 'authentic' means possible."[16] Lean had been warned about the dangers of presenting such an indelicately "authentic" incarnation of Fagin, though the director persistently refused to heed these warnings and subsequently paid a heavy price for his stubbornness. In the United States, representatives of the Anti-Defamation League and the American Board of Rabbis condemned the film as anti-Semitic; the American premiere was postponed indefinitely.[17] In Germany, demonstrators rioted to prevent the film from being shown, and several people were injured in the physical violence that followed. An anonymous article in a 1949 issue of the *Daily Telegraph* describes the extremely volatile circumstances surrounding the German premiere:

> Fewer than 100 Polish Jews, many of whom are known to the Berlin police as black market operators, again stopped the show at a British sector cinema here to-day of the British film "Oliver Twist." They staged a demonstration outside the cinema, in the course of which German police made baton charges, used a fire hose, and fired warning shots from revolvers. Jews yesterday forced a withdrawal of the film in protest at the portrayal of Fagin in what they regard as a role discreditable to Jews. [...] Several of the demonstrators received head wounds from truncheon blows. A number of policemen were also injured.[18]

Though *Oliver Twist* has always been regarded as a controversial novel, the riots inspired by the Lean film far eclipse any storms engendered by the original text, and the issue of Fagin's Jewishness continued to haunt many writers and directors long after the demons of Lean's adaptation had finally been exorcised. Bart would repeatedly struggle with this matter in the writing and staging of *Oliver!*

In spite of (or perhaps because of) this controversy, the influence of the Lean film on the public's memory of *Oliver Twist* is astounding. It is so astounding that it has had an impact on the shape of nearly every adaptation that has followed. The only adaptation of *Twist* that has exerted more of an influence on the popular impression of the novel than Lean's adaptation is *Oliver!*, though Bart acknowledged his own debt to Lean's film. It is a curious debt in light of the wide divergences between these artists' creative visions, and Bart's revisionist take on *Oliver Twist* seems antithetical to Lean's "authentic" approach. Still, thanks largely to Lean's efforts, the culture text of *Oliver Twist* had been repossessed by the English at the time that Bart began work on *Oliver!*

IDENTITY CRISES, EMPIRE, AND ANGRY YOUNG MEN

Although *Oliver!* emerged from a theatrical tradition that dated back to the late 1830s, Lionel Bart was a man of his time. His musicals reflected the ideals of a decade that was characterized by working-class empowerment, youthful frivolity, and, of course, pop music. It was also a period in which the traditional middle-class escapism of the English stage was displaced by a spirit of experimentation and cockney rebelliousness. However, the journey from Lean's *Oliver Twist* toward Bart's *Oliver!*—and more generally, from postwar austerity toward 1950s vitality—was convoluted.

The word *austerity* has become ingrained in the historical narrative surrounding this period, and it encapsulates the grimness and scarcity facing the English populace in the wake of the Second World War. The influential writer and critic Cyril Connolly observed that the wounded postwar London symbolized the general decline of English society, for the injured metropolis was "now the largest, saddest and dirtiest of great cities with its miles of unpainted half-inhabited houses, its chopless chop-houses, its beerless pubs [...] its crowds mooning round the stained wicker of the cafeterias in their shabby raincoats, under a sky permanently dull and lowering like a metal dish-cover."[19] Nevertheless, this melancholy belies the fact that the English had much to be proud of in the wake of the Second World War. As Peter Mandler writes in his study of English national identity, "[t]he outcome of the Second World War seemed to vindicate the English national character. [...] The people that had seemed to be dwindling to a passive, narcissistic nothingness in the period of appeasement had proved their mettle when their backs were against the wall."[20] Mark Donnelly concurs that the success of the English war campaign ostensibly "provided a striking vindication both of the British way of doing things and the character of its people."[21] Still, it did not last: "By the late 1950s, comment on the strength and virtues of the English national character—of a kind that had been standard for a generation among both the English and admiring foreigners—was dying out."[22]

The rise of a globalized Western culture, one dominated by the United States, obviously played a significant role in this shift; the postwar period would see the American influence on personal values and cultural trends reach new heights. As will be discussed later in this chapter, the American impact on popular music and stage music would exert a significant effect on the buildup toward *Oliver!*, as Bart's ironic ability to adopt and simultaneously counter these trends was essential to his success as a composer of pop music and a writer of stage musicals.

While the temptation to blame the "upstart Americans" for the decline of Englishness in the period following World War II is understandable—Mandler sardonically mentions the enduring temptation of the English "to unsheathe the sword of national character to ward off these alien invaders"[23]—many of the fundamental changes to the concept of English national character came from within. The basic fact that English identity had been so thoroughly connected to the English empire meant that, in an age of imperial decline, an identity crisis was inevitable. The 1956 Suez Crisis, regarded as a defining moment in this shift, highlighted the divergence between the prewar and postwar generations. Since England had avoided "the trauma of invasion and occupation" during World War II, historian Dominic Sandbrook points out that the "national myths were never challenged," at least up until that time.[24] For the postwar youth, however, the Suez Crisis was an indication of their country's status as a postimperial power. Nevertheless, at the exact same time that the old national myth of an empire on which the sun never set was waning, a new national myth that epitomized the concerns of postwar youth began to materialize. It emerged as a result of groundbreaking changes in the realm of the English theater and the arrival of a group of "angry young men."

The postwar period was marked by "a general surge in interest in the stage."[25] Though the percentage of Britons who visited the theater remained relatively small, the cultural cachet of this particular form of entertainment rose significantly, in large part owing to the tendency of critics to look toward the theater as a source of social commentary. The radicalism of the 1950s British theater may seem tame by today's standards, but its significance in its own era is undeniable as rebellious playwrights introduced subjects that had previously been labeled taboo, while visionary directors experimented with new staging techniques. In *Society and Literature*, Alan Sinfield characterized the radical ethos of the postwar theater as defined by a "disrespect for traditional middle-class attitudes, expressed directly and through aggressive presentation of other lifestyles."[26]

It seems providential that John Osborne's *Look Back in Anger* debuted the very same year as the Suez Crisis. Though Osborne would engage this historical event more directly in *The Entertainer*, the cultural, generational, and identity-based crises described above were all essential to his 1956 tour de force.[27] Jimmy Porter's contempt for his own generation is matched only by his contempt for his forebears, but he simultaneously acknowledges that "[t]he old Edwardian brigade do make their brief little world look pretty tempting. [. . .] If you've no world of your own, it's rather pleasant to regret the passing of someone else's."[28] Similarly, while his most memorable line—"There aren't any good, brave causes left"[29]—became the catchphrase for an entire generation, the statement is prefaced by his reflection that "I suppose people of our generation aren't able to die for good causes any longer. We had all that done for us, in the thirties and the forties, when we were still kids."[30] This reflection contributes to the notion that Jimmy's struggle is defined not by a strictly class-based frustration but by a sense of inadequacy in the face of the previous generation's achievements. As the great Colin MacInnes put it, "John Osborne's play exists within the context of the old order, and only takes on its meaning by being, in a sense, a part of it."[31] The inability of the postwar youth to find viable opportunities and outlets for surpassing their predecessors, as dictated by the shallowness and cultural bankruptcy of postwar England, is central to the play's meaning. David Ian Rabey eloquently observes that

> 1950s Conservatism emphasised the passive goal of 'affluence'—the dubious analogy between social progress and the growth of material wealth, extension of leisure and consumerist choice—rather than honourable conflict or release of energy. Osborne and [Arnold] Wesker attack 'the deadening effects of prosperity' more frequently than the uncomfortable confines of poverty.[32]

In spite of Prime Minister Howard Macmillan's memorable 1957 assertion that people in postwar England "never had it so good," Osborne and his peers resented the intellectual, moral, and cultural stagnation that came to epitomize postwar Englishness.[33]

Osborne's most noteworthy contemporary and counterpart among the angry young men, Arnold Wesker, conveyed a similar sense of longing and conflict in *The Kitchen*. Here, the "good, brave" causes worth fighting for are impeded by a lack of communal connectivity, as Paul bitterly recalls having encouraged a neighbor during a labor strike but having been spurned by the same neighbor for participating in a peace march: "And the horror is this—that there's a wall, a big wall between me and millions of people like him. And I think—where will it end?"[34] Marango, the beleaguered restaurant owner, raises similar questions in the final moments of the play. Bewildered by Peter's destructive actions, he cannot understand this angry young man's desire for a bigger, better life: "What is there more?"[35] It is a memorable final line, though Wesker crafted an even more memorable final refrain for Sarah Kahn in *Chicken Soup with Barley* as she warns her cynical son Ronnie that "if you don't care you'll die."[36] Much as Jimmy's subconscious striving toward the romantic heroism of the previous age in the face of the disillusioning realities of the 1950s is rendered even more powerful when juxtaposed against the Suez Crisis, Sarah's refusal to renounce her East End idealism and communist politics in the face of her family's disillusionment is particularly poignant when set against the USSR's 1956 invasion of Hungary.

One of the striking incongruities of the plays of Osborne and Wesker is that the playwrights can attack their country while simultaneously promoting an idealistic belief in the greatness of the English, whether it is through the intellectual vitality of Jimmy Porter or the communal compassion of the Kahn family. Such postwar incongruities were not surprising, as the younger generation's cultural skepticism, along with the eventual rise of the leftist counter-culture of the sixties, should not be viewed as repudiations of Englishness. In fact, it was perfectly feasible for a person to be both leftist and nationalist. In his reflections on the Campaign for Nuclear Disarmament, Sinfield writes,

> [i]t aspired, by withdrawing Britain from NATO, to liberate the county from Untied States domination. And it imagined that England, in the organised Labour movement and the radical intelligentsia, had access to an authoritative moral tradition that would make a unilateral renunciation of nuclear weapons a compelling example to the rest of the world. Both these factors involved an uninspected assumption that England was a world power capable of acting by itself and likely to be marked by others.[37]

Sinfield's words frame Jimmy's bitter sense of impotence in the globalized atomic age and Sarah's hopeless commitment to the labor movements as distinctly English struggles, reinforcing the notion that one could condemn the status quo while simultaneously promoting English cultural nationalism. Dickens had proved this to be true in the previous century, thereby cementing his unique place among the

Victorians: even as the postwar period rejected the values of the age that he had defined and immortalized, Dickens remained culturally relevant.

Although the concerns described above initially seem far-removed from *Oliver!*, such issues and ideas heavily shaped the theatrical and cultural context from which Bart came forth as the dominant force in the postwar musical theater. In spite of the "timelessness" granted to *Oliver!*, Bart's musical reflects many of the concerns that dominated the postwar English stage, including the struggle to define a new Englishness in the face of a globalized culture. Moreover, if the central contrasts between the prewar and postwar British theater are best exemplified by the decline of Terence Rattigan and the rise of John Osborne—the rejection of the drawing-room comedy and the acceptance of the kitchen-sink drama—Bart's musicals convey a similar shift away from the glitzy and glamorous world of the prewar operetta and toward a gritty, working-class musical genre. In spite of its musicality, through both its visual design and its thematic elements *Oliver!* would embody the same sort of "grittiness" that characterized its nonmusical kitchen-sink predecessors.

The famed producer Sir Cameron Mackintosh asserts that whatever the thematic, tonal, and generic differences between the two works, *Oliver!* "was the musical equiv-alent of *Look Back in Anger*"[38]:

> *Look Back in Anger* completely transformed the British playwrights; it suddenly, overnight, made Noël Coward and Terence Rattigan seem as if they belonged to a bygone era. Theatrically, *Oliver!* did the same, because the [musical] hits before that in the 1950s were *Salad Days*, *The Boy Friend*, *Irma La Douce*, and suddenly, this piece came, which then was considered very dark and different. I mean, it was the first time that the lights in the theatre were shown to the audience, not hidden; it was the first time that there wasn't a frontcloth and you went up on this dark and mysterious set and it all changed in front of you. From the moment it came on, the musical theatre was literally never the same in this country.[39]

It is fitting that Mackintosh should support his comparison with a discussion of the set. Sean Kenny's brilliant designs were essential to establishing the stark tenor of Bart's Dickensian musical, a starkness that tied the piece to its non-musical coun-terparts from the postwar era (see Chapter 3); as critic Caryl Brahms later noted in her review of *Oliver!*, "[t]he piece takes place in the shadows and cellars of a London as violent as any contemporary Ted-play."[40] The portrayal of class relationships in *Oliver!* is likewise evocative of *Look Back in Anger*, with Mr. Brownlow serving as a musical counterpart to Osborne's Colonel Redfern. Much as Redfern "finds himself in a world where his authority has lately become less and less unquestionable,"[41] Brownlow finds himself in a musical where his Victorian middle-class morality is outshined by Fagin and Nancy's postwar working-class dynamism.

Wesker seems a more obvious influence on Bart given their shared roots as Jewish East Enders. Several of the events that shape the Kahn family in *Chicken Soup with Barley*, including the Battle of Cable Street and the news from the Spanish Civil War, had exerted a significant effect on the Begleiter family during Lionel's forma-tive years.[42] Furthermore, like Wesker and the Kahns, Bart was a member of the

Communist Party. In light of these connections, Wesker's revelation that he almost sold the rights to his plays to Bart is not as surprising as one might think; in a 2012 interview with Michael Billington, Wesker explained that while he was trying to raise funds for Centre 42, he offered to sell Bart "the rights to all my plays for £10,000. He said no, thank God."[43] It is an ironic disclosure given Bart's eventual loss of the rights to his own works.

Billington's article somewhat offhandedly refers to Bart as "creator of the Oliver [sic] musical,"[44] dismissively depriving the piece of its trademark exclamation point and any corresponding sense of excitement. Still, such a dismissal ignores several of the intriguing correlations between Bart and Wesker's theatrical and ethical conceptions. Though *Oliver!* was based on a Victorian source that unhesitatingly endorses middle-class morality, the true moral center of Bart's musical adaptation, as in *The Wesker Trilogy*, is the working-class East End community. As in *Chicken Soup with Barley*, however, the fragility of that community is made apparent to the viewer: the breakup of the Kahn family and the breakup of Fagin's gang convey a similar sense of disillusionment. As Rabey observes, "Wesker identifies a 'melancholy optimism' to be a recognisable (and recognisably Jewish) colour in his work."[45] Though Bart struggled to find a suitable ending for his Dickensian adaptation, he eventually settled on a similarly "melancholy optimism" based heavily on the Jewishness of his main character. The Jewish rhythms of Wesker's characters' speech patterns would find their musical equivalent in the Jewish motifs of Fagin's songs, just as Sarah Kahn would later find her musical counterpart in Mrs. Blitzstein, the heroine of Bart's *Blitz!*

Given the significant emphasis on the angry young man movement in the critical and historical discourse surrounding the postwar English theater, it is important to acknowledge the indirect influence of this movement on the gestation of *Oliver!* However, as noted above, the angry young men became a new mythos in the face of postwar turbulence, and like any myth, it was dependent on continued retelling. As Jack Reading puts it in a letter to author Dominic Shellard,

> the claim now made for the play [*Look Back in Anger*] as the water-shed of post-war theatre is something developed *after* the event. It did not seem so at the time. Its importance is a myth which, like all myths, feeds on itself, aided, and very much aided, by that brilliant coinage of Angry Young Man. This has given journalists and writers a caption head-line much in the same way as the later catch of 'Kitchen Sink' had to explain the exploration, dramatically, of every-day working and low life.[46]

Certainly, in recent decades theatrical historians have acknowledged that the critical, cultural, and commercial "hype" surrounding *Look Back in Anger* was essential to its success, as prominent theater critics like Kenneth Tynan and Martin Esslin did everything in their power to facilitate the transformation of the postwar English theater by promoting new English works such as Osborne's play.[47] The unfortunate side effect is that this situation has prompted some writers and critics to disparagingly reevaluate the play and to treat it—and the angry young man movement in general—as little more than a glorified marketing campaign.

People can debate the quality of *Look Back in Anger* (and its squirrelly ending); the overall success of the movement behind it is indisputable. Osborne's play became a cultural and national phenomenon that notably tapped into a new youth market; Royal Court did everything in its power to exploit this market, promoting themselves as a theater for young English voices.[48] In his indispensable review of *Look Back in Anger*—tellingly titled "The Voice of the Young"—Tynan repeatedly drew attention to the topic of youth, noting that Osborne's work was "the best young play of its decade."[49] Esslin, a similarly vital force in the postwar theater and in the promotion of *Look Back in Anger* as a cultural phenomenon, would later note that "[i]n a period of steady decline of British power British artistic achievement has played an important part in keeping the country's prestige high."[50] The emphasis on "youth" and "vitality" in the discourse surrounding *Look Back in Anger*, along with the nationalistic celebration of a triumph of the English theater in the face of a waning sense of cultural identity, is perhaps the most noteworthy connection between Osborne's play and *Oliver!* This correlation warrants an extended discussion in Chapter 4, which details the reception of Bart's musical and the celebration of its Englishness.

POP RECORDS AND POSTWAR YOUTH

In keeping with the notion that *Look Back in Anger* exploited the postwar fixation on English youth, it is important to note the correlation between the advent of the angry young men and the rise of rock 'n' roll. Shellard mentions the alliance between the hype behind *Look Back in Anger* and "other cultural movements by young people as ways of disrupting consensus and challenging notions of respect (with all its class and generational implications)."[51] The carefree joy of rock and pop music may seem antithetical to Jimmy Porter's anger, and also to Osborne's longing for English music hall in *The Entertainer*, but such contradictions did not seem to bother the young audiences who snapped up both phenomena. It was a time of great excitement as "[t]he first expresso bars were spreading across southern England; students were huddling around coffees and cigarettes in their distinctive duffel coats; the first skiffle musicians were finding a mass audience."[52] Sandbrook's description, as quoted above, is especially noteworthy when one considers that this setting is the very scene in which Lionel Bart would first make a name for himself.

If history is written by the victors, then it seems fitting that the history of postwar Britain was written by the baby boomers, as the 1950s witnessed the triumph of youth culture. This emphasis on English youth was a sudden development,[53] and Bill Osgerby observes that "it is easy to get the impression that youth culture simply did not exist before the war, that it suddenly and spontaneously materialized in the 1950s amid a wave of rock 'n' roll records, coffee bars and brothel-creeper shoes."[54] The newfound fiscal influence of the teenaged generation played a significant role in English society's sudden interest in youth culture, and MacInnes assessed this correlation in his celebrated essay collection, *England Half-English*: "Today, youth has money, and teenagers have become a power. In their struggle to impose their wills upon the adult world, young men and women have always been blessed with energy but never, until now, with wealth. [...] They are a social group whose tastes are studied with respect—particularly by the entertainment industry."[55] The economic power of teenagers is especially important to consider in light of the fact that teen culture was shaped heavily by working-class culture. Osgerby reveals that working-class young people "flexed the greatest economic muscle"[56] in the 1950s and thus exerted a particularly strong influence in the definition of popular youth fashions; it seems difficult to distinguish between "postwar youth culture" and "postwar working-class culture" for they were very much intertwined.[57] The rise of postwar pop music thus reflected the prominence and economic power of working-class youths in the 1950s.

As Sandbrook perceptively points out, the ascendancy of pop music and rock 'n' roll was best understood as a manifestation of the larger shifts in English society, specifically the increased consumer clout of teenagers.[58] Although some traditionalist forces in Great Britain were disturbed by the emergence of rock 'n' roll, and more generally, by working-class youth culture, the more conspicuous target for the older generation's ire was the Americanness of this musical phenomenon. The wartime generation was inclined to label the postwar Americans as a frivolous, acquisitive people, though as noted in the previous section England was rapidly adopting the same materialist values; the postwar youth culture was the central link between these trends, for just as young Britons embraced American music, they were likewise prone to consumerism.[59]

MacInnes explicitly classified the pop song as "an American invention" and noted that "its greatest practitioners have undoubtedly been Americans."[60] His wry reflections on the pop music phenomenon reveal the derisive views of the arrival of this American craze:

> Although these songs are despised by educated persons (who never hear them) and, even more so, by lovers of serious jazz music (who, with pain, occasionally do), there is no denying that pop songs have a certain artistic quality which resides, almost exclusively, in the art of the individual singers. The tunes and lyrics in themselves are often of meagre quality—although manufactured with extreme competence—and the emotions they evoke are almost invariably synthetic: that is, they are songs about the idea of life, but rarely about life itself.[61]

The author's attitude toward American pop music is one of good-natured condescension as opposed to genuine distaste. Nevertheless, his wariness regarding the loss of English identity, even as a result of such a "trivial" phenomenon, is likewise apparent: "Until some forty years ago, the English song about English life resounded boisterously in the Music Halls. Since then, new American musical idioms, potently diffused by the cinema, radio, the gramophone and now TV, have swamped our own ditties."[62] MacInnes's remorseful invocation of the lost art of the English music-hall song is yet another parallel to Osborne, though his comments are particularly noteworthy in light of the fact that Bart successfully combined the genres of pop and music hall when he wrote *Oliver!* Indeed, Bart's standing as one of the foremost composers of 1950s pop songs, coupled with his East End background, allowed a unique blending of the disparate art forms.

Though MacInnes predicted that, whatever strides the English made in the development of their own pop music, English pop would never truly epitomize Englishness "since the commercial forces behind the American pop are so tremendous [. . .] and, at all events, it's certain that if English pop songs, as well as singers, do appear, they'll be profoundly influenced by America,"[63] he saw hope in the form of Tommy Steele, noting that the young singer's pop hits, as written by Bart, "possess[ed] a certain English essence of sentiment and wit."[64] "Sentiment and wit," brought together in songs sung by a working-class Englishman: it was the very same combination that had all but defined the ballads of the English music halls. MacInnes was eager to see Bart and Steele take this Englishness one step further in the hope that "we will hear once again, for the first time since the decline of the Music Halls, songs that tell us of our own world."[65]

The rise of Tommy Steele, which prefigured the emergence of British pop as a global force in the 1960s, disproved the popular belief that only Americans could produce pop music, much as the debut of *Oliver!* would disprove the popular belief that only Americans could write musicals. Bart was instrumental to both refutations, and it is fitting that he would eventually become friends with the Rolling Stones and the Beatles, as the transcendent success of these rock groups would—like the triumph of *Oliver!*—mark a uniquely similar English cultural victory over the Americans in a genre that the Yankees had ostensibly conquered. These two separate yet related triumphs became intertwined on a historic date in English pop-cultural history, February 9, 1964, "as millions watched the Beatles on CBS's *The Ed Sullivan Show*, [and] rock 'n' roll ceased to be an exclusively American art form."[66] On this same installment of Sullivan's show, Georgia Brown appeared with members of the Broadway cast of *Oliver!* to perform "As Long as He Needs Me."

AMERICAN INVASIONS AND ENGLISH MUSICALS

The tendency to disregard the English pop stars of the 1950s in the wake of their globally popular 1960s successors is surpassed by the unfortunate tendency to disregard the English stage musical tradition, though as in the case of the former this indifference is due partly to the American dominance of the genre. It seems difficult to accept that England fell behind the United States in the development of modern musical theater, especially given that the comic operas of W. S. Gilbert and Arthur Sullivan, works that prefigured the emergence of the modern musical, were fundamentally English.[67] Curiously, Gilbert and Sullivan did not truly inspire other English composers to pick up where they had left off. It was up to the American composers of the early twentieth century to move musical drama forward. By the early 1920s, English musical theater was already being dominated by musical trends from other cultures; Kurt Ganzl observes that most of the new British musicals being produced in the West End were basically "imitations of foreign shows—American or Continental."[68] Sheridan Morley echoes this sentiment, asserting that "the shows that came to us from New York for the first half of this century were much more energetic, more enthusiastic than the shows born here, and that did not just start from *Oklahoma!*"[69], though the London debut of Rodgers and Hammerstein's land-mark musical marked a critical moment in the history of West End musical theatre. Whereas most of the devastation facing England in the 1940s was the result of the Luftwaffe, the near destruction of the English musical was not attributable to the threat of German invasion during World War II but rather to the reality of American invasion in the postwar period; as Morely once joked, "the bomb that fell on West End musicals did not come from an enemy power at all: it was first detonated on Broadway in March 1943, in the shape of *Oklahoma!*, but its impact would not be felt in London until four years later."[70]

In spite of its unapologetic Americanism, *Oklahoma!* proved a West End hit. English traditionalists may have been tempted to turn up their noses at the American musical, greeting its arrival with the same disregard that defined their response to American pop music, but there was no denying that the Americans had come to mas-ter a captivating new form of theater. *Oklahoma!* was followed by a string of American musical imports including *Annie Get Your Gun* (Coliseum 1947), *Carousel* (Drury Lane 1950), *Kiss Me Kate* (Coliseum 1951), *South Pacific* (Drury Lane 1950), *Porgy and Bess* (Stoll 1952), *The King and I* (Drury Lane 1953), *Guys and Dolls* (Coliseum 1953), and *Pal Joey* (Prince's 1954).[71] The unfortunate side effect was that the English musical, which had already stagnated, now seemed in danger of extinction.

The apotheosis of the modern stage musical has long been attributed to the American emphasis on "integration," that is, the technique of synthesizing the plot, the songs, the dialogue, the dances, and the orchestrations into a coherent narrative.[72] Though supposedly "perfected" by Rodgers and Hammerstein,[73] this methodology was traceable back to earlier shows, including *Show Boat*, a musical that historians eventually came to regard as the true breakthrough in the develop-ment of the American "formula."[74] More recently, however, the idea of integration as the panacea for the perfect musical has become increasingly dubious. Geoffrey Block and Mark N. Grant both cite the negative critical/scholarly response to the megamusical as evidence of this shift, for the megamusical, with its operatic score and "sung-through" quality, represents total integration.[75] Scott McMillin takes the matter one step further in *The Musical as Drama*, labeling the megamusical as a variation on Wagner's *Gesamtkunstwerk*, though he views this form of theater as far-removed from the traditional American musical.[76] McMillin thus articulates his disagreement with the basic discourse on integration in regard to the golden age of Broadway, noting that

> the real cultural work being carried out by these writers and practitioners of the musical, I propose, was that of turning Broadway's skill at song-and-dance routines into a new format in which the numbers had important work to do because they were being inserted into the book as a different element, a change of mode, a sus-pension of the book in favor of music.[77]

Such a description flies in the face of the traditional emphasis on "seamless inte-gration," though Block, Grant, and McMillin's assertions carry particular weight when one considers the aforementioned failure of the English musical to reach

the heights of its American counterpart during the golden age of Broadway—
this in spite of the fact that the prewar English musical was virtually defined by
integration.

Certainly, the musical works of Ivor Novello—works that basically defined
English musical theater in the years leading up to World War II—are fundamentally
integrated. The transition from speech to song is almost always seamless because
the character is oftentimes called on to sing; consider that the lead characters in
Glamorous Night and *The Dancing Years*, Novello's greatest works, are musical performers—opera singers, professional songwriters, pianists, and crooners (Noël
Coward would employ a similar device in his most enduring musical, *Bitter Sweet*).
This means that most of the songs in these works are, to use McMillin's term,
diegetic: "The term *diegetic*, borrowed from film criticism, is coming to be used for
numbers that are called for by the book. It is meant to cover the backstage musicals
plus any other occasions on which characters deliberately perform numbers for other
characters."[78] A diegetic song is an instance of total integration as the libretto is actually justifying the transition from speaking to singing. Returning to the subject of the
potential limits of integration, the failure of the English musical to modernize in the
wake of Novello's death, coupled with the lamentable contemporary obscurity of his
works, reinforces the notion that integration is not an infallible principle.

What then accounts for the prominence of the American musical in the postwar
period? McMillin cites the basic improvement of the musical libretto in the 1940s
and 1950s as the true cause of the American musical's maturation,[79] much as the
acclaimed conductor Lehman Engel famously cited the libretto as the most important component of the Broadway musical.[80] Considering that integrated musicals are
occasionally referred to as "book musicals," this emphasis on the libretto seems well
founded. Rodgers and Hammerstein may not have perfected the integrated formula
(a concept that was, in and of itself, imperfect), but they certainly succeeded in raising the stakes of the Broadway musical by seeking out sophisticated and challenging
stories or stage properties as the sources for their librettos, which in turn granted
new opportunities for songs to carry greater weight.[81] Perhaps the golden age of
Broadway is defined less by the concept of integration and more by the fundamental
complexity of the plots, characters, and themes of classic musical shows. In the case
of *Oklahoma!*, the superficial simplicity of the story belies the dangerous and dramatic elements of the piece.[82]

The high stakes of the postwar American musical libretto stand in sharp contrast
to the books of the two most popular and successful English musicals from that
same era: Sandy Wilson's *The Boy Friend* and Julian Slade's *Salad Days*. John Snelson
labels these two musicals as "a strike back at the American repertory,"[83] and in his
review of *Salad Days* Cecil Smith asserted that there was finally "a challenger to the
long line of American hits."[84] The overt Englishness of both these shows is connected to an upper-middle-class nostalgia evocative of both Coward and Rattigan.
In both cases, this Englishness was a cause for celebration among West End theater
critics.[85] Still, the subject matter of both *Salad Days* and *The Boy Friend* is unashamedly trivial... perhaps startlingly so in the case of the former. Snelson humorously
recounts that

[a]n interviewer told [Jerome Robbins] the plot of [*Salad Days*] and quoted a few of
its lyrics. After a short silence Robbins's response was a stunned 'You're kidding!'.
How could you explain to one of the creators of such a socially aware show as *West
Side Story* that its main London British rival, seen by some five million people by
then, concerned a magic piano that made people dance?[86]

In spite of this dichotomy, several English critics who touted these homegrown
shows as remedies for the American invasion cited their innocent simplicity as their
most estimable trait. Anthony Cookman of the *Tatler* noted that, like its 1920s pro-
genitors, *The Boy Friend* "had a great deal more gaiety than the solemn musicals of
today,"[87] while a reviewer at the *Sketch* praised *Salad Days* for its "gaiety, youth, [and]
spring fever."[88] Though Timothy and Jane's central song is entitled "We Said We
Wouldn't Look Back," the tone of the ballad is ironic, promoting the very nostalgia it
denies.[89] *The Boy Friend,* which ends with all of the couples happily united and dancing the Charleston, embraces a similarly wistful conception of a frivolous bygone era.
The rub is that none of these couples possess the passion of their American counterparts. How could Timothy and Jane or Tony and Polly ever hope to compare to Curly
and Laurey, Billy and Julie, Emile and Nellie, the King and Anna, or Tony and Maria?
Even in their native England, Timothy and Jane stood in complete contrast to Jimmy
Porter, who would turn "looking back" into an infinitely more fiery pastime.

Still, the wistful tones of *Salad Days* and *The Boy Friend* reinforce one of the dominant historical contrasts between American musicals and British musicals: whereas
the American musical was constantly pushing forward and exploring new sources,
subjects, styles, and sounds, British musicals tended to look back toward a longer,
more fanciful tradition of comic opera. Snelson observes that "[t]his approach is a
constant one in British musical theatre."[90] Although Lionel Bart would take a similarly nostalgic approach, his use of the cockney idiom and his dark subject matter
set him apart from Slade, Wilson, Novello, and Coward. Furthermore, in spite of
the nostalgic elements in Bart's music, there is a contemporary emphasis on the
habits and heartaches of working-class characters that fits the conventions of the
postwar English stage. Perhaps most importantly, the more serious and wrenching
Dickensian elements of *Oliver!*, however mild in comparison to those presented in
the original text, are far-removed from the light whimsy of *Salad Days* and *The Boy
Friend*; as Mackintosh suggests, the correlation between *Oliver!* and *Look Back in
Anger* is most apparent when one contrasts Bart's musical with the two most popular English musicals of the 1950s. The very fact that Bart was willing to turn to a
Dickensian source when conceptualizing his musical hints at the sort of American
"enlargement" described by McMillin,[91] and the threat of Sykes,[92] like the threat of
Jud in *Oklahoma!*, fundamentally separates Bart's musical from its predecessors.

Salad Days and *The Boy Friend* were hardly the only two homegrown musicals of the
era to garner any attention. Just prior to his death, Novello completed his final musical, *Gay's the Word*. Here, Novello revealed his ability to self-deprecate, as *Gay's the
Word* spoofs the Ruritanian tradition of the prewar West End musical and acknowledges the ascent of the Broadway musical: "Since *Oklahoma*[sic]/We've been in a
coma."[93] He maintained his emphasis on diegetic singing, and his plot was incredibly

lighthearted, particularly in comparison to his heavier operatic works; nevertheless, Novello was clearly aware that the postwar West End musical would inevitably be measured against the benchmark of the American musical and would thus have to modernize if it ever hoped to compete. Sadly, his sudden passing precluded his using this realization as an impetus for writing contemporary English musicals.

Other noteworthy musicals from the period included *Grab Me a Gondola* and *Expresso Bongo*. Again the stakes of the librettos are low, but there is a cleverness and vitality to both shows that seems reminiscent of the American musicals of the period. Regrettably, the subject matter of the two musicals has prevented them from enduring beyond that era: the basic premise of *Grab Me a Gondola* is built almost entirely around the exploits of the 1950s British sex symbol Diana Dors, while *Expresso Bongo* is a riotous but dated satire of the 1950s English pop music industry and coffee-bar culture.[94] This reality not only impeded the enduring power of these two shows but likewise precluded their journeying to Broadway. Finally, there was the risqué French import *Irma La Douce*, which had an earthiness that seemed somewhat revolutionary in comparison to the airy *Salad Days*. As in Bart's *Oliver!*, the audience falls in with a group of housebreakers, pickpockets, and prostitutes—a sharp divergence from the clean-cut and sterile world of Slade. Still, unlike the American musicals of the era (and later *Oliver!*), *Irma La Douce* never takes itself seriously; the comic misunderstandings drive the story, and the result is an enjoyable romp as opposed to a musical drama.

The timelessness of Dickens inevitably helped *Oliver!* to achieve a transcendence that its contemporaries lacked, though the maturation of the West End libretto via the Dickensian novel/culture text played a significant role as well. Furthermore, the transatlantic appeal of Dickens allowed *Oliver!* to attain a global cachet that its predecessors lacked entirely.[95] Still, the buildup toward *Oliver!* seemed a period of continuous frustration for those who wished to witness a rebirth of the British musical theater and a reverse in the traffic flow between Broadway and the West End.

The London premiere of *My Fair Lady* added insult to injury given that the Americans had succeeded in creating a musical masterpiece based on an overtly English source. In spite of its deviations from Shaw, *My Fair Lady* received almost universal affirmation from the British press, with Tynan asserting that "it treats both the audience and 'Pygmalion' with civilised respect. [...] This winning show honours our intelligence as well as Shaw's."[96] Tynan and other critics likewise observed that *My Fair Lady*'s success validated the American musical formula in which "[e]verything in the score grows naturally out of the text and the characters"[97]—another indication of the power of the integration myth in its own age.[98]

Though the British press and public embraced an adaptation that might very well have been dismissed as an audacious American bowdlerization, *My Fair Lady* was a frustrating "tease"; it was so tempting to claim this show for the English, for as Morley notes, "if *My Fair Lady*, based by Alan Jay Lerner and Frederick Loewe on Bernard Shaw's *Pygmalion*, designed by Cecil Beaton and starring Rex Harrison and Julie Andrews and Stanley Holloway and Robert Coote, was still not a British musical, what is?"[99] The answer to the question is not a simple one, especially considering that Lerner and Loewe preserved the vital cockney idiom, employed music-hall inspired songs (through the character of Alfie Doolittle), and featured a music-hall performer (through the inimitable Stanley Holloway). The "Americanness" of *My Fair Lady* is perhaps the inevitable result of Lerner and Loewe's most noteworthy change to their source: the romance between Eliza and Higgins. David Walsh and Len Platt astutely assert that the musical "takes up issues of gender, power and love in an American way," fundamentally, by reimagining the drama as a love story and placing significant emphasis on the idea of Eliza as a "modern Cinderella."[100] Like Shaw's version of the character, Lerner and Loewe's Eliza is a true lady from the beginning, but she likewise attains an American independence via the power she gains over Higgins; in the Shaw play, there is no true equivalent to Higgins's singing of "I've Grown Accustomed to Her Face."[101] Whatever its English roots, *My Fair Lady* was an American adaptation.

Notably, *Oliver!*—which would debut in the West End just two years later—would take far greater liberties with its source than Lerner and Loewe had dared take with *Pygmalion*. Still, like *My Fair Lady* before it, *Oliver!* enjoyed widespread acclaim in England. If English critics and theatergoers could forgive two Americans for tinkering with Shaw, surely they could forgive a fellow Englishman for reinventing Dickens. Indeed, for English audiences, *Oliver!* would prove a double triumph. Not only did Lionel Bart create an entertaining adaptation of one of the most popular novels written by a fundamentally English author, but he likewise wrote an English musical that had just as much appeal, dramatic integrity, and dynamic energy as any American musical.

"I'VE MET THIS WONDERFUL NUTCASE CALLED LIONEL BART"

My Fair Lady proved that a cockney flower girl could become a duchess; *Oliver!* proved that a cockney-Jewish East Ender could change the history of the English musical forever. Any discussion of Lionel Bart's life and career must be prefaced by acknowledging the fact that the story of his journey from rags to riches (and back again) has fallen into the realm of theatrical lore. Bart played a significant role in transforming a life story into a larger-than-life story, and he was known for stretching the truth to its breaking point. This tendency extends all the way to his very name; there are multiple conflicting accounts of how exactly Lionel Begleiter became Lionel Bart.[102]

He was the last of seven surviving children born to Maurice and Yetta Begleiter, a pair of Jewish refugees from Austria-Hungary; the Begleiters settled in the East End of London, and Bart's formative years were spent on Brick Lane and in Stepney Way.[103] Bart's Jewishness and East End upbringing are arguably the defining traits of his life story, his personality, and his career; they are also, in many respects, the defining traits of his dramatic/musical canon, and their relevance to the conception and execution of *Oliver!* cannot be overestimated. Ironically, a theater artist whose work was defined largely by his experiences in the East End would go on to write musicals that would transform the West End.

In spite of the entertainment empire that he briefly controlled, Bart never truly "escaped" the East End, though many of his collaborators viewed this as his greatest creative asset. In a touching tribute following the composer's death in 1999, the great Ron Moody concluded that the key to Bart's success in writing *Oliver!* was his ability to define the musical characters by using the melodies and dialects that characterized his own background: "He went back to his roots. Back to his East End, Cockney, hei-mishe Jewish roots, where cockles and mussels (you should excuse the expression) formed an uneasy alliance with salt beef on rye mit a pickle."[104] By staying true to these roots, and writing in the traditions of a culture that he knew intimately, Bart was able to create songs that conveyed a sincerity belying their ostensible melodic simplicity.

For Bart, the cockney idiom was more than just the "native language" of the East End; it was also the language of the people. As will be discussed later in this chapter, his exploration of this dialect reinforces the fact that *Oliver!* not only debuted at a key moment in the history of the British theater but likewise made its own distinctive contribution to a more widespread theatrical movement. Mackintosh recalls that Bart "was, by nature, someone who loved to write for ordinary people to under-stand,"[105] a sentiment Moody echoed in his tribute: "Lionel Bart will [someday] be acknowledged as one of the great folk composers of his day. Burl Ives defined folk music as 'a people using music as its own personal expression', and Lionel's vernacu-lar characters certainly did that."[106] Bart's East End background comes to the fore-front of many of his most beloved theater songs through the cockney lyrics, but the bouncy melodies to his songs also bring to mind impressions of both the harmonious chaos of London street life and the brash vocables of the British music halls.

The other vital component mentioned above, Bart's Jewish heritage, was likewise indispensable to his conception of *Oliver!* and remains perhaps the most ironic para-dox stemming from *Oliver!*: remarkably, a Jewish East Ender conceived of a stage musical in which the hero is based on a Victorian literary character who embodies abhorrent anti-Semitic stereotypes. Bart's reinterpretation of Fagin was more than a literary (or musical) license on the part of an adaptor; it was a bold attempt to present Fagin in a unique and sympathetic light. His version of Fagin was therefore a reclamation in multiple respects. Not only did the composer redeem the character, but he likewise reclaimed him for the Jewish people.

An additional paradox relating to *Oliver!* is the fact that its creator was not for-mally trained in music.[107] In yet another merger between the East End and the West End, Bart combined working-class chutzpa and respectable humility when reflecting on his creative abilities:

I'm really just an ordinary cockney bloke who can whistle a tune. I've never spent more than an hour on a song. I think up a tune, hum it into a tape recorder, and if it's not working I put it away and listen to it again in three days. If it's still not working I throw it away. Thinking up tunes is second nature to me. Sometimes if I'm stuck I tap it out with one finger on the piano, change it around, then change it again, until it sounds right. Then I work out the orchestrations and arrangements in the same way.[108]

This is not to say that he never received any sort of formal instruction. As a young man, he started taking lessons on the violin, though his instructor was less than encouraging: "[He] tried to teach me to play the violin for about six months, and I got as far as the Bluebells of Scotland [sic]. [...] And this dear man said you're never going to be a musician Lionel, stick with the painting—I've heard you can draw, you know."[109] While this anecdote regarding Bart's lack of formal training bears testament to his intuitive musical genius, it likewise reinforces a certain "limited sticking power,"[110] a trait that would sadly serve to inhibit the composer in the latter stages of his life and career.

Even without formal instruction, Bart received a great deal of unofficial training over the course of his musical "education." Years after writing *Oliver!*, the composer would nostalgically recall that the abstract musicality inherent in his working-class upbringing proved essential to the writing of the score: "I don't know where it came from. I just know that I have always heard music in my head, wherever I am. I was in the street as a kid and I could reproduce all kinds of marching tunes that I had heard, one after the other, running a stick along the park railing to keep the time. I think that's how 'Consider Yourself' started."[111] Bart's childhood was obviously characterized by a wide diversity of musical idioms, from the cockney ballads of the music hall to the Jewish folk songs of the Yiddish theater, to the vibrant street cries of the East End buskers. Notably, these diverse traditions came together in the character of a charismatic yet frightening East End Jew who might very well have planted the idea for Bart's greatest character. In later life, the composer recalled an elderly busker by the name of Solomon Levy, who "had a grotesque clown effect, and a little dog. And he'd come along singing this song and of course he was frightening. My sister used to run and hide in the outside lav in the back yard when he came down the road."[112] The image of the frightening yet clownish East End Jew who has the power to entertain and to terrify simultaneously is at once evocative of Fagin, and the conventions of the music-hall singer, the temple cantor, and the East End busker would all find their way into *Oliver!*

Though Bart initially sought to become a graphic artist, the solitary nature of visual art was ultimately less enticing than the collaborative potential of the theater. Over the course of his national service with the Royal Air Force, Bart met John Gorman, a young printer who would prove to be a lifelong friend and confidant. The two bonded over their shared interest in art and eventually made plans to go into business together. Still, Gorman took note of his friend's capacity for musical experimentation: "He had a clever way of rhyming unlikely words and squeezing long lines into short bars, a portent of his brilliant future as the best lyricist of the sixties. [...] [He was able] to string words together with an ease that matched his natural ability to draw and paint."[113] Gorman had an early window into Bart's various talents. He also may have been granted a unique glimpse into a key moment in the gestation of *Oliver!* On an unauthorized trip to Gloucester, the pair visited the cinema to watch David Lean's *Oliver Twist*:

> It was a memorable film, and on our way back to camp Lionel said, 'One day, I'm going to write a musical based on that story and it will be better than any American musical.' It was an extravagant claim, even for Lionel whose imagination is untrammeled

by the boundaries that limit other mortals, but ten years later as I watched the opening night of *Oliver!*, which won Lionel universal acclaim and adulation, I thought
back to that afternoon of truancy and his prophetic words.[114]

Though there is no corroborating evidence that Bart watched the Lean film with
Gorman, the chronology fits. However, given the countless (and conflicting) accounts
of how the seed for *Oliver!* was first planted, it is uncertain that experiencing the
Lean film marked the precise moment of *Oliver!*'s conception. Nevertheless, the cen-
trality of the Lean film to the narrative arc of *Oliver!*—and to Bart's basic concept of
Oliver Twist—is unquestionable.[115]

Following their time in the national service, Bart and Gorman founded G&B Arts
in 1950, a printing business on Elderfield Road in Hackney.[116] Even as his vocation as
a businessman/artist began to take shape, however, Bart felt the pull of the theater.
Fortunately, the organization that would foster his theatrical development would
likewise offer him an outlet for his talents as a painter and designer.[117] Nevertheless,
it is fitting that Lionel Bart's most significant contributions to Unity Theatre were
musical.

The postwar theatrical discourse was dominated by talk of Royal Court and Theatre
Workshop; Unity Theatre was the "elder statesman" of the leftist troupes. Alumnus
Jack Grossman recalls that in the 1950s, "the Royal Court had opened up. Stratford
East had opened up. They were all doing that groundbreaking work which was not
acceptable to the establishment until Unity introduced it."[118] Though Bertolt Brecht
eventually became an idol of the postwar English theater, Unity had staged the very
first British production of a Brecht play in the years leading up to World War II.[119]
Similarly, Unity prefigured the arrival of the angry young men; in a promotional pamphlet produced by the organization, Ted Willis noted that "fifteen or twenty years
ago dramatists like Wesker and Osborne [...] would have turned naturally to Unity
as the only outlet for their plays."[120] Just as the dramas of the angry young men were
defined by their realistic depiction of working- and lower-middle-class environments,
Unity was committed to showing ordinary people in everyday situations, specifically,
situations involving work and labor.[121] Grossman echoes the sentiment, asserting that
"Unity was utterly groundbreaking. There was nothing like it. It was an amateur theatre that set professional standards, and I think that was the distinction, apart from
the material."[122] The material was, of course, leftist, if not fully communist.

Since Unity encouraged its members to immerse themselves in all the elements
of staging a show (acting, writing, music, set design, etc.), Bart was given an unparalleled "hands-on" education in the theatrical production process. Furthermore, in
light of Bart's aforementioned interest in folk music, it seems fitting that he began
his theatrical career under the tutelage of a group of artists who were committed
to preserving the entertainment traditions of the working classes. Just as music
hall would prove essential to Bart's shows, it was likewise an integral part of the
Unity repertoire: "[Lionel] came from an East End tradition and we did all that stuff
for Unity. Old time music hall was a very large part of the company."[123] Bart's fondness for the Jewish theaters of the East End provided yet another link to Unity, as
many Unity artists emerged from this same tradition.[124] Moreover, Unity Theatre

and the *Daily Worker* frequently praised and supported the efforts of the Yiddish theaters, including the Grand Palais. Yiddish theater was a community event, and given Unity's overarching goal of building a community of workers, its appreciation for the popular appeal of the Jewish theaters is understandable.[125]

Bart joined Unity Theatre in the early 1950s; on becoming a Unity player, he also became more heavily involved with the Communist Party. Though this was not a prerequisite for entering Unity, Bart was "[a]lready sympathetic to the Party on many issues" because of his East End roots.[126] Nevertheless, fellow Unity member Harry Landis, who worked alongside Bart on several projects, recalls that Bart was never an overtly political artist: "He put his mind to it and wrote some very leftwing songs. [...] Lionel was an East End boy from an area where there were struggles of working people, so he was kind of semi-involved but not all that committed."[127] Even so, there is no denying that Bart made an impact during his time at Unity. His roles were numerous and diverse, as he painted sets, designed posters, acted, and wrote songs.[128]

It seems natural that many of Bart's most noteworthy creative contributions to Unity were made in collaboration with Jack Grossman, given their similar backgrounds. They were sons of Jewish refugees who had been raised in the musical traditions of both the East End and the Yiddish Theatre.[129] Grossman met Bart while performing in *The Wages of Eve*, and the two men forged a successful working relationship. Though Grossman had more theatrical and musical experience, he immediately noticed Bart's talent for churning out songs in spite of his technical limitations with music. "I've described Lionel, perhaps unfairly, as a one-finger merchant," says Grossman. "He couldn't write music. He couldn't read music. He couldn't play. Nor could Noël Coward or Irving Berlin. And I remember it vividly, going to the house he lived in then, sitting in this room and we'd plunk about on the piano. And he'd do the one finger thing and I'd plot a number."[130] The two most significant products of the Bart/Grossman partnership were their musical contributions to the revue show *Turn It Up!* and the political pantomime *Cinderella*, for which the two young men wrote the score.

Bart gained much from his time with Unity Theatre, including experience with a collaborative and somewhat frenetic production methodology that would come to define many of his theatrical projects. Looking back on his career, Bart later stated, "I hate working alone. I'm not interested in sitting at a piano doing my scales three hours a day. [...] I'm not too good at working unless I'm working to a deadline with a team."[131] It is a description that seems evocative of his early theatrical upbringing at Unity. Fittingly, it was Unity Theatre that staged the very first Bart musical: a modernized adaptation of Ben Jonson's *Volpone* entitled *Wally Pone, King of the Underworld*. Produced in 1958, *Wally Pone* reset the story of Jonson's foxy con artist to postwar Soho, and the themes and settings of the piece reinforce Bart's understanding of "the fashionable coffee-bar culture which preceded the Swinging Sixties."[132] Surprisingly, the musical was not a success. In his comprehensive archival text on Unity Theatre, Colin Chambers states that the adaptation "played to practically empty houses for ten weeks."[133] Grossman and fellow Unity alumnus Julian Glover both acknowledge that the show had great potential and that Bart's ideas were both creative and engaging; the audience simply was not there.[134]

The failure of *Wally Pone* may account for why the Unity chapter of Bart's career has never received the full attention that it deserves regarding his development as a theatrical composer. Landis speculates that Lionel himself thought "it sounded better to have started his career with Joan Littlewood's theatre; he did work with her, but it was after Unity. I think he preferred it to look like he'd started there because there was more fame in it."[135] Landis's assessment may not be a fair assumption, for on the heels of *Oliver!*'s success Bart openly acknowledged the influence that Unity exerted on his development as a theater artist; in an interview with the *Belfast News-Letter*, the composer boldly stated that working at Unity was "the real turning point of my life."[136] In the very same article, however, Bart went on to cite the centrality of Littlewood's contributions to his career: "Writing for the stage, that was almost a closed shop. If I hadn't met Joan Littlewood, I really don't know what would have happened."[137] This "friction" between Unity Theatre and Theatre Workshop regarding the development of Lionel Bart's career is fairly ironic given that the goals and methods of the two troupes were strikingly similar. Nevertheless, the tension is perhaps inevitable given that Bart's first true theatrical success, though produced by Theatre Workshop, was a show that had its roots in Unity. Jack Grossman recalls that "some of the numbers and some of the ideas from *Wally Pone* basically became *Fings Ain't Wot They Used T'Be*."[138] Notably, the song "G'Night Dearie," which provides a boisterous opening to *Fings*, had actually been written for *Wally Pone*.[139]

This situation has fueled the belief that Bart lost sight of his Unity roots: "Unity Theatre got in touch with him and said, 'Could we have a royalty, because some of the material you took was from *Wally Pone*?' And I saw the letter where his agent [Jock] Jacobsen wrote back and said 'I've asked Lionel and Lionel's refused', which, you know, really surprised me."[140] Similarly, Jacobsen had played hardball when negotiating the contract for Bart's producing *Wally Pone* at Unity. Bart was cautious about some of the provisions outlined in his original contract, particularly terms specifying that certain percentages of the gross from potential future productions of the musical at other theaters should be paid to Unity.[141] Bernard Heniz, then the general manager at Unity, countered that "[a]s a theatre which has never been out of serious financial difficulties, [Unity] risks its very existence with each new play it puts on. We feel that if one of these plays creates attention and is transferred to a more profitable climate [...] then Unity should get a proper financial return for its enterprise."[142] Heinz went on to point out that "[Bart's] present, well-deserved success must in no small measure be due to the opportunity this theatre gave him to develop his talent," reinforcing the notion that the composer "owed" Unity.[143] The entire episode seems to epitomize the controversy regarding Bart's alleged failure to support the institution to which he owed much of his education in the theater. Such allegations overlook the fact that in spite of Bart's 1960s spending sprees, he nevertheless contributed to Unity in the years of his success; a 1963 version of the theater's "Here Is Drama" pamphlet listed him as one of the organization's financial sponsors.

Nevertheless, the tumultuous legacy of Bart's involvement with Unity is also peppered with allegations of plagiarism, as Bart purportedly adopted and adapted two of Grossman's melodies while composing numbers for *Oliver!*: Fagin's "Be Back Soon" was a variation on the melody to a song that Grossman wrote for Unity's *Cinderella* called "Be a Man, John Bull" (for which Bart cowrote the lyrics), while Mr. Bumble's haunting "Boy for Sale" was a modified version of another Grossman song, "Green Jungle," which first appeared in *Turn It Up!*[144] Grossman reflects on the entire episode with good-natured amusement:

> I met Lionel again about a year before his death. I was at a small dinner party with Bill Owen, who was a lifelong friend, and his wife Kathleen O'Donohue. She and I had performed together in Unity and the old time music hall. Anyway, I hadn't seen Lionel for years. [...] He said, 'Hallo Jack,' and we had a convivial evening, and then, he said, 'You know something, Jack, you used to write some good stuff.' I was very flattered. Then he said, 'I believe I pinched some of it.' [...] Lionel had chutzpah; that was his secret weapon. He turned around after that and said 'I believe I pinched some of my own stuff!'[145]

These controversies belie the fact that the Unity Theatre alumni who worked with Bart, including Grossman and Landis, continue to regard him with feelings of warmth and frustrated affection. The most contentious and obscure case of Bart's collaborations with fellow members of Unity is that of Joan Clarke Maitland Lerner (referred to simply as Joan Maitland from this point forward), who maintained a close working relationship with Bart following his time at Unity and who contributed to the development of his librettos, though this particular issue is best reserved for Chapter 2.

Even as Bart was developing as an artist of the theater, a separate and unique thread of his career was simultaneously evolving. "Lionel was *the* star pop composer [of the postwar period]" says Mackintosh. "When anybody wanted a hit they'd go to Lionel Bart and it was almost like that was his day job and the night job was turning out musicals."[146] At the time, Bart alluded to pop songwriting as a "means to an end,"[147] his ultimate goal being to break into the theater and write musical plays.[148] As the young Bart tried to balance his involvement in theatrical projects with his new career as a pop songwriter, he simultaneously set himself on the path that would eventually lead him to *Oliver!* The "poperetta" approach that defined his musical adaptation allowed him to find the proverbial best of both worlds.

Bart's successes as a pop songwriter were largely the result of his understanding of his time period. His first pop song, "Oh for a Cup of Tea," would poke fun at the postwar youth culture's fixation on trendy coffee bars. The song expresses a nostalgic lament for the prewar British culture, which was more definably English, in contrast to the globalized postwar culture symbolized by the Italian coffee fad (and the ever-growing taste for American popular music, epitomized by the jukeboxes that helped make the coffee bars a popular retreat for teenagers).[149]

Ironically, the success of the abovementioned song would lead Bart to a wildly profitable partnership that was largely driven by the very same coffee-shop craze. "Oh for a Cup of Tea" caught the attention of bandleader Billy Cotton, who played it on his show, making it the first Bart song to hit the airwaves.[150] While celebrating this achievement at the Yellow Door in Waterloo, Bart met a young seaman merchant by the name of Tommy Hicks, who was shortly due to change his name to Tommy

Steele and become the primary pop idol of the postwar period.[151] As noted, MacInnes perceived Steele's rise to fame and fortune as something of a "counterattack" against the Americans, as "[English] teenagers have hoped for, and now found, a troubadour with whom they can identify themselves more fully than they ever could with Elvis."[152] Bart's role in Steele's ascent is another foreshadowing of his granting England its own postwar musical tradition. As Steele's pop career blossomed, Bart's music started to reach wider audiences, thus earning him popularity, prestige, and prosperity.[153] In 1957 alone, he won three Ivor Novello Awards for songwriting, followed by an additional four in 1959, and, perhaps his crowning achievement, "Show Business Personality of the Year" in 1960. That was the year of *Oliver!*'s debut, though Bart had already achieved a significant reputation in the West End theater as a result of two early musical hits.

FINGS AIN'T WOT THEY USED T'BE AND LOCK UP YOUR DAUGHTERS

Fings Ain't Wot They Used T'Be developed under the supervision of one of the most important forces in the postwar English theater: Joan Littlewood. Littlewood holds a unique place in Bart's biography, as she was involved with the two projects that symbolize the alpha and omega of his theatrical career. It was Littlewood who recruited him to work on *Fings*, his first true success in the realm of musical theater. She also helped direct his disastrous Robin Hood musical *Twang!!* (before unceremoniously leaving the project), the show that marked a drastic turning point in Bart's career. Whatever *Twang!!*'s infamous legacy, the positive elements of the Bart-Littlewood relationship far outweigh the negatives, as Littlewood facilitated Bart's continued development as a theatrical composer. Granted, the improvisational tenor of Theatre Workshop's production process was antithetical to the notion of the sophisticated musical narratives of Broadway; Mackintosh wryly reflects that "Lionel basically liked the process of being put in the corner by Joan Littlewood—with plenty to drink—and told 'write a song about this, write a song about that, will you?' That was his idea of doing theatre."[154] Still, Littlewood's emphasis on working-class entertainment resulted in her drawing heavily from the traditions that would epitomize Bart's approach to musical theater.

Though Littlewood's early focus on cultivating a working-class theater was centered on socialist politics and agitprop, the postwar period marked a significant shift in her approach. The materialism of the 1950s, coupled with the "Red Scare," witnessed an understandable decline in the socialist elements of Theatre Workshop projects.[155] Nadine Holdsworth notes that "Littlewood replaced Theatre Workshop's earlier political and social agenda with a rousing knockabout East End 'knees up' style of theatre that owed a great debt to popular variety entertainment."[156] Robert Leach concurs that Theatre Workshop came to revolve heavily around the concept of "the cockney," and that for a time the troupe actually succeeded in drawing the interest of East End audiences.[157]

Theatre Workshop productions were built around the theory of performance as opposed to authorship.[158] As such, the scripts were composed through collaboration and improvisation, and they were hardly binding contracts, as Littlewood experimented with virtually every style of performance, oftentimes combining them in unique and radical ways that fundamentally resisted the plays' being constrained in the form of a publishable, reproducible text. As Ossia Trilling noted in her assessment of the postwar theater,

> [w]hat distinguishes the Littlewood manner from that of the other try-out theatres in London and the British provinces is the peculiar quality to which the term *commedia dell'arte* might very well be applied, not in the classical sense of the expression (by which is meant the formal use of the classical Italian masks), but in the widest sense, according to which all the contributory arts of the popular theatre, including improvisation, dance, music, song, and mime, for example, are given their fullest expression within the framework of a rich and truly popular dramatic dialogue.[159]

In light of Littlewood's 1950s fixation on the cockney, it is hardly surprising that the most dominant performance style at Theatre Workshop was that of the English music hall. Indeed, virtually all of the Theatre Workshop plays staged in the era of *Fings* were touched in some way by the conventions of English music hall: in *A Taste of Honey*, "[t]he addition of jazz interludes and the traditional 'music-hall' interpretation which was given to the role of the mother at least in London and New York were among the distinctive features that gave this play its singular appeal."[160] In Brendan Behan's two Theatre Workshop masterpieces, *The Quare Fellow* and *The Hostage*, music-hall motifs and performance routines dominate, particularly in the latter: "The debt to traditional music-hall entertainment and vaudeville is unmistakable and must be an essential metaphor in any production."[161]

Although Littlewood's fondness for music hall connects her to Osborne, her more chaotic and radical employment of music-hall conventions confirms another divergence between Littlewood and her angry young male contemporaries: Littlewood more deliberately embraced the theories of Brecht. Whereas the revolutionary elements of *Look Back in Anger* were based in its content, Littlewood was more concerned with matters of form, as she believed that the only way to reach the working classes was to rethink the very format of the theater. Margaret Eddershaw describes Theatre Workshop as having been "Brechtian in a number of ways":

> It was organised as a collective, believed in long rehearsal periods and drew eclectically on a wide range of sources of materials and production methods. Interested in performers from a variety of backgrounds as well as actors from the legitimate theatre, Littlewood instigated an intensive programme of company training, which comprised a mix of mime and physical exercises, and music hall and cabaret-style performance techniques (which brought them close to Brecht).[162]

Still, Leach asserts that Littlewood's work on *Mother Courage* was her "only serious encounter with Bertolt Brecht"[163] and he labels the results as disappointing.[164] Ironically, Littlewood's attempt at staging Brecht's greatest work was a failure, in spite of her receiving the benison of Brecht himself. Nevertheless, whatever his skepticism regarding the English understanding of Brecht, Esslin concedes that "Joan

Littlewood and Peter Brook's work on plays by other authors must, on the whole, be regarded as the most positive result of Brechtian influence on the art of stage directing in England."[165] Esslin is especially gracious in his praise of Littlewood's understanding of the Brechtian view of stage music, noting that of all the Brechtian musicals that debuted in the postwar era, "Joan Littlewood achieved the largest measure of success in this direction."[166] *Oh What a Lovely War*, Littlewood's most enduring work, remains a monumental achievement in the application of Brechtian musical principles.

In the context of *Fings*, Eddershaw's praise for Littlewood's reaching out to working-class audiences can be paired with Esslin's praise for her successful use of Brechtian music, for Brecht's emphasis on geistic music allowed him to break with the bourgeois traditions of opera and bring stage music down to the boards. The incomparable Kurt Weill understood this as one of the principal goals of Brecht's greatest musical work, *The Threepenny Opera*, "putting us in touch with an audience which was previously ignorant of us, or at least would never have believed us capable of interesting a circle of listeners so much wider than the normal concert- and opera-going public."[167] Like Brecht, Littlewood understood the power of music hall as a working-class cultural institution. Furthermore, the interactive nature of music-hall entertainment was conducive to creating the type of theatrical environment that Littlewood hoped would draw working-class patrons to Stratford East.

Bart's relationship with Littlewood reinforces the radicalism of his early theatrical career. Moreover, Bart was inevitably intrigued by Littlewood's use of music to foster camaraderie between the audience and the cast: "All the plays [at Theatre Workshop] had songs of some sort in them," Bart noted, "and I felt an infinity [sic] with that from my childhood days. In the Yiddish theatre which had that same kind of audience artiste thing."[168] Fittingly, Bart's first project with Littlewood was based heavily on that "same kind of audience artiste thing."

When Bart met Littlewood, *Fings* was still a highly abstract project. Though Frank Norman had not conceived of the play as a musical, Littlewood saw potential for merging the working-class themes of the piece with a working-class musical score: "It should be a musical, or anyway have a few songs in it. I've met this wonderful nutcase called Lionel Bart, I've already talked to him about it and he's agreed to write some songs."[169] Though initially enthusiastic, Norman grew frustrated as his writing was discarded in favor of increased improvisation.[170] Still, it is fortunate that Littlewood selected Bart to write the score, for Bart's own cockney background helped to preserve the basic tone of Norman's play even as the script changed. As Eric Johns noted in his review of the original West End production,

> [t]he bright, breezy, tuneful score is intimately woven into Frank Norman's play, as if the words and the notes had been created simultaneously. They are essentially created in the same idiom. Whether the characters speak or sing, their roots are still firmly embedded in the soil of Soho; there is no question of their stepping out of the picture whenever a musical number comes along.[171]

Johns's description implies that the show is written in the same vein as the integrated musicals that defined postwar Broadway, though this is not the case. Bart's songs spring up suddenly, even randomly, and the characters do "step out," or at the very least "step forward" to do a music-hall turn before singing. Nevertheless, there is a strong sense of cohesion due to Bart's masterful incorporation of Norman's cockney argot.

Fings was of great interest to Bart largely because of its relevance to a culture/language that he had known from his early life onward, and simultaneously, because of its innovativeness in exploring that culture/language (and its musical potential) onstage; he supposedly told Littlewood that it was the "[f]irst time I've heard cockney as she is spoke."[172] Certainly, the issue of language is central to understanding *Fings* in the context of Theatre Workshop's goals. In a prefatory note to the libretto, Littlewood reflected on the fact that in the traditional English theater, "the voice of the Cockney was one long whine of blissful servitude. [...] This refined and treasured theatre could not attract nor touch the vulgar populace, our theatres were kept pure and innocent, with the charm of an aged Peter Pan."[173] Her note concludes with an appreciation of the fact that this new musical would appeal to a different class of patrons, "most of whom, like Frank Norman, had never been in a theatre in their lives."[174] For Littlewood, the desire to transform the theater by speaking in the language of the people was fundamental, and it stemmed from her negative experiences at the Royal Academy of Dramatic Art and her negative impression of the middle-class traditions of the West End stage.[175] As noted, drawing-room comedies had confined the cockney dialect to servants; Barbara Windsor, who starred in the original West End production of *Fings*, perceived the show's importance in opening up new opportunities for cockney actors and singers: "[Before *Fings*] I would never have stood a chance of starring in anything. I was always the maid who opened the door and said, 'Oh yes, tea is ready m'lady. [...] [Afterward], it became very fashionable to talk like me. [...] I owe that to Lionel."[176] This truthful representation of an unglamorous yet passionate culture connects the musical to the kitchen-sink dramas of the period, and Mackintosh's linking of Bart's career to Osborne's thus becomes more tenable.

It may be somewhat ironic to assess *Fings* as a revolutionary musical given that the very title of the piece seems to reaffirm the British tendency toward "looking back." Nevertheless, the nostalgia that runs throughout *Fings* is unique in its connection to East End working-class entertainment. This is arguably the musical's defining theme, as Scott Miller declares that *Fings* is "a British music hall lament for the loss of community in modern times."[177] The music hall had been an institution devoted to fostering such a community, and Fred's chief motive in surpassing French Herbert and Meatface has less to do with his financial goals and more to do with his desire to recapture the kinship of the past. Miller's invocation of the music-hall lament, defined by Barry J. Faulk as a genre "in which what was most vital and most endangered about the English people could be found in the music hall," [178] is essential, not only because it underscores the aforementioned connection between Bart and Osborne, but also because such laments were central to cultural discourses on Englishness. In the music-hall lament, "[a] community of mourning is addressed, imagined, and created in these essays, mobilized as a psychic defense to compensate for the loss of vital music hall, or—it amounts to the same—essential Englishness."[179] As will be discussed in Chapter 4, these narratives, however exaggerated, indirectly helped to promote the idea of *Oliver!* as a distinctly English musical and a triumph of postwar Englishness.

From a narrative perspective, *Fings* leaned toward the Brechtian model of musical performance and thus seems more evocative of "concept musicals" than "book musicals." Much as Kander and Ebb's *Chicago* would use vaudeville routines to convey the thematic relationship between criminal trials and show business, *Fings* uses music-hall songs/routines to convey the thematic relationship between the decline of the music hall and the fractured sense of postwar community.[180] Nevertheless, *Fings* lacks a tight sense of integration, even on a basic conceptual level: Bart's role was to write songs, not to set Norman's narrative to music. Bart would later assert that "I would never call [*Fings*] a musical per say [sic], it was a play with songs."[181] The fact that the characters indicate the shift from speech to song by moving downstage reinforces the piece's Brechtian quality; as in *The Threepenny Opera*, there is a "separation of the music from all the other elements of entertainment offered."[182] *Oliver!* would certainly embrace a more integrated model, and the fact that it prefigured the megamusical movement hints toward a Wagnerian vision that seems anathema to Brecht's own theories. Yet, as will be discussed in subsequent chapters, *Oliver!* hardly comes across as Wagnerian, particularly given its music-hall techniques and its emphasis on conscious performance in Fagin's den. Perhaps what makes *Oliver!* so analogous to the American musicals of the golden age of Broadway is not its use of integration but rather its successful alternating between operatic concepts of unity and disruptive performance.[183]

Morley claims that there were many people "who believed that the triumph of Bart's *Fings* and *Lock Up Your Daughters* meant a kind of Brechtian change, whereby audiences would be prepared to accept extremely unglamorous low-life musicals with maybe also a social message,"[184] though he likewise notes that most of the musicals that were produced in the same spirit failed.[185] Still, audiences and critics recognized *Fings* as "a new kind of musical—brash, irreverent and 100 per cent working-class English."[186] Although it repeatedly earned the ire of the lord chamberlain, *Fings* ultimately found its way to the Garrick Theatre, where it would play concurrently with *Oliver!* for the first few years of the latter musical's run.[187]

Bart's other early success, a loose adaptation of Fielding's *Rape Upon Rape* entitled *Lock Up Your Daughters*, was another highly collaborative project. Bart served as lyricist, setting words to the melodies of Laurie Johnson; they had previously worked together on *The Tommy Steele Story* before being recruited by the musical's librettist and producer, Lord Bernard Miles.[188] In spite of its lusty comicality and catchy songs, it has not aged as well as *Fings*; the thematic emphasis on the notion that a woman can "cry rape" when there is in fact no rape taking place inevitably offends contemporary sensibilities. Still, if *Fings* was an important precursor to *Oliver!* because of its tone and theme, then *Lock Up Your Daughters* was an equally important predecessor from a more practical standpoint. Two of the men who worked behind the scenes on *Lock Up Your Daughters* would prove indispensable to the success of *Oliver!*: director Peter Coe and designer Sean Kenny.

Coe was born to a lower-middle-class family in Camberwell, though his ex-wife Tsai Chin recalls that the director preferred to think of himself as "working-class":

> Peter would call himself working class because at that time it was very fashionable to be working class after *Look Back in Anger*. He was of the new school. At that point, we were in the middle of change. It was just after the Second World War, and the theatre was shifting from the polite theatre—the Coward era theatre when people came to rehearsals in suits and ties—to people coming in their jeans and sweat-shirts and being less and less polite. [...] We were there for the first night of all these wonderful plays: *Waiting for Godot, Look Back in Anger*, all that. When you think about it, it was just incredible. Peter fit in right there because he was working-class, anti-establishment.[189]

Like Bart, his journey to the stage was gradual. After being awarded a scholarship to study at the London Academy of Music and Dramatic Art, Coe eventually settled on education as his vocation: "'My parents and I decided that I should be a teacher so I studied and qualified'. After discovering an aptitude for theater and a distinct disability for teaching, he spent a stormy three and a half years as an actor. Stormy, because besides acting, he had to find work in turn as a farm hand, a crane driver, a factory worker, a clerk and a postman."[190] West End producer Michael MacOwan eventually took an interest in Coe and asked him to teach acting at LAMDA. In a two-year time frame, Coe turned professional producer and became director of productions at repertory theatres in Carlisle, Ipswich, and Hornchurch. While at Hornchurch, his work caught the attention of Miles, who offered him the post of first resident director at the Mermaid. Coe was a neophyte regarding musical theater when he took on *Lock Up Your Daughters*, and he did not hold the genre in particularly high regard.[191] Nevertheless, his lack of fondness for this theatrical form may in fact have contributed to the success he eventually achieved as a director of musicals, for much of this success can be attributed to his unique perspective.[192]

Sean Kenny, whose set design for *Oliver!* later won near universal acclaim from critics in both England and the United States, was likewise new to musical theater—in fact, he had always considered himself an architect as opposed to a set designer. Moreover, like Coe, Kenny was a man of diverse interests and professions; before pursuing theatrical design as his primary vocation, he spent time searching for gold, living among the Apaches, and traveling aboard a scientific vessel exploring the South Seas.[193] His unconventional pursuit of his architectural education reflected his adventurous approach to life.

A fervent admirer of Frank Lloyd Wright, Kenny undertook the long journey from his hometown of Tipperary, Ireland, to Arizona in 1950 so that he could study under the master himself. Kenny revered Wright as "the greatest architect of the century. He was involved with people not just buildings, unlike many modern architects who build monuments to themselves."[194] Just as Bart's desire to work collaboratively with others inspired him to transition from commercial artist to theater artist, so did Kenny's own interest in working closely with other people inspire him to employ his architectural education in the realm of the English theater. Furthermore, much as Bart found his "big break" working with Littlewood at Theatre Workshop, Kenny cited his work on the set for *The Hostage* as "the beginning for me and from there, everything snowballed."[195]

Kenny's experimental approach to the possibilities of theatrical set design would contribute immeasurably to the success of *Oliver!* His involvement in *Lock Up Your Daughters* served as a fitting precursor in this regard given that the Mermaid Theatre aptly fit his vision of what a modern theater should be. The Mermaid was one of the first theaters to experiment with new stage layouts, a key step toward creating what Kenny called "a multi-purpose theatre."[196] For Kenny, the constrictions created by traditional theater buildings impeded creativity: "The strait jacket of the (present) theatre building is what we spend half our time trying to outwit."[197] Thus, Kenny was interested in new approaches not only to set design and staging but also to a complete reimagining of how the physical space of a theater was constructed. It is natural for a period that saw revolutions taking place regarding the form and content of British plays to likewise witness revolutionary new approaches to the concept of theatrical space; Irving Wardle would later write that "[t]owards the end of the fifties it did seem that there might be an upheaval in theatre building to match the upheavals in production. There was a lot of fighting talk about the 'tyranny of the proscenium arch', and a big welcome for the Mermaid—with its curtainless end stage enclosed in the same room as the auditorium—when it opened in 1959."[198] The Mermaid was the ideal spot for Kenny to ply his trade.

The three men who helped bring *Oliver!* to life were all under the age of thirty when they began work on *Lock Up Your Daughters*, meeting two of the three criteria associated with the "angry young men" moniker. Though the full potential of this triumvirate would not be tapped until they worked together on *Oliver!*, the fact that Lionel Bart had two hit shows running simultaneously so early in his career was a testament to both his growing popularity and his indefatigable creativity.[199] The East End pop songwriter was rapidly becoming a pioneer in English musical theater, and his energetic celebration of cockney culture seemed to match the vigor that had made American musicals so popular on the West End stage. At this point, Bart had already set to work writing a musical adaptation of the story of Dickens's first child hero, Oliver Twist. His program bio in the *Lock Up Your Daughters* souvenir program hinted toward this unique theatrical endeavor: "Later this year his musical version of 'Oliver Twist' will be presented in the West End. For this he has produced the book, music and lyrics—he also hopes to make a little on the side selling pickled herrings in the foyer!" In actuality, the show that would earn him eternal fame was still a year away.

CHAPTER 2

⌒∿⌒

"The image for the show came to me from a candy": Writing *Oliver!*

In his youth, Lionel Bart frequented a candy shop near his parents' house that sold penny chocolates. One such sweet was a chocolate bar produced by Terry's of York. The candy bar was called an "Oliver Twist" and featured a bright label with a picture of a little boy eagerly putting forth his empty bowl. Of course, the child presented on the wrapper looks nothing like Dickens's Oliver Twist; he is a cheery, healthy-looking lad with a bright smile. Instead of sporting a ragged parish uniform, he wears a schoolboy's outfit (see Figs. 2.1, 2.2). The wrapper's bright colors stand in sharp contrast to the dark and squalid Dickensian world depicted by George Cruikshank.

All of the aforementioned changes to the imagery surrounding Dickens's character were necessary from a marketing standpoint. Who would buy a chocolate bar with a dull-colored wrapper depicting a terrified and ragged urchin pathetically holding out his bowl for more gruel? Nevertheless, the Terry's candy bar is a deceptively powerful representation of how the exploitation of Dickensian characters and images can carry significant reverberations regarding the overall perception of Dickens: the memory of this obscure treat stayed with Bart into his adult years. In a souvenir program article entitled "One of the Worldwide Family," Bart claims that "[t]he image for the show came to me from a candy,"[1] and it is not surprising that *Oliver!* opens with the scene in which the title character asks for more.

The candy bar story has become part of the lore surrounding *Oliver!*, and the fact that *Oliver!* was inspired in part by a marketing campaign designed to make money off a well-known literary character, as opposed to its being inspired by the novel itself, obviously raises questions as to whether or not *Oliver!* emerged from an artistic tradition, or rather from the transcendent commercial appeal of Dickens. Granted, these two traditions are connected in several respects, thanks to the culture text of *Twist* reflecting and reinforcing the aforementioned commercial elements: as noted in the previous chapter, Jackie Coogan's market-ability in the role of Oliver Twist drew American filmgoers to the cinema, thus allowing the Lloyd film to shape the culture text. Nevertheless, the happy-go-lucky Oliver presented on the wrapper is the antithesis of Boz's downtrodden orphan, and while the Terry's chocolate bar can do little harm to Dickens, it underscores the tendency to simplify and sentimentalize the author's works for the purpose of popular consumption.

Whatever the incongruities between the literary character and his commercial counterpart, Dickens himself had turned the "asking for more" scene into a market-able image simply by having Cruikshank depict it in his illustrations. Though it seems blasphemous to connect Cruikshank's exceptional pictures to advertisements, the fact remains that illustrations were essential to the marketing of Dickens's novels. Dickens serialized *Oliver Twist* in *Bentley's Miscellany*, and publisher Richard Bentley

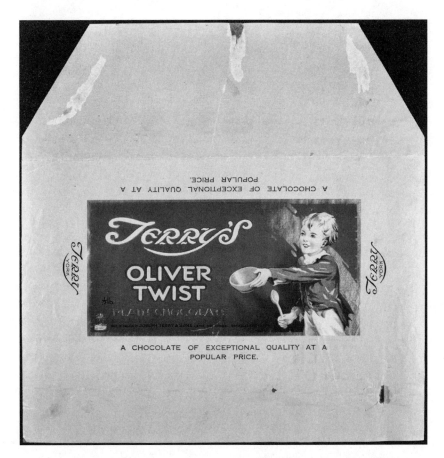

Figures 2.1 and 2.2 (continued on next page): Wrappers to the "Oliver Twist" candy bars by Terry's of York confectionary company.
Source: Reproduced from the originals in the Borthwick Institute for Archives, University of York.

Figures 2.1 and 2.2 (Continued)

insisted on all of his authors including highly visual scenes so as to facilitate the inclusion of illustrations.[2] Furthermore, in the early stages of his career, Dickens was aware that Cruikshank's marketability exceeded his own; his willingness to consider giving Cruikshank "equal billing" in the title to *Sketches by Boz* reinforces this fact.[3]

More generally, Dickens's own commercial sensibilities endowed him with a genuine appreciation for marketing and merchandising, as Jay Clayton notes that "he was never averse to commercializing these enterprises: his serials carried advertising from almost the beginning, and he took pleasure in noting the spinoff products from his imagination, such as the Little Nell Cigar and the Gamp Umbrella, even though he received no royalties from their sale."[4] If Dickens encouraged lending Little Nell's name to a brand of cigars, it seems hypocritical to fault Terry's for lending Oliver's name to a chocolate bar. Simultaneously, it seems impossible to fault Lionel Bart for having been inspired by a promotional campaign given the remarkable presence of Dickens's characters in advertising.

SWEET CONFECTIONARY, STARK FILM, SOURCE TEXT

The chocolate bar, with its commercially viable representation of Dickens's character, may have provided Bart with the "image" for a musical adaptation of *Oliver Twist*, but it offered little in the way of concrete guidance. Bart therefore turned to another key source of inspiration: the 1948 David Lean film. Though the Lean adaptation was a direct antecedent to *Oliver!*, it seems a highly unlikely foundation for Bart's project. Lean's stark conception of the story is the exact opposite of the cheerful representation of Oliver on the candy bar wrapper, much as Alec Guinness's depiction of Fagin as a terrifying corruptor seems the exact opposite of Bart's revised vision of the old man as a wily rascal. Whatever these contrasts, the Lean film provided the composer with a point of reference for the story, along with an effective outline for the plot.[5]

Almost all of the scenes in *Oliver!* have a corresponding scene in the Lean version. Both versions feature Oliver's abuse in the workhouse, Oliver's asking for more gruel, Mr. Bumble's flirtations with Mrs. Corney, Oliver's apprenticeship to Mr. Sowerberry, his mistreatment at the hands of Mrs. Sowerberry and Noah Claypole, his subsequent altercation with Noah, his journey to London, his introduction to the Artful Dodger and Fagin, his awakening to discover Fagin counting his treasures, the pick-pocketing "game," the picking of Mr. Brownlow's pocket, Oliver's arrest, Sykes and Fagin's plot to get Oliver back, Oliver's good treatment by Mr. Brownlow and Mrs. Bedwin, his subsequent abduction by Nancy and Sykes, the Bumbles' domestic troubles, the death of Old Sally, Nancy's secret meeting with Brownlow, her murder at the hands of Sykes, the pursuit of Sykes and his subsequent death, and finally, the safe return of Oliver to Mr. Brownlow. One of the only significant differences between the two adaptations regarding the storyline is that Lean includes an abridged version of the Monks subplot while Bart excises this element entirely.

If the Terry's chocolate bar planted the seed for *Oliver!*, the Lean film gave Bart the resources necessary to grow that seed. But what about the primary source for Bart's *Oliver!*: Dickens's *Oliver Twist*? Bart's own recollections of his level of familiarity with the Dickensian text are ambiguous at best, as he later reflected that "I kind of felt a great ifinity [sic] with that story, and somehow I'd always known the story. I guess I must've read it or had it read to me or been involved with it as a young kid. I know the image of the kid asking for more with the bowl was always with me."[6] On a basic narrative level, there was little reason for Bart to return to the original text; adapting Dickens's novel for the musical stage would necessitate a great deal of excising so as to leave room for music and song, and the Lean film had already streamlined the plot in such a way as to create a more fast-paced and coherent story from which Bart could work. Still, in spite of the narrative efficiency of the Lean film, the austere tone and brutal cruelty that define this adaptation leave one with the feeling that there is very little to sing about in this story. By comparison, the original novel conveys clearer musical potential. As the melodramatic Victorian stage tradition indicates, there are numerous emotional highpoints in the original text that could serve as appropriate moments for characters to transition from singing to speaking. Bart later reflected on the project as a "musical staging of this world-known classic melodrama," the ultimate goal being to preserve "the inherent Dickens mood and period atmosphere, translate it into a modern entertainment, [and create] a new expression of the 'musical' form."[7] *Oliver!* would thus reimagine the story of *Oliver Twist* without ever becoming wholly unfamiliar.

TOO YOUNG FOR FAGIN, TOO OLD FOR THE DODGER

Bart first began publicly alluding to his Dickensian musical project in 1959 on the heels of *Fings*; in a March 1959 interview with Jenny Firth, the composer explained that in spite of his successes as a pop songwriter, he was turning his attention to more substantive projects: "I'm working on Frankie Vaughan's film, 'Heart of a Man', and 'Tommy Steele, The Toreador' but I'm concentrating on more serious songs. They give more satisfaction."[8] Toward the end of the interview, Bart optimistically alluded to his future projects; with *Lock Up Your Daughters* due to open in a few short months, the composer believed that he would ultimately "have three shows in the West End [...] 'Fings', 'Lock Up Your Daughters', and a musical adaptation of 'Oliver Twist'."[9] It is fitting that Bart would mention his *Oliver Twist* musical in an article that recapped his recent cinematic work, for initially these very different projects may have shared a common link in the form of Tommy Steele.

Many years later, while reflecting on the conception of *Oliver!*, Bart recalled that "it was my job at this time to provide material for film stories for Tommy Steele. This was the original incentive for me dissecting Charles Dickens [*sic*] 'Oliver Twist'. [...] Of course, Tommy Steele was too young to play Fagin and too old to play the Artful Dodger. So I had to forget about it as an idea for him."[10] The notion of *Oliver!* as a Steele project is yet another unique plot twist in the story of the adaptation's early development, though Steele himself supposedly had no memory of any discussions with Bart regarding an *Oliver Twist* musical.[11] This contradiction immediately throws the entire issue of *Oliver!*'s emergence into question, though Bart's notion of framing his Dickensian musical as a Tommy Steele film may have been due to pressure from his music label, Peter Maurice, Ltd.

While writing pop songs for the London-based music company, Bart had tried to stir up interest in his Dickens project, but when he approached the management, "[h]e remembered Mr. [James] Phillips saying 'Show business is all right for your own amusement but why don't you sit down and write a hit song for Tommy Steele?'"[12] The only time that the executives allegedly expressed any interest in *Oliver!* was when it was framed as a potential Steele project: "Mr. Bart said he talked about 'Oliver!' to

Mr. James Phillips, managing director of Peter Maurice, while they were on a train journey. Mr. Phillips said it might be a good idea if Tommy Steele took the lead."[13] The fact that the Tommy Steele films of the 1950s were basically "vehicles" for furthering the lead performer's pop career recalls the omnipresent issue of marketing. Promoting *Oliver!* as a glitzy, pop-oriented musical project for postwar youth would likely have eased some of the difficulties that Bart faced in finding backers, though the end results would have diverged significantly from what he eventually envisioned as a more genuinely Dickensian adaptation about a suffering child's tireless search for love.[14]

The tension between the "teenybopper" approach to adapting *Oliver Twist*, as promoted by James Phillips, and Bart's own quest for "legitimacy" in the realm of the postwar theater is somewhat ironic given that Bart's fame was based heavily on his ability to reconcile such tensions. Still, it is doubtful that *Oliver!* would have achieved the timelessness of other canonical musicals had it been developed as a "pop" project. Though Bart embraced the glitz of the pop music industry, and though his pop sensibilities guided his approach to *Oliver!*, the final vision of the adaptation fostered the creation of a musical whose enduring power directly contradicted the quick consumption associated with postwar pop. Furthermore, although dynamic "American-style" musicals such as *Expresso Bongo* and *Grab Me a Gondola* were noteworthy predecessors to *Oliver!*, the fact that these musicals were steeped in the popular culture of 1950s England precluded their revival in subsequent decades. Given the timelessness of Dickens's stories—particularly *Oliver Twist*—Bart was cultivating a legacy for his musical even before the piece had been fully realized.

Nevertheless, if Bart saw great promise in the *Twist* project, the producers and theatre managers with whom he shared his ideas were far less enthusiastic, "rejecting it as morbid."[15] Given that the last major adaptation of *Twist* had been the David Lean film, it is hardly surprising that people were skeptical of a musical version of what was now perceived as an incredibly dark story of cruelty, crime, neglect, and punishment. Bart's struggle to stimulate interest in *Oliver!* likewise harkens back to the previously discussed contrasts between the American and English views of the musical theater. British theater critic W. A. Darlington noted that in the postwar era "[t]he Americans have come to believe that almost any story can be made into a musical play. [...] There has grown up in New York a belief that almost any kind of story can be set to music, however little of romance it may contain."[16] While *Oliver Twist* certainly contains its share of "romance," the romantic elements are largely overshadowed by the dark subject matter and harsh social criticism. Furthermore, in the conflict between allegorical romanticism and stark realism that defines the original text, it is clear which side the Lean film takes.

An unwaveringly dark story about a neglected child, a sinister group of criminals, and a prostitute trapped in an abusive relationship with a man who eventually bludgeons her seems an unlikely source for a musical.[17] Bart's willingness to consider the musical possibilities of *Oliver Twist* seems to intimate an "American" approach to the composition process, though this Americanness had less to do with integrated models of musical narratives and more to do with a willingness to experiment with nontraditional sources. As noted in the previous chapter, the continued improvement of the musical libretto during the thirties, forties, and fifties was arguably more vital to the advent of that golden age of American musical theater than the "perfecting" of the integrated formula. Bart's basic use of a Dickens novel/narrative as the source for his libretto invariably raised the stakes of his project in comparison to contemporary West End musicals such as *Salad Days* and *The Boy Friend*.

DONALD ALBERY, *OLIVER!*'S MR. BROWNLOW

For a time it seemed as though *Oliver!* would never make the transition from conception to production. However, Bart eventually managed to find a supporter in the prominent theater impresario Donald Albery, who would prove to be a driving force behind the success of *Oliver!* Albery came from an old theatrical family that, at the time of *Oliver!*'s emergence, controlled three theaters, though his theatrical tastes diverged significantly from those of his father, Sir Bronson Albery. Whereas Bronson was devoted to staging the classics, Donald "had catholic taste, and several times chanced his arm on plays which seemed to be vehicles of misfortune at the time, but turned out to be recognized as masterpieces."[18] Notably, he helped stage Beckett's *Waiting for Godot* "at the Arts Theatre Club, directed by the young Peter Hall, and later [...] at the Criterion (of all theatres), where it ran for some months to polite but puzzled audiences."[19] Though West End crowds were not instantly won over by Beckett's extremely unorthodox play, there was no denying that Albery had brought something unique and daring to the West End. He eventually formed his own production company, Donmar, which became known for its innovative theatrical endeavors.

Albery was not solely interested in the artistic elements of theater; he was also a savvy businessman with a keen sense of how to create box-office successes. In several respects, Albery was ahead of his time in his ability to conceptualize a West End that functioned as a transatlantic commercial center. Just as his son Ian Albery would become a dedicated examiner of theater attendance patterns in the 1970s and 1980s, Donald Albery was one of the first impresarios to "assess the value of the great numbers of tourists to the West End theatre."[20] To that end, Albery "conducted a survey, asking people to fill in a form, stating how and why they had come to such-and-such a show. This yielded much data of commercial value, and confirmed what ought to have been self-evident, that the American tourist was exceedingly important to the theatre economy in this country."[21] Furthermore, like Lionel Bart, Andrew Lloyd Webber, and Cameron Mackintosh, Albery understood the transnational (and eventually, global) possibilities of West End musicals.

Albery's roles as theater owner and impresario granted him the privilege of taking an active part in the supervision of Donmar productions. Indeed, another fundamental element of Albery's approach to the production process was his hands-on role in the running of his theatrical empire on both macro and micro levels: "He is a man who likes to see things done properly. The staff in his theatres are ordered to be polite. [...] He is firm with his backers—or angels, as he calls them. They back all or nothing. Once they back out, they don't back again. 'Can't have them picking and choosing', he says."[22] Notably, the article that put forth this description was published *subsequent* to the triumphant success of *Oliver!* As will be discussed shortly, the impresario was not quite so self-assured during the long and suspenseful buildup toward *Oliver!*'s debut; several of the backers for Bart's musical were reluctant to "back all," and Albery could not afford to take such a hard-line approach.

Throughout the latter part of the 1950s, Albery played a significant role in promoting Theatre Workshop. It was another bold move on the part of the producer, for Littlewood and her company were still being marginalized by traditionalists.[23] Albery later commented that "[t]he press had never made me feel I ought to go to Theatre Workshop. They had the reputation of being a left-wing theatre and the attitude of established West End managements seemed to be prejudiced against them."[24] The West End transfers of several Theatre Workshop shows were carried out under his supervision: *A Taste of Honey, The Hostage,* and, most importantly, *Fings Ain't Wot They Used T'Be* all reached the West End as a result of his efforts. It was through Littlewood and her theater company that Albery first became familiar with Lionel Bart.

Albery's business savvy and pioneering spirit were both central to his decision to take a chance on *Oliver!*, which was still an unfinished show. Tellingly, the impresario was convinced to invest in the musical adaptation simply by listening to a tape of Bart and Joan Maitland singing the songs that the composer had written—a genuine testament to Bart's creative magnetism and the appeal of his melodies.[25] On May 6, 1959, Bart's manager, Jock Jacobsen, sent Albery's assistant, Anne Jenkins, the signed contract that established the terms of the parties' relationship regarding *Oliver!*; Albery took an option on *Oliver!* for the sum of £400.[26] In a note enclosed with the contract, Jacobsen wrote, "I sincerely hope that this will be the beginning of a very happy association."[27] Though the relationship between Albery and Bart would not always be particularly happy, it would prove unquestionably successful for both parties.

At this point, however, *Oliver!* existed as an abstraction, and the seemingly interminable delay from May 6, 1959, to June 30, 1960—the night of *Oliver!*'s West End premiere—is indicative of the long and winding road that the adaptation would follow as it evolved. In one of the souvenir booklets printed during *Oliver!*'s West End run, Albery himself explained that the delay in the production could be attributed not to any one problem but rather to an overarching sense of uncertainty regarding the very "form of the production." Albery does not elaborate on this assertion, though it seems obvious that he is not simply referring to the physical staging of the adaptation (granted, this issue would inevitably shape the "form" of the entire production as Sean Kenny worked tirelessly with Lionel Bart and Peter Coe in conceptualizing the piece). Rather, *Oliver!* seemed torn between several potential identities: was it a musical, a pantomime, an operetta, a pastiche, or a straight Dickensian adaptation? *Oliver!* may have been slated to reach the stage in 1959, but Bart's musical had to journey through the inferno of "developmental hell" before reaching the paradise of record-breaking West End success.

OLIVER! IN DEVELOPMENT

Oliver! was assigned a decidedly modest budget of just £15,000. Ultimately, Albery was able to raise £14,350 from a diverse group of backers that included family members, like his son, Ian Albery; fellow West End producers, like Emile Littler; and artists, like Margot Fonteyn de Arias.[28] Understandably, some of the backers were nervous and displayed the sort of indecisive behavior that Albery criticized in the abovementioned article. Littler, a West End impresario best known for his panto-mimes, had invested in several of Albery's previous shows and had originally agreed to put £3,000 into *Oliver!* though his fears regarding the potential for the show's suc-cess led to his reconsidering that sum. In a letter to Albery, Littler claimed "I do not think that I want to have £3,000 in this musical. [...] I do not think this is a very good time of year to do a new show."[29] He suggested instead that he would be willing to contribute only £1,000 because, "with the Press in their present mood of slamming everything, one has to be cautious"[30] though he assured Albery he was not backing out entirely. Littler's complete withdrawal from the list of backers might have been better for Donmar in the long run, as working with Littler would ultimately prove dif-ficult.[31] Nevertheless, the full sum raised by Albery meant that Donmar would need to invest only £650 in the show, a figure that was a cause for some concern within the company; if *Oliver!* proved to be the hit that they were all hoping for, a larger invest-ment would have meant greater returns. An undated memo from Jenkins to Albery suggested that the company refund part of Littler's investment and put up the rest of the money through Donmar.[32] Jenkins's surprise regarding the low sum that Donmar would need to invest in *Oliver!* is an indirect indicator of Albery's enthusiasm regard-ing the musical—an enthusiasm so palpable that he was able to generate sufficient interest among backers to the point where practically the entire budget was covered before Donmar invested its own money.

Albery's skills at raising funds were matched only by his skills at cutting costs. Table 2.1 reveals that when the musical was finally ready for its West End debut, the production was under budget.

Though Bart was working diligently on the score to *Oliver!* and Albery was just as busy tending to production matters, both men were actively involved in the process of finding a director. Since the stage musical was still viewed as a genre dominated by Americans, it is not surprising that Albery's first instinct regarding possible directo-rial candidates for *Oliver!* was to turn to an American source for guidance: Broadway producer David Merrick. A 1959 telegram from Albery to Merrick conveys Albery's eagerness to find an American director: "Can you suggest any first class American musical comedy director who might be unexpectedly free this autumn capable of directing Dickens [sic] Oliver Twist as musical. [sic] Enormous possibilities. Score really hot stuff. Any suggestions greatly appreciated."[33] Merrick replied a week later to inform Albery that almost all of the top American musical directors were currently swamped with projects which were set to open that same year; committing to assist in the development of a new musical like *Oliver!* would not have been possible.[34]

With the option of an American director ostensibly off the table, Albery turned his attention back to his native England. It is surprising and simultaneously under-standable that Joan Littlewood was an early candidate for the post. Even though Littlewood's Theatre Workshop projects stand in sharp contrast to mainstream musi-cals such as *Oliver!*, she had worked closely with both Bart and Albery previously; additionally, the music-hall motifs in the score to *Oliver!* coincided with her own interest in working-class musical trends. Finally, Littlewood had experience as an

Table 2.1. *OLIVER!* BUDGET (BRITISH POUNDS)

Director—Peter Coe	350
Designer—Sean Kenny	800
Choreographers—Eleanor Fazan	100
—Malcolm Clare	150
Scenery	3,066
Wardrobe, Properties, and Equipment	3,194
Orchestrations and Music—Eric Rogers	500
—Eric Lambert	132
—Misc.	12
Printing and Publicity	995
Rehearsal Expenses	677
Salaries—Artistes	639
—Staff	697
Stage Labour	335
Management Fee	300
Production Fee re Ian Albery's services	150
Legal Charges	100
John Wyckham (production manager)	125
Fares, Taxis, Transport	560
Insurance Premiums	75
Audition Expenses	63
National Insurance	57
Stagesound	32
Accountancy	210
Misc.	194
Wimbledon week 1 expenses	425
London week 1 expenses	779
Total	**14,717**

Source: Sir Donald Albery Collection, DAT 194.002. Harry Ransom Center, University of Texas at Austin.

adaptor of Dickens's texts. She had written stage adaptations of *A Christmas Carol* and *The Chimes* that were staged at Stratford East during the holiday season in 1953 and 1954, respectively; true to the overwhelming popularity of its source, the former was revived in 1958.[35]

As discussed in Chapter 1, Littlewood's use of stage music was regarded by some critics as the most successful English attempt to duplicate Brecht's approach to musical narratives, with *Oh What a Lovely War* standing out as her masterpiece in this regard. However, *Oh What a Lovely War* was more of a performance-based experience than a scripted narrative. When Methuen published an official version of the script in 2000, the piece was attributed to Theatre Workshop as opposed to its being assigned one specific author. Littlewood's introductory note likewise states that "[t]his is not a conventional play and will not come to life if treated as such. It was first performed by a company of fifteen skilled dancers and singers, accustomed to improvisation and guided by a director."[36] She boldly instructs the actors and directors to "[t]hrow out your ad libs after one usage. However good they were, there are plenty more where they came from."[37]

It is intriguing to contemplate how Littlewood would have shaped the nebulous *Oliver!* in her own image had she agreed to serve as director. Given Bart's sentimental investment in the project, along with his desire to reach a broad audience, any attempt by Littlewood to capture the alienation effect of *The Threepenny Opera* would likely have met with resistance from the composer; the notion of a projector displaying appalling statistics regarding the deaths of Victorian workhouse orphans while the child chorus sings "Food, Glorious Food" is an intriguing dialectic, but it would hardly make for a pleasant evening of West End musical theater. Nevertheless, Littlewood's appreciation of rollicking, carefree music-hall performance techniques seems fully reconcilable with most of the songs that make up *Oliver!*'s score. Brechtian distancing would have run counter to Bart's vision, but a Brechtian musical narrative featuring overt "turns" during which the characters acknowledge their transition from speaking to singing (as they subtly do in *Fings*) is hardly inconceivable. In fact, had Littlewood undertaken such an approach, *Oliver!* would probably have looked a great deal like its most prominent and successful Dickensian musical successor, Rupert Holmes's *The Mystery of Edwin Drood* (see Epilogue).

Ironically, though *Oliver!* was touted as a fundamentally English musical and embraced as such by the English press (see Chapter 4), it is conceivable that a production of *Oliver!* with Littlewood at the helm would have been more pronouncedly English because of her overt emphasis on music hall and pantomime performance techniques in various Workshop plays; the latter of these performance styles would likely have exerted a noticeable effect on the Littlewood version of *Oliver!* given that the show would theoretically have debuted around Christmastime and would have continued the 1950s tradition of Dickensian Christmas shows at Stratford East. Nevertheless, Bart's desire to create a "new musical form" while building off Dickens's Victorian melodrama seems to have been directed toward an integrated vision as opposed to a Brechtian "theory of separation,"[38] and the megamusical movement that emerged in the wake of *Oliver!*'s success was defined in part by Wagnerian unity. As discussed in Chapter 1, however, the significance of integration in relation to the success of the American musical during the golden age of Broadway has become an oversimplification of a more complicated evolution, and it is doubtful that taking an integrated approach to the musical narrative was the only means of ensuring *Oliver!*'s success.

Bart was writing in an age where the concept of integration had ostensibly become a universal truth, and where the Americans had presumably cornered the market on the musical format. It seems improbable that he would not have been affected by these trends. Although it is paradoxical to imply that Bart—"the father of the modern English musical"—was "selling out" to the American model, in his resistance to Littlewood, Bart repeatedly emphasized commercial concerns, not only in regard to her approach to the project but also regarding the possible limitations of staging the musical at Stratford East. By August 1959, Albery and Littlewood had discussed the possibility of her taking on *Oliver!* as a Christmastime Theatre Workshop production, though Bart was wary: "Having thought about the whole aspect of 'OLIVER' [*sic*] starting at Stratford, I am still worried, but it looks as though this is the only way Joan will even think about it. We must be prepared to lose out on the element of large spectacle and lush sound."[39] Bart conceded that whatever their creative differences, Littlewood's participation would inevitably enhance other elements of the piece: "We will certainly gain on 'Dickens' and style."[40] The question was whether the possible "literary" and "performance-based" benefits of hiring Littlewood as director outweighed the potential commercial limitations of *Oliver!* as a Littlewood-style musical mounted at Stratford East.

Though Bart had forsaken the "teenybopper" approach advocated by Peter Maurice, Ltd., the marketability of the musical was still of significant importance to him, and his emphasis on glitz and spectacle at the expense of the Dickensian element reinforces the centrality of his "pop" sensibilities to his vision of the project. Nevertheless, these same sensibilities may ultimately have saved *Oliver!* from enduring the nightmarish preproduction process of its infamous Littlewood-directed successor *Twang!!* The difficulty of reconciling Littlewood's improvisational approach with Bart's concept for a coherent, large-scale West End production could have proved disastrous. More importantly, Littlewood's commitment to spontaneous theatrical performances, combined with her downplaying of scripts and texts, would have made it difficult to define the already elusive and abstract *Oliver!*

The issue of Littlewood directing *Oliver!* at Stratford East eventually became moot, possibly as a result of scheduling conflicts, though by December 1959 it was clear that any hope of doing *Oliver!* as a Christmas show had long since passed.[41] Concerns about the feasibility of Stratford East would likely have grown as Sean Kenny's grand vision for the *Oliver!* set began to evolve. In fact, the entire creative vision behind *Oliver!* was continuing to expand in both size and scope, though the final product would simultaneously exude the music-hall intimacy that Littlewood strove for in her own musical productions.

With Littlewood out of the running, Albery eventually sought out Peter Coe. Coe had previously worked with Bart on *Lock Up Your Daughters*, and with Albery on *The World of Suzie Wong*. The young director's reputation had grown immeasurably as a result of these two plays, particularly the latter.[42] His work on *Oliver!* would not only establish the definitive staging of Bart's musical, but it would likewise establish him as one of the foremost directorial talents in British musical theater. Sadly, the full degree of Coe's contributions to *Oliver!* remains unknown, though it extended well beyond the staging of the musical. A letter from Albery to agent Milton Goldman notes that "[t]he script [to *Oliver!*] has now been partly rewritten by Peter Coe."[43] Alastair Davidson, who served as deputy stage manager on the original West End production, corroborates this assertion, recalling that "the shape of the script was Lionel Bart. But the script, as it was finished in the theatre, was mainly Peter Coe."[44]

Unfortunately, there is no comprehensive record of what changes the director made to the script, owing to the lack of surviving draft materials. Still, there are some clues as to the nature of Coe's revisions, and it is clear that Coe's creative vision oftentimes diverged from Bart's. These textual issues will be discussed at length later in this chapter.

THE CONTROVERSY SURROUNDING THE *OLIVER!* LIBRETTO

With so many individuals contributing to the basic shape of the adaptation, and thus exerting a pronounced effect on the text, it is understandable why one of the most significant controversies regarding *Oliver!* relates to the writing credits, for since its debut performance the book, lyrics, and music to *Oliver!* have been attributed solely to Lionel Bart. The collaboration between Bart, Kenny, and Coe was indispensable to the writing of the libretto, but it is Joan Maitland who proves to be the most indistinct and controversial figure regarding the composition of *Oliver!* In the literature surrounding the musical, Maitland has oftentimes been identified as Bart's "secretary," though this designation may be misleading. Maitland worked closely with Bart over a period of several years and undertook the arduous task of helping him manage his affairs; however, she likewise participated actively in her own theatrical and musical endeavors outside the scope of Bart's projects.[45] Her connection with Bart eventually led to her most enduring contributions to the English musical theater through her work on the librettos to *Oliver!* (for which she received no credit) and *Blitz!* (for which she received formal credit as Bart's coauthor). The relationship was reciprocally beneficial, for just as Bart relied heavily on Maitland, Maitland later tried her hand at songwriting and turned to Bart for tutelage in writing lyrics.[46] In spite of this once happy and fruitful friendship, surviving letters reveal that the relationship between the two gradually degenerated, wavering between nostalgic affection and increasing frustration. Most of these conflicts seem to have stemmed from the financial difficulties that plagued both parties throughout the 1960s.[47]

Maitland's official role in the writing of *Oliver!* was never established. Years later, Bart's business manager, Stephen Komlosy, guardedly acknowledged that Maitland "was instrumental in the earlier days, to a certain extent, in complying [sic] ideas for *Oliver!*"[48] Former Unity Theatre member Harry Landis takes the matter infinitely further, fully crediting Mailtand with the writing of the libretto.[49] It is obvious that Bart did not depend entirely on Maitland in crafting the script, as surviving notebooks and draft materials contain his own scenes and dialogue, as adapted directly from Dickens's text. Furthermore, the circumstances surrounding *Oliver!*'s composition precluded close collaboration between the two. In the summer of 1959, Bart took a long trip to Spain, during which he devoted much of his time to writing *Oliver!*[50] Bart was in continuous contact with Maitland over the course of the trip, relying on her to run his business affairs while he was abroad, though surviving letters offer no concrete details regarding the extent of Maitland's creative contributions.

Indeed, it is impossible to determine the very nature of Maitland's contributions, for both Maitland and Bart completely obscured her involvement from the public. In a curious *Daily Mail* article published in March 1961, Maitland briefly acknowledged that although she received royalties from *Oliver!*, "the payment does not mean she gave any creative help to Lionel Bart, the musical's author. 'It's just that Lionel is a very generous man', she explained."[51] The notion that Maitland would receive a percentage of the show's profits and royalties in spite of her not having done any "creative" work on the project seems implausible, and during the buildup toward *Blitz!* Maitland's work on *Oliver!* received more formal notice in the press, most notably in a *Daily Telegraph* article by Winifred Carr which went so far as to acknowledge that "Miss Maitland [...] helped 'Bart' as she calls him, to write 'Oliver' [sic]."[52] Such comments may have contributed to the growing tension in Bart and Maitland's relationship; in a 1965 letter, Maitland chastised Bart for his supposed protectiveness of the "narrative" of *Oliver!*'s development, as Bart was purposefully ambiguous whenever he referred to Maitland in interviews, using neutral descriptions such as "colleague of long standing"[53]; Maitland found such descriptions unflattering, though she was willing to continue playing the role of uncredited collaborator in regard to *Oliver!*[54]

Landis speculates that Bart's hesitancy regarding any public acknowledgment of Maitland's work on *Oliver!* stemmed from his wish to be recognized as the sole creative force behind the written components of the musical.[55] Maitland thus received no formal acknowledgment at the time of the show's debut. Still, given her lifelong reticence regarding the details of her contributions to *Oliver!*, Maitland was obviously more than willing to sacrifice "credit" for cash: the royalties were significant.[56] She displayed a similar willingness years later when the possibility of a film adaptation of *Blitz!* seemed tenable.[57]

The fact that the libretto was reworked by Coe in the months leading up to *Oliver!*'s premiere may ultimately render the final question of Maitland's contributions futile. As will be discussed later in this chapter, the final drafts of the libretto ultimately diverged from Bart's earliest conceptions while simultaneously building on the foundations that he—and Maitland—had established. Moreover, the fact that *Oliver!* was constantly evolving in terms of its very form (transitioning from a potential Theatre Workshop Christmas show to a musical spectacular modeled on the ethos of the golden-age Broadway musical) seems fundamentally antithetical to the very concept of authorship: no one "author" could have written the "text" for *Oliver!* because the writing of the text was no simple matter of putting words on a page.

Oliver! was hardly the exception to the rule in this regard. The truth is that authorship is oftentimes a vague construction, as opposed to a distinct reality, in the realm of musical theater. Jim Lovensheimer deconstructs this issue in *The Oxford Handbook of the American Musical*: "How many times have the phrases 'Leonard Bernstein's *West Side Story*' (what would Jerome Robbins have said about that?) or 'a Stephen Sondheim musical' been used to identify a work that in actuality was the result of a collaborative team, whose members share the responsibility for the musical's success or failure?"[58] Naturally, Sondheim's success in the musical theater allowed him to develop a "brand name" that subsequently witnessed his fully embracing the role of "author" even as he continued to collaborate with other artists, and although

Mark N. Grant acknowledges the collaborative nature of creating a musical, he also states that

> individual voices do emerge out of the collaborative process; sometimes one voice does dominate, and sometimes there is synergy—a metavoice, the collaborative chemistry greater than the sum of its parts. But the only sure road for an individual to attain guaranteed personal expression in the Broadway musical is to first achieve enormous commercial success in the collaborative mode. That way, one gets the power and becomes the 'muscle.'[59]

Bart's desire for acknowledgment as the sole writer on *Oliver!* may have been based in a larger desire to cultivate and secure the abovementioned "power," and certainly, the success of *Oliver!* guaranteed Bart the "muscle" described by Grant, though his subsequent emphasis on "personal expression" in musical productions proved detrimental to later projects, particularly *Twang!!* (see Epilogue).

Fundamentally, in formally establishing himself as the "author" of *Oliver!*, Bart may have hoped to circumvent what Raymond Knapp describes as the "diluting" tendency of musical theater as a collaborative art, for "individual genius" is tempered and rendered indistinguishable against a background of continuous teamwork.[60] As Roland Barthes once noted, "[t]o give a text an Author is to impose a limit on that text, to furnish it with a final signified, to close the writing,"[61] and Bart may have sought such closure by ascribing all the written components to a single writer. The fact remains, however, that even after these three written elements of *Oliver!*—the music, the lyrics, and the libretto—had been attributed to Bart, the "text" was far from "closed." Like all musicals, *Oliver!* would be fully realized only in performance, and thus could be fully developed only in the theater through the contributions of the director, the actors, the choreographers, the stagehands, etc.

Ironically, Bart's theatrical education at Unity and Theatre Workshop had instilled him with an appreciation of this reality:

> Basically, I'm of the theater. I can work as a performer and go to a rehearsal and treat my script as bones to grow from. For instance, I've scripted crowd scenes as counterpoints of dialogue, and I expect actors to grow from that. People are not just going to see my script; they are going to see a work of art made by the writer, the lighting director, the scenic artist, the producer and the actors, etcetera, and I don't go to rehearsals with the idea that my script is the Holy Bible. What I think is true in writing may not be true in rehearsal, and I have a first-hand demonstration of whether my script is working.[62]

Here, Bart demonstrates a clear awareness of the artificial nature of authorship in relation to performance-based texts, an awareness that ostensibly contradicts his desire for sole writing credits (though the previous quotation reaffirms his desire for authorial authority—e.g., "my script"). Whatever these contradictions, Bart's dedication to *Oliver!* and his creative investment in the conception and composition of the musical's written components are incontrovertible. The desire for professional authorship—and the equally potent desire for professionalization in the realm of West End musical theater—belies what was, for Lionel Bart, a highly *personal* desire: a commitment to cultivating and executing a meaningful musical project that had the potential to forever change the West End musical. Through the combined efforts of all the "authors" involved in composing the performance-based "text" of *Oliver!*, Bart's desire came to fruition.

THE EVOLUTION OF *OLIVER!*'S NARRATIVE

Though the undocumented collaboration on the libretto is a significant impediment to the construction of a coherent "biography" of *Oliver!*, the deficient paper trail tracing *Oliver!*'s origins is even more obstructive. Various materials were lost or discarded in the years of Bart's creative/financial slump, and by the time Brenda Evans undertook the overwhelming task of organizing and archiving Bart's papers, the composer had resorted to storing many of his materials in unlabeled bins. Because most of the surviving materials from the early stages of *Oliver!*'s conception are undated, the only way to craft a satisfactory chronological approximation of *Oliver!*'s evolution is to trace the changes that were continuously being made to the adaptation over the course of its development. What follows is an attempt to create a linear and logical narrative "arc" for the biography of *Oliver!* on the basis of surviving drafts, archival materials, and interviews.

The musical that became known as *Oliver!* was designated *Oliver Twist* in the earliest draft materials. It gradually evolved into an adaptation that Bart called *Oh, Oliver!*[63] The curious "Oh" in this second working title could connote several meanings, though the exclamation point following the lead character's name seems to imply a callout or summoning. It is a fitting interpretation given the sheer number of characters who interact with the protagonist and shape his destiny. The oldest surviving relic from *Oliver!*'s developmental period is not a script but rather a chart that delineates the structure of the story as Bart conceived it. Notably, the chart includes a column labeled "Pages," and it is clear that the page numbers listed in this column refer to the passages/sections of the original novel containing the relevant scenes as written by Dickens, reinforcing the fact that whatever Bart's familiarity with Dickens before he began work on *Oliver!*, the original text came to serve as a vital source.[64]

The breakdown of the score is a particularly arresting component of the table, for even though the name and placement of the songs vary widely from the latter drafts of the adaptation, there are significant parallels between certain early numbers and their imminent counterparts. The opening scene is described as featuring the "Boys—bowls & spoons"[65] and the opening number is titled "There's Going to Be a Change in the Workhouse." This same song would carry over to the *Oh, Oliver!* draft before eventually evolving into the musical's beloved opening number, "Food, Glorious Food." Bart knew from the beginning that his adaptation would open with the scene/image that had remained with him from his childhood: Oliver's request for more.

Similar "seeds" for *Oliver!*'s songs are scattered throughout the early outline, though of the numbers described in the chart only four truly endured in a virtually unadulterated state; from the beginning, Oliver's "Where Is Love?", Bumble's "Boy for Sale" (originally called "Oyez, 'Boy for Sale'"), Fagin's "Pick a Pocket or Two" (originally called "You Have to Pick a Pocket or Two"), and Sykes's "My Name" (originally called "My Name Is") were included. Nevertheless, other now-classic songs from *Oliver!* were clearly conceived. Oliver is listed as singing a song with Bet that Bart simply labeled an "Ingenuous Love Song" (which would become "I'd Do Anything") while Nancy is later given a "Beery Song" in the Three Cripples (which would become "Oom Pah Pah"). Furthermore, in the table outlining the show's final act, Bart indicates the need for a "He's My Man sort of song," which Nancy would sing after her meeting with Brownlow; clearly, "As Long as He Needs Me" was part of Bart's vision from the beginning. Finally, a song that Bart initially described as "Morning Cries" would later evolve into the memorable depiction of London street-singing, "Who Will Buy?"

The ambiguous but suggestive descriptions of the abovementioned songs reveal that certain elements of *Oliver!*'s narrative were clear to Bart from the start. Furthermore, even songs that moved beyond the realm of vague, descriptive titles and toward actual concrete musical numbers can be identified as forerunners to the songs that would appear in the final score. Oliver's request for more is followed by a song with the somewhat unoriginal title "Oliver Twist Has Asked for More"—a precursor to the title song, "Oliver." Later, when Oliver first meets the Dodger, a song titled "I'm Going to Seek My Fortune" serves as the placeholder for the now immortal "Consider Yourself."[66] Toward the end of the show, Fagin grows more and more fearful of Sykes. The scene description states that the old man "reviews the situation," though the song he sings is titled "There Isn't the Profit There Used to Be in Crime." Eventually, the descriptive caption became the title and refrain of the song.

Of all the numbers listed in the original chart, only two can truly be singled out as having ultimately exerted no real impact on the final incarnation of the adaptation. A song sung by Mr. Bumble and Noah called "That Boy Was Born to Be Hung"—the title obviously lifted from the morbid refrain of Dickens's most obnoxious workhouse bureaucrat, the gentleman in the white waistcoat—seems to have been cut early, despite the outline leaving room for a reprise by Bumble and Mrs. Corney later in the show. The other song that was lost to posterity is titled "Now There's a Proper Gentleman, If You Like," a cheeky number in which Dodger parodies the manners of Mr. Brownlow. Though parody would remain an important element of several songs, this particular number ultimately proved impractical as the plot began to change.[67]

Although the musical clues drawn from the early outline intimate that Bart's initial vision of *Oliver!* was quite similar to the final product, at least from a narrative perspective, the scene breakdown proves otherwise. In spite of the enduring criticism from purists that *Oliver!* is unfaithful to its source, this epic, three-act version of the story included significantly more material from the novel than several prominent stage and film versions of *Oliver Twist*. Bart even went so far as to bring back characters who had been cut from the Lean adaptation, including Rose Maylie in the revised role of Brownlow's ward.[68]

Table 2.2. LISTING OF SONGS IN *OLIVER TWIST* DRAFT OUTLINE AND THEIR
EVENTUAL SUCCESSORS IN *OLIVER!*

Original Version	Final Version
"There's Going to Be a Change in the Workhouse"	"Food, Glorious Food"
"Oliver Twist Has Asked for More"	"Oliver"
"Oyez 'Boy for Sale'"	"Boy for Sale"
"Where Is Love?"	"Where Is Love?"
"I'm Going to Seek My Fortune"	"Consider Yourself"
"You Have to Pick a Pocket or Two"	"Pick a Pocket or Two"
Ingenuous love song	"I'd Do Anything"
Beery song	"Oom Pah Pah"
"My Name Is"	"My Name"
"Morning Cries"	"Who Will Buy?"
"There Isn't the Profit There Used to Be in Crime"	"Reviewing the Situation"
He's My Man sort of song	"As Long as He Needs Me"

The early outline follows the novel closely in tracing Oliver's journey from the
workhouse to the Sowerberries' shop, to London, and finally to the thieves' kitchen.
Nevertheless, the draft begins to diverge slightly following Oliver's first day "on
the job" with the Dodger. After the failed attempt to pick Brownlow's pocket, both
Oliver *and* the Dodger are brought before Magistrate Fang. The sympathetic and
compassionate Brownlow decides not to press charges against the boys, however,

Table 2.3. MAJOR REPRISES IN *OLIVER TWIST* DRAFT OUTLINE

"There's Going to Be a Change in the Workhouse"	Originally sung by Oliver and the workhouse orphans, reprised by the same in the final scene of Act III
"That Boy Was Born to Be Hung"	Originally sung by Noah and Bumble in Act I, reprised by Bumble and Mrs. Corney in Act II
"Where Is Love?"	Originally sung by Oliver in Act I, reprised by Rose in Act II when Oliver recovers from his wounds during the botched robbery, and again by Rose in Act III after she meets Nancy
"My Name Is"	Originally sung by Sykes in Act II, reprised by him in the same act after he conscripts Oliver to help in robbery
He's My Man sort of song	Originally sung by Nancy in Act III, reprised as a duet between Nancy and Sykes in the same act just before Sykes murders her

and ultimately "tells Oliver not to do anything unlawful again, gives him 2/6 and [a business] card."[69] This scene would have set up the "Proper Gentleman" number, as the Dodger is not impressed by Brownlow's middle-class morality, though it leaves a distinct impression on Oliver and thus foreshadows his eventual ascent to the middle class.

Though this entire section of the adaptation was ultimately cut, it reveals Bart's strategy of combining critical moments from Dickens's novel; in this case, he would have been able to merge the disparate trials of Oliver and the Dodger into a single scene.[70] Similarly, rather than send Oliver home with Brownlow following the trial, this early draft sees the orphaned hero willfully journeying back to the thieves' den in the company of the Dodger, which again facilitates the combination of different threads of the original plot: Brownlow and Rose will reappear later and adopt the roles played by the Maylies in the original text as would-be robbery victims turned caretakers.

The implications regarding Oliver's character here are intriguing, for by this point Oliver has discovered the true nature of Fagin's "profession," and yet, unlike his novelistic predecessor, he still desires to be a part of the thieves' community. However, the orphan begins to question his place in the thieves' kitchen after meeting the villainous Sykes, who is introduced in the next scene. Here too, Bart combines elements from two sections of the novel, for Oliver's introduction to Sykes involves the villain's eagerly seizing the 2/6 note—an obvious parallel to the point in the novel where the thief relieves Oliver of the five pound note entrusted to him by Brownlow—and recruiting the unwilling Oliver to assist him in a robbery. However, instead of the "Chertsey job," Sykes has set his sights on Brownlow's house.[71]

The attempted robbery of Brownlow's house introduces one of the chief problems with this early incarnation of the narrative in that it sets up a cyclical pattern that hinders the pace of the story. As in the novel, the botched robbery sees Oliver wounded and left behind by the thieves. Brownlow and Rose take pity on him once more and decide to take him into their household. Oliver thus finds himself in the exact same situation that he would have been in had they taken him in immediately following the courtroom scene. Consequently, virtually every scene that takes place between the trial and the attempted robbery comes across as filler. It is not difficult to see why many of these scenes were ultimately cut, consolidated, and rearranged over the course of the preproduction period.

The aforementioned redundancy inevitably resurfaces as Oliver's eventual abduction by Sykes and Nancy leads to yet another confrontation between the orphan and the housebreaker upon Oliver's return to the thieves' kitchen. The scene that follows, in which Oliver is stripped of his finery and Brownlow's books/cash, is a virtual duplication of the scene in which Sykes steals the 2/6 note. Here again, there is a sense of "delaying the inevitable," as having the robbery take place *before* Oliver's abduction makes the child's second return to the thieves' den anticlimactic.

In spite of these noteworthy differences, the final scenes documented in the draft—scenes that revolve primarily around Nancy's attempts to save Oliver—proceed in largely the same way as they would in the final libretto. The only major exception is that Bart reintroduces Noah and Charlotte so that he can use Noah to "peach" on Nancy and set up the final tragedy—another indication of his fidelity to the novel at this stage in the project's development. The return of these characters in the latter part of Dickens's text has never been a popular plot point with playwrights or screenwriters, possibly thanks to the overly coincidental nature of this development; the notion that Oliver's chief tormentor from the early sections of the novel would return in the latter sections and fall in with Fagin is beyond implausible.[72] Nevertheless, the excision of this element of the story can create several difficulties in moving the plot toward its climax, given that Noah ultimately plays a critical role in the novel's denouement as the spy who betrays Nancy to Fagin. As will be discussed shortly, Bart wrestled with this complication on excising Noah's return.[73]

The finale outlined in this particular draft varies widely from both the original text and the final product. In the concluding moments of the musical, Oliver journeys back to the workhouse with Rose and Brownlow to surprise his fellow orphans with treats and shillings. There is an even bigger surprise in store for the group, however, as Fagin, fed up with the dangers of being a criminal, happily takes Mr. Bumble's place as the parish beadle and proves a benevolent caretaker to the orphans. This is, of course, a ludicrously sentimental conclusion, though it is simultaneously an unequivocally uplifting ending in comparison to the more ambiguous culmination of Fagin's journey in the final version of the play. Fagin's fate proved another controversial sticking point for Bart throughout the development of the adaptation, and the composer eventually found himself in conflict with several other members of the creative team who offered starker alternatives to the story of the "merry old gentleman."

Given the inclusion of key episodes from the novel that were ultimately excised from the final version of the script, most notably the trial of the Dodger, the scene in Fang's courtroom, the botched robbery, and Noah and Charlotte's return, it is fair to state that the earliest conception of Bart's musical interpretation of *Oliver Twist* was grounded more fully in Dickens's text. Furthermore, the early outline created opportunities for greater development of the supporting characters: Noah, Mr. Bumble, Mrs. Corney, Charlotte, and Bet all play significantly larger parts in this version of the piece. The same can obviously be said of Rose, Toby Crackit, and Magistrate Fang, for all of these characters would ultimately be struck during preproduction.

THE LOST SUPPORTING WOMEN OF BART'S *OLIVER TWIST* MUSICAL

The prominence of Rose and Bet in Bart's earliest conception of *Oliver!* is particularly arresting. The table notes Oliver's reactions during his first meetings with these two young women. In the first two thieves' kitchen scenes, "Oliver falls for Bet," and then "tries to copy Dodger to impress Bet."[74] After meeting Brownlow, "Oliver [is] overcome by Rose's elegance and beauty."[75] Clearly, Bart hoped to include a wider variety of female characters in the earliest version of the piece and sought to highlight their relationships with Oliver. While the final version of the libretto includes examples of Dickens's monstrous matriarchs such as Mrs. Sowerberry and Mrs. Corney, this early draft provides room for angelic counterparts through the compassionate Rose and the equally sympathetic Bet.

The eventual decision to delete Rose and turn the play into the proverbial "one-woman show" (with Nancy as the only major heroine) may have been inevitable. From the nineteenth century onward, Nancy has exerted a more pronounced impact on the culture text of *Oliver Twist*. In spite of Bart's desire to keep Rose in the show, he seems to have been aware of her limitations. The early outline does not include any sort of defining solo number for the character, save for her reprises of "Where Is Love?"

Although Rose never made it past the developmental stages of the musical, Bet survived the "final cut," even if her presence in *Oliver!* is something of an afterthought in comparison to her infinitely more significant role in the early drafts. The fact that Bart saw such potential in Bet's character is perhaps still more striking than his early desire to include Rose. Though her role in the original novel is very small, Dickens's Bet obviously would have appealed to Bart on a basic level given her low-class, cockney background. Similarly, her status as a streetwalker ties her directly to the supporting prostitutes who appeared in *Fings*. Perhaps the most noteworthy potential that Bart saw in Bet relates to the theme of "Where Is Love?" as the defining motif of the adaptation. In the early versions of the script, Bet offers Oliver the chance for another type of love that is widely divergent from virtually every other "love story" presented in the adaptation. The innocent and playful romance that Bart initially scripted between the two characters is arguably the only love story that fosters long-term potential regarding Oliver's development as a character. If we interpret "Where Is Love?" as a plea for maternal love, then the questions posed in the song are ultimately answered by Nancy, who proves a loving mother figure for Oliver and who, like Agnes, sacrifices herself for him. However, in this early version of the piece, we might likewise interpret "Where Is Love?" as the search for romantic love. If so, the "sweet hello" that Oliver is searching for in this particular incarnation of the story is ultimately provided by Bet, who outlives Nancy and who is effectively "betrothed" to Oliver by the end of the musical, as they are both taken in by Mr. Brownlow.

The struggle to find a place for Bet in the narrative as her role continued to decrease in significance proved difficult for Bart, and the character never reached the full potential that the composer had initially seen in her. This fact may have related more directly to the vital significance of Nancy than to any other factor. It is a fairly ironic development given that Bart's ability to perceive untapped possibilities in the character of Bet echoes Dickens's eventual realization of the potential that existed in Nancy herself, whose role expanded greatly over the course of the novel's serial run.

FROM *OLIVER TWIST* TO *OH, OLIVER!*

The earliest outline of Bart's adaptation suggests a longer, more complex version of *Oliver Twist*, though the eventual excision of some of the scenes and characters included in the original outline ultimately aided in the creation of a more coherent, lively, and linear adaptation. The fact that virtually none of these additional scenes included songs seems to indicate that, even from early on in the project's development, Bart was aware of the true heart of the musical narrative. As *Oliver Twist* evolved into *Oh, Oliver!*, however, the narrative arc remained convoluted.

The pre-production documentation for *Oh, Oliver!* intimates that this adaptation was modeled very heavily on the outline that Bart created when he first conceived of an *Oliver Twist* musical. Frustratingly, the surviving script to *Oh, Oliver!* is incomplete and cuts off after Oliver's first meeting with the Dodger, which is particularly unfortunate given that the first several scenes of this version of the show play out almost identically to the final product. In spite of this, the *Oh, Oliver!* libretto provides several insights into how the show (and, more specifically, the show's score) was evolving.

"Where Is Love?" remained the musical centerpiece; for Bart, the song not only crystallized the theme of the musical but simultaneously allowed him to turn his attention back to the true source of the story. He later reflected, "I like to believe it is a song about what Charles Dickens was looking for in his life."[76] For certain, the image of the suffering child locked in a terrible enclosed space and crying out for compassion is evocative of many Dickensian child heroes, including David Copperfield, the fictional protagonist whose roots most fully mirror those of his creator. Whatever the potential biographical implications of the song, Bart understood "Where Is Love?" as the lynchpin of his adaptation, stating that "all the other songs in the show belong to that song."[77]

At this point in the show's development, Bart's conception of the number had grown in terms of both its scope and its potential staging; the libretto indicates that subsequent to Oliver's singing of the song and drifting off to sleep, a "Ballet Sequence About His Mother" begins.[78] This unproduced "dream ballet" is obviously reminiscent of the famous closing to the first act of *Oklahoma!*, and Bart preserved the sequence through virtually all of the drafts that preceded the final version of the libretto. The idea of building a dream sequence around the deceased Agnes reinforces the centrality of the absent-yet-angelic mother figure to both Bart and Dickens's conceptions of the story. Pages from a later version of the script describe the scene in detail, transforming the number into a ballet/pantomime that retells the story of Oliver's parents:

> As [Oliver] sleeps the lighting changes to reveal a dream portico from which emerges an elegant young lady in a crinoline, [sic] bonnet and parasol. She has auburn ringlets. 'Where is Love' [sic] is reprised in the style of a minuet, and suitors for the lady appear in the garb of a dashing guardee, a hussar, a romantically be-cloaked poet, etc. The suitors and the young lady dance variations of quadrille steps. The young lady finally sends away all her suitors except the dashing guardee, who whisks her off her feet and off away as the light fades. The "Where is Love?" Theme develops dramatically as a ragged girl with the same auburn ringlets appears now carrying a tiny baby in the fold of her shawl. She struggles painfully to reach a forbidding gateway which suggests the Workhouse. She settles her baby at the foot of the gate, and dies before it. As she dies, the music becomes celestial and the lighting reveals a group of angels.[79]

The scene culminates with a heavenly chorus reprising the refrain to "Where Is Love?" None of this carried over to the final version of the adaptation, though the dream ballet vividly reinforces Bart's fondness for experimentation with different musical genres and conventions, another facet of his talent that was essential to the success of *Oliver!*

The centrality of "Where Is Love?" is hardly surprising, but by contrast the continued absence of "Consider Yourself" from the *Oh, Oliver!* draft is quite striking.[80] "I'm Going to Seek My Fortune" is not included in this script, and the libretto is unclear as to how exactly the musical interactions between Oliver and the Dodger should proceed.[81] Oliver's journey to London includes a short song entitled "Off to London" that he is supposed to reprise with the Dodger, but handwritten notes indicate that Bart was already second-guessing this number.[82] These brief annotations suggest that the composer had started to envision the Dodger-Oliver duet as a transitional song—one depicting the boys' journey through London. Bart's marginal notes also include room for another song entitled "Going Where the Going Is Good," which seemingly serves as yet another placeholder for "Consider Yourself."[83] Though the lyrics and melody to the song have been lost, Bart's annotations seem to indicate that this song was far closer in its overall purpose to its successor than the other predecessors, serving as a ballad of welcome and celebration.

By the time *Oh, Oliver!* began evolving into *Oliver!*, the structure of the plot began to stray from its original conception. An updated plot outline—notably lacking the show's trademark exclamation point—offers the "middle ground" between the earliest version of the show and the final incarnation. It includes several characters and plot points from the original outline that were eventually cut, but it simultaneously moves the libretto closer to its final incarnation by trimming the fat. As in the original breakdown, there is a scene set in Fang's courtroom, with both Oliver and the Dodger facing the judge, though Oliver's subsequent return to the thieves' kitchen alongside the Dodger is excised. Instead, the narrative follows the novel, as Oliver journeys home with Brownlow immediately after the trial while the Dodger reports back to Fagin and Sykes. The botched-robbery scene from Dickens's novel is then reimagined as a botched kidnapping, as Sykes attempts to break into Brownlow's house so as to bring Oliver back to the thieves' kitchen.

In some respects, this particular plot outline presents the most coherent and fully realized version of the story, surpassing even the final draft of the libretto; the omission of the courthouse scene in the final script leaves an almost fatal gap in the story's narrative. Similarly, this version sensibly and seamlessly integrates the Dodger's trial and the "Chertsey job" into the plot, thus enabling a more complete retelling of the story as it was originally written by Dickens. Table 2.4 provides a condensed outline of this version of the show.

The only other surviving Bartian artifact from the period spanning the show's evolution from *Oh, Oliver!* to *Oliver* (and toward *Oliver!*) is a red spiral notebook. Bart wrote out the dialogue for several of the scenes listed in the previous table, though the notebook likewise provides updated titles for many of the show's songs, another noteworthy indication that the adaptation was slowly but surely approaching its final incarnation. "There's Going to Be a Change in the Workhouse" had

Table 2.4. PLOT OUTLINE OF *OLIVER* SUBSEQUENT TO *OH, OLIVER!* REVISIONS

Act I	Workhouse opening	"There's Going to Be a Change in the Workhouse"
	Oliver asks for more; punished by Bumble	"Oliver Twist Has Asked for More"
	Bumble and Mrs. Corney's flirtations	
	Sale of Oliver to Mr. Sowerberry	"Oyez, Boy for Sale"
	Oliver left alone in the coffin shop	"Where Is Love?"
	Oliver's confrontation with Noah; escape from the Sowerberries	
	Oliver meets the Artful Dodger on the road	"I'm Going to Seek My Fortune"
	Dodger and Oliver reach central London	Lusty song
Act II	Oliver meets Fagin and the gang, including Nancy and Bet; Oliver goes to sleep in the den for his first night with the gang	"Pick a Pocket or Two", "For the Right Girl I'd Do Anything" "Pick a Pocket or Two" (reprise as lullaby)
	Fagin-Oliver treasure chest scene	
	Oliver continues to grow close with Bet (wishes to impress her by being like Dodger)	"For the Right Girl I'd Do Anything" (reprise by Bet and Oliver)
	In Fang's courtroom, Oliver and Dodger have been brought before the judge for picking Brownlow's pocket; after exoneration, Brownlow takes Oliver home; Dodger departs with Brownlow's business card	
	Three Cripples introduction; Nancy performs just as Sykes arrives	Beery song, "My Name Is"
	Dodger reports on what's happened; Fagin and Sykes plan to get Oliver back; Bet and Dodger worry about Oliver	"My Name Is" (reprise)
	Bumble is miserable married to Mrs. Corney; he finds the pawn ticket for a locket that belonged to Oliver's mother and is curious as to what has become of Oliver	

(Continued)

Table 2.4. (CONTINUED)

	At Brownlow's house, Oliver is cared for by Rose; sees portrait of Agnes for the first time	"Where Is Love?" (reprise)
	Sykes spies on Oliver through the window but is seen before he can abduct the boy	
Act III	Oliver listens to the street vendors while running errand for Mr. Brownlow; he is abducted by Nancy, Bet, and Sykes; Mr. Brownlow witnesses the kidnapping and quickly sends for the police	"Morning Cries"
	Bumble and Corney arrive in London and make plans to go and see Brownlow about Oliver	"Oliver" (reprise)[125]
	Oliver is brought back to the den and abused by Sykes; Nancy intervenes and confronts Sykes; Bet and Oliver comfort one another; Fagin begins to grow wary and weary of Sykes	"There Isn't the Profit There Used to Be in Crime"
	Bumbles visit Brownlow and badmouth Oliver; Brownlow disappointed	
	Nancy arrives to see Rose; Nancy and Rose plot to rescue Oliver from Sykes	He's My Man song, "Where Is Love?" (reprise)
	Nancy attempts to rescue Oliver; caught by Sykes; Oliver dragged back to the den by Sykes's henchmen while Sykes kills Nancy; Brownlow and Rose arrive to find her dead and summon the police	He's My Man song (reprise)
	Sykes is caught and arrested; Brownlow takes in Oliver and Bet; Fagin escapes and finds an ad for a new vocation	
	Oliver returns to the workhouse with Rose, Bet, and Brownlow to give money and food to the orphans; Fagin arrives and is given the post of beadle, eagerly roasting sausages for the boys	"There's Going to Be a Change in the Workhouse" (reprise), "Oliver" (reprise), "Ask for More and the Lot!"[126]

now been renamed "Gruel," but annotations within the notebook indicate that Bart had a more appealing title in mind, as the unappealing "Gruel" was scratched out and replaced with the more inviting "Food, Glorious Food." Indeed, many of the songs were now drawing closer to their progeny: "Oliver Twist Has Asked for More" was now "Oliver," "Oyez Boy for Sale" was now "Boy for Sale," and "There Isn't the Profit There Used to Be in Crime" was now "Reviewing the Situation." Amazingly, "Consider Yourself" had yet to be added; Bart seemingly wavered once again and replaced the recently revived "I'm Going to Seek My Fortune" (as listed in the previous table) with "Going Where the Going Is Good" as the Dodger's introductory number.[84]

Notably, several of the scenes contained in the notebook reinforce the continued importance of the Oliver-Bet storyline to Bart's vision, as Fagin and Nancy play matchmaker with their young charges:

FAGIN: I was just telling young Oliver that to make a proper show—he must have a
   lady....Now Nancy is spoke fore [sic] aint [sic] you nancy [sic] dear
BOYS: Good Ole Bill
FAGIN: So that leaves [Bet] my love.[85]

Nancy notes Bet's obvious attraction to Oliver and compliments Fagin on the match, while the Dodger promptly begins instructing Oliver in how to court Bet, which leads into "For the Right Girl I'd Do Anything." It is surprising that this number originally centered so squarely on the relationship between Oliver and Bet (to the point that the two characters would reprise it together), given that it is oftentimes mistakenly remembered as a duet between Nancy and Oliver. As will be noted in Chapter 7, this error is likely due in no small part to the influence of the Reed film. Still, even as the show's narrative was drawing closer to its final outline, Bet remained a vitally important character. Bart was more convinced than ever that Bet was the person who Oliver was searching for in "Where Is Love?", as an updated outline describes the nature of their relationship: "Fagin [sic] Bet, Dodger. (will [Oliver] take up Crime? [sic]) (Has he found love—Bet?)."[86] The outline likewise notes that when Oliver is enjoying his life with Brownlow, he is "happy except for Bet," that is, except for Bet's absence.[87] For Bart, the central tension driving the Brownlow scenes would relate to Oliver's feeling torn between his loyalty and gratitude toward Brownlow and Rose, and his love for Bet: "Will he stay with the Brownlows and renounce gang...Bet?"[88]

Bart's interest in the Oliver-Bet subplot is further epitomized by two other scenes the composer scripted in his notebook: the first is a brief conversation between Bet and the Dodger following the pickpocket's explanation of what transpired during the trial. Bet is concerned, upon learning of Oliver's ordeal, and inquires as to what happened:

BET: Did he get hurt bad?
DODGER: He got a proper shiner.
BET: And he went on account of me. Poor Oliver.[89]

Later, when Oliver is forced to return to the thieves' kitchen, it is Bet who consoles him; though upset at having left Brownlow behind, Oliver takes comfort in being reunited with his sweetheart:

BET: I'm sorry—I'm sorry you had to come back to this place.
OLIVER: Are you Bet? I'm not sorry—[90]

This dialogue prompts Oliver to reprise their duet once more.

It is somewhat remarkable that a character who was once so vital to the very fabric of the adaptation was eventually reduced to a virtual nonentity in the final version of the script. Still, with Nancy acting as Oliver's chief defender and advocate throughout the second half of the adaptation, Bet's role seems somehow superfluous. The tension between the two roles is made tangible in a surviving scrap from an undated draft written during the "middle period" of the show's development. In this scene, Nancy tries to help Oliver escape the thieves' den and return to Mr. Brownlow and Rose, though Oliver's loyalty to Bet holds him back:

NANCY: Can you guess who you are going to meet tonight, Oliver, in this dark place?
OLIVER: It *is* dark. Why couldn't you tell me before, and why did we have to come all the way here?
NANCY: It's a gentleman who was very good to you, and his daughter, and I wish to heaven I'd never taken you from them!
OLIVER: Rose! Rose and Mr. Brownlow. Oh, Nancy, are they really coming here?
NANCY: Yes and they're coming to take you home again with them, Oliver, and away from Fagin's and all of us.
OLIVER: Home! To that lovely house again! I can't believe it Nancy. But how did you...?
NANCY: I put a sleeping draught in the drink tonight, so that I could get you out without Bill or anyone knowing...
OLIVER: But what will they do to you, Nancy, when they find out?
NANCY: There's time enough to think about that
OLIVER: (thinking for a while) Then let's go back and get Bet.
NANCY: We can't Oliver. I belong there, and so does Bet—besides it's too late now.
OLIVER: Then I can't go. I can't go and leave Bet there.
NANCY: Don't you want to go back to those kind people, that will love you and give you a home? I'll tell you something but it's a great secret, because I think they would like to tell you themselves. They are your very own family, Oliver. Rose's sister was...your mother.
OLIVER: My mother! My family! You mean I really belong somewhere?! I knew I did. Oh, Nancy. Thank you for telling me. But I still can't go—I couldn't leave Bet like that. Unless she can come too, I can't go.
NANCY: Don't worry about Bet, Oliver. She's used to that life. Besides I'll look after her.[91]

The central problem with this scene is that it tries to balance several divergent issues; whereas the emotion should be centered on the relationship between Nancy and Oliver, and the looming danger of their discovery by Sykes, the tangential discussion of Oliver's fondness for Bet seems to draw attention away from the enormous risk that Nancy is taking on his behalf.[92] Furthermore, it establishes a conflict between the two characters, in that Oliver wishes Bet to accompany him into the world of the middle class, while Nancy wishes for her to remain a part of her own circle. Although this tension is not explicitly discussed, it is clear that the two characters have very different agendas regarding Bet's future, and the divergence detracts from the bond between them, which should theoretically be driving the entire scene.

Perhaps there simply was not room enough for both Bet and Nancy in the adaptation; the relationship between Bet and Oliver diverts the audience's attention from the relationship between Nancy and Oliver—a relationship that, in several respects, has come to define the entire adaptation thanks to the popularity of the film version and the Palladium/Drury Lane revivals. Nancy's redemption is dependent on her plumbing the depths of this maternal love for Oliver to the limit and tragically realizing that it is a love she cannot reconcile with her equally palpable—but ultimately destructive—love for Sykes. The prominent presence of another innately loving and noble-hearted girl within Fagin's den who shares a similar interest in Oliver's safety and happiness would ultimately serve to detract from Nancy's tragic story arc.

The other main casualty of Nancy's prominence, Rose, was also still an important character at this point in the show's development, though her role had been revised from that of Brownlow's ward to his daughter. Bart thus managed to further combine the Brownlow and Maylie families into a single unit, preserving Rose's role as Oliver's aunt and transforming Brownlow into Oliver's grandfather.[93] By this point, Bart had come to picture Rose as Oliver's central confidante in the world of the middle class; it is Rose who shows Oliver the portrait of Agnes, thus providing him with the first clues to his mother's identity. The draft script likewise indicates that Rose is the one who meets with Nancy to work out a plan for Oliver's rescue.[94]

The inclusion of the latter scene is particularly arresting in that the confrontation between Nancy and Rose is one of the key moments in Dickens's novel. When Rose resolves to help Nancy escape the miserable life she has known for so long, she refers to the girl's "terrible infatuation,"[95] a fitting description of her extremely unhealthy relationship with Bill. However, Rose is unsuccessful in persuading Nancy to renounce this life. Notably, Bart addresses Rose's inability to comprehend Nancy's tendency toward self-destruction in this draft of the script: Nancy actually sings "As Long as He Needs Me" in front of Rose so as to try to explain her devotion to the housebreaker.[96] The idea of Nancy performing her all-important soliloquy in front of Rose makes for a powerful musicalization of one of the novel's most memorable scenes and allows Rose and Nancy to develop an understanding they never quite achieve in Dickens's text.

As in the case of Bet's reduction, the eventual deletion of Rose might likewise be connected to Nancy's centrality, though it remains a somewhat unfortunate excision. Whatever her limitations as a character, Rose offers a unique perspective in comparison to Bet and Nancy, and the juxtaposing of Nancy and Rose as mother figures for Oliver, like the juxtaposing of Fagin and Brownlow as father figures, would have supported a more dynamic exploration of class conflict. Mrs. Bedwin serves as something of a substitute; however, her role is never as significant as Rose's part was originally intended to be.[97]

FINDING A SUITABLE ENDING

Fundamentally, the middle period in *Oliver!*'s development was defined by a more linear narrative, as the creative team worked to condense the story. An outline from the latter stages of the show's development entitled "Suggested New Version" alludes to these cuts, as the courthouse and kidnapping scenes have been scratched out. Simultaneously, the revised table indicates that the musical score is reaching its ultimate design: "Consider Yourself" has *finally* been added to the score, and the only two songs missing from this particular outline are "That's Your Funeral" and "I Shall Scream." [98] The former would not be written until the last minute of the production process, while the latter was already being conceived, as the need for a "Bumble courting song" was listed on a separate page of notes.[99]

Regarding the roles of the supporting characters, Rose and Bet were still being featured prominently at this time, and the annotations to this "Suggested New Version" allude to the addition of yet another supporting character: Mr. Brittles. In Dickens's text, Brittles is the incompetent but well-meaning servant who assists the Maylies' butler, Mr. Giles. Here, he is reinvented as a stately and cynical butler serving Brownlow, and the character acts as a sort of amalgamation of Mrs. Bedwin, Giles, and Mr. Grimwig: like Mrs. Bedwin and Giles, he assists in caring for Oliver, but like Grimwig, he is suspicious of Oliver's true character.[100] As will be discussed, however, Brittles presented Bart with a unique opportunity to try to resolve an overarching problem he faced regarding the ending to the play.

By this point in the show's development, there were three major difficulties regarding the structure of the story: the gradual unfolding of the mystery surrounding Oliver's birth, the circumstances surrounding Sykes's murder of Nancy, and the final fate of the "likable villains," Fagin and the Artful Dodger. The issue of Oliver's true pedigree had proved something of a stumbling block for Bart from the very beginning, for he had never planned on including Monks, the character who drives this particular plot thread in Dickens's novel. Without someone actively conspiring to prevent Oliver from discovering his roots, there is no conflict or tension surrounding this issue. Having reinvented Fagin as a lovable rascal, Bart thus turned to Monks's co-conspirators, the Bumbles, as a means of weaving this plot thread into the narrative. In the early drafts, the subplot centered primarily on Agnes's locket, which the Bumbles eventually tracked down via a pawn slip; the later drafts include a brief appearance by Old Sally, who reveals to Mrs. Corney that she took the piece of jewelry that holds the key to Oliver's identity.[101]

The second issue, the motivation behind Sykes's murder of Nancy, returns us to the previous discussion of Noah's expanded role in the early scripts; by bringing Noah back, Bart could use this unlikable and irredeemable character to tip off Sykes, as opposed to using Fagin, the Dodger, or one of the sympathetic criminals. In a memo regarding Coe's suggested changes to the script, Bart indicates his unwillingness to compromise on this particular issue: "Do NOT like and will NOT have the scene of Fagin grassing on Nancy.... The same applies to using Dodger as a grass. I wish Dodger and Fagin to be sympathetic characters. If someone is to grass on anybody, make it Noah Claypole or someone like that."[102] Though there is no surviving

Table 2.5. SEQUENCE OF SONGS INCLUDED IN "SUGGESTED NEW VERSION," HIGHLIGHTING MAJOR DEVIATIONS FROM THE FINAL INCARNATION OF *OLIVER!*

Act I	Song	Deviations
	"Food, Glorious Food"	n/a
	"Oliver"	n/a
	"Boy for Sale"	n/a
	"Where Is Love?"	n/a
	"Consider Yourself"	n/a
	"Pick a Pocket or Two"	n/a
	"I'd Do Anything"	Song is used to establish a bond between Bet and Oliver; Nancy is not listed as participating in the song.
	"It's a Fine Life"	Song is ostensibly used as an introductory number for Nancy and revolves around her interactions with Bet; it is implied that the song takes place outside the den as opposed to inside.
	"We'll Be Back"	Renamed "Be Back Soon" in final version.
Act II	**Song**	**Deviations**
	"Oom Pah Pah"	n/a
	"My Name"	n/a
	"Where Is Love?" (reprise)	Ostensibly sung by Oliver and Rose (as opposed to Mrs. Bedwin) in Bloomsbury.
	"Who Will Buy?"	n/a
	"I'd Do Anything" (reprise)	Following his abduction by the gang, Oliver and Bet comfort one another in Fagin's den.
	"Reviewing the Situation"	n/a
	"As Long as He Needs Me"	Having informed Rose of her desire to help Oliver, Nancy explains her love of Sykes and her inability to give him up.
	"As Long as He Needs Me" (reprise)	As Nancy lay dying, her final thoughts convey her love for Sykes via a brief snatch from the preceding number.
	"Food, Glorious Food" (reprise), "Consider Yourself" (reprise), "I'd Do Anything" (reprise)	Sung-through finale featuring return to the workhouse to cheer up the orphans.

record of the abovementioned sequence as written by Coe, the outline to his version of the libretto included a scene between Fagin and Sykes at the Three Cripples— Act II, scene 7—in which Fagin, like his literary predecessor, betrayed Nancy to the vengeful housebreaker.[103] It is clear that Coe was more willing to compromise the integrity of the thieves than Bart, who was adamant about preserving their benevolent characteristics.[104]

The conflict over Dodger and Fagin's role, or lack thereof, in Nancy's death can be connected to the last of the three troublesome plot points that impeded *Oliver!*'s libretto as it reached the final stages of its development: the ultimate fate of the two abovementioned characters. By this point, the idea of Fagin becoming a beadle had been abandoned completely, but this did not mean Bart had fully discarded the idea of presenting a new beadle to close out the show. Oddly enough, he had begun to consider this new vocation as a potential "happy ending" for the Dodger. If the idea of Fagin as the parish beadle is ridiculous, the idea of the Dodger filling that part seems even more outlandish.[105] In the previously discussed memo on Coe's modifications, Bart inquires: "Does Peter Coe not like my idea of the Dodger taking the vacant job as the Beadle in the workhouse. [*sic*] This may be fantasy but will surely do more for audience warmth in the finale."[106] The separate page discussing the role of Brittles offered another solution: "Dodger come[s] back as assistant Footman to Brittles instead of as Beadle. Or query let the lordly Brittles take the Beadle's place and Dodger become the Brownlows [*sic*] somewhat unusual manservant."[107] Thus, the inclusion of Brittles may have been little more than a means to an end regarding the Dodger's redemption.

Even as these plans were discarded, the creative team left a window open for a potential happy ending for the Dodger, as a later document called "Suggested New Breakdown (B)" notes that the musical would culminate with a return to the workhouse so that Oliver could rescue the Dodger (who was inexplicably sent there following his arrest).[108] However, this conclusion never came to fruition, a somewhat disappointing development given that the Dodger is easily one of the most memorable and lovable characters in the piece. The idea of his winding up in prison or facing transportation adds a decidedly darker dimension to the musical's climax.

Fagin's fate proved an even greater challenge for Bart and the creative team. Though Dickens's (and Cruikshank's) depiction of Fagin's "last night alive" has endured as one of the most powerful, primal, and vivid scenes that the author (and illustrator) ever created, it is obvious that this particular scene does not fit the scope of Bart's adaptation. Even Lean, who had created an irredeemably evil Fagin, was willing to forgo the condemned cell scene. The early version of the ending, in which Fagin replaces Bumble as the workhouse overseer, clearly met with resistance, and although Bart was willing to move beyond the idea, he was determined to preserve the old man's "happy ending." This may have led to further conflict with Coe, for the director seems to have put forth the idea that Sykes, the Dodger, and Fagin should all be arrested in the penultimate scene, though, as mentioned, the Dodger would ultimately be rescued from the workhouse in the final reprise.[109] Bart's memo regarding Coe's changes to the script reveals his passionate conviction that Fagin did not deserve to be arrested: "[I] [w]ill NOT have Fagin led away to prison. Establish that he has had a change of conscience early in the play. Therefore he has no introvert [*sic*] wickedness, but sincere like for Oliver."[110] The composer never wavered in his belief that this incarnation of Fagin was a decent person in spite of his criminal lifestyle.

The debate over Fagin's fate dragged on far longer than many of the other conflicts over the creative vision of the piece. An item toward the bottom of the notes page tellingly reveals "Fagin's fate? . . . . . No agreement yet"—this in spite of the fact that the document mentions several songs that were added late in the production process, such as "Be Back Soon" (then called "We'll Be Back") and "It's a Fine Life."[111] The two major parties trying to work out this agreement were likely Coe and Bart, and the divergences in their approaches to the story are indicative not only of Coe's closer adherence to the original text but, likewise, of the cultural differences between them. The kinship that Bart felt with Fagin, and the fear of his Jewishness being misinterpreted, remained contentious issues even after the show premiered.

Coe's own vision for the finale is something of a mystery, though interestingly, in the table outlining the Coe version, Fagin does not sing "Reviewing the Situation" until the very end of the show, subsequent to Sykes's downfall. In all of the previous outlines/drafts this number was sung far earlier in the second act, either just before or just after Oliver's return to the thieves' kitchen. Coe seems to have preferred the idea of using the song as an "eleven o'clock number" at the very end of the play. Indeed, Bart's memo implies that Coe envisioned Fagin's big solo as an appeal to both the audience *and* the other characters (namely, the choral "mob" that pursues Sykes); Coe apparently wanted the song to be sung in front of the chorus as opposed to its being sung by Fagin on a bare stage. Bart steadfastly resisted the idea: "Will NOT have Fagin singing his song called 'Reviewing the Situation' to a stagefull [*sic*] of people. The scene is obviously a soliloquy which are his thoughts [*sic*]."[112] Notably, this item on Bart's list of changes immediately precedes the note insisting that Fagin must not be led away to prison, which seems to imply that if Coe had indeed planned on Fagin's using "Reviewing the Situation" as an appeal, the plea was ultimately intended to fall on deaf ears—an intriguing and perhaps even quasi-Brechtian ending for the ostensibly happy musical.[113] Such ideas were obviously far-removed from Bart's conception of the project.[114]

Bart eventually settled on an ending that was neither the unreservedly happy conclusion that he had envisioned nor the bleak conclusion put forth by Coe. In the notes referencing the Coe version of the script, Bart imagined a new vision for Fagin's finale: "Having learnt to live with this conscience in himself, and having his treasure chest taken away by the police he may even wander away to Israel or somewhere— friendless."[115] Though transforming Fagin into a "wandering Jew" may confine Bart's Fagin to the same stereotypical realm as his literary predecessor, Bart's view of Fagin as a misunderstood outsider is conveyed in this statement. Furthermore, the idea of Fagin's returning to Israel adds a spiritual dimension to the old man's redemption, though it is a bittersweet climax given that the price of salvation was the final dissolution of the thieves' kitchen (and the sacrifice of the Dodger). In some ways, Bart's final vision of Fagin's fate directly prefigures the conclusion to another English musical that would go on to enjoy unprecedented worldwide success: Andrew Lloyd Webber's *The Phantom of the Opera*. Like Fagin, the Phantom is redeemed and allowed to escape, but he must likewise concede the loss of Christine and the cessation of the "Music of the Night." Similarly, though Christine finds happiness and peace with Raoul, the audience is left to wonder if she will ever enjoy the same level of passion and imagination that defined her relationship with the Phantom; this situation is virtually identical to the scenario facing Oliver as he commits himself to a life of middle-class domesticity (see Chapter 5).

The contrast between Bart and Coe's vision of what should happen to Fagin is just one small example of the divergences between their visions of *Oliver!* Though the full extent of these contrasts will likely remain a mystery owing to the lack of surviving drafts, there are several key pieces of evidence regarding Coe's vision of the script. Among these artifacts is a detailed scene breakdown (likely compiled by Bart) enti- tled "Oliver—Peter's Version." What is perhaps most striking about this chart is its near equivalence to the final version of the adaptation—a fact that bears testament to the influence Coe ultimately exerted on the shape of the musical.

Indeed, Coe's vision of the show features only a few major deviations from what would eventually become the final version of *Oliver!* before it debuted at Wimbledon. Notably, rather than use "I'd Do Anything" as a thieves' den song between Bet and Oliver, Coe recommended "It's a Fine Life" instead and suggested "I'd Do Anything" be rewritten as a courtship song for the Bumbles. On a general level, Bart preferred

Table 2.6. SEQUENCE OF SONGS INCLUDED IN "OLIVER—PETER'S VERSION" HIGHLIGHTING MAJOR DEVIATIONS FROM THE FINAL INCARNATION OF *OLIVER!*

Act I	Song	Deviations
	"Food, Glorious Food"	n/a
	"Oliver"	n/a
	"Where Is Love?"[127]	n/a
	"I'd Do Anything"	Used here as a courting song between the Bumbles
	"Consider Yourself"	n/a
	"Pick a Pocket or Two"	n/a
	"It's a Fine Life"	n/a
	"We'll Be Back"	Renamed "Be Back Soon" in final version
Act II	Song	Deviations
	"Oom Pah Pah"	n/a
	"My Name"	n/a
	"As Long as He Needs Me"	n/a
	"Who Will Buy?"	n/a
	"Reviewing the Situation"	Sung by Fagin following Nancy's murder and Sykes's downfall; apparently, sung in front of the mob as opposed to being sung as a soliloquy
	"Food, Glorious Food" (reprise), "Consider Yourself" (reprise)	n/a

"I'd Do Anything" over "It's a Fine Life," viewing the former as the superior song.[116] Furthermore, Bart's preference for "I'd Do Anything" was strongly connected to his unceasing desire to preserve Bet's role as Oliver's love interest; "I'd Do Anything" had initially been conceived as an "Ingenuous Love Song" between Oliver and Bet, and Bart perceived the number as central to defining the love that Oliver discovers in the thieves' kitchen, while Coe ostensibly preferred the more generalized and celebratory lust for life conveyed in "It's a Fine Life."[117] Bart lumped the issues of Bet's role and the debate over the two abovementioned songs together in his critique of Coe's libretto, stating "[I] [d]o NOT agree with the exclusion of Bett [sic]. Do NOT agree with the placing of 'It's a Fine Life' in the middle of the scene. If we are to use 'It's a Fine Life' at all, this must be a front clothe [sic] type number performed in a music hall area to convey a street feeling."[118] In the end, the two songs would become virtual bedfellows, as they were juxtaposed to chronicle the introduction of Nancy and Bet, and Oliver's gradual acclimation to the thieves' kitchen.

Though the chart is clearly a useful tool in evaluating the director's vision of *Oliver!*, Bart's response to Coe's changes is arguably an even more important piece of evidence, for it not only serves to outline several of Coe's contributions on a macro level, but likewise provides the only real opportunity for timing *Oliver!*'s development. Dated February 4, 1960—nearly five months before the debut of *Oliver!* at the New Theatre—this document supports the notion that by this point in the production process, the show had been placed in Coe's hands. This is not to suggest that Bart had surrendered creative control of the project, as the very existence of his memo regarding Coe's edits reveals that he was still firmly involved in the creative process (and that he likewise possessed "veto power" regarding the director's alterations/ decisions). Even so, he clearly had an appreciation for Coe's ability to streamline the adaptation[119]: "I feel that Peter has economised with sets and simplified the general conception. Also to his credit he has allowed more upon [sic] the premise of Oliver's search for love and his frustration in this cause."[120]

Bart was less pleased with Coe's decisions regarding the Dickensian characters, however, as he opined that Coe had "be-laboured [sic] the script with too many scenes containing grey old ladies and gentlemen and has robbed the script of glamour. I feel that Nancy is not sufficient, and that we need beautiful girls like Rose Brownlow and the young sprightly appeal of Bett [sic] and Dodger."[121] Bart's assertion that Nancy was incapable of carrying the female dimension of the show on her own is somewhat ironic given that she would go on to do precisely that. He may have underestimated just how strongly the character would resonate (and continues to resonate) with fans of the show.

Significantly, Bart's critique reinforces the creative differences between the two men: the composer's concerns with "glamour" and "sprightly appeal" underscore his connections with the pop-music scene and his keen marketing sensibilities in relation to the youth culture of the period. Coe's attempts to include the idiosyncratic and, at times, terrifying characters from the original novel underscore his artistic vision and fidelity to the text's Dickensian roots. Years later, the director explained the importance of this approach to his basic theatrical philosophy: "I always return to first sources—Lionel Bart's script for *Oliver!* was hardly satisfactory and we needed

Dickens."[122] This critique may seem somewhat misleading given that Coe ultimately cut several scenes Bart had based on chapters from the original text, though Coe's overall interpretation was far more Dickensian in terms of its tone. Coe's dialogue was likewise more fully grounded in the text, as Davidson recollects that the director "simply went back to the book."[123] Bart may have been tempted to sentimentalize the script, as indicated in the melodramatic dialogue between Nancy and Oliver quoted above, but Coe gave the dialogue a more sober directness (ironically, via the Dickensian source). Cameron Mackintosh would later reflect that Coe's "sterner" approach to the material was vital to the show's success: "[Peter] was a rather astringent individual, not sentimental at all—which is one of the reasons that Lionel Bart's version of *Oliver Twist* works. [Peter] actually provided the grit that the production needed."[124] Much of this "grit" was to be found in the novel, which remained Coe's primary source.

In spite of Bart and Coe's creative conflicts, the combination of both of their approaches was vital to the overall success of the show: Bart's emphasis on glamorous spectacle ensured that the adaptation would resonate with a mainstream audience, while Coe's devotion to the Dickensian component ensured that style never eclipsed substance. It is doubtful that *Oliver!* would have exerted as profound an effect on the culture text of *Oliver Twist* were it not for Coe's contributions. As will be discussed in the next chapter, Sean Kenny played an equally important role in this regard, and so too did the gifted actors who would embody the Dickensian characters.

CHAPTER 3

✧

"There is no reason why the show should not be a big success": *Oliver!*'s Evolution

One unique facet of Lionel Bart's working relationship with Peter Coe—and, more especially, with Sean Kenny—was their ability to alternate between methods of conceptualization. Bart and Kenny, both gifted visual artists, exchanged drawings and storyboards during the initial phases of the creative process: "In the early stages bothe [*sic*] director Peter Coe, and myself filled a room with drawings; [*sic*] while Sean stopped drawing and filled my type-writer with fresh outlines for plot-development and script construction. The aim was to bring about a perfect marriage of words, music, actor and scenic effect."[1] This emphasis on amalgamation reinforces Bart's desire for an integrated musical narrative, and though the composer listed "scenic effect" last, one could argue that Kenny's set served as the central unifying device behind that narrative. The surviving draft materials from *Oliver!*'s preproduction period reveal Coe's version as the most "stageable" incarnation of the musical up to that point in time, for Coe was able to reduce the number of scene changes, improve the narrative's fluidity, and condense the overall length of the play. However, just as Coe's blocking was dictated by the parameters of Kenny's massive, mobile set, Coe's vision of a unified, flowing plot correlated with Kenny's determination to keep the story moving forward—even when the scenery was moving.[2]

SEAN KENNY'S SET AND THE *OLIVER!* NARRATIVE

As his vision for the *Oliver!* set evolved, *movement* remained the driving idea behind Kenny's concept for the scenery: "I walked through the old parts of London. What I visualized was a great millwheel—an enormous turning thing—with wooden beams, bridges across streets, heavy wooden doors."[3] This image proved central to Kenny's design scheme, which seems somehow fitting in light of the Victorian roots of the source. The preceding description calls to mind the intimidating factory

machinery of nineteenth-century industrial society, or, perhaps even more appropri-
ately in the case of *Oliver Twist*, the Victorian treadmill. Still, in spite of its harshness,
Kenny's set did not achieve the same stark critique of Victorian industrial capitalism
as Eugene Lee's similar scenery for Stephen Sondheim's *Sweeney Todd*, though this
disparity is understandable given the inestimably more optimistic tone and theme of
Bart's adaptation. Had Kenny pushed his austere, industrial vision to its limits, he
might very well have created a jarring dialectic between the dreamy musical celebration taking place onstage and the nightmarish industrialized setting on which it was
unfolding. Still, in spite of its quasi-Brechtian components, Kenny's set was simultaneously Wagnerian in its function, for it was wholly integrated into the overarching
vision of Bart's musical (see below).

Kenny eventually described the main revolve—"this wooden O"[4]—as a nucleus for
the creative vision of the show and a microcosm of "the whole world of Dickens,"[5] and
the designer's use of a revolve, along with his correlating emphasis on movement,
certainly seems appropriate given the picaresque traits (and peripatetic tendencies)
of Dickens's title character. In fact, Kenny deliberately sought to connect his scenery to the titular character; much as Lean captured the vulnerability of Dickensian
childhood by filming from Oliver's perspective, Kenny attempted to achieve a similar
effect by purposefully enlarging the set: the bigger the scenery, the smaller and more
vulnerable Oliver became in comparison.[6] Moreover, the anti-realist qualities of the
set could be connected to Oliver's juvenile subjectivity: "I wanted places to hide and
places to run round and it became now not a toy so much as a child's dream of this
world. This building became something which a child's imagination could create."[7]

As intimated in this quotation, the set likewise provided Oliver with a great
deal of space to move about, and the revolve could be used to simulate movement
between wide and diverse spaces. Whereas Dickens's novel gradually stops moving—indeed, given the tediousness of the Maylie chapters, some might say that the
narrative "grinds to a halt"—Bart and Coe's libretto emphasizes Oliver's continuous progress: from the workhouse, to the undertaker's shop, to the London streets,
to Fagin's den, and finally, to Bloomsbury. Kenny's set facilitated this movement,
and the physical journey underscores the lead character's thematic journey from
the loneliness of the workhouse to the communal friendship and boisterousness of
working-class London, to the final discovery of his roots in the middle-class world of
Mr. Brownlow's house.

Movement was more than the defining characteristic of Kenny's concept for
Oliver! It was also the defining characteristic of his approach to producing plays, and
to living life. In an interview with Vivien Hislop, Kenny revealed his disregard for
material possessions, claiming that they engulf people instead of granting them the
flexibility necessary for achieving true contentment through continuous movement
and creativity: "Why surround yourself with things? [...] If you collect enough it just
weighs you down. What you need are two marvellous suitcases."[8] A separate interview with Carol Wright further emphasizes his interest in movement:

> Rather like the moving scenery in *Oliver* [sic], Sean Kenny's ideal house would be
> made up of moving parts to create change: lights would change colour schemes,

enlarge or diminish sizes; screen walls would move; roofs would raise according to the weather and floors would change. Outside uniformity should be avoided with walls set at different angles, patterns of stone used to create identity and pleasant outlook; aluminum, which needs no paint, is a material he would like to see more used.[9]

Kenny later noted that his ideal form of theater would not take place in a building (because of the rigidity of the structure), but rather in a tent, and that the production process would be equally flexible, as "a group of writers, directors and actors" would collaborate on the schematic for the show.[10] Kenny's ideal methodology is strikingly evocative of Joan Littlewood's vision of theatrical production, and it is not surprising that Kenny—like Lionel Bart before him—found an outlet for his talents at Theatre Workshop.[11] Much as Littlewood was setting the postwar theater free by placing the amorphous and extemporaneous performance above the concrete text, Kenny was attempting to free the practice of theater from the concrete confines of the playhouse.

Kenny's prominent yet controversial reputation in the postwar English theater was centered squarely on his interest in demolishing traditional conceptions of theatrical space. In his view, such a demolition should take place on a literal level as well as a theoretical level. In a 1967 article, theater critic Irving Wardle explained that Kenny was "in no great hurry to put up theatres. He thinks the main thing is to demolish the inherited lumber, and turn out actors to play in all kinds of temporary structures until they arrive at a fresh understanding of what the theatre really is."[12] For Kenny, such an understanding centered around the idea of theater as "'a kind of happening', not a building, but an activity inside a free space."[13] Again, one cannot help but think of Littlewood and her performance-based sensibilities.

In spite of this connection, some people associated with the rapid evolution of the postwar British theater resisted Kenny's vision. Kenneth Tynan was an early champion of Kenny's creations; in a review of Theatre Workshop's 1958 production of The Hostage—a production for which Kenny served as set designer—Tynan cited the Irishman's immense talents and praised the show's scenery as "by far the best in London."[14] Two years later, in his review of Oliver!, Tynan unhesitatingly acknowledged Kenny as "the hero of Oliver!,"[15] though he glibly qualified this opening statement by noting that Kenny's "smoky, oaken, restlessly revolving, gargantuan setting" was the true hero.[16] Tynan continued to recognize Kenny's genius in the years that followed, but, as foreshadowed in his Oliver! review, he eventually began to express skepticism (and even scorn) toward Kenny's work due to the tendency of the scenery to eclipse the human element; Dusty Vineberg wrote that "[Tynan] confessed himself 'a bit afraid' of Mr. Kenny's machines."[17] Tynan was quoting himself, as he had put forth the same sardonic critique in his markedly negative review of Bart's first post-Oliver! musical, Blitz!—a show that employed an even grander Kenny set than its predecessor. After harshly criticizing Bart's musical, Tynan opined,

[Blitz!] does, however, have Sean Kenny's scenery, and herein may lie its true significance. Belasco and Novello went pretty far in the direction of spectacular realism;

but in *Blitz!* there are distinct signs that the sets are taking over. They swoop down on the actors and snatch them aloft; four motor-driven towers prowl the stage, converging menacingly on any performer who threatens to hog the limelight; and whenever the human element looks like gaining control, they collapse on it in a mass of flaming timber. In short, they let the cast know who's boss. They are magnificent, and they are war: who (they tacitly inquire) needs Lionel Bart? I have a fearful premonition of the next show Mr. Kenny designs. As soon as the curtain rises, the sets will advance in a phalanx on the audience and summarily expel it from the theatre. After that, the next step is clear: Mr. Kenny will invent sets that applaud.[18]

Tynan's critique seems to foreshadow the trademark negative response that many critics would put forth regarding the massive mechanized spectacle that defined the megamusicals of the 1980s—a telling indication of *Oliver!*'s status as the chief forebear to the shows that defined the modern West End approach to musical theater (see Chapter 4). Notably, Kenny once described the *Oliver!* set's pair of revolving staircases as "the most important feature of the entire show. The story is really set around them and they are in every scene."[19] Many years later, John Napier, the set designer on Boublil and Schönberg's *Les Misérables*, would assign an equal amount of importance to the physical setting of the barricade: "My starting point was the centre of the play's biggest moment, the barricade (196A). Once that was solved everything else fell into place."[20] The idea of building a musical around the movement of an "authoritarian" piece of scenery—whether it is the rotation of a staircase or the rise of a barricade—seems to run counter to the more traditional notion that music is the central narrative force.

In *The Musical as Drama*, McMillin devotes an entire chapter to the subject of technology and its relation to narrative in the musical theater, specifically, the narratives of megamusicals. In a passage that seems strikingly relevant to discussions of the Kenny set, which, seemingly of its own volition, revolved before the eyes of delighted audience members, McMillin reflects that "[s]tage technology has advanced to the point where the set can move itself into position before the eyes of the audience, as though magic or the almighty were creating the effect for us."[21] Like many critics of the megamusical, McMillin expresses reservations about this trend, hinting at the tendency of such scenery to overwhelm the musical element.[22] However, McMillin pushes the matter further, framing the "excessiveness" that defines megamusicals as the natural consequence of the "doubling up of all-knowing forces—the orchestra in the pit, where omniscience belongs, and the computerized lighting and set design, which covers song-and-dance with another layer of infallibility."[23] McMillin's theory of the narrative omniscience of the musical orchestra is important to my reading of *Oliver!* in Chapter 5, and I would argue that the orchestra ultimately eclipses the Kenny set in terms of its discursive power. On the other hand, the very fact that Bart had to write extra music for the moments during which the Kenny set was revolving hints toward the set's dominance over the narrative. Still, the two elements ultimately work together in a way that McMillin finds problematic from a narratological standpoint; when a piece of scenery, such as the revolving Kenny set, asserts itself, "[t]he stage technology is merely showing its omniscience, while the orchestra plays some underscoring from *its* position of omniscience, and the interlocking systems of unseen authority have taken over the drama."[24]

For McMillin, the megamusical set epitomizes the Wagnerian tendencies that govern this particular musical genre, as the various components of the piece are forcefully united under the yoke of an all-encompassing technology.[25] However, in the case of *Oliver!*, this Wagnerian propensity seems to conflict with the Brechtian elements of the show's design. Kenny alluded to this conflict in his personal reflections on the set. Although he put forth the Brechtian complaint that British theater sets had "too much decoration,"[26] he likewise advocated a Wagnerian emphasis on unity between drama and design, decrying scenery that was "quite separate from the play and [did] nothing to push it across nor to help the audience understand anything about it."[27] The very function of the Kenny set epitomizes this contrast: the scenery may dictate the flow of the narrative according to its rotations, but, as will be discussed in detail shortly, it likewise shatters the traditional illusions of the theater and draws attention to the artificiality of what is transpiring onstage (ironically, by the same act of rotating). When *Oliver!* received its megamusical makeover for the 1994 Palladium revival, the Kenny set was abandoned in favor of a grander, more cinematic set that effortlessly preserved the very illusions that the Kenny set had previously destroyed (see Chapter 7).[28] Kenny's scenery can thus be read as straddling two separate—perhaps even antithetical—theatrical concepts and movements, which is fitting given that Kenny was both a man of his era and a creative visionary. Moreover, Bart's musical score straddled similar concepts, for although Bart's "poperatic" score leaned toward the *Gesamtkunstwerk* concepts that would be made manifest in the megamusicals of the seventies and eighties, the music-hall roots of several key numbers hinted toward a more Brechtian vision.

In the years following *Oliver!*'s debut, Bart boldly asserted that Kenny's input had been important to him from the beginning, and that the two had "spent an entire week swapping drawings before I wrote word-1 or note-1."[29] While this statement is likely an embellishment, it reinforces just how central Kenny's ideas were to the composer. In spite of Coe's work on the script, Cameron Mackintosh asserts that the final incarnation of *Oliver!* as it appeared onstage can largely be viewed as a product of Sean Kenny's imagination: "Sean Kenny was in a way the co-genius with Lionel. In fact, Lionel always said that Sean was his amanuensis, that he really liked to develop shows in the writing with Sean."[30]

Bart and Kenny had shared a common theatrical education through their work with Unity and Theatre Workshop.[31] Although his theatrical designs made him famous, Kenny, like Bart, had his hand in countless other projects, walking the fine line between the experimental and the absurd (a line that Bart himself frequently crossed). In a 1967 speech, Kenny noted that he was hard at work on "an underwater complex," explaining "it's a theatre under the water. It might seem crazy but I think that it is going to be built. The audience is encased in two tubes and glass domes. By entering the tubes, one arrives in the glass domes under the sea. Outside the glass domes is the entertainment, underwater performers with sea animals."[32] In his interview with Wright, Kenny spoke of a "'fantasy ride' in which the public is carried through [...] Outer Space, falls through a volcano crater and finally is swallowed up in

Figure 3.1: Concept art of Mr. Bumble by Sean Kenny
Source: Used by permission of the Lionel Bart estate.

the jaws of a 30 ft. monster crab."[33] Though some of his projects, like those of Lionel Bart, never made it past the borders of the imagination, several of these nontheatrical endeavors, including an underwater restaurant constructed from glass and a multilevel stage for the Dunes Hotel in Las Vegas, actually reached fruition.[34] His greatest theatrical accomplishment may very well have been his work on the Mermaid's 1968 production of *Gulliver's Travels*; through a combination of movie projections, lighting effects, and sheer imagination, Kenny brought Lilliput and Brobdingnag to life onstage.[35]

Bart's collaboration with Kenny was one of those rare relationships in the theater where the two artists did not simply build on one another's talents but moreover brought out the very best in each other. Furthermore, Bart trusted Kenny implicitly in matters of staging, as Mackintosh recalls that "Lionel would throw ideas up and Sean would actually give him the geography of the set. He literally directed a lot of that show; Peter Coe staged it but the actual vision that made the show so enormously successful came from Sean Kenny's genius."[36] In public interviews and personal correspondence, Bart proudly touted Kenny's brilliance, asserting that "I suppose people would call him a genius. If I knew the meaning of the word, so would I. He is, to my knowledge, second to none in the aesthetic utilization of space, movement, shapes, texture and light for dramatic purposes."[37] It is not surprising that Kenny would actually prove to be a leading contributor to Bart's work throughout the rest of the composer's career; he went on to design the scenery for later Bart musicals such as *Blitz!* and *Maggie May*. He likewise played a major role in helping Bart dream up various musical projects in the late sixties and early seventies, though many of these projects never made it beyond the planning stages. Unproduced Bart musicals, such as *Quasimodo*, were touched heavily by the hand of

Kenny during the development period, and Bart's vision for the Hugo project was based around Kenny's concept for reproducing Notre Dame onstage.[38] The two men even worked together to outline a spectacular musical adaptation of Tolkien's *Lord of the Rings* trilogy that would presumably have combined both dramatic action and animation.[39]

Sadly, the bond between Kenny and Bart was not simply creative but also biographical in that both men would go on to face significant financial and personal turmoil in the years following *Oliver!*'s success. Kenny became caught up in the "sex, drugs, and rock 'n' roll" lifestyle promoted by the swinging sixties and endured several failed marriages as a result of his unpredictable behavior (including a tumultuous marriage to model/actress Judy Cook).[40] Like Bart, Kenny faced bankruptcy in the late 1960s, though the files detailing his finances have been sealed. Kenny's sudden and premature passing in 1973 would prove yet another devastating blow to Bart's life and career. It would likewise play a role in the composer's retreat from the world of show business.[41] The lure of the theater seemed less vibrant and inviting without the presence of his beloved friend and collaborator.

THE PARADOXES OF THE KENNY SET

It is difficult to overestimate the importance of the Kenny set to the success of *Oliver!*, though as noted previously the set presented yet another example of the countless paradoxes that defined Bart's adaptation, including the aforementioned dichotomy between the Brechtian and Wagnerian elements of Kenny's design scheme. Though *Oliver!* was not directly affected by the Brechtian discourse that was dominating the British stage at the time, its set was regarded as a prominent example of Brechtian staging.[42] Furthermore, since the Brechtian movement in the postwar theater was confined mostly to ideas about what Brecht stood for as opposed to a direct understanding of what Brecht was advocating, elements of theatrical production, such as scenery and staging, oftentimes proved more conducive to displaying the impact of Brecht on the English stage. As Martin Esslin noted,

> because hardly anyone in the English theatre knows any German, [Brecht's] impact chiefly manifested itself in those spheres that remained unaffected by the language barrier: in stage design and lighting and in the use of music. Indeed, as far as design is concerned, one can safely say that practically *all* British stage design [...] today derives from the work of the main Brechtian designers.[43]

Esslin cites "flexibility and mobility" as the driving principles behind Brechtian staging, and these two qualities were essential to Kenny's vision of the set for *Oliver!*[44] Through the use of a revolve and two flanking trucks, Kenny succeeded in creating a set that could be transformed into any one of the play's seemingly innumerable locations simply through the principle of rotation: the workhouse, Mrs. Corney's parlor, Mr. Sowerberry's shop, the streets of London, Fagin's den, the bookseller's storefront, the Three Cripples saloon, Mr. Brownlow's house, and, perhaps most spectacularly, London Bridge all came to life in front of the audience without the lowering of a frontcloth.

In another paradox, Kenny's set could be celebrated as an artistic triumph even though its form and function were utilitarian. Designer Roger Hardwick, who worked with an upgraded version of the Kenny set during the national and international touring productions in the 1970s, notes that the revolving set provided a logical means of speedily transitioning between the diverse locations that shape Oliver's destiny: "I suppose the thing that Sean grasped was how many different scenes there were, and with his particular design of this show you actually flow from one to another by the movement of the scenic pieces."[45] Whereas a traditional set would require countless potentially disruptive scene changes to move the main pieces on and off the stage, Kenny found a way of streamlining this process so that Oliver's journey could go forward unimpeded.

Finally, even though the exposed set seemed fundamentally modern, it was simultaneously evocative of the decayed, ramshackle world of Dickensian London; the prevalent use of timber seemed at once reminiscent of the nineteenth century, for as Kenny stated in an interview with the *Epsom and Ewell Herald*, "[m]ost of the architecture during the Dickensian era was made of wood, such as the staircase in the old tenement, and I set out to capture that atmosphere."[46] As noted above, Kenny viewed the staircases as the show's central feature. Aside from their rickety design, Hardwick observes that "the way the stairs were painted or decorated gives [the set] this kind of drabness which people imagine Dickensian London was like."[47] The prominence of the bare wooden rafters, beams, and stairs that lead up and down to strange and oftentimes terrifying spaces is particularly evocative of the settings that Dickens himself created in many of his novels, including *Oliver Twist*. Still, the innovative designs that facilitated the creation of these Dickensian locations were the product of Kenny's postwar theatrical sensibilities.

For all of the innovations that defined the set, the principles behind the movement of the scenery were decidedly old-fashioned. "The actual mechanization, the way it worked, was what you might call very basic, because the moving unit had people who actually pressed the buttons and pulled the levers," recalls Alastair Davidson. "Computerization, at that time, was not even being thought of."[48] To say that several of the assistant stage managers took a hands-on role in working with the set would be something of an understatement, in that certain members of the crew actually had to position themselves *within* the construct so as to activate its moving parts. Davidson explains:

> There was an ASM [assistant stage manager] inside the main revolve, hidden in a compartment under the stairs, who pulled the lever which operated the wheel that operated the revolve. So it was actually operated by a wheel on the main stage underneath the revolve. The other pieces, the flying pieces, they were all counterweighted; there wasn't a counterweight system in the New Theatre, but they put counterweights on the flying pieces so that they could be operated easily from stage level. The two stage trucks were simply operated by pushing buttons. You pushed

a start button to start them moving and then a stop button to stop them on their mark.[49]

Whatever the technological limitations of the original scenery, Kenny's construction captured the imagination and attention of a global community of theatergoers. "The control was absolutely basic," reflects Davidson, "but it worked in a way that no other set had ever operated. And it was magical. It was a bit of theatre magic."[50] Such magic came at a price, as a large portion of the show's budget was allocated to the scenery, to the properties, and to Sean Kenny himself; tellingly, Kenny's salary was more than twice that of Peter Coe. Still, it was a highly profitable investment. Not only did the Kenny set contribute heavily to the positive response to *Oliver!*, but it likewise made the entire adaptation feasible. Without the Kenny set, it would have been impossible to trace the full scope of Oliver's journey with the same degree of fluidity.

Though Tynan objected to the basic principles behind Kenny's settings, claiming that the reliance on machines would lead to the "mechanization" of the theater, Kenny understood that machinery was necessary "as a means of showing people that you can have different kinds of stages. Stages that come out over the audience; stages that appear in the walls; ceilings that move; floors that move."[51] For all of his creative gifts, however, Kenny was a designer, not an engineer. In order to transform his dream of a mobile set into a reality, the services of Donald Albery's son, Ian, were required. According to Davidson, Ian Albery "was the person who was able to realize the set and actually get it on stage."[52] Furthermore, as the set evolved toward a more formally mechanized, electronic incarnation subsequent to the show's success, it was Ian Albery who found ways of improving the overall functionality of the scenery; such developments were essential to the feasibility of both domestic and international touring productions of *Oliver!*[53] Like Kenny, Ian Albery saw mechanization as necessary to the evolution of theatrical scenery and to the basic functionality of the *Oliver!* set.[54]

THE KENNY SET: FORM AND FUNCTION

Essentially, the set was made up of three main parts: the revolve in the center, which consisted of two turntables, and one "truck" on each side. Each side truck contained its own separate mechanical unit chain drive, which connected to a wheel on a curved track. When the set needed to be changed, the revolve turned, and, on the basis of its movement, the trucks were likewise shifted to create the new location. Table 3.1 details the various positions for the set and the number of degrees that the revolve needed to rotate in order to create these new locations.

The economy of Kenny's design was perhaps just as impressive as its functionality. Extra pieces were placed onstage in different scenes, but Hardwick recalls that these pieces were used "mainly for decoration": "There are, as I recall, only six or seven flown pieces apart from lights, and they're all dressing pieces: there's one for the kitchen, coffins for the Sowerberry scene, a window for the Three Cripples scene, a window for Brownlow's, and London bridge—and they just come in and land either on the stage or on the revolve to set up a new visual for the playing of the scene."[55]

Table 3.1. *OLIVER!* SET ROTATION CHART

Act I	Actors Right (O/P) Truck	Revolve	Actors Left (P/S) Truck
Workhouse	Upstage	360°	Upstage
Corney's Parlour	Upstage	360°	Downstage
Undertaker's	Upstage	A/C 179°	Upstage
Paddington Green	Upstage	A/C 89°	Upstage
Consider Yourself	Upstage	CL 360°	Upstage
Thieves Kitchen	Downstage	A/C 198°	Downstage
Robbery	Upstage	Ch. 360°	Upstage

Act 2	Actors Right (O/P) Truck	Revolve	Actors Left (P/S) Truck
Three Cripples	Downstage	Lined with P/S Truck	Downstage
Brownlow's	Downstage	A/C 271°	Upstage
Recapture	Downstage	C/L 284°	Upstage
Thieves Kitchen	Downstage	A/C 198°	Downstage
Corney's Parlour	Downstage	C/L 259°	Downstage
Brownlow's	Downstage	C/L 259°	Upstage
Bridge	Intermediate	C/L 62°	Upstage

Source: Cameron Mackintosh Archive, Cameron Mackintosh Ltd.

Employing the revolve meant that the basic elements defining the show's set were constantly being used and reused. As noted, Kenny had also designed a set that made it possible for scene changes to take place in front of the audience:

> There are many scenes in 'Oliver!' [...] and it would become boring for an audience if the curtain was to drop every five minutes. They know what goes on when the cloth drops for a scene change—so they might just as well see it. [...] Dropping the front cloth for scene shifting is old-fashioned. [...] The theatre has always had it, and it's really rather pointless. I have built my sets for all my shows [...] with the story in mind—to enable it to carry on right through without any delays. The scenery is part of the story.[56]

Kenny viewed the future of set design as revolving around this concept of a fully visible and movable set as opposed to the traditional use of the curtain and sliding flats. This is in keeping with the designer's overarching philosophy of mobility.

The fact that the set changed in front of the audience was just one of several elements in the staging of *Oliver!* that granted the audience unprecedented access to the practice of stagecraft. Besides the omission of the frontcloth, no attempt was made to mask the lights. Although this nonrealist technique is evocative of the Brechtian tendency toward breaking down the illusions of the theater, Davidson maintains that "it all happened for practical reasons":

Figure 3.2: Original set for *Oliver!* designed by Sean Kenny
Source: Photographer unknown; print owned by Cameron Mackintosh Archive.

Because of the way things were hung in the flies, it was impossible to mask the lights. We attempted to at Wimbledon, but it was then decided to just leave them bare. It was practical consideration, not artistic consideration. As far as the back wall was concerned, we had no backing when we were at Wimbledon and what Sean Kenny wanted was to have projections on the back wall. But [...] we weren't allowed to spend any more money because the Albery management had a disaster the week before we opened and any further expenditure on *Oliver!* was vetoed completely. So Sean Kenny and a painter sat down and painted the back wall. The back wall was simply a view of old London.[57]

The nontraditional elements of the show's staging may have been incidental, but the very fact that Kenny considered using a projector seems to strengthen the connection between *Oliver!* and the postmodern staging tendencies of the postwar theater, many of which had been influenced by the increasing prominence of Brecht in Britain.

Moreover, like Littlewood and Brecht, Kenny strove toward reaching a broader audience. In 1966, Kenny again spoke out against the constrictiveness of traditional theaters, claiming that the English theater was "loaded down with theatrical experts, and with cumbersome old-fashioned buildings. And because of this we're forgetting the theatre's real function as a live speaking voice that people will listen to: a man

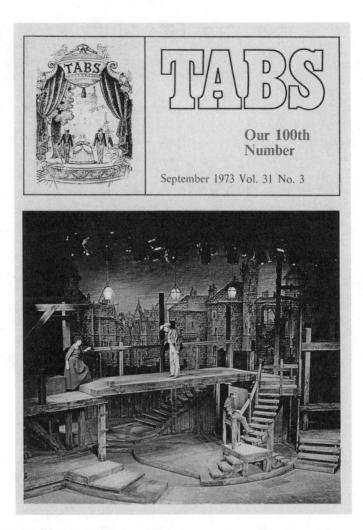

Figure 3.3: Photograph of Sean Kenny's *Oliver!* set
As printed on the cover of *TABS* magazine, 31.3 (September 1973). *Source*: Philips Strand Lighting.

telling a story. At the moment nobody listens. It's a museum tucked away and visited only by the committed few."[58] Kenny's comments are at once evocative of the mission statements put forth by Theatre Workshop and Unity Theatre in their attempts to reach working-class audiences, and although class does not enter directly into his assessment, Kenny clearly perceived the untapped potential of nontraditional theatergoers: "I don't like the theatre of gold cupids blowing kisses across the proscenium—nor the theatre of Noël Coward and Terence Rattigan. Coward has taken the theatre away from the people. I don't mean the communistic people, but ALL people."[59] This desire for a theater of "the people" reinforces Kenny's conception of architecture as an art of the people, and it may explain why he ultimately achieved his greatest success as a theater designer.

FINDING A HOME, CASTING THE LEADS

The Kenny set epitomized the architect's understanding of what a set should be, but finding a theater that suited this particular set was more difficult. The scale of the set was clearly an issue, but the overall "size" of the production was small by today's standards and thus required an intimate theatrical space. It is intriguing to imagine what the original production would have looked like had Sean Kenny designed both the set *and* the theater; nevertheless, it was Coe and Albery who undertook the task of finding a suitable venue for *Oliver!*'s debut, and likewise for its West End transfer. One possible location was the theater where Coe had cut his teeth as a director: Bernard Miles's Mermaid. The Mermaid seemed a natural fit given Coe's connection to the theater and Kenny's work on the set for *Lock Up Your Daughters*, to say nothing of the building's unique concept of theatrical space. Albery was on friendly terms with Miles and corresponded with him about the possibility of producing *Oliver!* at Puddle Dock.

Miles's theater presented several advantages over Stratford East; not only could it seat more patrons, but it likewise permitted the exploration of a larger dramatic space. Miles considered the matter closely before politely declining in January 1960. In a letter to Albery, he explained "I don't think OLIVER [sic] is right for our next production and I have decided against it. This in no way diminishes my admiration of it. Indeed, I think you have a great work on your hands and I envy you possessing such a property. And thank you for giving me the opportunity of being in on it."[60] This letter provides yet another clue regarding the show's sluggish evolution, for Miles's reference to *Oliver!* as a potential "next production" seems to indicate that the show was set to debut sooner rather than later. Even as the winter moved forward toward the spring, however, there was no clear indication of when or where *Oliver!* would open.

The management eventually decided that the play would debut at the Wimbledon Theatre before its West End transfer. Coe visited the theater personally and found that its size and equipment were sufficient for the needs of the scenery, though he was worried "that possibly the acoustics might be a bit bad as he sat at [sic] the back and though they were using mics he had difficulty in hearing."[61] In spite of these concerns, Wimbledon was formally established as the site of *Oliver!*'s debut performances. As for its West End premiere, Albery managed to procure one of the Albery family theaters: following the Wimbledon previews, *Oliver!* would relocate to the New Theatre on St. Martin's Lane. Seventeen years later, when the New Theatre had already been renamed the Albery Theatre (today, it is the Noël Coward Theatre), it would again play host to Lionel Bart's musical. The revival would be a happy homecoming for all those involved in the project, including a young producer by the name of Cameron Mackintosh.

The topic of casting is yet another curious stumbling block in tracing the chronological history of *Oliver!*, as auditions for the show were taking place as early as December 1959. An audition schedule dated December 23, reveals just how premature this casting call may have been, as several of the actresses read for the part of Rose.[62] The existence of this sheet confirms that *Oliver!* was originally slated to debut far earlier than its eventual premiere in the summer of 1960. The difficulties in finding a location and the continued changes to the form and content of the show undoubtedly prolonged the preproduction process, but casting proved controversial as well and served as a frequent source of friction between various members of the creative team.

Discussing the casting of *Oliver!* presents a unique situation, for the title character is a role meant to be played by a preadolescent. However, given the strenuous nature of live theater, the stringent laws regarding child performers on the English stage, and the unavoidable fact that children tend to grow up rather quickly, there was always a sense of evanescence regarding the role. By the end of his first year as Oliver, Keith Hamshere, the young actor who originated the role, had outgrown the part. A 1961 memo from Anne Jenkins to Monty Berman, the costumier, noted that she had already found "a splendid new boy to play Oliver as Keith has now got [*sic*] too tall."[63] Hamshere was thus the first (but hardly the last) Oliver to come up against a foe that was even more terrifying than Bill Sykes: puberty.

In order to preserve the youthful vulnerability of Oliver's character, it was decided by the management that as soon as a young performer grew "too tall," he was to be replaced by a newer, shorter actor. Understandably, this policy created a great deal of turnover. Trevor Ray, who starred as Noah Claypole in the original West End production, recalls that the production "had a lot of new blood coming in and out of it all the time."[64] Though every effort was made to successfully prepare replacement children and understudies for the lead parts, the hectic pace dictated by the children's schedules oftentimes made it difficult to fully familiarize new cast members with old cast members. Humorously, Ray recalls a particular performance in which he played out the confrontation between Noah and Oliver with a young actor whom he had never met. He fondly reflects that this impromptu pairing gave new meaning to Noah's initial inquiry to Oliver: "Are you the new boy?" Even before its first West End run had concluded, *Oliver!* had featured an uncharacteristically large number of child performers.[65] Sadly, the young actors cast in the title part were unable to "grow into" the role of Oliver; rather, the tendency was for actors to "grow out" of the part as Hamshere had done.

"BOY[S] FOR SALE"

The strictness of the postwar licensing laws for English child actors reflects the conservatism that continued to surround the British theater even as the actual productions staged in the West End became more experimental. Still, the desire to protect young children from potential exploitation and overwork in the exhausting world of theater is understandable and perhaps somewhat fitting in the case of *Oliver!* given the source text's horrific depiction of child exploitation. Nevertheless, there were several peculiar instances of "life imitating art" regarding the experience of the children in *Oliver!*, and, as in the case of Dickens's title character, there was a certain sense of commoditization regarding the children; in a letter to Bart, Albery ironically informed the composer that although Donmar was constantly on the lookout for new boys to put in the chorus, "the market is not unlimited."[66] Even Fagin and Mr. Bumble would have blushed at such a description.

A 1950 report to the Home Department on the subject of child actors revealed the contentious debate over whether children under the age of thirteen should be granted licenses, considering that thirteen was "the minimum age for general employment,"[67] this in spite of a 1918 law that had set the minimum age for attaining a theatrical license at twelve.[68] Nevertheless, child actors had been a staple of English pantomime, and "[c]hildren appearing in troupes form[ed] the majority of licensed children and they normally act[ed] as another row in the chorus."[69] Though *Oliver!* would present its own unique variation on a chorus of children, its emphasis on a child protagonist (and a young co-protagonist in the Artful Dodger) was particularly striking. Notably, in the report quoted above, the committee reflected that the parts assigned to children in West End plays were typically quite small,[70] a fact that prompted some debate over whether minimal age limits were even necessary: "We do not expect that the removal of the minimum age limit for child actors will result in the outburst of new plays requiring small children."[71] The minimum age requirement remained in place up through the period of *Oliver!*'s West End debut, however; though special licenses could be obtained, Anne Jenkins and the Donmar production team were meticulous in making certain that no child under the age of twelve was ever cast in *Oliver!*[72]

Perhaps more significant than these age requirements were the strict laws dividing the child cast members from their adult counterparts. Actress Edna Doré, who took over the role of Mrs. Sowerberry early in the show's run, recalls that "the law said that we were not to mix with [the children], so they were kept in a separate dressing room with separate chaperones."[73] Ironically, though this statute was meant to protect the child performers, it may have contributed to the transformation of these young actors into pathetic and overwrought workhouse children, at least according to the adult cast members who wished to ease their burdens and make them feel more at home in the theater. Doré recalls, "that was something that did upset me, was those little boys [who] would come straight from school and eat sandwiches and do their homework, and then do the show, and to me they all looked gray and tired. I felt sorry for those children."[74] The law was unyielding on this matter, however, and mandated the formal hiring of matrons to look after the child actors and "to ensure that as far as is possible the children [did] not mix with the adult members of the cast."[75]

The use of matrons seems another *Twist*ian irony surrounding *Oliver!* Moreover, though one would hope that the overseers employed by theater producers in the postwar era were a vast improvement on the matrons who populate Dickens's novel, this was not always the case; the 1950 Home Department report mentioned at least one instance of a matron who "ran the food side of her responsibilities as a profit-making business. Some children were found in tears after the lunch hour; the matron, for a punishment, had deprived them of their lunch."[76] It seems as though this particular matron had taken a page out of the book of *Oliver Twist*, and more specifically the book of Mrs. Mann, the most monstrous of Dickens's workhouse matrons:

> The elderly female was a woman of wisdom and experience; she knew what was good for children; and she had a very accurate perception of what was good for herself. So, she appropriated the greater part of the weekly stipend to her own use, and

consigned the rising parochial generation to even a shorter allowance than was originally provided for them. Thereby finding in the lowest depth a deeper still; and proving herself a very great experimental philosopher.[77]

Like the literary character he was bringing to life onstage, Keith Hamshere was forced to deal with the overbearing presence of matrons, including one particularly hostile woman who contributed to the stress of the early weeks of the production.[78] Thankfully, whatever the difficulties of being a child actor on the English stage, they paled in comparison to the difficulties of being a Dickensian orphan; unlike Mrs. Mann's baby farm, there is no report of a child "sicken[ing] from want and cold, or [falling] into the fire from neglect, or [getting] half-smothered by accident"[79] whilst working on *Oliver!*

Among the children cast in *Oliver!* was actor Tony Robinson, who starred in the original West End production as one of the chorus boys:

> When I was about thirteen, my mom read an advert in the newspaper which said that they were looking for kids to be in a new show in the West End. They asked me if I'd like to audition for it, which I did. I think I had, in total, about six auditions. With each one, I got more excited, as it felt like I was getting more and more sucked into it. At the end, I was offered a part in this new musical based on *Oliver Twist*.[80]

Robinson's reflections provide unique insights into what it was like to be a child performer who suddenly found himself cast in one of the most important productions of the postwar era, and he describes "the whole thing [as] this great adventure where suddenly I'd been wrested out of school into this hyper world of show business."[81] Transitioning from elementary school to Fagin's school was not as difficult a shift as one might think, for the general precociousness of the young pickpockets that made up Fagin's gang was reflected in the precociousness of the boys who brought these characters to life onstage. "All of us kids who were in it knew the whole show from beginning to end. I used to go home with Keith Hamshere, who lived quite close to my family, and on the way home, Keith and I would sing and recite the whole show. It wasn't a studied act of cleverness on our part, it's just that kids absorb this stuff, don't they?" says Robinson.[82] Since *Oliver!* transformed the dark world of Dickens into a more inviting and playful world, it is not surprising that the young members of the cast embraced the show in spite of the exhausting routines.

Nevertheless, the abovementioned scheduling issues created a fair number of difficulties for the young performers, and Doré's sympathy for the preadolescents in the cast was not unwarranted. Robinson states that "compared with child actors nowadays [. . .] we were always tired. Kids went to bed much earlier than they do now, and we weren't going home until about 11:30, which, for a child of that age, night after night, was quite a toll."[83] The fact that the boys were able to maintain the strenuous pace of the production is a testament to their lively appreciation for the show, and likewise, to the firm hand of the management.

Robinson's recollections of the rehearsal period likewise reinforce the previously discussed contrasts between Peter Coe and Lionel Bart's visions of the show and the personal differences between the two men. The stern and sober Coe focused heavily on the "adult" elements of the show, while the playful and effervescent Bart celebrated the comical and "childish" elements of the adaptation:

> There was this rather serious atmosphere orchestrated by Peter Coe, who was a very tall and austere man. In a way it was like being at school but a very glamorous school. I suppose it was like being at Hogwarts. [...] Lionel was an incredibly attractive person for a youngster to be around. He was very playful. He reveled in what he was doing and he reveled in the fact that there were lots of kids around. He was by far the most playful person there with the exception of Ron Moody. I perceived that the two of them got on very well together and they always seemed to be on our side. There was the more passionate, serious side of the rehearsal process with Peter and Georgia [Brown], and the producers who didn't have that sense of playfulness.[84]

In spite of the rigorous production and rehearsal schedule, Bart and Moody worked to create a comfortable environment for the boys in the chorus by accentuating the spirit of "play" that defines the thieves' kitchen.[85]

Though the bond between Fagin and his charges is vital to the musical's theme and narrative, the aforementioned rules set forth by the Home Office encumbered the formation of such bonds backstage. Robinson recalls that "we weren't allowed to become familiar with the other people in the show. We weren't allowed to climb the stairs to the next floor above us. So we didn't really mix very much with the dancers and the singers, except in the wings"[86]—this in spite of the fact that the adult cast members, like Moody and Doré, were supportive of and sympathetic to their juvenile co-stars. Thus, the brief periods of interaction between the two sects brought out the parental instincts in several actors, though there was a sharp difference between the stern oversight of the matrons and the maternal nature of the female cast members: "I remember in the wings, two of the young women who played prostitutes were very affectionate, in that sort of maternal way that young women often are, toward Keith and myself. We used to sit on their laps and they would cuddle us. It was probably the most erotic memory of the first twenty years of my life; she seemed the epitome of what womanhood ought to be."[87] The amusing dichotomy between the maternal instincts of the chorus girls and the proto-erotic infatuations of the boys in Fagin's gang—who were perched precariously on the edge of puberty—gives new meaning to Bart's assertion that the multiple interpretations of "Where Is Love?" are the musical's defining theme.[88]

FAGIN AND NANCY

This dichotomy between the adolescent and adult elements of Oliver! is likewise reflected in the contrast between the leading adult and child roles. Given the heavy turnover associated with the parts of Oliver and the Artful Dodger, the adult roles of Nancy and Fagin seem more consequential regarding the question of which actors originated the parts. In many respects, these roles would ultimately define the careers of the leading performers.

Figure 3.4: Ron Moody and Georgia Brown remain the definitive Fagin and Nancy for many
Oliver! devotees
Source: Photofest.

Georgia Brown's early biography reads like a virtual duplication of Lionel Bart's
childhood. Like Bart, she was born in the East End to Jewish immigrants; like Bart,
her father was a clothier; like Bart, she left London during the Blitz; like Bart, she
changed her name upon entering show business—she was born Lillian Klot and took
her stage name from the songs "Sweet Georgia Brown" and "Georgia on My Mind."[89]
Bart had actually known Brown since childhood: "I can remember a very glamorous,
mature-before-her-years, 14 year old [...] parading down a back street, as a gang of
scruffy ragamuffins led by scruffy little Lionel Begleiter stood gazing on in awe at this
unapproachable creature of beauty."[90] They were reunited by happy happenstance
years later when she auditioned for the part of Nancy. Though Bart was initially distracted by memories of his past associations with Brown, "she managed to convince us
all that nobody else in the world could be considered for Nancy; we had [not] seen and
we're [sic] not likely to see anybody else with as much earthiness, vitality, and soul."[91]
    Brown's journey from working-class roots to theatrical stardom was gradual. She
started out as a nightclub and cabaret singer in London and eventually worked her
way up to performances on the radio and in television specials. Her first truly significant theatrical role was as Lucy in the Sam Wanamaker revival of *The Threepenny
Opera*, a role she played in both London and New York.[92] Given the thematic links
between Brecht's musical and *Oliver!*—and the "professional links" between several
of the women in Brecht's play and Nancy—it seems fitting that she would go on to
originate the role of Bart's "prostitute with a heart of gold."

Though Brown awed her fellow cast mates with her vocal talents, it was her kindly and open personality that most endeared her to them.[93] To Lionel Bart, she became more than a beloved colleague; like Sean Kenny, she was a muse. In his tribute note, Bart admits that he wrote *Maggie May* with the intention of casting Brown in the title part, and he envisioned several other projects built squarely on her talents: "During the rehearsals for 'OLIVER!' we grew closer together, and I realised that there was no other artiste in life with whom I had as much rapport and mutual background."[94] To this day, Brown remains the definitive Nancy for many fans of *Oliver!* Not only did she originate the role on the West End, but she also played the part in the first Broadway production three years later. Like most members of the original cast, however, Brown did not reprise her role in the 1968 motion picture adaptation. Consequently, we are left without any true archival recording of Brown performing the role of Nancy, though she did make an appearance on the *Ed Sullivan Show* during *Oliver!*'s initial Broadway run to perform "As Long as He Needs Me."[95] In spite of the fact that she did not play the part in the film version, Brown's enduring power in the role has not been inhibited, as her renditions of "As Long as He Needs Me" on both the original West End cast recording and the original Broadway cast album have cemented her legacy in the part.

Even more assured is Ron Moody's legacy in the part of Fagin. In fact, Moody's popularity in the role of the "merry old gentleman" has become almost transcendent, which makes it all the more difficult to believe that he almost did not get the part. Both Albery and Bart had initially hoped to cast an established star or singer in the role.[96] Moody's audition was largely accidental, as Gerry Raffles of Theatre Workshop encouraged him to try out for the part:

> I auditioned, did my guitar act, and then I sang 'Nessun Dorma,' a chunk of it [because] they wanted to hear if I could sing, and that was all right. And then [Peter Coe] said, 'Well can you read a bit?' I said, 'Well, I can't possibly improve on Alec Guinness.' I said, 'All I can do is do an imitation of Alec Guinness'. [...] It was a ghastly anti-Semitic stereotype, but I said it was all I could do.[97]

Given that the Guinness performance and Moody's own performance in the film version of *Oliver!* remain the two most important cinematic depictions of the character, it is fitting that this link should exist between them, though the paternal and loveable Fagin that Moody portrayed on film seems leagues removed from Guinness's devilish corruptor.

The fact that Moody did not even meet Lionel Bart during his audition is indicative of the lukewarm response that his try-out provoked in both Bart and Albery. Moody recalls that "[Bart] was sitting in the dark, you know, in the recesses of the New Theatre, and I was auditioning for Peter Coe. [...] I don't think Lionel wanted me, or Donald Albery. They had their ideas of what they wanted for Fagin, but Peter Coe just saw something there and he kept on. He said, 'Come back in a week and I'll work on it with you'."[98] It was Coe who ultimately recommended him for the role, and while Albery eventually took to the idea, Bart remained cautious; the conflict over whether or not to cast Moody seems to have been one of the more contentious issues raised during pre-production. Kurt Ganzl notes that "Ron Moody was brought back again and again but Bart would not agree to his engagement."[99] Bart eventually dropped his protestations, though he would maintain his wariness of Moody's approach to the character for months thereafter. That mistrust would eventually evolve into a messy conflict with the actor, and the fact that Moody chose to adopt Guinness's mannerisms seems a fitting prelude to this conflict (see Chapter 6). Nevertheless, the enduring popularity of *Oliver!* is intertwined with the enduring popularity of Moody's Fagin, an interpretation that has not only shaped the perceptions of *Oliver!* but likewise exerted a significant effect on the culture text of *Oliver Twist*. In a 1983 interview, Moody reflected that both he and Bart "felt an obligation to get Fagin away from a viciously racial stereotype and instead make him what he really is—a crazy old Father Christmas gone wrong."[100] Many Fagins in subsequent adaptations of the novel have borrowed heavily from Moody's approach to a character who had, up until this point, been perceived as little more than a monstrous boogeyman. Following Moody's performance in the West End, and perhaps more directly, his portrayal of the character in the film adaptation, Fagin would never quite be the same again.

Ron Moody was born Ronald Moodnick, thus making him the third of three talented Jewish artists (all of whom took new stage names) whose contributions were essential to *Oliver!* His father was a master plasterer who worked at Elstree Studios, and Moody's first job saw him working for the studio as a clerk.[101] After four years of national service with the Royal Air Force, Moody began to study sociology at the London School of Economics "not for any vocational reason but because I wanted to know what made people tick."[102] This fascination with sociology and psychology would manifest itself throughout his career as an actor, not only in his talent for impressions and his multifaceted approaches to tragicomic characters, but also in the various interviews he gave regarding his performances; indeed, Moody's reflections on Fagin provide fascinating insights into the character and reveal the sheer intelligence of the man who brought him to life: "a sociologist is trained to perceive, and so is an actor. I had all these tools which came from my academic background, but fitted right into show business."[103] The overlap between his educational interest and the emergence of his career as a performer became especially discernible toward the end of his schooling.

While working on his thesis, Moody began writing and participating in revues at LSE, and "on the last night two showbiz casting people came backstage and said: 'Would you like to turn professional?' "[104] This marked the beginning of his career as an actor, though Moody had always been something of a performer. He had proved a talented impressionist at family gatherings and school revues before his actual discovery: "I'm an extrovert in the sense that I'm 100 percent aware of the environment. [...] It's a family trait. My mother's lot—from Lithuania—were very musical, and my father, who was born in Hackney, was always performing parlour poetry."[105] Given these particular interests and talents, it is fitting that revue proved to be the theatrical format through which Moody first found success. Though little archival material survives from his "Intimate Revue" performances, Moody earned a reputation as both a gifted impressionist and a popular comedic performer. Following his time in revue, Moody landed his first role in a major musical in 1959: the Governor of Buenos Aires in a London production of Leonard Bernstein's *Candide*. The musical, which had flopped on Broadway in 1956, did not fare much better in London. It mattered little, however, for Moody was rapidly approaching the role that would define his theatrical career.

Much has been written about Moody's performance as Fagin, but perhaps Sheridan Morley puts it best in his text on the history of the British musical: "Moody will never do anything in his career that is better than that Fagin, and there will never be a musical Fagin that good: the part defines the career and the career is dominated by the part, one he also happily immortalized in the film version."[106] As Morley points out, there is a sense of symbiosis regarding Moody's Fagin in that Moody will forever be remembered for his performance, and simultaneously that every Fagin must inevitably be evaluated against Moody. Building on Bart's foundation, Moody succeeded in creating a multifaceted character who cannot be defined by a single trait and who refuses to serve as the pure vice character epitomized by his literary forebear. As Fagin memorably quips in "Reviewing the Situation" (Moody's most successful number), "I'm finding it hard to be really as black as they paint."[107] Moody's ability to paint in shades of gray distinguishes his Fagin from virtually every incarnation of the old man that preceded his interpretation. Moody's Fagin is angel and devil, clown and corrupter, song-man and sinner. In some ways, he is an antagonist who poses a distinct threat to Oliver's attaining middle-class domesticity. In other ways, he is a sympathetic co-protagonist who manages to steal the central storyline right out from under the titular character's nose. Moody's ability to capture the multifaceted elements of the character proved both entertaining and artistically significant.

Perhaps even more impressive is his enduring attraction to the character and the energy that he still manages to convey regarding the part that made him famous. In the 2005 Boxing Day special, *Celebrate Oliver!*, Moody reprised the role of Fagin to sing "Reviewing the Situation" in full makeup and costume. At eighty-one, the actor showed that he had not lost his touch, and the comedy and patter that had helped to define the number when Moody first sang it forty-five whole years earlier were still alive and well in his new rendition. More recently, on the night of *Oliver!*'s fiftieth anniversary, June 30, 2010, the eighty-six-year-old actor came out onstage following the performance to entertain the audience with a rendition of "Pick a Pocket or Two."

WIMBLEDON AND BEYOND

Albery, Coe, and Bart had managed to assemble a talented cast and crew for *Oliver!* and the musical eventually entered a brief rehearsal period in the late spring of 1960 during the weeks leading up to the Wimbledon premiere in June. Though the show had evolved significantly, it was still in a state of "trial and error." The continued experimentation that defined the rehearsal period was due to numerous overarching factors, including Bart and Coe's own tendencies to improvise, the changes necessitated by the Kenny set, and of course the contributions of the actors. This last factor is an important clue to understanding Coe's interest in casting Moody. Davidson asserts that Coe "wasn't a director in what I would call the classic style. Still, there are a number of people in the show who loved working with him because it was mainly improvisation."[108] For Moody, Coe's approach was ideal in that it allowed him to explore the broad, comic dimensions that he perceived in Fagin without restraint. It likewise permitted him to draw on his revue show roots. The actor later recalled that "Peter Coe allowed me to do whatever I wanted. All he said to me, the only note he gave to me, was, 'Now make it real', which is one of the best notes that any director can give to an actor."[109] This sense of understanding between Coe and Moody underscores Coe's role as Moody's chief supporter throughout the original West End production, and Moody clearly appreciated Coe's willingness to trust the actors. Though Bart would grow frustrated with Moody's embellishments subsequent to the show's premiere, he was very much in favor of this experimentalism in the rehearsal period, as he himself was still experimenting with Fagin, and indeed, with the rest of the show.[110]

As the date of *Oliver!*'s West End premiere approached, most of the cast and crew were optimistic that the show would prove a success, though the preview performances at the Wimbledon Theatre did not inspire as much confidence as Albery had hoped for regarding the project. The discrepancies between the lukewarm reception that the show received at Wimbledon and the overwhelmingly enthusiastic reception that it received at the New Theatre have become part of the myths surrounding the story of *Oliver!*; in fact, the popular understanding is that the Wimbledon run flopped, though this is overstating the matter. A party of Theatre Workshop alumni, including John Junkin, journeyed to Wimbledon to experience *Oliver!* and were amazed by what they saw:

> We sat there knowing absolutely nothing about what was going to go on, and suddenly, this incredible piece of magic started with the kids in the workhouse, and we sat there with that little tingle that comes over you when you know that you're seeing something new, and incredible, and marvelous. And as it went on, you just got higher and higher and higher. The songs, I remember, hitting you like a blow. [...] And at the end of it, we went back[stage]. [...] And I can remember [the cast and crew's] almost disbelief when we rushed in and erupted with the praise that came pouring out of us. 'Is it really that good?' They had gotten so close to it in the development that they hadn't realized that they had reached the peak, that they had reached the point that they were ready for the West End, they were ready for the world, they were ready for anything. Even Lionel, who was not a man who was renowned for lack of confidence, was very tentative to accept our praise at face value.[111]

Nevertheless, while Junkin and Bart's other friends from Theatre Workshop were convinced that the show was ready for its West End debut, the creative team knew that some important adjustments would have to be made.

Fortunately, several of the problems relating to the Wimbledon production stemmed from issues presented by the theater itself as opposed to any noteworthy flaws in the show. Coe's initial fears regarding the acoustics at the theater were well founded, and the audibility of the actors was frequently problematic. Speaking and singing clearly while using a realistic street accent was a difficult balancing act for the performers, and doing so in an enormous theater with poor acoustics made the matter even trickier. Davidson recalls that "the Wimbledon Theatre is a barn of a place, and in fact, the original production of *Oliver!* was what one might call an intimate musical."[112] Though *Oliver!* would prove to be one of the biggest British musicals of all time (in terms of not only its scope but also its reception), and though it would help to pave the way for the epic English musicals of the 1980s, its true power lay in the close, music-hall style bond that it sought to create between the audience and the lead characters, particularly Oliver, Fagin, Nancy, and the Dodger. The theater allowed sufficient room for the set to revolve freely, but the size of the stage and auditorium prevented the show from achieving the level of vocal "nearness" that the production demanded, as Davidson claims that the show's theme, and even the massive Kenny set, "[were] fairly lost on the stage at the Wimbledon Theatre."[113]

The problems at Wimbledon likewise prompted a drastic reimagining of how certain numbers should be staged. From the beginning of the rehearsal period, there had been significant conflicts between Coe and the show's choreographers; Cameron Mackintosh humorously reflects that the show supposedly went through five choreographers, a fact that may underscore the "astringency" that he attributed to Coe's personality.[114] Nevertheless, in a last-ditch effort to make the crowd and street scenes fit more seamlessly into the overall vision of the show, Coe boldly decided to eliminate the choreography entirely.[115] "Originally there were two big dance numbers that [Coe] threw out and the only real bit of dancing was a sort of step sequence at the end of 'Consider Yourself'," recalls Davidson.[116] These alterations were another indication of Coe's interest in improvisation, as the director transitioned the chorus from choreographed dances to spontaneous crowd scenes so as to give the songs a more believable conception of London street life:

> [Initially] there was what I would call conventional musical dancing with men and women doing steps and lifts and things like that. This happened in the middle of "Consider Yourself" and in "Who Will Buy?" in the second act. In those days, I mean, your ensemble consisted of singers, dancers, and actors, and the three things were entirely separate. Peter Coe made them into an ensemble as you have today.[117]

In this endeavor, Coe was assisted by the gifted ballet master Larry Oaks, who helped to block out certain movements for the crowd scenes and who was later given the task of assisting Davidson in the training of new cast members and understudies.[118] The result of Oaks and Coe's efforts was a more dynamic vision of London, and the organized chaos of the improvised crowd scenes gave the songs a uniquely Dickensian feel—one reminiscent of many of the vibrant crowd scenes featured in Boz's novels, crowd scenes that were frequently captured and preserved in a picturesque tableau through Cruikshank and Phiz's brilliant illustrations.

Regarding the narrative, the version of *Oliver!* that premiered at Wimbledon was not exceptionally different from the version that would premiere at the New Theatre, though there were a few noteworthy divergences in the order of the scenes and songs, as documented in the Wimbledon libretto licensed by the lord chamberlain on June 1, 1960. In the opening scenes of Act I, the flirtatious interactions between

Mr. Bumble and Mrs. Corney—including their comical duet "I Shall Scream"—were awkwardly incorporated *after* Oliver's apprenticeship to Mr. Sowerberry. Moreover, this scene included the first appearance of Old Sally, thus sowing the seeds for the mystery of Oliver's parentage far earlier in the story. This sequencing created a more suspenseful subplot, but it simultaneously impeded Act I from progressing at a brisk pace by jumping back and forth between the workhouse and the undertaker's shop instead of simply moving Oliver forward from one location to the next. Kenny's emphasis on linear movement, though ironically dictated by the revolving set, seems antithetical to such a "circular" staging of the pre-London scenes.

Act II likewise diverged from its final incarnation regarding the order of songs. "As Long as He Needs Me" was originally slated to be sung toward the very end of the show, just before Nancy's death; moving it to the first scene of Act II added greater intensity to the Nancy-Sykes subplot that dominates the second act. Similarly, Fagin's showstopper, "Reviewing the Situation," was initially set to be sung at the beginning of the final thieves' kitchen scene, before the melodramatic confrontation between Nancy and Sykes; moving the song to the end of the scene ultimately ensured a more dynamic conclusion to this final sequence, even if it broke up the continuity of the Nancy-Sykes subplot by putting Fagin center-stage. This modification also supported the brilliant notion of rotating the set as Fagin sings the last verse of the song and inquires as to who will "change the scene" for him.[119]

The surviving Wimbledon script indicates that the lyrics to the songs were still in a state of flux, as several of the songs featured in this libretto contain words that were ultimately cut or revised for the final version of the show.[120] Notably, the lyrics to some songs were omitted entirely; others were pasted in haphazardly on separate scraps of paper. Bart was still working feverishly to revise the old songs, and simultaneously to create new songs to fill out the score. In fact, the score was still incomplete just days before *Oliver!* premiered at the New. The beloved comic performer Barry Humphries, then an eager young actor who had just relocated to London from Australia, was cast in the part of the morbid Mr. Sowerberry, and Bart was so impressed with his performance that he decided to create a song specifically for him. "That's Your Funeral" was thus written at the proverbial "last minute."[121]

Unfortunately, the positive word of mouth so essential to a successful transfer to the West End was not quick in coming following Wimbledon. Both Bart and Moody would later recall that the previews had failed to generate much hype for the new musical; in his retrospective article, Bart reflected that "[w]ord wasn't that great after Wimbledon,"[122] and Moody echoed this sentiment, asserting that "it wasn't terribly successful. People came to see it, and one or two of them, I remember Bill Bourne, the *Evening Standard* show business journalist, *he* liked it [...] he was saying 'I think you've got something, got a hit there', but nobody else seemed to be very impressed."[123] Undaunted, Bart continued to work with the creative team in hopes of perfecting the adaptation. He would later recall that changes were made "right up until the opening night."[124]

Bart's eagerness to see *Oliver!* succeed was matched only by Albery's, who still believed in the project, though he was wary of the Wimbledon setbacks. Joan

Littlewood had attended the debut performance at Wimbledon and sent Albery words of encouragement, but his reply letter reveals his frustrations:

> Thank you very much for your telegram of good wishes. I personally found the first night disappointing, as I expected so many of the artists to have been better, and it worried me that many of them were inaudible. I think it was partly the theatre and partly their elocution. However, on the Saturday night it was quite a different cup of tea, and they did make a real effort to be heard, and the audience enjoyed themselves hugely.[125]

Before closing his letter, Albery added "[t]here is no reason why the show should not be a big success, but of course nobody can be quite sure of anything these days,"[126] a fatalistic assessment, particularly in comparison to his early enthusiasm for the property. Still, there was little time left for speculation regarding the chances for the show's success: *Oliver!* was set to open at the New Theatre.

CHAPTER 4

cᴧᴕ

"This was the real Dickens": The Triumph of *Oliver!*

As *Oliver!*'s opening night drew closer, the question of whether or not Bart's Dickensian musical would prove to be the groundbreaking hit that Bart and Albery had envisioned seemed uncertain. Years later, Albery would recall the general feeling that "[w]e had a flop on our hands."[1] Tellingly, no opening night festivities were planned for the show's premiere.[2] Fortunately, the debut performance of *Oliver!* would present its own sense of revelry.

OPENING NIGHT

Oliver! premiered at the New Theatre, as scheduled, on June 30, 1960, at 7:30 P.M. in the midst of a blistering summer heat wave, though the initial reaction to the piece was decidedly frosty. "They were not a warm audience. They were expecting a disaster," Alastair Davidson recalls.[3] The opening numbers were politely received, but the overall reaction to the show was staid. The introduction of the Artful Dodger gave the show a much-needed boost in terms of audience enthusiasm, effectively breaking the ice between the cast and the crowd; Albery later opined that "[a] good Artful Dodger [...] can make a great deal of difference to the effect of the production."[4] Given the Dodger's status as the chief representative of the kinship and hospitality that characterize the thieves' den, which is arguably the defining component of Bart's creative vision, it is fitting that he helped to "sell" the show to the opening night crowd.

It was "Consider Yourself" that truly marked the turning point, however, and this ditty deserves its prominent place in the canon of Lionel Bart's songs. "Consider Yourself" transformed the very tenor of the opening night performance: "During 'Consider Yourself', they just went mad. It was one of these things in the theatre that happen once in a lifetime. It was extraordinary. After that, they just went absolutely mad."[5] The tumultuous applause following this number was so great that the start of the next scene had to be delayed. Though the set had revolved to reveal Fagin's den, and though Ron Moody was onstage to start the next segment of the show, he had to wait several minutes before he could begin his performance.[6] "Consider Yourself" had proved itself a "show-stopper" in every sense of the term.

Amazingly, Bart did not witness this transition. Though the composer had always maintained confidence in the project, his nerves were raw and he left the theater early on to "take a walk around London."[7] His wanderings supposedly took him to Piccadilly Circus, and then, to the Garrick Theatre, where the West End production of *Fings Ain't Wot They Used T'Be* was playing. Bart sought comfort from his friends in the cast; Barbara Windsor vividly recalls, "he was in such a state, Lionel, and said, 'It ain't gonna work. It's gonna flop'."[8] By the time he returned to the New Theatre later that evening, the show was over. Bart found himself witness to an enormous standing ovation—one that had lasted over twenty curtain calls and a seemingly endless string of reprises of "I'd Do Anything" and "Consider Yourself."[9] In a letter written two short days after the premiere, Albery ecstatically recounted the electric response to *Oliver!* on its opening night: "The play has had the most vociferous reception I ever remember in London. The whole house was cheering and would have stayed all night with reprise after reprise if we would have let them."[10] Nevertheless, even after all the reprises had been sung and all the bows had been taken, the audience continued its boisterous shouts of "Author!" and "Speech!" Bart humbly began his speech by acknowledging Dickens, though this acknowledgment was framed as an apology: "May the good Dickens forgive us."[11] His apologetic words were a testament to the fact that he understood how fundamentally he had modified his source, though given the reaction of the opening night crowd, it seemed that no apology was necessary.

Some of the younger cast members were naïvely unaware of what they were witnessing. Tony Robinson recalls "there was something like 26 curtain calls. It felt like everybody came up to take a bow, including the stage carpenter. And yet, I didn't know that that was unusual. Everyone was heaping praise on it, and I thought, 'Well, why wouldn't they?'"[12] For the adult cast members, however, it was a once-in-a-lifetime moment. Years later, Ron Moody would remember "a kind of electrical magnetism around the theatre. I've never known it since. It's something called success but it's more than that. It's huge success. Excitement. It sizzled. You felt it in the atmosphere all the time we were in there."[13] The opening night of *Oliver!* inaugurated an incredible six-year run in the West End that would play a record-breaking total of 2,618 performances.

Oliver! thus proved to be more than just a passing craze; the fanfare surrounding the show would last well beyond its opening night. Throughout the next several years, Bart's musical continued to attract enthusiastic West End audiences who were always left "asking for more." Albery's files contain copious copies of fan letters praising the merits of the show and complimenting the producer and the creative team on the success of *Oliver!* Coupled with these fan letters were countless requests to try to get hold of some piece of *Oliver!*, either for sentimental reasons or for the desire to make a profit. Various schoolchildren wrote to Albery in hopes of getting permission to perform songs from the show in recitals, while numerous audience members requested signed photos of the cast members, most often of the children portraying the lead roles of Oliver and the Artful Dodger. Some theatergoers did not even bother to ask permission, and instead smuggled cameras into the show to shoot pictures of their favorite orphans and pickpockets.[14]

As a precursor to the transatlantic success that the show would eventually enjoy, various American tourists who saw *Oliver!* while visiting London were frustrated by the fact that copies of the LP were not available in their home country. Furthermore, Harrods was unable to ship the record across the Atlantic because of legal restrictions.[15] Nevertheless, *Oliver!*'s songs would eventually find their way onto American turntables thanks to black market sales of the soundtrack (see Chapter 6). The songs would likewise appear on countless pop singles from prominent singers of the period, including Shirley Bassey, Nancy Sinatra, Sammy Davis, Jr., Dionne Warwick, Lena Horne, Tony Bennett, George Feyer, Al Hirt, Marilyn Maye, Eydie Gorme, and Jack Jones.[16]

While British and American recording artists were capitalizing on the popularity of Bart's songs, British businessmen and advertisers were eager to incorporate lyrics from these same songs into various ad campaigns: J. Clarke of the Clarke Agency contacted Duncan Melvin, the New Theatre's press representative on August 15, 1961, with a request to quote "Pick a Pocket or Two" in an ad for Cleveland Motor Service Ltd. (included in the letter was a cartoonish caricature of Fagin flipping through a large wad of currency).[17] The banking firm, Glyn Mills & Co., used a similar marketing ploy. The business took out an advertisement in the *Oliver!* playbill with a tiny caricature of Fagin singing happily to giant bags of English pounds. The ad misquotes his song, stating that "In this world / One thing counts / In the bank / Large amounts"; it goes on to affirm that "Glyn Mills & Co will be happy to keep your 'large amounts' safe for you at any of their branches [...] *Our* Mr. Oliver will gladly give you details."[18] Perhaps the cleverest of these marketing ploys was by North Thames Gas, which also took out an advertisement in the original program. The ad features the headline "Asking for more?" and reads "Is yours a Bleak House in winter? Then, like Oliver Twist, you're justified in asking for more."[19]

As a result of its pervasive presence in the popular culture of the 1960s, *Oliver!* quickly ingrained itself in the larger perception of Dickens's *Oliver Twist*, forever changing the view of the original text. The Artful Dodger was now the singer of "Consider Yourself" instead of the snub-nosed pickpocket who is ultimately transported for life. Fagin was now the roguish song-man who deserved a second chance as opposed to the devilish corruptor who warranted a trip to the gallows. Although the deviation of the musical from the novel held little meaning for the countless children who embraced the show, adults and critics familiar with Dickens's works were aware of the fact that Bart had created a very loose adaptation of Boz's text. Nevertheless, the appreciation of British audiences for *Oliver!* in the face of its divergences from the source is one of the most fascinating elements surrounding the reception of this musical in England.

OLIVER!, OSBORNE, AND ENGLISHNESS

Assessing the response to the very first production of *Oliver!* in England, one finds a palpable sense of pride in the reactions of many critics. Bernard Levin of the *Daily Express* wrote that "[i]t is a very long time indeed since I came out of the theatre after a musical whistling the tunes. So before all else I salute Mr. Lionel Bart—who has also written the book and lyrics of this, the most ambitious *British* musical of recent years—for his score."[20] Levin was just one of a seemingly endless number of theater critics who chose to focus on the "national identity" of *Oliver!* in his review; Robert Muller of the *Daily Mail* proudly dubbed *Oliver!* "[a] British musical [...] that will and must charm audiences all over the world,"[21] while Harold Conway of the *Daily Sketch* tried to capture the electricity of the opening night premiere in his introductory paragraph: "A warming, wonderful thing to hear last night. Resounding, uproarious cheers for a British musical—roars of pleasure from stalls and gallery in unison."[22] Notably, Conway celebrates not only the cultural unity promoted by *Oliver!* but an equally important class-based unity reminiscent of the late Victorian music hall. Martin Shulman echoed many of Muller's and Conway's statements about the revolutionary nature of *Oliver!* in a review entitled "This One Could Start an Avalanche." Though he was referring to an avalanche of Dickensian adaptations as opposed to an avalanche of English musicals—a prophetic statement in light of the Dickensian musical fad initiated by *Oliver!*—Shulman made certain to conclude his article by encouraging all of his readers to go and see "this imaginative, virile, pulsating and melodic British musical."[23] These reviews are representative of the pervasive sense of patriotism surrounding *Oliver!*, and this almost nationalistic reaction to Bart's musical is underscored by the fact that numerous peers of the realm and members of the royal family repeatedly came to see the show over the course of its initial West End run. The Queen Mother, Princess Margaret, Prince Philip, Princess Anne, the Duchess of Gloucester, the Duke and Duchess of Windsor, Lady Monckton, Field Marshal Lord Alexander and Lady Alexander, and Queen Elizabeth II herself all experienced *Oliver!* during its first year in the West End.[24]

The notion that the debut of a stage musical could be regarded as a culturally significant event is a testament to the more general prominence of the theater in postwar English society, as described in Chapter 1; the changes within the English theater and the rise of the angry young men became touchstones for measuring larger cultural shifts. Returning to Cameron Mackintosh's assertion regarding the parallels between *Oliver!* and *Look Back in Anger*, I find it important to consider that both the specific discourse and the general energy surrounding *Oliver!* in the English press were reminiscent of the enthusiasm for Osborne's play. Granted, there was no single theatrical review that did for *Oliver!* what Tynan's review had done for *Look Back in Anger*; Tynan's own reaction to *Oliver!* was positive but sedate in comparison to many of his contemporaries. Still, the celebratory tone surrounding both works as powerful expressions of English culture was incredibly similar. David Ian Rabey writes that Tynan and the other promoters of the *Look Back in Anger* "industry" were actively "ushering in an age of specifically English indigenous theatrical dominance"[25]; Dominic Shellard concurs with this assessment, citing the "relief that, at last, an indigenous playwright had written something that could start to challenge the notion that only the French could write stimulating works on contemporary dilemmas."[26] Although Bart's victory was not over the French experimental drama, but rather over the American musical tradition, both *Look Back in Anger* and *Oliver!* marked powerful instances of English insurgence against globalized cultural trends. If Osborne had proved that the English drama could reassert itself in a pronounced English fashion, Bart had done likewise for the English musical.

Just as Tynan had embraced the youthfulness and vitality of *Look Back in Anger*, critics honed in on the same qualities in *Oliver!* In Osborne's play, the "blazing vitality"[27] manifests itself through the unbridled emotionalism and passionate anger of the central characters; as a musical, *Oliver!* could rely on the less irate but equally passionate power of song, and the reviews quoted above hint at the palpable energy surrounding Bart's adaptation. On the topic of youth, T. C. Worsley concluded his review by noting that "[t]he combined talents which have gone into bringing off [*Oliver!*] are among the youngest and most adventurous the theatre has thrown up lately."[28] It was easy to focus in on the youthfulness of *Oliver!* given its emphasis on child characters, though its working-class energy likewise connected it to the general shifts that defined both the postwar youth culture and the postwar theater. Robinson perceptively observes that *Oliver!* was part of "this extraordinary transition from an internationally dominated West End to a British theatre culture which was asserting its own Britishness, and in particular, its own working-class roots. The idea that there were ordinary people to be celebrated built upon the work of Osborne, Wesker, and the plays of Joan Littlewood's theatre."[29] As in the case of these revolutionary plays, the Englishness of *Oliver!* was more than an inert, passive trait; it was an active theatrical element and a fundamental cause for celebration. The boisterous, youthful, working-class energy behind that Englishness made it all the easier for audiences to become part of the celebration.

Of course, the idea of a "rebellious" play becoming an English cultural institution as a result of a brilliant marketing campaign threatens to push the play across the fine line between irony and hypocrisy; as noted in Chapter 1, the indispensability of media publicity to the success and cultural dominance of the angry young men has exerted a negative impact on the legacy of *Look Back in Anger* to a certain degree.[30] Like all musicals, *Oliver!* has faced its own problems in attaining "artistic legitimacy" because of the inescapable reality that the musical genre has always been a heavily commercialized form of theater. Nevertheless, the commercial success of these two works was vital in facilitating their cultural significance. In reflecting on the triumph of *Look Back in Anger*, Rabey asserts that this play ultimately demonstrated "the adaptability of commercialism, responding to offset a fear of national decline."[31] In this case, a media marketing campaign became a tool for helping to combat English anxieties in the postwar period, as the object of that campaign provided forceful proof that English culture still had a great deal to offer. *Oliver!*'s triumphant (commercial) success counteracted similar fears, specifically fears of the unceasing American dominance of the West End musical theater.

Muller boldly asserted that *Oliver!* is "as professional as anything the Americans have sent us: mobile, high-spirited, squeezing every last ounce of drama and comedy from the book,"[32] thus heralding what he viewed as the first true signs of counter-attack against the American invasion of the West End. Tellingly, both Allan Hale and Roy Shepherd compared *Oliver!* to *Oklahoma!* in their reviews, though they did so while touting the same Englishness cited above; Hale happily titled his review "Musical Hit...and made in Britain" before noting that Bart's adaptation "has London in the greatest tiz since 'Oklahoma' [sic],"[33] while Shepherd predicted that *Oliver!* "will become as firm a favourite as 'Oklahoma'[sic] [...] and most important, it's ALL BRITISH."[34] What is especially noteworthy about these two reviews—aside from their omission of *Oklahoma!*'s trademark exclamation point—is the celebration of *Oliver!*'s Englishness juxtaposed against *Oklahoma!*, an American show celebrating American themes written in American idiom by two American writers who had seemingly perfected an American form of theater. Much as Rodgers and Hammerstein's musical achieved transatlantic success in spite of that palpable Americanness, Bart had succeeded in creating an English musical that would achieve a similar global dominance even as it promoted a distinctive national character, a fact that only fueled the British boasting. The very week after *Oliver!* debuted, an article in the *Evening News* proudly asserted that the battle was on for the rights to the first Broadway production: "It must be a very long time since the Americans showed so much interest in a British musical as they are doing for 'Oliver!' A week after it opened it is still getting cheers every night and anything from 15 to 20 curtain calls."[35] Perhaps the least subtle instance of this patriotic provocation of the Broadway community was on the part of C. B. Mortlock, who ostentatiously titled his *Oliver!* review "We can do this as well as Americans."[36]

MOURNING THE MUSIC HALL: *OLIVER!*, OSBORNE, AND ENGLISHNESS REVISITED.

It may be tempting to label the cultural phenomenon of *Look Back in Anger* as inauthentic given the PR movement behind it, and *Oliver!*, as a musical and as a loose adaptation of a Dickens novel, is inevitably subject to similar skepticism regarding its authenticity. Such accusations ignore the fact that however artificial these texts may seem, the cultural turbulence to which they were reacting was very real; anxiety over imperial decline (and the fear of embracing a chauvinistic nostalgia for that same Empire) remains a prominent component of postwar discussions of English national character. In their analysis of contemporary Englishness, Andrew Gamble and Tony Wright note that although then Prime Minister Gordon Brown "argued that Britain should not retreat into the 'nineteenth century conceptions of blood, race, and territory'" he simultaneously conceded that England's most significant achievements "lie in a receding past. Britain is no longer able to celebrate its empire in the way that it did one hundred years ago; it no longer has daily proof of its own greatness."[37] Though this assessment hints at a purely internal struggle, the external pressure of Americanization has been an important element since the postwar period; as Jimmy Porter laments, "I must say it's pretty dreary living in the American Age— unless you're an American of course. Perhaps all our children will be Americans."[38]

In defining the current trends in English "cultural nationalism," Richard Hayton notes that "[t]he attempt to capture what is supposedly essential or distinctive in the national character of the English, clearly arises against a backdrop of a host of socio-economic and geo-political changes, as well as some ongoing pressures, notably the impact of American values and culture."[39] *Look Back in Anger* and *Oliver!* offered their own unique rebuttals to the American trends of postwar Western culture, and Bart may actually have eclipsed Osborne in this regard since he was writing in a genre that had been cultivated and dominated by American writers and composers up to that point in time; while Osborne was reestablishing a strong English voice in the English theater, Bart was beating the Americans at their own game.

Still, the question of authenticity takes on new dimensions when one considers that the entire concept of "Englishness" is potentially inauthentic, particularly in the context of contemporary theories of nationhood and national character as construc- tions. As noted in the Introduction, however, the falseness that defines the creation of an imagined community should not negate the powerful influence of these com- munal identities on populations, nor reduce them to "imaginary." In his rebuttal to Benedict Anderson, Antony Easthope claims that "[a]ny theoretical opposition which would contrast some notion of authentic identity with the inauthenticity of national identity has to be rejected."[40] Cultural narratives regarding Englishness have proven incredibly influential and powerful, and the potent cultural narratives surrounding the angry young men and *Oliver!* were significant representations of this discourse in the postwar era.

As examples of the power of narrative and discourse to shape and contribute to perceptions of national identity, *Oliver!* and the angry young men seem unique exam- ples of Easthope's argument, and yet the works of Osborne and Bart simultaneously seem to embrace what Easthope derides as

> a nostalgic and sentimental desire to believe that face-to-face contact is real [...] while opposed to this the larger, more impersonal groupings constructed by moder- nity are imaginary, false, unreal. In the pre-national culture, the lost organic com- munity where everyone knows everyone else, people are supposedly directly present to each other without mediation while in the nation they are not.[41]

Granted, for Osborne and for Bart, the "pre-national culture" is the culture of a pre-globalized England as opposed to a pre-national England, but in both instances, the "lost organic community" is represented by an English institution that was of the foremost importance to both writers: the English music hall.

Certainly, *Oliver!* and Osborne were just two prominent examples of the larger theatrical trend toward music-hall performance on the postwar English stage, and this trend was essential to the revitalization of the English theater. As early as 1911, G. H. Mair was complaining that "the English theatre has no artistic vitality what- ever,"[42] while the English music hall boasted "the best English acting—perhaps the only live English acting."[43] In spite of this hyperbole, which is in keeping with the exaggerated and sentimentalized celebration of the music hall as England's "one pure-blooded native amusement,"[44] Mair's comments are noteworthy in the context of the music-hall movement in the 1950s theater; the unbridled passion and desire for human connection that define so many of the characters in the plays of the angry young men is less in keeping with the traditional acting methods of the English stage and more in keeping with the unashamed emotional directness of the English music hall.

Osborne's most sustained and insightful exploration of the relationship between the music hall and Englishness was *The Entertainer*; in the author's note, he warned that "[t]he music hall is dying, and, with it, a significant part of England. Some of the heart of England has gone; something that once belonged to everyone, for this was truly a folk art."[45] Here, the decline of English music hall becomes a metaphor for the decline of England itself and the more general decline of a sense of English communal identity in the wake of postmodern globalism. Though Bart makes greater use of this same allegorical premise in *Fings Ain't Wot They Used T'Be* than in *Oliver!*, his magnum opus presents a similarly mournful commemoration of a dying art, as the portrayal of Fagin's gang is a compelling reminder of the working-class camaraderie and imaginative energy that had once defined the English music halls. As will be discussed in the next chapter, the breakup of the gang, and the forced retirement of Fagin (the character who most adamantly believes in the power and promise of music hall), adds a pronouncedly melancholy quality to *Oliver!*'s ostensibly happy ending. Here, the destruction of the thieves' kitchen becomes an allegorical representation of the destruction of the halls, and perhaps for the larger destruction of English community in the face of capitalist materialism.

Oliver! and *The Entertainer*'s emphases on the decline of music hall are part of a much broader cultural discourse on the same subject, one that predates World War II. Indeed, rumors of the untimely death of English music hall had been greatly exaggerated in the decades leading up to the Second World War. In all of these instances, the mourning of music hall's passing reflected a larger mourning of some element of English identity or national character that had supposedly gone extinct.

OLIVER! AND MUSIC HALL

Given the cultural connections between the music hall and English national character, it seems somewhat odd that the English author who helped to define English national character at the height of its power largely ignored this cultural institution. Despite his exploration of many types of Victorian popular entertainment forms in his novels, "Dickens pays surprisingly little attention to the music hall."[46] Still, he made use of the institution in *Oliver Twist*, depicting the Three Cripples as an early music hall. The portrait is hardly favorable. In Chapter 26, Fagin journeys to the tavern:

> It was curious to observe some faces which stood out prominently from among the group. There was the chairman himself, (the landlord of the house,) a coarse, rough, heavy-built fellow, who, while the songs were proceeding, rolled his eyes hither and thither, and, seeming to give himself up to joviality, had an eye for everything that

was done, and an ear for everything that was said—and sharp ones, too. Near him, were the singers: receiving, with professional indifference, the compliments of the company: and applying themselves, in turn, to a dozen proffered glasses of spirits and water, tendered by their more boisterous admirers; whose countenances, expressive of almost every vice in almost every grade, irresistibly attracted the attention, by their very repulsiveness. Cunning, ferocity, and drunkenness in all its stages, were there, in their strongest aspects; and women: some with the last lingering tinge of their early freshness, almost fading as you looked: others with every mark and stamp of their sex utterly beaten out, and presenting but one loathsome blank of profligacy and crime: some mere girls, others but young women, and none past the prime of life: formed the darkest and saddest portion of this dreary picture.[47]

Given these sentiments, it is hard to believe that Dickens did not support his fellow middle-class reformers in their attempts to close down the music halls, but it is important to note that the sentiments put forward here are conveyed by the novel's moralizing narrator, who, though an expression of Dickens's authorial voice, does not necessarily speak for the author.[48] Furthermore, one cannot ignore the fact that the camaraderie of the Three Cripples, though debauched and corruptive, is infinitely more alluring than the miserable loneliness that defines the workhouse; as will be discussed in the next chapter, this contrast is important to understanding some of the more subversive qualities of Bart's interpretation of Oliver Twist.

Besides this fictitious presentation in Twist, Dickens published two noteworthy essays on the subject of music halls in Household Words and All the Year Round, the first written by himself and the second by his colleague Richard Halliday.[49] Both pieces feature a fictional character visiting some entertainment spots associated with the lower classes. In Dickens's piece, he insists that the working class has a "right to be amused"[50] and decries the efforts of reformers to close down these saloons or revoke their licenses:

> Ten thousand people, every week, all the year round, are estimated to attend this place of amusement. If it were closed tomorrow—if there were fifty such, and they were all closed tomorrow—the only result would be to cause that to be privately and evasively done which is now publicly done; to render the harm of it much greater, and to exhibit the suppressive power of the law in an oppressive and partial light. The people who now resort here, *will be* amused somewhere. It is of no use to blink that fact, or to make pretences to the contrary. We had far better apply ourselves to improving the character of their amusement.[51]

Just over a decade later, Dickens's eldest son, Charles Dickens, Jr., then the editor of All the Year Round, published a strikingly similar assessment of the late Victorian music halls:

> There is perhaps no one to be found who is less an admirer of these 'institutions' than myself, but I can see plainly enough that it is of no use to loftily ignore them, or to write of them as if they were pest-houses, when all those who have the slightest

acquaintance of them know better, and so are led to judge of the remainder of any
hostile arguments from the unfairness displayed in that.[52]

Though the anonymous author of this article assumes an even more patronizing air
than Dickens, he is willing to acknowledge the better qualities of the genre.[53] This is
a milder form of the general snobbery that defined the middle-class response to the
Victorian music hall. As will be discussed shortly, however, the eventual inclusion of
the middle classes in music-hall entertainment was essential to its gaining sufficient
cultural cachet to qualify as a symbol of the English nation.

Whatever his reservations about music-hall entertainment, Dickens clearly perceived that the halls were essential to cultivating a sense of community among the
working classes—the very same sense of community that defines Bart's vision of
Fagin's den in Oliver! As Peter Bailey writes, "[t]he rhetoric of music-hall friendship
was all-inclusive, promising universal membership. In this we can recognise a genial
cognate of other omnibus and ideal categories of Victorian Britain as a liberal democ-
racy—associationism, social citizenship, respectability—combining the proprieties
of voluntarism, equality, dignity and earned inclusion."[54] Bailey's description of the
idealized rhetoric by which the Victorian music hall defined itself is strongly evocative of the community that Oliver discovers on arriving in London and meeting
the Artful Dodger. Here, a group of working-class characters embraces the power
of song and performance as a way of creating a sense of cooperation and unity,
and the fact that the thieves are constantly performing and singing in front of one
another reinforces the centrality of the music hall to Bart's vision; music-hall community was shaped heavily by the intimate relationship between the audience and
the music-hall singers. Fagin's gang thus embodies the working-class musicality that
had defined Bart's own upbringing in the East End. Given his lack of formal training,
this upbringing was essential to Bart's musical "education," and he later stated that
throughout his childhood "the music was just part of living and part of the life."[55] As
befits a stage musical, music is likewise "part of living and part of the life" in Bart's
vision of Dickensian London.

Nearly all of the most memorable songs from Oliver! contain elements that reflect
the traditions of the music hall, which is in keeping with the folkish qualities of Bart's
music as described in Chapter 1. However, these songs are also theater songs, serving
to advance, or at the very least enhance, a theatrical narrative. Surprisingly, despite
the Englishness of music hall and the Americanness of the stage musical, the divide
between a music-hall song and a show tune is not a particularly wide one. In his
assessment of music-hall songs, Peter Gammond writes that "they borrowed from
the theatre-song and folk-song in almost equal measure to produce a particularly
strong and stable compound," though he simultaneously acknowledges that they
were "never theatre-songs in the true sense."[56] Still, the traditional music-hall song is
quite similar to the "Tin Pan Alley" song, a genre that was a critical precursor to the
show tunes of the American musical. Raymond Knapp and Mitchell Morris describe
the Tin Pan Alley song as follows: "The vast majority of Tin Pan Alley songs use a
verse-chorus structure, in which the 'verse' either narrates a story or establishes a
dramatic situation, and the 'chorus' either acts as a punctuating refrain or represents

the song promised by the dramatic setup."[57] Knapp would also write that Tin Pan Alley songs were built around repetition of key words and key musical phrases.[58] These descriptions can easily be applied to traditional music-hall songs, as classic numbers such as "Wot cher!", "The Man Who Broke the Bank at Monte Carlo," "It's a great big shame," and "I'm Henery the Eighth" all employ the "verse-chorus structure" described by Knapp and Morris: the verses advance the (comical) narrative, but the chorus, with its continued repetitions and catch phrases, is the part of the song that the audience remembers (and sings along with). For Knapp and other scholars of American musical theater, the evolution of the Tin Pan Alley song both shaped and reflected the evolution of the Broadway musical from interpolation toward integration.[59] Music-hall songs thus allowed Bart to bridge the gap between folksong and show tune, which is especially significant in the context of *Oliver!* in that the folkish elements of his music-hall songs, including the cockney and Yiddish conventions that characterize these numbers, are vital to the theatrical vision. These elements not only help to define the Dickensian personalities of the lead characters but likewise produce a coherent musical narrative steeped in the traditional Englishness associated with Dickens.

The clearest example of music-hall influence in *Oliver!* is "Oom Pah Pah," the opening number to the play's second act. Not only is it a funny and bawdy song with a catchy melody, but it is also one in which the audience is encouraged to participate as Nancy has the chorus members join her whenever she repeats the song's refrain (meanwhile, the verses each put forth a funny, coarse story). The lyrics to the song, though not explicit, focus on drinking and sex, two of the most common topics of early music-hall songs. The refrain is likewise reminiscent of the music hall; in his archival text on music-hall songs, Christopher Pulling writes about the typical chorus to a music-hall ballad, which might have gone something like, "'Tooral-li-ooral-li-ooral-li-ay' or 'Tiddie-iddie-iddie-iddie-ol-lol-li-do', or 'Fol-de-rol-de-ri-do.' Superior persons are apt to claim that that was all the old music-hall songs *did* consist of."[60] Of course, music-hall songs were more than just popular ballads featuring vocables, but this trait was nevertheless one of the common conventions of the ballads sung in music halls, including the immortal American import "Ta-ra-ra-boom-de-ay."

Other songs reveal a similar influence. Like several classic music-hall songs such as "I'm Henery the Eighth" and "The Galloping Major," "Consider Yourself" is a boisterous 6/8 march. Though the Dodger's cockney idiom is the most overt indication of this connection, the melody and structure of the song can likewise be traced back to songs made famous by Dan Leno and Harry Champion. The Dodger's song follows the same AAB pattern as "I'm Henery the Eighth," and the boisterous opening bars to both songs create a "fanfare" heralding the cockney cheek that will define the singers' personalities. The subject matter of the Dodger's song, which includes the question of how to make up the rent, can be found in several music-hall songs, including another popular number performed by Champion titled "Have You Paid the Rent?" Though the Dodger's song is subversive and bold, it is not a revolutionary call to arms, nor a ballad for class equality; instead, "Consider Yourself," like many music-hall ballads, presents "an acceptance of things as they are. This is not, however, apathetic acceptance [...] but a down to earth awareness of the real conditions of the life lived."[61] Whereas Oliver strives for something more in his personal ballad, "Where Is Love?", the music-hall ballads of the Dodger offer joyful endorsements of camaraderie as a cure-all for social inequality.

The Dodger is not the only character to adopt music-hall conventions in his numbers. "I Shall Scream," the Bumbles' courting song, is set to the tempo of a polka, a staple of many music-hall songs including "Following in Father's Footsteps," "One More Polka," and "Just One Little Polka." The fact that the Bumbles' marriage will prove unhappy further underscores the music-hall roots of the song; as Gammond notes in his description of music-hall songs about married life, "[b]y this time, the enslaved couple have awoken from love's dream and found themselves in a pretty pickle. They may have already found out that they cannot stand the sight and sound of one another."[62]

Coupled with this cockney comicality is an emphasis on parody that also connects the thieves' kitchen and its denizens to the music hall. The Dodger, Nancy, Bet, Fagin, and the rest of the gang repeatedly mock the pretensions of the upper orders, keeping with the traditions of the "Toff" songs of the music hall. The Dodger, who proudly introduces himself as a "gent," particularly enjoys mocking middle-class pretensions, most especially in "I'd Do Anything," during which he steps into the role of the "lion comique" and shares a mock romance with Nancy, who assumes the airs of the "shy maiden." Nevertheless, the lyrics to "I'd Do Anything" are not written in the sardonic and mocking tone of a "swell" song; rather, it is a genuinely affectionate love duet. Even music-hall songs, best remembered as being bawdy and mocking, had their sentimental side, and in spite of the rough boisterousness of cockney culture, Peter Davison concurs that "it is among the Cockney music-hall songs that are to be found some of the best 'songs from the heart' sung in the halls."[63] Sentimental music-hall songs such as Chevalier's "My Old Dutch" and "The Future Mrs. 'Awkins" epitomize this cockney schmaltz. The juxtaposition of the tender sentiments and comical satire in "I'd Do Anything" provides unique insight into the dichotomy that defines the thieves' kitchen in Bart's adaptation. This is in keeping with "a rare quality of insight and expression" that Davison felt defined the Victorian music hall's conflating of the sentimental and the sardonic, and Chevalier's songs frequently present "that conflict of tone which is so remarkable a feature of many of the best comic music-hall songs and acts."[64]

Fagin's two main numbers, "Pick a Pocket or Two" and "Reviewing the Situation," though defined largely by their Jewish rhythms, can be traced back to the music hall in terms of their comic patter. Deborah Vlock describes the patter song as "a type of comic song typical of music-hall entertainment. It consists of sung portions interspersed with spoken dialogue. The spoken dialogue, or patter, is generally wordy and unwieldy, with lapses in grammar and logic that make it somewhat difficult to follow."[65] "Pick a Pocket or Two," with its highly alliterative refrain, is evocative of the patter-style song, but "Reviewing the Situation" is even more obvious in this regard, for parts of the song are more "talked through" than sung. There is also the same sort of wordiness and unwieldiness described by Vlock as Fagin tries to outline a course of action for himself, and then repeatedly second guesses his logic. Like the characters created by renowned music-hall performers, Bart's Fagin presents a unique opportunity for comicality, though the humor grows out of the character's ability to combine song and sketch, music and patter, in his solo numbers. Ron Moody's early roots in revue, a direct descendant of music hall, helped to emphasize this connection.

Fagin's inherent musicality is particularly noteworthy given the links between Jewish culture and music-hall culture, for Jewish music became a prominent part of music-hall performance in the late nineteenth and early twentieth century. In the aforementioned *All the Year Round* article, the author tactlessly and tastelessly states "I must leave it to others to explain why [...] Jews are so exceedingly fond of dramatic and musical entertainments; why they furnish so many aspirants for music-hall honours; and why, proverbially cautious as they are, Jewish money is always forthcoming for theatrical or musical speculations."[66] The critic asserts that nearly one-third of all music-hall artists are Jewish, though, many sing "under titles by no means suggestive of their race"[67]—a comment that takes on additional significance when one considers the artists who helped to create *Oliver!*

The rise of the music hall in the mid-to-late nineteenth century coincided with a period of increased Jewish immigration. Districts in the East End became "shtetls," and though life in the East End was difficult, the sense of community that defined Jewish neighborhoods in Whitechapel and Spitalfields helped to ease the burdens of the people. The communities were likewise defined by their unique musicality and theatricality, as Yiddish drama became "the main form of entertainment for the immigrant working class."[68] This emphasis on working-class audiences meant that the tenets and practices of Yiddish theaters were quite similar to those of the early English music halls. Meier Tzelniker claimed that whereas general theater separates plays into genres such as comedy, drama, and musicals, "Yiddish theatre [...] incorporate[s] them all into one, thereby hoping to satisfy the palate of the Yiddish theatre audience. A zing, a lach un a trer. (A song, a laugh and a tear.) If they don't hear a song, have a good laugh and cry their eyes out, all at the same time, they don't get their money's worth."[69] This blending of different genres and the emphasis on audience reaction implies the same sort of rhetorical relationship between performer and audience that defined the London halls.

In her study of Jewish music, Marsha Edelman defines traditional Jewish music as "folk music," "the spontaneous, anonymous creation of songs with universal appeal and simple-enough musical content to allow virtually anyone to learn and sing them."[70] Though Bart was not a religious man, Jewish traditions were important to his sense of identity, and it is hardly surprising that Bart's main interests in Jewish culture were musical and theatrical. It likewise seems natural that Bart, with his folk musical sensibilities, would be drawn toward the conventions of Yiddish, for Yiddish was the language of the people. It was also the language of the major Jewish cultural centers that defined his Brick Lane upbringing:

> My mother used to take me to a Yiddish theatre [the Grand Palais], which was down the Commercial Road. And they played the same plots of these old middle-European stories by Sholem Aleichem. [...] People who went to see these plays, Jewish people, they knew them; they knew the plays. I used to make a beeline for the pit and lean over and get close to the actors so you could really see the greasepaint.[71]

For Bart and many East End Jews, the Grand Palais was both a social outlet and a cultural institution devoted to the preservation of Jewish traditions. A 1957 article in the *Times* cited the Grand Palais as "[the only] theatre in London where you might buy *matzos* in the bar and where they play two national anthems before the show begins—Israel's 'Hatikva' and then 'God Save the Queen'. It is not in the West End but in the East."[72] Notably, the tone of this article conveys a sense of fond-yet-bittersweet nostalgia that defined many postwar newspaper articles addressing the analogous subject of the decline of the English music hall.

The productions that characterized the Grand Palais—productions that undoubtedly resonated with the young Bart—were highly musical: "Most of the productions are of a musical comedy kind—not musical comedy on the glittering scale that the West End knows but rather a simple skeleton of a play, with a few songs and dances briefly interrupting the flow of homely humour."[73] The columnist's description of the "good will [that] flows strongly between players and audience"[74] is strongly evocative of the tone and tenor of the English music halls. David Mazower reinforces this characterization in his historical text on the Yiddish theater, describing audiences as "unsophisticated but discriminating; generous in their applause and loudly critical of any shortcomings."[75] It is a description that could easily be applied to the patrons of English music halls.

These close ties between East End Jewish culture and cockney music-hall culture are crystallized in *Oliver!*, as both elements are combined in the character of Fagin and in the general representation of the thieves' kitchen. Furthermore, Bart's account of the Grand Palais immediately calls to mind images of Moody made up as Fagin, the heavy greasepaint, red wig, and whiskers transforming the thirty-six-year-old actor into Dickens's "merry old gentleman." Though the Yiddish theater and the British music hall fell into decline in the years following World War II, Bart nostalgically adopted and adapted the traditions of both institutions in writing *Oliver!* Moreover, though *Oliver!* was a boisterous musical, it lacked the "glittering" qualities mentioned in the *Times* article, as the creative team substituted working-class grit for operatic glitter.

Granted, characterizing Fagin's music as Jewish is somewhat problematic. "Pick a Pocket or Two" and "Reviewing the Situation," with their pronounced use of the tambourine and the violin, along with their Yiddish cadences, strike the listener as Jewish, and for certain they are written in a Jewish idiom by a Jewish composer, but does this mean they are Jewish songs? The fact that Fagin never deviates from the central melody in either song seems to underscore the Jewish element, for, as Jack Gottlieb writes, "the music of the Jewish people has been preeminently single-line vocal melody for solo voice."[76] Edelman concurs that this is the chief distinction between Jewish "folk" music and Western "art music," citing "the melodic line [as] primary; harmony as we know it (the coincident sounding of two or more different pitches) does not exist."[77] Here, the links between the Jewish and music-hall components of Bart's score, as relating to the "folkish" quality of both idioms, are further reinforced.

This discussion of Fagin's character, and his prominence as a music-hall "performer," brings to light another definitive element of Bart's adaptation that reveals the centrality of music hall to his creative vision. The emphasis on musical performance in *Oliver!*

and the performance-oriented traits that define Bart's approach to songwriting create a distinct link between the two elements. Mark Steyn reflects that

> If you look at when Lionel Bart writes with other composers, [when] he just writes the lyrics—you know, you look at *Lock Up Your Daughters*, where Laurie Johnson [...] did the music for that. [...] Lionel Bart's words are okay, but they're [just] words on notes. [...] [In *Oliver!* Bart uses] big fat words that land on the notes. [...] If you can write words, sung words, to characters, the fact that you don't know how to put those little notes down on paper has nothing to do with it. You can pay a guy $20 to do that. [...] [Bart] is a songwriter not a composer.[78]

For Steyn, this distinction relates to the fact that the singers themselves—that is, the characters—are so vital to Bart's understanding of his own work. Bart perceived lyrics as "words to be sung, and words that are in the rhythm of those characters."[79] This focus on performance is one of the defining traits of music-hall songs: their vitality was bound up in the actual *performance* of these works by music-hall singers with distinctive stage personas/personalities. Ronald Pearsall notes that "[s]tyle, deportment and delivery were as important as the material."[80] Similarly, in one of his numerous articles celebrating the music hall as an English institution, Max Beerbohm commemorated Dan Leno by noting the importance of this specific performer in relation to the songs: "Partly, again, our delight was in the way that these things were uttered—in the gestures and grimaces and antics that accompanied them; in fact, in Dan Leno's technique."[81] Like Fagin, Leno's stage personality and stage presence played an inestimably important role in the overall success of the songs; when a Fagin song is sung by someone besides Fagin, or when a Dodger song is sung by someone besides the Dodger, the full impact of the song decreases. On paper, the lyrics and melodies to Bart's songs may seem simple, but in performance—and, specifically, when performed by the characters for whom they were written—they take on a vitality, catchiness, and grandeur that belie this simplicity.

Perhaps most significantly, like all good music-hall songs, Bart's songs are infinitely singable; as Steyn points out, "there's a good eight, or nine, or ten songs in [*Oliver!*] that absolutely land, land those lyrics, they hammer them home to you, so that kids—people—love to sing them. It's not just that *Oliver!* is a great show to watch. It's a great show to do."[82] Robinson agrees that the songs themselves, and the energy surrounding the performance of these songs, are the primary reasons for the show's success and enduring power:

> The quality of the music is so supreme. Sometimes, a particular show captures the writer at some mysterious moment in their career where everything they touch turns to gold. I think that's true of Lionel and his songs from *Oliver!* I can't think of one that I don't like, and I'm sure I can easily think of every single song in that show. Even the songs that are just a bit too umpty dumpty and don't have the astonishing tunefulness of the other ones, they're positioned so well and provide such a springboard for a good performer to operate off, that actually, they do their job just as well as all the tuneful songs.[83]

As in the Victorian and Edwardian music halls, the lifeblood of the songs was neither in the music nor in the lyrics but in the actual *singing*.

THE IMAGINED COMMUNITY OF THE MUSIC HALL

Through communal vitality and music-hall performance, Fagin and his gang temporarily offer Oliver a respite from the loneliness and misery that has defined his life, though as noted above, it does not last. As in the case of plays like *The Entertainer*, *Fings*, and even *Look Back in Anger* (which, in one of the few light and joyful moments in the piece, features Jimmy and Cliff imitating the music-hall caperings of Flanagan and Allen)[84], *Oliver!* can be read as a postwar "music-hall lament," an intriguing literary and cultural phenomenon that celebrated the music hall as a representation of true Englishness while simultaneously mourning its decline as a metaphor for a larger national deterioration. In his outstanding text *Music Hall and Modernity*, Barry Faulk assesses the "striking paradox" of this phenomenon, noting its "simultaneous aspect as statement of national pride and narrative of cultural decline."[85] Certainly, the postwar emphasis on music hall embraced both of these components, and the latter was particularly significant in the wake of World War II. Still, people had been "lamenting" the decline of music hall since the early twentieth century; indeed, the aforementioned inability to come to a clear consensus regarding when music hall "died" hints toward the potential disingenuousness of this lamentation.

1912 ostensibly marked the apex of the music hall, when King George V specifically requested a performance from a popular troupe at the Palace Theatre in London.[86] For many critics, however, the "respectability" of the latter-day music halls meant a fundamental loss of the most vital elements of the institution itself. Roger Wilmut labels 1912 as "the peak and at the same time the swan-song of the old Victorian music-hall [...] there was less of the everybody-sing-along type of act, less of a free-and-easy feel to the proceedings, and gradually the presentations—though still in a similar format—became more of a *theatrical* experience."[87] The notion that the music hall declined as a result of its becoming respectable is an intriguing paradox, and many music-hall lamentations echo the notion that as the music hall became more mainstream (e.g., more middle-class), it lost its essence as authentic, English entertainment.

In his essay commemorating the great Marie Lloyd, T. S. Eliot touted the legendary music-hall singer as

> the expressive figure of the lower classes. There is no such expressive figure for any other class. The middle classes have no such idol: the middle classes are morally corrupt. That is to say, their own life fails to find a Marie Lloyd to express it; nor have they any independent virtues which might give them as a conscious class any dignity. The middle classes, in England as elsewhere, under democracy, are morally dependent upon the aristocracy, and the aristocracy are subordinate to the middle class, which is gradually absorbing and destroying them. The lower class still exists; but perhaps it will not exist for long.[88]

Eliot's commentary seems strikingly relevant to any discussion of the postwar theater—and more specifically, to *Oliver!*—in regard to the "morality" of the working
classes; Fagin, Nancy, the Dodger, and the boys may be thieves, but they are simultaneously the most vital and admirable characters in the musical. Still, Eliot likewise
refers to the fragility of the working class as a community (and of the music hall as a
form of entertainment): "With the decay of the music-hall, with the encroachment
of the cheap and rapid-breeding cinema, the lower classes will tend to drop into the
same state of protoplasm as the bourgeoisie."[89] Eliot was decrying cinema with the
same fervor with which 1950s music-hall lamenters would decry television and pop
music, and yet even before the ascent of these forms of media, people were publicly
lamenting music hall's decline.

   Faulk scrutinizes Eliot's comments in relation to similar articles by Beerbohm and
Elizabeth Robins Pennell: intellectual literary and cultural critics who embraced the
music hall as authentic "folk" culture, as a potential cure-all for middle-class con-
formity, and as a profound yet fleeting representation of native Englishness.[90] As
Faulk points out throughout his text, however, many of these laments were oversimplifications, generalizations, and exaggerations. Bailey has likewise debunked many
of the sentimentalized narratives surrounding music hall and its representativeness
of English community and working-class "folk" culture, for even in its heyday the
music hall was a heavily commercialized institution.[91] Indeed, Bailey goes so far as
to suggest that music-hall culture was actually a "culture for the people not of the
people,"[92] its values and traditions shaped by middle-class entrepreneurs as opposed
to working-class patrons or singers.[93] Certainly, many of the owners, operators, and
perhaps most notably songwriters were middle-class,[94] and, whatever the rough-
ness or baseness of the song and the subject matter, the sentiments were oftentimes
conservative.[95] The emergence of the stage cockney as the dominant figure on the
music-hall boards hints at the manufacturing of a marketable persona as opposed to
the presentation of a truthful folk culture.[96]

   In the end, the music-hall lament ironically manufactured a community by fostering a sense of communal loss (and a larger sense of lost English identity) as epitomized by the decline of the English music hall. The notion of a music hall as an "imagined community" seems difficult to accept given that the popular perception of the
music hall is that of an institution so devoted to fostering English community that it
ultimately came to stand for the nation itself. Still, perhaps this is the decisive indication of the "imagined" quality of music hall; in spite of its face-to-face interactions
and its emphasis on audience-performer intimacy, it was ultimately, like the nation, a
construction. This viewpoint is reminiscent of the previously discussed issues regarding the "artificiality" of the angry young man movement and *Oliver!*, though as in
the case of these phenomena, the sheer proliferation of the music-hall lament is
yet another powerful indication of the importance of narratives to constructions of
nationhood. Though the realities of the English music hall may have complicated the
idealized picture of cockney community and working-class camaraderie in the face
of penury, it did not compromise it entirely; certainly if the music hall had remained
a closed-off subculture forever inaccessible to the middle class, it is doubtful that it
could have taken on the dimensions necessary to serve as a representation of the

English nation (even as "purists" decried the middle-class presence). Furthermore, as in the case of *Oliver!* and *Look Back in Anger*, the angst that was fueling the celebration of Englishness via the celebration of music hall was all too real.

Following the two world wars, the decline of the music hall became a rallying cry for mourning the decline of traditional Englishness, or at the very least the communal Englishness that had existed before the fracturing influence of the modern and postmodern ages. In the early 1940s, Ernest Walter hinted at the increased importance of the music hall (and its signature songs) as a representation of Englishness following the shell shock of World War II: "They reflected that Cockney spirit of cheerfulness and courage and steadfastness which the Luftwaffe was never able to kill, or even bring to earth. Perhaps it would not be too much to say that spirit soared too high in a realm of its own ever to be conquered."[97] The invocation of the Luftwaffe indicates just how significant a stake the English public had placed in music hall as a representation of English culture, and it adds an even more tragic dimension to this particular lament; although Britain remained unconquered, the England that rebuilt itself after the war had seemingly lost sight of some essential part of itself. "The music-hall lament was an expression of lost hopes and diminished expectations,"[98] writes Faulk, and that diminishment plays a fundamental role in fueling the anger of Jimmy Porter, Archie Rice, and the other music-hall devotees of the postwar English stage. In addition, it was possible to reconcile the nostalgic, conservative lament for the music hall with the progressive, rebellious experimentalism of the postwar theater, as the type of Englishness promoted by music-hall narratives was working-class and vigorous as opposed to middle-class and repressed. Whatever the institution's Victorian roots, the celebration of music-hall Englishness was a "safe" form of nationalism, unburdened by what Faulk calls "the imperial hubris or expansionist bravado scholars of nationalism usually analyze and critique."[99]

In the context of such a pervasive and powerful cultural discourse, the music-hall dimensions of *Oliver!*'s score take on an added significance. Certainly, the celebratory Englishness that critics and audiences so embraced in *Oliver!* was directly connected to this component of Bart's musical, which likewise served to connect it to two of the most powerful voices in the postwar theater, Osborne and Littlewood. Furthermore, although the breakup of Fagin's gang places *Oliver!* in the genre of the music-hall lament, the predominance of music-hall songs in the score allows Bart's musical to revive a dying English tradition as opposed to simply mourning it. In spite of the loss of community both onstage and outside the theater, Bart's musical was a significant reminder of the power of English music-hall songs (and English music-hall narratives) to promote a shared sense of national character and national camaraderie.

OLIVER!'S AUTHENTICITY AS A DICKENSIAN MUSICAL

Oliver!'s celebration of the traditions of English music hall endowed it with an "authentic" Englishness, thanks to the centrality of music hall to narratives of English national identity, but it is important to recall that the stage musical as a genre has traditionally wrestled with issues of authenticity. Is there any hope for

truth in a theatrical genre that involves people transitioning from speaking to singing? Here it is useful to return to the writings of Raymond Knapp. In his essay on
performance and authenticity in the American musical, Knapp questions whether
"authenticity or idealism [can] be advanced through the blatantly artificial modes
of performance offered up in musicals."[100] Notably, Knapp compares the American
musical to other indigenous forms of American music, including jazz and rock, which
have usually been granted a greater sense of legitimacy by musicologists and cultural critics. Though Knapp rejects such distinctions as fundamentally *in*authentic,
he also acknowledges that this discrepancy is based on "a centuries-old tendency to
find musical authenticity among the working and peasant classes."[101] It is an assessment that seems particularly applicable to any assessment of *Oliver!* given the determination to create an "authentic" English musical by turning to the "authentic"
working-class Englishness of music hall. Yet, as noted above, this entire narrative
of music-hall Englishness is based on an oversimplified vision of music-hall culture.
Comparing and contrasting *Oliver!* and English music hall according to the issue of
authenticity seems an exercise in futility, and it is more productive and intriguing
to consider the fact that both of these performance-based mediums, whatever their
inauthenticities, contributed to a legitimate celebration of English national character
and culture. In the case of *Oliver!*, such celebratory sentiments were much needed in
an age of ostensible national decline and genuine music-hall decline.[102]

In this context, Knapp remains an excellent source for analyzing *Oliver!*, particularly in light of his emphasis on the American musical's centrality in forming
American national identity.[103] The golden age of the American musical coincided with
America's rise to global dominance, and there is a sharp contrast between the sense
of American cultural ascendancy that framed *Oklahoma!* and the sense of English cultural decline that framed *Oliver!* Still, there are likewise several similarities between
these two landmark musicals; much as *Oklahoma!* strove toward constructing an
authentically American vision by means of its idealized portrayal of the American
West and country folk, *Oliver!* embraced a similar sense of cultural legitimacy by creating an idealized vision of the working-class communities of the English music halls.
Moreover, just as Knapp voices his skepticism toward *Oklahoma!*'s wholesome vision
of Americana, noting its somewhat self-satisfied determination to "reassure a nation
of its own essential goodness,"[104] one might be tempted to decry *Oliver!*'s nationalistic hype as an attempt to recapture an outdated and smug sense of Victorian
Englishness steeped in imperial arrogance. Nevertheless, such a viewpoint ignores
the fact that America and England needed to reaffirm their belief in their national
myths at a time of great social upheaval.

In both *Oklahoma!* and *Oliver!*, there is a vital emphasis on community. Granted,
Oklahoma! ends with a marriage, signifying the building of a community. Though
Oliver! does not end in death—Fagin thankfully escapes the gallows—the conclusion
places a melancholy emphasis on the destruction of the vital, loving, and musical
community of the thieves. In spite of these important contrasts, both musicals promote a communal sense of national identity built around a key national mythos: in
the case of *Oklahoma!*, the American frontier; in the case of *Oliver!*, Dickens and
music hall.[105]

The mention of Dickens brings up one of the central questions surrounding *Oliver!*'s authenticity: its relationship to its source. Before proceeding to this point, however, it is prudent to address the question of how authentically English *Oliver!* is (or can be), given its use of American musical conventions. The musical narrative certainly seems to embrace the concept of integration. Donald Pippin, who served as the conductor and musical arranger for the first American tour/Broadway production of *Oliver!*, attributes the show's success to Bart's willingness to adopt the American musical "formula":

> When *Oliver!* came along, by that time, believe me, the American musical had had a tremendous effect on writers in London. America really developed what we call the musical theatre [...] Lionel Bart and I had a little talk about this one night. Every show he said was his favorite show was an American show. He'd been so influenced by the musical theatre from the States [...] *Oliver!* followed [the American format] to a tee. It had the main plot, the subplot, the heartbreaking ballad, the show tunes, all the elements of American musical theatre.[106]

Similarly, an anonymous author at the *Times* commented on the importance of the format of the American musical to British approaches to postwar musical the-ater: "Since the war [...] the musical has often looked for considerably more solid foundations; it demands that songs and dances appear with dramatic relevance, and a doctrine seems to have developed to the point at which it can be hotly argued that neither is permissible unless it carry the narrative forward."[107] Here, the author is clearly articulating the influence of American trends on British perceptions of the musical genre, and a review of the soundtrack to *Oliver!* in *Plays and Players* praised Bart for his having written a show in which the music and songs were fully inte-grated, declaring that "this is a show in which story, characterisation, atmosphere, production and music are each of equal importance—which is as things should be in a stage musical."[108] Much as the "narratives" surrounding the aforementioned dis-cussions of Englishness, though steeped in oversimplifications, became universally accepted, the narrative of "integration" as the universal solution to any questions regarding musical plots clearly held (and continues to hold) a great deal of power.

Bart was willing to acknowledge the American influence on his approach to his craft, though, as an interviewer at the *Times* noted, "[t]his is a territory over which Mr. Bart has obviously travelled carefully; one feels that he has spent some time in defining the position he holds in relation to the great musical shows that have trav-elled across the Atlantic."[109] The composer cited the transatlantic "exchange" that had shaped the early roots of American musical theater, pointing out that "[t]he American musical [...] having been influenced over the years by Britain—a great deal by Gilbert and Sullivan—eventually came up with *Oklahoma!*"[110], thus acknowledging the Rodgers and Hammerstein piece as a landmark in the evolution of the musical; however, he likewise noted that the integrated formula, as patented by Rodgers and Hammerstein, "didn't go on from there. American musicals became stereotyped, and the only departure has been *West Side Story*, which is a brilliant marriage between drama and dance. [...] It has influenced me to the extent that it has shown me the importance of truth on stage; I've tried to give shows with guts."[111] Clearly, Bart wished to push the musical formula even further, and given that the very title of this interview hints toward his desire for an "epic" musical,[112] and that his definition of musical success appears based on pushing the concept of integration to its limit, the notion of his being an unofficial "founding father" of the megamusical movement seems all the more significant.

As noted in Chapter 1, however, *Oliver!*'s success may have had less to do with the concept of integration and more to do with Bart's determination to create a show with "guts," particularly in relation to the libretto. By incorporating brutally serious scenes (such as the abuse of Oliver and the death of Nancy) and brutally serious songs that build off these scenes (such as "As Long as He Needs Me," which is a frank and fundamentally modern depiction of a woman in an abusive relationship), Bart was able to push the English musical toward the dramatic significance of its American counterpart. The author of the previously mentioned article noted that "[o]ne of the most surprising and enlivening features of the postwar theatrical scene has been the emancipation of the 'musical' from bondage to a soft-centered conventional type of day-dreaming romanticism,"[113] distinguishing Bart's gritty, "socially valuable"[114] musicals from the blithe and romantic English musicals of the preceding era; when one considers the general seriousness of Broadway musicals such as *Carousel, South Pacific,* and *West Side Story*, it is not surprising that the author labels this an American trend, and it is perhaps a much more important trend regarding the maturation of the modern musical than the trend toward integration.

Certainly, Bart raised the stakes of the West End musical libretto by turning to Dickens as his source, and the role of Dickens in the triumphant success of *Oliver!* cannot be overestimated. Besides the palpable patriotism that defined the English response to *Oliver!* the initial English reviews present a unique assessment of the musical as a Dickensian adaptation. Given the traditional British view of Dickens as more than an English novelist, but simultaneously as an English institution, one might assume that many English critics would have decried Bart's modifying Dickens so heavily and setting him to music. Nevertheless, the general reaction to the Dickensian element of Bart's show was remarkably positive. In his review, Conway admitted that "[Bart] takes gaily-audacious liberties" but he immediately followed up this assertion by stating that "liberties don't matter."[115] Rather than limit his assessment to the tenets of fidelity criticism, Conway chose to focus on the electricity of the premiere performance; similarly, Muller praised the libretto to *Oliver!* as "[a] clean-cut book, no more than a digest, a strip-cartoon version of *Oliver Twist,* that nevertheless manages to be so succinct, so true to the spirit of the original, so neatly constructed that it makes everybody ask for more."[116] "True to the spirit" is the trademark phrase used for justifying adaptations that stray from the original source, but more important than Muller's somewhat clichéd assessment is his willingness to justify *Oliver!* as a Dickensian adaptation.[117] Numerous British critics expressed the same sentiment. J. C. Trewin quipped that "the musical play is Dickensian in its spirit, if not the letter, so I do not believe that Mr. Bart will be haunted by a bearded shade with a geranium in its buttonhole,"[118] and added that "I believe that Dickens will always be mined. When an explorer comes up with such riches as Mr. Bart has found [...] the task seems worth-while."[119]

In a separate column for the *Illustrated London News*, Trewin took the point further by noting that coupled with its Dickensian "spirit" was a separate spirit of celebration (analogous to the "electricity" and "magnetism" to which his fellow critics alluded) that rendered its deviations from its source inconsequential: "We are far too occupied in trying not to join the company in full song during 'Consider Yourself' and 'I'd Do Anything', to worry about textual departures from Dickens."[120] He reiterated that "[t]he spirit of the book is here; the music helps mightily."[121] For Trewin, the music-hall fervor generated by the almost participatory nature of *Oliver!*'s songs offered the audience so much in the way of joyful celebration that the departure from Dickens, whether textual or spiritual, seemed something of a moot point; however, the spiritual fidelity that many perceived in *Oliver!* was likely bound up in that same celebratory English spirit. As Pulling articulately noted in his archival text, "[t]he old music-hall songs were a national product, and for that reason cannot be considered negligible."[122] Of course, the nostalgic view of music-hall culture in the thirties and forties was similar to the nostalgia that defined Dickensian London for many Britons. Walter directly connected the two in his 1942 article "London's Noisy Music Halls Embodied the Cockney Spirit," noting that

> [music halls] really originated back in the early days of Dickens, when entertainments were put on in 'pubs,' a fore-runner, indeed, of today's cabaret show. Dickens himself speaks of being taken to a public house, where he was stood upon a table to recite. You will recollect, also, how in 'Bleak House' you make the acquaintance of Little Swills, 'the comic vocalist,' who used to perform in the Sol's Arms, Cook's Court, off Cursitor Street. Dicken's [sic] description of 'the Harmonic Meeting hour' in an early music hall is worth re-reading any day.[123]

If Dickens has become the unofficial touchstone of Victorian Englishness, the music halls were similarly defined by their emphases on English community and culture in the songs and lyrics that defined the genre. Furthermore, like Dickens, the music halls repeatedly displayed a "fascination with language"[124] and this language was "not only a means of communication but a form of being in its own right."[125] In this sense, *Oliver!* remains true to the "spiritual" Englishness of Dickens even as it deviates from the "spirit" of his text.

Even those theatergoers most deeply invested in Charles Dickens and his legacy expressed the highest regard for *Oliver!*; the Honorary Secretary of the Dickens Fellowship, J. Greaves, sent Bart a letter praising his musical adaptation. Notably, the letter was printed on the stationary of the Dickens Fellowship, which included a graphic of 48 Doughty St., the very house in which the young Dickens wrote *Oliver Twist*. Greaves admitted that he went into *Oliver!* with "'fear and trembling' at the thoughts of what might have been done to Dickens" but quickly reassured the composer "that Dickens comes through wonderfully and I have seen many a dramatic production that has done far less justice to the original than your production of 'Oliver' [sic]. I feel sure that the old master himself would have been very pleased with it and have enjoyed it thoroughly."[126] In a reply letter, Bart humorously admitted his own "fears" regarding *Oliver!*, claiming that "I let my musical [...] loose upon the world with some trepidation, particularly bearing in mind organizations such as yours."[127] The Dickens Fellowship's endorsement was thus all the more gratifying.

Bart had felt compelled to apologize to Dickens, and yet most critics and audiences were more than willing to forgive his infidelities to his source, in part thanks to the incredibly entertaining results, but perhaps even more so because the composer had created the possibility for a bold new period of English musical theater: "After the gruesome inadequacy of some recent musicals, how good to welcome one which is entirely successful!" exclaimed Muller.[128] Trewin likewise opined that *Oliver!* had premiered at precisely the right time, arriving "at an hour when the British 'musical' needed something as downright and as likeable."[129] The fact that Bart had adapted a Victorian novel by a Victorian author who was regarded as a bastion of Englishness certainly made *Oliver!*'s celebration of English identity all the more palpable, as Peter Mandler labels the nineteenth century as "the century of national character."[130] Moreover, whatever his middle-class biases, Dickens, like music hall, offered a "safe" celebration of Englishness: his working-class characters, his subversive satire, and his emphasis on social reform provided a sense of national identity that was ultimately compatible with a post-Victorian world.

In spite of the English press's positive affirmation of *Oliver!* as a Dickensian adaptation, the very fact that many critics felt the need to comment on *Oliver!* in relation to *Oliver Twist* evokes the specter of fidelity criticism. The central problem with using fidelity as the primary factor in assessing adaptations is that it creates an automatic imbalance, for as Thomas Leitch writes, "fidelity as a touchstone of adaptations will always give their source texts, which are always faithful to themselves, an advantage so enormous and unfair that it renders the comparison meaningless."[131] In the case of *Oliver Twist*, fidelity criticism does a disservice to the culture text of the novel, as the countless adaptations of the story are partly responsible for the longevity and continued relevance of the Dickensian text; that is, the legacy of the source on stage and screen has eclipsed the limitations and inconsistencies of the text itself thanks largely to the creative reimaginings of that source for theater and film.

Though the energetic frivolity of *Oliver!* seems far removed from the original Dickensian text, it is nevertheless reflective of the enthusiasm for Dickens and the English nostalgia that surrounded (and continues to surround) him in the postwar era. As such, one critic at the *Liverpool Post* offers perhaps the highest praise any critic could heap on Bart's play, at least from the perspective of "fidelity": "This was real Dickens."[132] The critic's perception of *Oliver!* as the "real Dickens" says much about the power of adaptations; here, *Oliver!* not only becomes the *real Oliver Twist* but also the *real* Dickens, dictating the larger perception of the entire Dickens canon. It likewise reinforces the power of images, sentiments, and energies to usurp meanings in a mass-culture society. Whatever its divergences, the essential Dickensian elements, as promoted through the boisterous musical score and unrelenting enthusiasm of the piece, precludes outcries of infidelity from all but the most inflexible of critics.

In many respects, the Liverpool critic's reaction is evocative of Frederic Jameson's definition of the postmodern "[approach to] the 'past' through stylistic connotation, conveying 'pastness' by the glossy qualities of the image."[133] Although there is a Dickensian "ness" (and a Victorian "ness") to *Oliver!*, the heavy stylization dictated by the theatrical genre in which Bart was writing, combined with Bart's own "pop" sensibilities, results in an interpretation that is something of a "glossy image" of its literary forebear. This is not particularly surprising given that the adaptation was inspired by such a glossy image—the Terry's chocolate bar wrapper—but the true strength of *Oliver!* lies in its ability to promote that image, thus allowing it to become the "real Dickens."

Still, the very notion of the "real Dickens," like the notion of the "authentic" music hall, is subject to scrutiny, and in spite of the rejection of fidelity as a trope, the previous analysis seems to do *Oliver!* a disservice by suggesting that its post-modern qualities are a betrayal of the authentic Dickensian roots. Dickens himself has been (and remains) subject to accusations of inauthenticity given his "indus-trial" approach to writing and publishing, his tremendous financial success, and his unwavering popularity. As Juliet John writes, "[i]n the current postmodern, mature age of mass culture, it is a commonplace to associate mass culture with inauthenticity and dishonesty. [...] But what Dickens's vision of mass culture has in common with some (post) modern manifestations is that they trade on the per-formance of the personal."[134] John's emphasis on mass culture is clearly relevant to discussions of music hall, which, for all of its supposedly "folkish" qualities, "became the prototype of the modern entertainment industry, rapidly commer-cialized as capital was invested, advertising techniques were developed to pro-mote stars, and a hierarchy of stars and supporting acts was evolved."[135] It remains a powerful representation of the Victorian anticipation of postmodernism. Moreover, the Broadway musical in general (and *Oliver!* specifically) embraced the possibilities of mass culture, which is yet another reason musicals have struggled in attaining legitimacy.

However, John's emphasis on performativity in Dickens's prose and its potential authenticity in advancing personal feelings (whatever its inherent "dishonesty") is even more striking in its relevance to *Oliver!*, particularly in light of *Oliver!*'s status as a musical and its roots in the performance-based culture of the music hall. Dickens's mass appeal, marketing savvy, and conscientious efforts to transform himself into a "name brand" may have compromised his "authenticity" as a novelist, but these strategies did not negate the powerful ideas and sentiments put forth in his nov-els, nor the palpable sense of Englishness that so defined his writing. Similarly, the commercialism of music-hall entertainment clearly did not impede its significance as an English institution, nor its potent celebration of communal culture and song. Indeed, the merger of Dickens and music hall—two fundamentally English insti-tutions, whatever their inauthenticities—in *Oliver!* actually serves to make Bart's musical more authentic, as opposed to less, for *Oliver!* embraces and embodies two definitive representations/constructions of Englishness. Although its postmodern mass culturalism may weaken its authenticity, both Dickens and the music hall had already proven to be mass-cultural institutions in spite of their (manufactured) folk-ish qualities. Perhaps in this sense, *Oliver!* is no longer a representation of Dickens in the postmodern age...*Oliver!* is in fact the *real* Dickens.

OLIVER! AND THE ENGLISH MEGAMUSICAL

Before concluding this chapter, it is useful to analyze *Oliver!*'s success in relation to another English cultural institution that epitomizes mass culture: the English megamusical. Although Bart succeeded in merging elements from several very different cultural and musical traditions, this multifaceted approach resulted in a final product that defied any clear-cut categorization. Even the English theater critics who touted its Englishness were quick to assert that *Oliver!* was a new entity. Here we must return to Andrew Lloyd Webber's description of Lionel Bart as the father of the modern British musical.

The most obvious connection between Bart and Lloyd Webber lies in the transatlantic success that they achieved as English composers operating in a primarily American genre; when *Oliver!* reached New York, it enjoyed the longest run ever attained by an English musical up to that point in the history of Broadway. Lloyd Webber's *Cats* would eventually break this record, and, as Sheridan Morley notes, Lloyd Webber essentially proved himself to be Bart's successor as an English composer capable of exploring the potential of English musicals to attain success in both the West End and on Broadway.[136] The connections between the two artists extend beyond the realm of transatlantic production, however. Both men likewise exerted a groundbreaking effect on the very foundation of English musical theater. Like *Oliver!, Cats* was a musical the likes of which nobody had ever seen before, and like *Oliver!* it was heralded as the start of an exciting new phase in the history of the English musical. Furthermore, like *Oliver!*, it was met with suspicion and hostility from traditionalist forces in the American theater community (see Chapter 6).

Granted, *Cats* and *Oliver!* diverge significantly in terms of content and theme, though Cameron Mackintosh notes a "spiritual" bond between the two works in terms of the global English vision of both Bart and Lloyd Webber: "When I first revived the original production [of *Oliver!*] in 1977, it still was current. But by that time, nearly 20 years had elapsed and we still hadn't got the new renaissance of the English musical, which was going to happen in 1981 with *Cats*."[137] Had Bart been able to sustain the momentum of his early career, it is likely that the aforementioned renaissance would have occurred sooner, though it took the emergence of Lloyd Webber to truly cultivate the seeds that Bart had sown through his writing of *Oliver!* As Steyn humorously observes in *Broadway Babies Say Goodnight*, "[t]his is how they divide history: BC—Before *Cats*—and AD—Andrew Dominant."[138] In this "chronology," *Oliver!* is basically lumped in with the musicals of the pre-Lloyd Webber era (in spite of its revolutionary qualities and canonical status) as opposed to its being designated as a turning point in the postwar English musical theater.

Nevertheless, there are several important connections between the technique that Bart employed in *Oliver!* and the format of Lloyd Webber's "megamusicals" that serve to reinforce the centrality of Bart to the emergence of the modern English musical. When Bart outlined his approach to writing *Blitz!*, a musical that he described as "epic," he explained his use of "period pastiche to create the atmosphere of those days," though he likewise asserted that "the dramatic statement is my own, and timeless."[139] The composer's reference to musical pastiche and grand sweeping themes is strongly evocative of the characteristics of the megamusical, and the same description could be applied to *Oliver!*

Music and song are the driving forces behind *Oliver!*, and although there is spoken dialogue, the ratio of sung words to spoken words is heavily balanced in favor of the former. The first ten to twelve minutes of the show contain almost no dialogue, as Bart uses songs and music to set up the entire story: the musical begins with "Food, Glorious Food" to establish the workhouse setting; transitions to the introduction of Mr. Bumble through instrumental underscoring; features an ironically sung prayer; uses more instrumental music to accentuate the rapidity with which the boys devour their gruel; and then shifts to another song, "Oliver." Throughout this entire scene, there are only fourteen spoken words. By the time Oliver reaches Fagin's den in the middle of Act I, the gaps between songs are virtually nonexistent, as "It's a Fine Life" leads right into "I'd Do Anything," which leads right into "Be Back Soon," which leads right into the instrumental sequence involving Oliver's first encounter with Mr. Brownlow.

Certainly, music is central to the basis of the narrative as conceived by Bart, and the songs in *Oliver!* dictate both the narrative pace and thematic significance of the story being presented onstage. On first reading the script, Ron Moody noted that the libretto seemed "sparse, with short bursts of dialogue alternating with a page or two of lyric. We soon discovered, however, that this simple balance played incredibly well."[140] As such, *Oliver!* proved a unique musical that not only combined the integrated technique of American musical theatre with English texts, tunes, and topics but simultaneously united the disparate traditions of operetta, music hall, and pop music.

One American reviewer, Henry Hewes, felt as though a new sort of musical label was necessary for *Oliver!*, noting that "the scenes and songs [...] [focus on] manufacturing reasonably entertaining vocal numbers which the familiar Dickens characters might sing if they spoke in the vernacular of today's popular songs. Indeed, for want of a better word, one might call 'Oliver' [sic] a *poperetta*."[141] Though critical of the omission of Dickens's social commentary, Hewes was willing to acknowledge that Bart had created something bold and new defying easy categorization from both a national and generic standpoint.

In a noteworthy interview with Anthony Brown, Bart likewise struggled to conceive an appropriate designation for a distinct theatrical genre that walked the line between opera and musical. When Brown referred to Bart's *Quasimodo* as an opera, the composer resisted the label, noting that "[i]t's only an opera, I suppose, because there's no chat in it."[142] Brown pushed the point, curious as to Bart's views on the differences between operas and musicals; Bart replied that "an opera has a libretto and an integrated score in which there's no dialogue, as such, it's all music. I would like to try and invent another name for such an entertainment."[143] He elaborated that the epic and serious *Quasimodo* was too big to be called a musical, and yet he continued to resist the term *opera*: "[W]hat can I call it?"[144] Had the term "megamusical" existed at the time, it seems as though it would have fit Bart's concept for his *Hunchback of Notre Dame* adaptation.

These debates would continue to shape discussions of British musical theater when Lloyd Webber rose to prominence in the seventies and eighties. Just as Hewes coined the term *poperetta* to describe Bart's approach to *Oliver!*, the word has been used by critics and musicologists regarding Lloyd Webber's work. It is an apt term given the composer's use of popular music and his habit of writing musicals that emphasize sung lyrics over spoken words.[145]

The aforementioned diversity of musical idioms presented in *Oliver!* provides another correlation between Bart and Lloyd Webber, for just as *Oliver!* allowed Bart to experiment with music-hall songs, pop ballads, Jewish folk songs, and show tunes, *Cats* granted Lloyd Webber the chance to experiment with pop, rock, jazz, and opera. The potential caveat of this approach is that the songs might be labeled as imitations; Jessica Sternfeld notes that " '[p]astiche' has become a word used so often in association with Lloyd Webber's music that it almost ceases to have meaning,"[146] and it is a term that could likewise be applied to the scores to several Bart musicals given the composer's above-quoted description and his admitted fondness for borrowing from different musical genres. As in the case of Lloyd Webber's Puccini-inspired scenes in *Cats*, Bart uses pastiche repeatedly and deliberately throughout *Oliver!*

In comparison to Lloyd Webber's "revue-style" shows such as *Joseph and the Amazing Technicolor Dreamcoat*, *Cats*, and *Starlight Express*, Bart manages to preserve a greater sense of narrative unity in his score thanks to the overarching Englishness of his vision and the use of a heavily plotted Dickensian source. Still, Bart invariably faced accusations that his songs were imitative. The goal of any writer of musicals is to create songs that stay with the audience after the final curtain has fallen; Trevor Ray only half-jokingly reflects that *Oliver!* was the sort of musical where the patrons went *into* the theater whistling the tunes.[147] Similar accusations of derivativeness have plagued Lloyd Webber for decades, despite the fact that "[w]hen critics or historians do go hunting for actual stolen tunes, they rarely find any. [...] He borrows from himself all the time, usually using tunes he has written for unfinished projects or for no particular project at all."[148] Bart was well aware of his own tendency to borrow from himself, or as he put it, to "pinch" melodies from his own repertoire when writing new works (see Chapter 1).

Perhaps the most obvious indication of *Oliver!*'s status as a forebear to the megamusical is the dominance of its set, which, as noted in the previous chapter, unsettled certain critics who resented Kenny's "mechanization" of the theater. The cliché that audience members leave megamusicals "humming the scenery" has been used as a blunt instrument with which to bludgeon the megamusical despite the fact that the visual effects that characterize many megamusicals are not meant to draw attention to themselves but rather to help move the story forward; as Sternfeld writes, the most noteworthy special effects from eighties megamusicals are "integrated moment[s] of visual spectacle" as opposed to mere diversionary displays.[149] Sternfeld's point reaffirms McMillin's assertion about the megamusical as a Wagnerian theatrical genre, for even the settings, properties, and special effects are integrated into the narrative (in fact, they oftentimes seem to control the narrative). Similarly, the Kenny set, though a remarkable piece of imagination, architecture, and engineering, was essential to the show's narrative on a fundamental level given the sheer diversity of settings that had to be presented onstage and the sheer breadth of the Dickensian narrative that Bart was trying to recreate. The Kenny set thus had its own distinct role to play in the success of *Oliver!*, and Roger Hardwick recalls that audiences would oftentimes react to the scenery in the same way they would react to a skilled performer: when it played its part (that is, when it rotated) the crowd would actually take time to applaud[150]—much as there is a temptation to applaud the flying tire, the falling chandelier, the rising barricade, and the landing helicopter. While the idea of an audience applauding a piece of scenery is anathema to some critics, the fact remains that had it not been for Kenny's genius, *Oliver!* would never have reached the stage.

Oliver!'s influence on the megamusical movement would extend beyond the advent of Lloyd Webber, eventually helping to serve as the inspiration for one of the most successful megamusicals ever produced. Mackintosh once related that when composer Alain Boublil went to see the aforementioned 1977 West End revival of *Oliver!*, "[h]e said that as he watched the Artful Dodger sing 'Consider Yourself', the character of Gavroche from *Les Miz* suddenly just jumped into his head. By the end of the show he had worked out roughly what he wanted to do with all the characters and afterward he immediately telephoned Claude-Michel [Schönberg] in Paris and said, 'I've got the subject for our next musical.'"[151] Mackintosh views *Oliver!* as the most noteworthy forebear to *Les Miz*, going so far as to label the latter musical as "the new version of *Oliver!* Very much the same dark, brooding, moving mass that conjured up amazing things out of your imagination as well as presenting you with a massive, great, theatrical barricade,"[152] though it is unlikely that this revolve show would have reached fruition had *Oliver!* not established the trend of representing the innumerable locations covered in a nineteenth-century serial novel through the use of a rotating set.

The connections between *Oliver!* and English megamusicals (and Anglo-French megamusicals) like *Cats* and *Les Misérables*, along with Lionel Bart's direct influence on the likes of Mackintosh and Lloyd Webber, have only served to reinforce *Oliver!*'s significance in the advancement of the postwar English musical theater. Nevertheless, *Oliver!*'s own Englishness actually far exceeds that of its megamusical successors. The megamusicals of the eighties purposefully embrace a global vision, as epitomized by their sweeping themes and fundamental emotional emphases, and though critics are tempted to attribute this quality to the general sense of wonder brought about by the spectacle of the megamusical, Sternfeld points out that this appeal is likewise grounded in the universality associated with the megamusicals' themes.[153] The consequence of embracing such a universal vision, however, is the loss a distinctive "sense of local and contemporary flavor."[154] As Steyn observes,

[AD] British musicals are about cats and trains and deformed creatures who live in the Paris sewers. For all they tell us about contemporary Britain, they might as well come from outer space. [...] But, twenty years Before *Cats*, for a few seasons, there was a distinctive native strain of contemporary London musical, written by a man who filled the stage with British types—Blitz babies from the forties, coffee-house spivs of the fifties.[155]

Steyn's subsequent assertion that Bart "gave Britain one of its own"[156] has several connotations. Although Bart may have given England its own version of the American success story gone wrong, he likewise gave Britain its own canonical musical of the golden age of Broadway, and, as Steyn astutely notes, that musical, like all of Bart's musicals, was unabashedly, overtly, and fundamentally *English*. The megamusical movement ensured English transatlantic dominance of the musical stage, but *Oliver!* remains a more identifiably English musical compared to any piece from the megamusical era, thanks to its emphasis on a specifically English community.

CONCLUSION

Setting aside these cultural issues described throughout this chapter, the debut of *Oliver!* inspired another important shift in the West End, as countless family audiences in London would share in the celebration of this musical. The transformation of Dickens's social polemic into "family entertainment" may have offended some purists, but *Oliver!*'s emphasis on the child-hero's quest for love resonated strongly with the young and the young-at-heart. If the working-class qualities of the score helped to market the show to a patriotically English yet socially diverse audience, the emphasis on child actors and childhood joys and terrors helped to market the show to different

Figure 4.1: *Oliver!*'s global popularity allowed Lionel Bart to create a "worldwide family" for himself; he is pictured here with the Broadway cast of *Oliver!*
Source: Photographer unknown; print owned by Lionel Bart Foundation Archive.

age groups. As Edna Doré recalls, "if you read the book of *Oliver Twist*, there's a very complicated story there, but [Lionel] just took out this magic little storyline about a little boy; and it's so beautifully done."[157] For several members of the cast, *Oliver!*'s emphasis on family carried over to real life; Doré's son eventually joined the orchestra for the show, while Robinson's happiest moment in his three-month run came when he stepped into the role of the Dodger for the first time: "They asked would I be prepared to go on and play the part of the Artful Dodger, which of course I was only too happy to do. [...] My dad was working about half a mile away, and I phoned him up and told him what I was doing, and he dropped everything and rushed to the theatre and watched me as the Artful Dodger."[158] The fact that Bart's musical brought families together to the West End is somewhat ironic given that his vision of *Oliver!* revolved squarely around the orphan's own search for love and family. For Bart, this success marked the creation of what he would later call a "worldwide family" of audience members who embraced his musical, sang his songs, and loved his characters.[159]

The triumph of *Oliver!* marked a critical chapter in the evolution of the English musical, and likewise in the life stories of the artists associated with the project. For many, including Bart, *Oliver!* would mark an apex. *Oliver!* thus not only told a Cinderella story but likewise contained its own unique Cinderella story regarding its arduous journey from conception to completion. Furthermore, the culture text of *Oliver Twist* was forever affected by the premiere of *Oliver!*; in spite of the numerous creative liberties taken by Bart, the popular perceptions of *Oliver Twist* would now forever be shaped by his musical. The basis for this popularity, as well as myriad other issues related to this adaptation, will be discussed in the next chapter, which presents a reading of the musical and further analysis of the various social and cultural negotiations that are evident within the very framework of the adaptation.

CHAPTER 5

༄

"Oliver! Oliver!": A Reading

Crafting a "reading" of *Oliver!* (or any musical) presents several unique challenges. As noted in the discussion of authorship in Chapter 2, a musical is not written (and therefore does not read) like a traditional text. Analyzing the libretto and the lyrics is certainly not enough, as the music and orchestrations contribute immeasurably to the narrative. Eric Rogers, the orchestrator on *Oliver!*, remains one of the show's unsung heroes in this regard; as will be discussed throughout this chapter, his orchestrations were essential to the show's musical narrative.[1] In the context of the formalist approach to narrative theory, one might (albeit awkwardly) label the libretto and the lyrics as the "story" and the music and orchestrations as the "discourse." Though such a distinction seems antithetical to the very concept of an "integrated" musical, in which the various component parts allegedly work together to create a coherent whole, such a separation has been central to traditional theories of narrative: "In Russian Formalism this is the distinction between *fabula* and *sjuzhet*: the story as a series of events and the story as reported in the narrative. Other theorists propose different formulations, whose terms are often confusing. [...] But there is always a basic distinction between a sequence of events and a discourse that orders and presents events."[2] In the case of a musical, the "order" of the events is actually set forth in the libretto and preserved by the musical discourse (for the order of the songs is laid out in the book). Nevertheless, the "presentation" of these events is dependent on forces beyond the libretto, given the centrality of the music to telling the story. A variety of musical "narrators," from the orchestra to the characters who sing solo, to the chorus, control the presentation of events by taking up the musical "discourse" at different points in the narrative.

This complicated relationship between numerous "texts" and "voices" becomes even more complex when dealing with a musical adaptation such as *Oliver!*, which built off a longstanding tradition of earlier adaptations of *Oliver Twist*. The intertextual dimensions of Bart's adaptation are highly suggestive of Roland Barthes's definitions of a literary text as "a multi-dimensional space in which a variety of writings, none of them original, blend and clash" and "a tissue of quotations drawn from the innumerable centres of culture."[3] Bart adapted numerous "texts" while simulta-neously working within the abstract "multidimensional space" that is the *Twist*ian culture text. As suggested in the previous chapter, evaluating the adaptation by com-paring it solely to Dickens's novel is taking a limited view of a much more complex relationship between adaptation and "source."

The very title of Bart's adaptation hints at these interrelationships. Gérard Genette asserts that the purpose of a title, as a paratext, is "(1) to identify the work, (2) to designate the work's subject matter, (3) to play up the work."[4] In spite of its apparent simplicity, the title *Oliver!* accomplishes all three of these goals. It identifies the work, though it wisely does *not* directly recognize the work as a Dickensian adap-tation. Calling the piece *Oliver Twist*, or *Oliver Twist!*, or *Oliver Twist: The Musical!* would immediately place the adaptation in a more stringent literary context by tying it directly to its novelistic source. The evolution from *Oliver Twist* to *Oh, Oliver!*, to *Oliver!* signifies a journey toward greater freedom in exploring the "multidimensional space" of texts and adaptations of texts. In regard to the subject matter, Bart's use of the exclamation point subtly places the piece in a musical context.[5] The exclamation point likewise achieves Genette's third goal by generating a sense of excitement.

Regardless of the multiplicity of texts at work in *Oliver!*, Bart's adaptation can also be read, on a basic level, as a musical variation on (or musical interpretation of) Dickens's story. In a 1960 letter to Ron Moody, Lionel Bart revealed what he consid-ered to be the four central plot threads of *Oliver!* in descending order of importance:

1. The story of a little boy searching for love against all opposition.
2. The story of a strange and seemingly fruitless romance between 'Nancy' and 'Bill'.
3. The story of a lonely Jew who is searching for love, and finds it from the children he fosters.
4. The comic and slightly macabre relationship between 'Mr. Bumble' and 'Widow Corney'[6]

Here are four very different love stories woven together into a single narrative and stemming from a common source: Oliver's "Where Is Love?" As Bart asserted, "musi-cally, it's the root theme for the rest of the songs. [...] The songs, which are character songs, come off of that tune."[7] Dickens's original text is about the power of good to survive in the face of evil; Bart's adaptation is about the equally enduring power of love. This thematic cornerstone can provide a useful catalyst for analyzing Bart's musi-cal. Rather than present a traditional "chronological" reading of the piece, this chapter analyzes the four aforementioned plot threads on a thematic and musical level.

A NOTE ABOUT NARRATION

As discussed in the previous chapters, the notion of *Oliver!* as an "integrated musi-cal," in spite of its being written in the golden age of the Broadway "book musical," is complicated by some of the assumptions that characterize this format/genre, and by *Oliver!*'s anticipation of the more overtly Wagnerian megamusical movement. In spite of these complications, there is no denying that song and music are the domi-nant means of discourse, even though the show is not sung through. Conversely, the discourse of Dickens's novel is defined largely by the over-the-top voice of the omniscient narrator. Both of these discursive strategies leave room for narrative tan-gents; McMillin's skepticism regarding the notion of integration has been touched on already, but his reading of numbers as moments during which the story is actually suspended rather than advanced is useful when comparing the discourse of *Oliver!* to the discourse of *Oliver Twist*.[8]

Certainly, Dickens's narrator frequently suspends the plot to offer his own phil-osophical treatises on the general selfishness and corruption of humanity, on the bureaucratic incompetence of local governmental officials, and on the necessity of middle-class compassion toward the poor. Similar "interruptions" occur throughout *Oliver!*, though these interruptive moments lie with the characters as opposed to the narrator. Private and introspective solo songs such as "Where Is Love?", "As Long as He Needs Me," and "Reviewing the Situation" furnish critical moments of personal reflection but actually do very little to advance the story, while diegetic songs such as "I'd Do Anything" and "Oom Pah Pah" are moments in which characters stop what they are doing in order to entertain one another.

However, McMillin's most interesting and applicable theory regarding musical narratives and musical narrations relates to the role of the orchestra, an entity that he describes in terms that are purposefully evocative of an omniscient Victorian nar-rator: "The orchestra knows everything. It knows when to introduce the numbers, when to bring them to a close, when to keep the beat, when to keep quiet. It knows the difference between book time and number time, and it knows how to set the two apart, or lead from one to the other."[9] McMillin's description accurately defines the narratorial power of the orchestra, but it seems problematic to describe the orches-tra as a substitute for Dickens's narrator. As noted above, the discursive tangents in *Oliver Twist* are shaped by the narrator's ostentatious personality, whereas the discursive tangents in *Oliver!* are dictated primarily by the characters; the orchestra helps to create the discursive tangent by cuing up the song and supplying music for the character to sing to, but the discursive power ultimately lies with the character.

This contrast between Dickens's narrator and *Oliver!*'s orchestrations reveals that Bart's characters have a narratorial ability that Dickens's characters lack since his narrator frequently places himself center-stage in a way that distracts from (and occasionally detracts from) the individuals who populate the novel. Although the narrator's ostentation contributes greatly to the satirical humor of the novel, it simultaneously tempers the overall effectiveness of Dickens's polemic; George J. Worth notes that "[w]hen depicting Oliver's deprivation and degradation [...] [Dickens] is sometimes not content to let narrative, description, and dialogue do their work but has his narrator engage in laboriously sardonic commentary on what is happening—commentary that tends to jar the reader in ways that vitiate much of what the author is trying to achieve."[10]

Karin Lesnik-Oberstein takes the centrality of the narrator even further, negat-ing his role as a "tool for conveying ideological positions"[11] (however effectively or ineffectively) and arguing instead that he "is not so much an instrument in and for the novel as that the novel is a tool or instrument for *him*: that he in fact creates the narrative to tell his *own* tale, the tale of how he exists as narrator, what it means to be a 'narrator'."[12] Building on the writings of Anny Sadrin, Lesnik-Oberstein notes that in spite of Oliver's status as the title character, his general passivity, reticence, and absence throughout the narrative stand in sharp contrast to the narrator's forward-ness, verbosity, and omnipresence.[13] Moreover, Oliver is repeatedly depicted as being incapable of telling his own story.[14]

Naturally, Bart's version of Oliver must be a more assertive individual than his literary forebear, for even though he is still a rather passive character, he has a power that his literary predecessor lacks: the power of song. The orchestra, like Dickens's narrator, speaks out on Oliver's behalf; however, it does so by supporting his own discursive voice—most obviously during "Where Is Love?"—rather than by usurping complete control of the narrative. Whereas Dickens's narrator asserts total narrative authority to the point of potentially laying claim to a text that is actually named for the title character, Bart uses music to create a storyteller who keeps the lead character (and the other leading characters) at the forefront of the discourse. Even when the orchestra goes off on tangents by harmonizing—again, most obviously in the underscoring to "Where Is Love?"—this tangential harmony is meant to lend support and encouragement to the character, as will be discussed in detail shortly.

THREAD 1: OLIVER'S SEARCH FOR LOVE

It is fitting to begin with this particular thread given its primacy on both thematic and chronological levels: the events of the story are initiated by Oliver. The narrator dominates the opening chapters of *Oliver Twist* with his satirical philosophical digressions, but the orchestra is far less assertive in the opening measures. Tellingly, the introduction to *Oliver!* is a brief prelude as opposed to a full-scale overture. Rather than incorporate movements and motifs from every song in the musical score, Bart simply alludes to the two most immediate numbers: "Food, Glorious Food" and "Oliver." The narrative thus centers on Oliver from the beginning, for these two songs define his early experiences in the workhouse. Furthermore, the brevity of the overture coincides with Bart's determination to move his narrative forward to the plot's seminal moment: the title character's request for more gruel. In so doing, Bart quickly grants the audience a familiar point of entry into the adaptation.

"Food, Glorious Food" seems a traditional "I want..." opening number, as Oliver and the boys sing of their desire for sustenance, though Oliver's major solo number, "Where Is Love?" fits the "I want..." label even more clearly.[15] In this later song, Oliver explicitly makes it clear what is driving him: the desire for love. The desire for food is a more immediate requirement as opposed to an overarching yearning. Still, from a practical and an artistic standpoint, it is appropriate for Bart to start out with this large-scale choral number as opposed to the private solo number. Oliver has not yet established himself as being any different from his fellow orphans; specifically, Oliver has not yet committed his rebellion by asking for more.

In Dickens's original text, Oliver stands out from the beginning; the reader knows that the text is named for him and is likewise made privy to his birth in the workhouse. However, these distinguishing characteristics are dependent on the narrator's commentary. It is the narrator who draws the reader's attention to Oliver and who talks us through his birth in Chapter 1. In Bart's musical, Oliver is just another workhouse orphan until he dares to step out from the crowd and ask for a second helping. This innocent action on the part of the protagonist allows him to become a distinct individual. He will become an even more distinct individual a few scenes later through the support of the orchestral narrator, though "Where Is Love?" can only be sung following the establishment of Oliver's particularized personality.

The opening measures to "Food, Glorious Food" are purposefully clipped and monotonous, as the boys sing a series of staccato notes, their vocal range largely restricted to three notes. Bart cleverly builds up to the word "gruel" by shifting from a series of six eighth notes and one quarter note to four eighth notes and two quarter notes in anticipation of the two half notes that make up the key word. The usually monosyllabic "gruel" is given two distinct and drawn-out syllables with two distinct and drawn-out notes, the second of which jumps up the scale. This emphasis is appropriate given the centrality of the word *gruel* to the cultural memory of *Oliver Twist*; more specifically, gruel, as a symbol of the boys' status, warrants such emphasis. Notably, the only notes that change when the aforementioned pattern repeats itself in the next four measures are the "gruel" notes.

The repetition of notes over the first eight bars of the song is coupled with a repetition of movements, as the prompt book from the original 1960 West End production of *Oliver!* indicates that the blocking of the number matches the music: methodical and mechanical.[16] In Dickens's novel, the inhabitants of the workhouse are disconsolate automatons expected to perform a task assigned to them by the administration unquestioningly and submissively (which is why Oliver's emotional and openhearted nature later arouses bewilderment and frustration in Mr. Bumble and the members of the parish board).

As the boys transition to actually singing about food, the song immediately becomes livelier. In the lyrics, the orphans mention that using their imaginations is one of the few freedoms granted to them, and the early flute harmonies add to the whimsical and imaginative quality of the song. These orchestrations are eventually replaced by rapidly ascending scales of sixteenth notes, which reinforce the boys' ever-increasing imaginative energy and enthusiasm. However, the enthusiasm is quickly curtailed by the introduction of the tyrannical Bumble, who uses music for oppression and domination as opposed to celebration, though his punishment of Oliver will provide a new source of entertainment for the other orphans.

As in Dickens's novel, Oliver's asking for more earns him scorn and castigation. The three-note phrase that defines the "Oliver" theme alludes to the punitive consequences of Oliver's "rebellion," for this phrase, so associated with the gait of the oppressive Bumble, conveys a disciplinary disapproval. The "UH uh UH" pattern of the notes insinuates the wag of a finger or the shake of a head. The song's primary objective is to make an example of Oliver before the other workhouse orphans, which harks back to Dickens's text:

> [Oliver] was carried every other day into the hall where the boys dined, and there sociably flogged as a public warning and example. And so far from being denied the advantages of religious consolation, he was kicked into the same apartment every evening at prayer-time, and there permitted to listen to, and console his mind with, a general supplication of the boys: containing a special clause, therein inserted by authority of the board, in which they entreated to be made good, virtuous, contented, and obedient, and to be guarded from the sins and vices of Oliver Twist.[17]

Bart obviously tames the source material, and the audience never witnesses Oliver's being beaten. The punishment of his protagonist is confined mostly to hyperbolic threats by Bumble, and though the song may refer to Oliver's being stuffed up a chimney, Bart saves his title character the trauma of almost being apprenticed to the brutal Gamfield. The humorous hyperbole in the lyrics tempers the fears we have about Oliver's fate, much as Dickens tempers such fears through the blatant sarcasm of the narrator and through the use of conventional fairy-tale motifs.[18]

Nevertheless, while Bart spares the rod, he makes certain to emphasize that Oliver is very much alone and vulnerable to such abuses. During the number, the other workhouse boys all turn on the title character and mock him. The musical score describes the boys as singing Oliver's name "tauntingly,"[19] while the prompt book states that "[a]ll the boys gather round Oliver mocking him."[20] Although the admonitory tone of "Oliver" seems contradictory to the celebratory tone of "Food, Glorious Food," the structure of the two numbers is strikingly similar in that the midpoints of both songs include the exact same key change. In both cases, the modulation signifies a heightening intensity, but the fact that the boys and the workhouse administrators follow the exact same pattern hints at the parallels between the two songs: for the orphans, energetically imagining increasingly harsh punishments for Oliver is just as satisfying as energetically imagining increasingly bounteous feasts.

Even though Bart's vision of the workhouse is not nearly as violent or repulsive as Dickens's, it is just as harsh in terms of the depiction of Oliver's solitude. The title character's nonconformity results in his being knocked even lower than his fellow workhouse orphans, and the moment he descends, the other boys flaunt their superiority. It is strikingly reminiscent of Dickens's narrator's assessment of Oliver's mistreatment at the hands of Noah Claypole:

> The shop-boys in the neighbourhood had long been in the habit of branding Noah, in the public streets, with the ignominious epithets of 'leathers,' 'charity,' and the like; and Noah had borne them without reply. But, now that fortune had cast in his way a nameless orphan, at whom even the meanest could point the finger of scorn, he retorted on him with interest. This affords charming food for contemplation. It shows us what a beautiful thing human nature sometimes is; and how impartially the same amiable qualities are developed in the finest lord and the dirtiest charity-boy.[21]

The predatory desire to assert power over the weak and vulnerable is essential to the characterization of the petty "bullies" who populate the musical's opening scenes, including Mr. Bumble, Mrs. Corney, Mrs. Sowerberry, Noah, and even the workhouse orphans. Conversely, the ethos of the London characters will offer a much more benevolent and supportive philosophy of camaraderie and solidarity in defiance of economic vulnerability.

For the time being, however, Oliver's loneliness and despair are pushed even further with the solemn and haunting "Boy for Sale." This interlude reemphasizes the dispassion of Oliver's guardians and also helps to prefigure the introduction of Mr. Sowerberry, as the ballad comes across like a dirge. The notes are consistently longer than in any of the previous songs, and the orchestrations grant the beadle's solo a solemnity that is lacking in the early numbers. The premise of "Boy for Sale" is actually an inversion of the corresponding scene in the Dickens text. In *Oliver Twist*, the workhouse board, eager to get rid of Oliver, offers a "reward" of five pounds to anyone who will take him on as an apprentice. Still, Bart's modification is highly effective, for the selling of Oliver by the parish advances the idea of the child as a commodity to be exploited as opposed to a human being to be loved. However, what is perhaps most ominous about Bumble's song is that his street-singing prefigures a more celebratory and joyful example of street-singing: "Who Will Buy?" in Act II. As will be discussed shortly, Oliver's participation in this later number signifies a sharp change in his values following his acclimation to the middle class.

Oliver's transition from the melancholy world of the workhouse to the morbid world of the Sowerberries does not offer much hope for his eventual happiness, though there is something grotesquely amusing (and thus highly Dickensian) about the Sowerberries. As mentioned in Chapter 3, "That's Your Funeral" was written at the last minute owing to Barry Humphries's memorable performance in the original Wimbledon production. This song, perhaps more so than any other number, epitomizes James Kincaid's assertion that the humor in Dickens's *Oliver Twist* is built on the topic of death.[22] In fact, "That's Your Funeral" almost plays as an extended version of several of the morbid jokes that Dickens includes in the original text, most of which are connected directly to Sowerberry's profession. When Bumble notes that the recent string of parish deaths will allow Soweberry to "make his fortune," the undertaker retorts that,

> " 'The prices allowed by the board are very small, Mr. Bumble.'
> 'So are the coffins,' replied the beadle."[23]

As in the text, Mr. Sowerberry clearly takes an unhealthy amount of pleasure in discussing death, and the contrast between the humor of the Sowerberries' song and the melancholy of Oliver's new situation fits in perfectly with the purposefully incongruous tenor of the early scenes in the original novel: "In denying the possibility of a comic society and yet provoking laughter, the novel continually thwarts and frustrates the reader."[24] The Sowerberries are quite entertaining, but they will hardly prove to be the loving and caring guardians that Oliver so needs and deserves. Bart will eventually break with Dickens on sending Oliver to London; there, Bart will fully endorse "the possibility of a comic society" even as he accepts the fragile and illusory qualities of that society.

The orchestra again shifts the tone of the scene following the conclusion of "That's Your Funeral," as Oliver is given the broken scraps of food meant for the dog and makes ready to spend his first night sleeping among the coffins in the undertaker's shop. It is a fitting lead-in for the cathartic singing of his major solo. Oliver's asking for more may be the key scene from Dickens's original text, but in this adaptation his singing of "Where Is Love?" must share that distinction.

In alluding to "his singing," I wish to draw attention to the fact that although the revelation of Oliver's innermost desires—as expressed in "Where Is Love?"— is of tremendous importance to understanding Bart's version of the character, the very act of singing is, in itself, central to the song's meaning in the larger context of the narrative.[25] The content of the song is obviously relevant, but McMillin's book emphasizes that the *performance* of songs in stage musicals is vital to their connotation.[26] Oliver has not sung a solo number up to this point, and his doing so here fully confirms that he is different from the other orphans at the workhouse. Actually, as the first "private" number in the musical, this song reveals that Oliver is different from every other character we have encountered up to this point, and "Where Is Love?" helps the audience to truly understand why this character is the hero of the story. By performing "Where Is Love?" Oliver is once again stepping out from the crowd, much as he did when he asked for more.[27]

Like many of its counterparts in the Dickens canon, *Oliver Twist* is frequently criticized as "melodramatic," and certainly there are instances of melodrama throughout the novel; yet, in spite of the emphasis on Oliver's suffering, Oliver himself is not a particularly melodramatic character in that he rarely uses the inflated rhetoric of stage melodrama. In fact, there is a certain simplicity to Oliver's idiom, and, much like Oliver's simple request for a second helping, the melody to "Where Is Love?" initially seems quite straightforward: Oliver does not jump about suddenly from note to note, but systematically works his way up the scale. The ostensible simplicity of the melody thus complements the ostensible simplicity of Oliver's question.

In both cases, however, there is an underlying complexity at work. Just as Oliver's request for more gruel has far greater symbolic resonance than the surface-level appeal for another helping, the question of "where is love?" runs deep. The world that has been presented onstage up to this point is a world in which love does not exist: the workhouse has effectively eliminated love and compassion (barring the purposefully harsh and unhelpful "God Is Love" sign). Similarly, the two adult couples who have been introduced have no true love for one another, nor any room in their hearts for Oliver. The fact that the song's title question is not easily answered reinforces the subtle complexity of Oliver's situation, a situation that will become even more complex as Oliver begins to interact with a wider diversity of characters.

The reality that the superficial simplicity of Oliver's solo number belies a deeper complexity is strongly reinforced by the orchestrations. Oliver's melody repeatedly follows a linear pattern up the scale, though the instrumental harmony is surprisingly elaborate (see Music Example 5.1). Throughout the first verse, these instrumental elaborations come through mainly during Oliver's held notes, but they grow more dominant in the second verse as the violin builds an ornate harmony on Oliver's scales. The strings create a similar effect during the bridge, deviating heavily from the sung melody and offering an airy, dreamlike "reply" to Oliver's inquiries. These elaborations not only add to the complexity of the song but simultaneously offer something of an answer to Oliver's question as the harmonies seem to signify that love is an intangible, transcendent, spiritual presence. In effect, the orchestra represents that presence, offering Oliver comfort and consolation during this, his lowest moment. Much as Dickens's narrator speaks out on Oliver's behalf in the original text, the orchestra proves to be a source of support and fulfillment for the orphan. However, the orchestra actually exceeds Dickens's narrator in this regard. Whereas the narrator's strategy for defending Oliver is to sarcastically attack his persecutors (and human nature in general), the orchestra remains more focused on Oliver himself, providing genuine emotional comfort and affirmation. This is the power of musical narrative: Oliver and the omniscient orchestral "narrator" are brought into dialogue with one another in a way that is unfeasible in Dickens's text.

Music Example 5.1 *Oliver!* musical score, 29

Like the superficially straightforward melody, the lyrics to "Where Is Love?" initially appear to be somewhat generalized. There are moments when it seems as though this song might be sung by anyone who is desirous of love. Nevertheless, "Where Is Love?" yields important insights into Oliver's character. The longing that Oliver expresses throughout this number is directed primarily toward the image of the mother he never knew. This emphasis on his deceased mother is taken directly from the novel, for even in death (and even as a "fallen woman"), Agnes embodies the compassionate and giving presence of the Victorian maternal ideal. When Oliver reflects on his mother with Mrs. Bedwin in Chapter 12, he reveals just how significant an impact Agnes has had on him, asserting that he has felt his mother's presence throughout his tribulations: "Perhaps she does see me [...] perhaps she has sat by me. I almost feel as if she had. [...] Heaven is a long way off; and they are too happy there, to come down to the bedside of a poor boy. But if she knew I was ill, she must have pitied me, even there; for she was very ill herself before she died."[28] Though the reflections that Oliver shares with his caretaker are overly sentimental, the spiritually affirmative vision he has created of his mother as a devoted and sympathetic protector is what allows him to find the strength to face a world that is openly hostile to his goodness. Though Agnes is gone, she is hardly forgotten, for she maintains a remarkably strong presence throughout the hero's journey. In the musical, her presence is most directly felt during "Where Is Love?" and the elaborate orchestrations are an overt indication of that loving, spiritual presence.

Though the orchestra provides Oliver with an intangible, spiritual support, he does not live in an intangible, spiritual world. A more concrete answer to the "where is love?" question seems contingent on his escaping the wretched people who have mistreated him throughout the opening scenes. Following his confrontation with Noah, Oliver flees from the Sowerberries and finds himself in London, where he meets the Artful Dodger. The search for love has finally yielded some promising results: a new friend. "Consider Yourself" also marks a shift for Oliver in terms of his use of music. In "Food, Glorious Food," Oliver sings as part of a chorus and does not truly stand out as an individual. In "Where Is Love?" he sings solo, but his individuality is marked by feelings of loneliness. Here, Oliver sings a duet with the Dodger, and the Dodger's use of the plural pronouns "we" and "our" as opposed to the singular "I" and "my" emphasizes the inviting hospitality of London. Although Oliver's parroting of the Dodger's verses occasionally ends in question marks, thus implying a mild uncertainty, he sings to the exact same tune as his companion. The score likewise notes that throughout the song, "Dodger illustrates various Cockney actions which Oliver tries to emulate."[29] Oliver's attempts to duplicate the Dodger are prophetic given that Fagin will encourage the orphan to make the Dodger his "model." Though the characters' idioms and personalities are widely different, Oliver and the Dodger share a close musical bond here.

More significantly, the Dodger offers Oliver a gateway into a community—not simply the community of the thieves' kitchen, but the greater community of London. Their duet gradually evolves into a larger chorus number, and as the scope of the song expands and the chorus grows, the entire city seems determined to welcome Oliver. Though the chorus in this number is made up of a wide variety of characters, the lyrics repeatedly imply that the characters singing this song are in difficult financial straits; however, they are unwavering in their optimism that things will get better. The Dodger's insistence on a "share-and-share-alike" philosophy is the play's first true indication of compassionate fellowship, and the Dodger proves that such fellowship can exist even among those who have very little.

Oliver continues to follow the Dodger's lead throughout the first act and into later numbers such as "I'd Do Anything," in which he duplicates the pickpocket's singing of the refrain. As noted in the previous chapter, "I'd Do Anything" is defined by its sentimentality and its parody of middle-class culture. The blocking is comedic, as the prompt book describes the interactions between Nancy and the Dodger when they sing the first verse of the song: "Dodger pulls stool d/s between Nancy. Nancy takes handkerchief from her bosom. Nancy dusts stool with hank—Drops hank to her R. Dodger kneels R of Nancy, picks up hank. & holds it up to her. Fagin rise, rush up steps of truck, grab Nancy's hank & runs back to fireplace, hang it on line."[30] Nevertheless, the sentiments expressed in the song recount the genuine fondness that these characters have for one another, and when Oliver takes up the song in its second verse, the warmth of these sentiments becomes all the more apparent given Oliver's innocent desire for love.

"I'd Do Anything" is oftentimes mistakenly remembered as a duet between Oliver and Nancy; notably, the song's title was adopted for the reality TV series that focused on the casting of these two roles for the West End revival at Drury Lane (see Chapter 7). However, Oliver and Nancy do not actually sing together in the original version. The song is structured as two separate duets: one between the Dodger and

Nancy, and the other between Oliver and Bet.[31] Through the juxtaposition of these two duets, Bart reinforces the importance of showmanship to the thieves and the other low-class characters as they are all constantly trying to entertain and cheer one another, a true indication that this environment is built around love (even as it satirizes traditional love songs and courtships). When Fagin and the rest of the boys get in on the act toward the end of the song, with Fagin humorously singing the female part while the boys mockingly sing of their devotion to him, the notion of parody is fully realized, though the truthfulness behind the sentiments remains unquestionable.

Furthermore, "I'd Do Anything" epitomizes the contrasts between the thieves' den and the workhouse. In the middle of the song, following Nancy's verse with the Dodger, Fagin and Nancy encourage Oliver to join in:

FAGIN: Now you Oliver ...
NANCY: You do everything you saw him do. And I'll tell you all the words you don't know.[32]

As in the case of "Consider Yourself," Oliver is invited to join in the celebration. The neglect of the workhouse and the Sowerberry household is replaced by the active interest of the thieves' kitchen, as Fagin, Nancy, the Dodger, and Bet show compassion toward a helpless child and make him feel wanted.

Unfortunately, this newfound optimism is compromised by the reality that the camaraderie of the thieves' den is funded by the boys' ill-gotten gains. Oliver's arrest at the end of Act I highlights the brutal realities that loom over Fagin's world. Although music, singing, and friendship can provide a temporary refuge from these realities, and can likewise provide a tenable answer to the question of "where is love?", the safe haven of Fagin's den is delicate and ephemeral. As Oliver is hauled away by the Bow Street Runners, the specters of abuse, misery, and loneliness seem set to reemerge, and the love of the gang can do little to help him.

Bart once again shields his protagonist from the horrors faced by his novelistic counterpart, as he excises the traumatic scene set in Fang's courtroom. By the time Oliver is reintroduced in Act II, he is already living a life of luxury in Mr. Brownlow's house. Oliver's first scene in this new environment features a brief yet noteworthy reprise of "Where Is Love?" sung by Mrs. Bedwin. Given that Oliver's solo song revolves heavily around his feelings towards his deceased mother, it seems fitting that the maternal Mrs. Bedwin would reprise it in this location, which will eventually be revealed as the former home of Oliver's mother. It is intriguing to think that Mrs. Bedwin, as a servant in the Brownlow household, may have sung this very "lullaby" to Agnes, and that Oliver's singing of the song signifies the spiritual connection to his deceased mother.

Even so, certain issues complicate the notion that Brownlow's house is the ideal location for Oliver (and the place that best answers the "where is love?" question). The very fact that Mrs. Bedwin is singing "Where Is Love?" as opposed to some sort of variation that states "*Here* is love..." implies that the question is still unsettled. Similarly, though Mrs. Bedwin is loving and maternal, she is also a servant, and the topic of class hierarchies is a central contrast between Brownlow's house and Fagin's den. These contrasts are revealed musically in the next big production number, "Who Will Buy?"

"Who Will Buy?" is somewhat analogous to "Consider Yourself" in its focus on working-class Londoners who use music to express themselves. However, there are also clear differences between the two songs. "Consider Yourself" presents a communal vision of London as the Dodger insists that everything is share and share alike. The vision of London presented in "Who Will Buy?" is more individualist and capitalistic. Whereas "Consider Yourself" repeatedly addresses the idea of trying to avoid making payments, "Who Will Buy?" implies that making payments is essential to the function of society. When the chorus begins singing in "Consider Yourself," it enters as a unified whole to sing about camaraderie in the face of hardship. Though "Who Will Buy?" eventually builds toward a unified choral number, it initially features a set of distinct individuals who retain their own unique wares, identities, and notes.

Oliver has already begun to subscribe to a new "transactional" point of view as he joins in the song. He is more focused on the spiritual sense of optimism and affirmation that he feels in this new environment, as opposed to any specific material comforts or possessions; nevertheless, he describes this joyous sentiment in materialist terms and expresses a desire to take possession of it. Oliver's desire to keep this lovely morning for himself is fundamentally antithetical to the Dodger's philosophy as expressed in "Consider Yourself," and moreover, to the philosophies presented in such songs as "It's a Fine Life," "I'd Do Anything," and even "Oom Pah Pah." These songs all focus on the collective sharing of food, drink, song, dance, and happiness, and the environment in which they are sung thus comes across as more genuinely loving even if that love is masked behind a cockney cynicism.

Moreover, the idea that Oliver must "buy" this wonderful morning as opposed to simply being able to enjoy it for free places the middle-class comforts of his new environment in contrast to the lower-class joys of the thieves' den.[33] Whereas the question of "where is love?" is not easily answered, the question of "who will buy?" seems rather straightforward. The comforts and joys of Bloomsbury are dependent on Brownlow, whose wealth guarantees security and leisure.

An even more striking comparison can be drawn between "Who Will Buy?" and "Boy for Sale." Although the keys and notes are very different, the "who will buy?" phrase seems reminiscent of Mr. Bumble's own three-note phrase (particularly in Bumble's final repetition of the phrase at the end of the song, which follows the ascending pattern of the "who will buy?" phrase). Obviously, the most direct connection between the two songs is the emphasis on street-singing, but the fact that the type of singing that characterizes Bloomsbury calls to mind Oliver's former status as a commodity is unsettling. In the original text, Oliver tries to convince Brownlow to allow him to stay in Pentonville by offering to become a servant in the old man's household. Although "Who Will Buy?" does not feature Oliver trying to "sell" himself to Brownlow, it does emphasize two of the defining traits of Oliver's new home: first, you cannot get something for nothing, and second, looking out for one's own material needs is a central element of the middle-class lifestyle.[34]

If Oliver's new environment is more capitalistic and self-centered than the thieves' den, it is likewise less lively from a musical point of view. Aside from Mrs. Bedwin's brief reprise of "Where Is Love?" and Oliver's quick chorus of "Who Will Buy?", no music is ever sung within Brownlow's house. Tellingly, Brownlow himself never sings, a sharp contrast to Fagin, Oliver's other protector and father figure, who is constantly using music to express himself and to entertain his pupils. Furthermore, there are no boys Oliver's age in Brownlow's house. Here, Oliver is constantly interacting with adults who act like adults, as opposed to Fagin's den, where he is interacting with people his own age, or with an adult who is almost childlike in his spontaneity. The absence of song here is a troubling indicator that the exuberant elements of life in London are confined only to the underprivileged characters like Fagin, the Dodger, Nancy, and Bet, who must use music to keep their spirits high. Oliver's life of calm and comfort will leave little room for song; furthermore, his new lifestyle makes any sort of companionship with the thieves impossible.

Oliver's return to the thieves' den following his abduction at the hands of Nancy and Sykes marks a turning point in the portrayal of the criminals, who have, until this moment, been depicted in a consistently positive light. In this scene, the group turns against Oliver, and the portrayal of the Dodger here is especially unfavorable.[35] Initially, the writing of the character seems uneven, for in the first act the Dodger is presented as a companion and role model for Oliver. Conversely, the second act portrays him as an antagonist and tormentor in the vein of Noah. Nevertheless, there is a solid basis for such a transition, and it relates back to the humorous depiction of the middle class in the earlier music-hall-style thieves' den songs. The Dodger and the other pickpockets enjoy mocking their social betters. On ascending to the urban gentry, Oliver has become the very sort of person that the boys all love to hate: a well-dressed and respectable member of the upper middle class. Though the Dodger and Oliver met on equal terms, Oliver's ascent means that he can no longer consider himself "one of the family."

It is ironic that Oliver's rise prompts the thieves to turn their backs on him: a paradoxical inversion of the traditional belief that a rise in social status makes one's former friends "unsuitable" company. What is even more ironic is the fact that we are left to wonder whether this ascent has truly been worthwhile, given all that Oliver has had to renounce in the process. The reality that he will lose Nancy while trying to get back to Brownlow's house highlights the costliness of a middle-class life; clearly, Victorian middle-class tranquility is oftentimes dependent on brutal working-class sacrifices.

Following Nancy's death and Sykes's failed escape, the show proceeds toward its conclusion as the rescued Oliver reunites with Brownlow for his well-deserved "happily ever after," though this resolution is bittersweet when set against the breakup of the thieves' den. Furthermore, Brownlow's inability to sing seems to reflect an inability to experience the intense emotions and joys that propel Fagin, Nancy, and the other musical characters to burst into song. Brownlow's middle-class existence is one of quiet respectability as opposed to the more dynamic, passionate world of the thieves—a world that better exemplifies Oliver's own passion. It is unlikely that the material comforts of Bloomsbury can resolve the spiritual and emotional longings that drove Oliver in Act I.

In spite of this ambiguity, the orchestra injects a strong optimism into the string of reprises that make up the curtain call. The very first song to be reprised is "Food, Glorious Food" and, as the workhouse orphans take their bow, Oliver arrives with Brownlow to share a food basket. Here, Oliver reveals that despite his new middle-class lifestyle, he will not turn his back on his roots. The reprise of "Consider Yourself," which immediately follows, emphasizes that Oliver is capable of applying the Dodger's share-and-share-alike philosophy even though he has now ascended to the middle class. Furthermore, Oliver has retained his own ability to use song as a means of expression despite having entered the staid middle-class world of Brownlow's house; he is the only character to sing solo during the curtain call. Oliver thus seems capable of balancing the best elements of both worlds, mixing the passion and music of the thieves' den with the charity and protection of Brownlow's house. The final reprise of "I'd Do Anything," which plays up the number's sentimental affection, provides a hopeful answer to the question of "where is love?" by reestablishing the bonds of communal, music-hall fellowship between the cast and the audience.

THREAD 2: NANCY AND SYKES'S RELATIONSHIP

Nancy is easily the most interesting and fully realized female character in *Oliver Twist*, and, more generally, one of the greatest female characters from Dickens's early works. Granted, her enduring power is partially the result of her dramatic afterlife, including Dickens's dramatization of her death in his public readings, but even without this added dimension Nancy stands out. The same is true of her musical counterpart. As noted in Chapter 2, Bart eventually had to rely on Nancy to carry the female dimension of the show, but she proved up to the task, as indicated by the role's continued popularity.

No discussion of the character can avoid the issue of her profession. Dickens does not directly identify Nancy as a prostitute, though he would later do so in the preface to the 1841 edition. Nevertheless, it is not difficult to pick up on the fact that Nancy and Bet are streetwalkers. In Bart's libretto, Nancy's character description lists her as a "graduate of Fagin's academy and Bill's doxy."[36] Even as the latter part of this description establishes her as a "fallen woman," the former seems to imply that she is a thief as opposed to a prostitute. Later, when Nancy is asked to sing "Oom Pah Pah" at the Three Cripples, the line is blurred further. London music-hall culture was repeatedly associated with the prostitution epidemic that plagued the city throughout the Victorian era. Still, Victorian music halls offered exciting new opportunities to women from a social and a professional point of view. J. S. Bratton writes that "[i]t is a commonplace of the more recent music-hall history that the halls provided working-class women with a rare opportunity to make their way to independence and even to fortune."[37] These freedoms, coupled with the discussion of sexuality in music-hall songs, scandalized many in the middle class, and a woman attending a music-hall performance without a chaperone had to deal with numerous assumptions regarding her livelihood: "Any woman who dared to leave her home in the evening unaccompanied by a man in order to go to a place of entertainment was automatically presumed to be a prostitute."[38] Nevertheless, there was no law against being a prostitute and visiting a music hall, so long as one did not solicit.[39] As such, proprietors generally accepted their attendance, "since the police, as a rule, sided with the proprietors rather than the magistrates in disputes about the presence of prostitutes in the halls."[40] With its emphasis on camaraderie between working-class men *and* women, and its inclusion of "fallen women," the early music hall defied prevalent Victorian prejudices.

The liberating nature of "music-hall morality" is conveyed by Nancy and Bet throughout "It's a Fine Life," as they mock the prudishness of those who cannot appreciate the love and conviviality of this working-class community. Notably, Nancy frames the song as a music-hall performance in that she has the boys, her audience, echo her whenever she sings the refrain. Still, "It's a Fine Life" is not an unequivocally merry song, as Bart drops hints that Nancy's fondness for the life she leads is tempered by the dangers of being a criminal and by her tumultuous relationship with Sykes. The orchestra likewise sets up an ambiguous final verse. After a quick key change prefigures a few energetic dance steps, the boisterous refrain abruptly transitions to a more reflective conclusion. Though Nancy may claim that "it's a fine life," she simultaneously expresses her wish for the kind of domestic happiness and tranquility that Sykes is unable to provide her, owing to his brutishness and his thievery.

The complexities of the Nancy-Sykes subplot cement *Oliver!*'s status as a fundamentally modern English musical in that Bart has raised the stakes of the English musical libretto. Here, he breaks completely with the light and airy notions of musical couples, as defined by Wilson and Slade, and instead offers a darker, more complex take on relationships, one that seems far more evocative of various groundbreaking American musicals. In many ways, Nancy fits neatly into a tradition of proud but mistreated heroines from the golden age of the Broadway musical, including the two Julies: Julie La Verne (*Show Boat*) and Julie Jordan (*Carousel*). Much like her two predecessors, Nancy is willing to endure emotional neglect and physical cruelty out of her devotion to the man she loves. Setting aside the issue of physical abuse, the general complexities of Nancy's feelings toward Sykes make her an infinitely more authentic musical character than many of her English predecessors.

Granted, Sykes contributes little to this complexity, and the difficulties surrounding Sykes's role can be framed in the context of more general "second-act problems" that traditionally seem to plague musicals[41], though in the case of Bart's musical the true culprit is the sheer scope of the original story.[42] *Oliver!* is an adaptation of a long and complex novel with an extremely complicated denouement. Though Act I follows the plot of Dickens's novel closely, this act covers only the first ten chapters of a fifty-three chapter novel. Consolidating ten chapters into a single act is difficult enough, but consolidating forty-three chapters is all but impossible. Still, Act I notably proceeds to its conclusion without any real conflict, as the previous antagonists have all been left behind; the momentum of the story lies in the lively depiction of the thieves. Act II must initiate some sort of tension to drive the rest of the narrative; enter Sykes.

It is a memorable entrance considering how thoroughly Sykes's introductory song, "My Name," diverges from Nancy's boisterous Act II opener, "Oom Pah Pah."[43]

Although Sykes has been spoken of (and sung of) several times prior to this scene, the audience cannot appreciate just how dangerous he truly is until he sings "My Name." The content of the song is actually traceable back to the novel, for during Sikes's introduction, as presented by Dickens, the character places especial emphasis on his name:

'Hush! hush! Mr. Sikes,' said the Jew, trembling; 'don't speak so loud.'
'None of your mistering,' replied the ruffian; 'you always mean mischief when you come
    that. You know my name: out with it! I shan't disgrace it when the time comes.'
'Well, well, then—Bill Sikes,' said the Jew, with abject humility.[44]

The concrete textual basis for Sykes's number is somewhat surprising given that he seems so unmusical a character, though the distinctive qualities of his solo reinforce these unmusical traits. His vocal range is limited; his singing lacks a fluid melody and, in performance, oftentimes suggests a recitative as opposed to a true "song." In *Carousel*, Billy Bigelow may be an unlikable and abusive man and a thief, but his ability to sing—and the musical and psychological complexity of his sung reflections, as epitomized by "Soliloquy"—ensures that the audience will never doubt his inner goodness. Conversely, Sykes is no true singer, and the lack of complexity to his musical expression reinforces his general lack of complexity as a human being. Like his textual predecessor, he is primarily defined by his physical brutality.

Though it is frustrating that the complexities of the Nancy-Sykes "love story," as presented by Bart, must be viewed solely through Nancy's eyes, there is a clear textual basis for this one-sidedness. Furthermore, Bart had little material to work with regarding Sykes's role. The Lean film's thuggish Sykes, portrayed by the great Robert Newton, is characterized mainly by his physical menace, his gritted teeth, his bulging eyes, and his violent behavior. Still, if "My Name" establishes Sykes's dangerous and volatile nature, it likewise establishes his possessiveness of Nancy. In the original staging, when a drunken patron begins flirting with Nancy and makes the mistake of touching her, Sykes grabs him and punches him. Nancy rests her head on his chest and he puts his arm around her.[45] Here, Sykes displays some sense of devotion toward Nancy though he is only capable of expressing it through violence.

Nancy and Sykes's relationship is indeed "strange" and "seemingly fruitless"; however, its unconventionality does not seem to degenerate into mutual destructiveness until Sykes forces Nancy to retrieve Oliver. Notably, Nancy's initial desire to avoid this task is self-serving: she does not want to risk being caught. Nancy has not yet resolved to put Oliver's needs before her own, though she will make that transition shortly, and "As Long as He Needs Me" is an important indicator of this shift as she begins to reevaluate her relationship with Sykes: if Sykes does not need her, perhaps Oliver does. Nancy's love for Sykes may come across as selfless, but the self-destructive quality of that love taints the nobility Nancy exemplifies in her devotedness to the housebreaker—we know Sykes is not worthy of her. Conversely, her purer love for Oliver allows her to attain true selflessness, as Oliver is indeed worthy of her devotion and of her self-sacrificing decency. As in the original novel, however, Nancy seems desperate to convince herself that the housebreaker truly loves her.

Nancy's status as a prostitute is of great significance here, for her living a "life of the flesh" ultimately leaves her open to physical abuse. Dickens repeatedly links Nancy's prostituting of herself and her relationship with Sikes to an overarching tendency toward self-destruction. Neither Rose nor Brownlow can persuade Nancy to leave Sikes, though Nancy seems fully aware of the fact that abandoning her lover (and her lifestyle) would allow her to find peace. Robert R. Garnett astutely notes that toward the end of the novel, when Nancy pleads with Sikes to spare her, there is an added dimension to her pleas in that she finally seems determined to break with the life she has known: "she pleads for freedom—freedom from her carnal life; freedom from Bill himself."[46] Nevertheless, the situation is complicated in the musical by the fact that Nancy's reckless hedonism, as conveyed in her early songs, does not carry the inherent stigmas that faced her Victorian forebear. Moreover, the lifestyle Nancy leads is never depicted as particularly unhappy; after all, she would hardly be capable of singing a song entitled "It's a Fine Life" if she were the degraded, alcoholic, self-loathing creature presented in Dickens's novel.

Still, up to this point in the adaptation, all of Nancy's songs have been sung in front of an audience: "Oom Pah Pah," "I'd Do Anything," and "It's a Fine Life" are all "public" numbers (the former two were also diegetic), as befits the music-hall tenor of these pieces. We get a private glimpse into the "real" Nancy at the end of "It's a Fine Life," and tellingly this glimpse occurs when she shifts her attention to Sykes. Similarly, "As Long as He Needs Me," Nancy's one private and personal song, focuses entirely on the subject of Sykes, and so she reveals parts of herself that are normally kept hidden from others—even Sykes, as she alludes to feelings of love that she has been forced to hide. Ironically, Nancy's search for love with Sykes is doubly futile. Not only does he refuse to acknowledge her love, but she is simultaneously incapable of displaying the full extent of her feelings for him, from the necessity of her showing strength in the face of his brutality. In spite of her physical relationship with Sykes, and her unashamedly hedonistic worldview, Nancy is startlingly repressed from an emotional point of view; "As Long as He Needs Me" is a moment of catharsis.

In contrast to her previous songs, where the rhythm is kept fairly constant, Nancy repeatedly switches back and forth between common time and cut time, using the latter whenever she deviates from the song's central theme. This strategy gives the number a sense of dramatic buildup, and it likewise permits unique insights into Nancy's psyche as the three cut-time sections are all moments of intense reflection. Whereas the "as long as he needs me" musical phrase is defined by its constancy, in terms of both its common time and its lyrical certainty regarding Sykes's need for her, the cut-time sections, which deviate from the main phrase, explore the uncertain and terrifying elements of the relationship. Nancy confesses her own emotional suppression, reflects on Sykes's behavior toward her, and finally admits that whatever her doubts regarding Sykes's need for her, it is her own loneliness and degradation that are fueling her commitment to this destructive relationship. "As Long as He Needs Me" is thus a direct follow-up to "Where Is Love?" in that both "private" songs focus on the singers' need for compassion and companionship.

Nancy's visit to Brownlow confirms that her loyalties have shifted from the thieves' den to Oliver, but this does not mean she is willing to betray Sykes. As in the novel, she refuses to do anything that will compromise her lover's safety. The subsequent reprise of "As Long as He Needs Me" reinforces this fact; whatever Nancy's change in loyalties, the "he" in the title never changes from Sykes to Oliver. Still, other subtler transitions capture the emotional conflict within her. The noticeable key change and the higher register of the notes grant the piece a greater intensity than its predecessor. Furthermore, unlike in the previous version, Nancy actually refers to Sykes by name, an indication of her need to forcefully emphasize her loyalty to the "he" in the title even as she plans on supporting another "he."

Tragically, Nancy's attempt to reconcile her loves for the two "he's" in her life proves fatal. Though Nancy's death on London Bridge is by far the darkest moment in the musical (and a powerful indication that the postwar West End musical had grown up), Nancy's redemptive sacrifice on behalf of Oliver makes it clear that her death was not in vain, and moreover that the search for love that has driven both characters is not hopeless since they have discovered the purest and most transcendent type of love. This realization underscores the connections between Nancy and Agnes (and between "Where Is Love?" and "As Long as He Needs Me"). It simultaneously reinforces Bart's initial point about the ultimate fruitlessness of the Nancy-Sykes relationship, which brings about the destruction of both participants. Sykes, who proves the true betrayer in the relationship through his senseless murder of Nancy, will endure a violent death of his own.

THREAD 3: FAGIN AND THE GANG'S LOVE

Although Fagin and his gang ranked third in Bart's hierarchy of love stories, these characters are arguably the true heart of the adaptation.[47] More so than any other characters, they embrace the performativity and diversion of music-hall entertainment that is so central to both the musical and thematic elements of the piece. In an ironic yet not necessarily incongruous break with the literary source, the thieves serve as the primary guardians of Dickensian values. This is not surprising given the overlap that Paul Schlicke perceives between Dickens's celebration of popular entertainment and his equally potent celebration of childhood: "The values which Dickens associated with popular entertainment—including spontaneity, freedom, fancy and release, as opposed to life-denying forces of hard-headedness and hard-heartedness—converged in the most important image in his art, that of the child."[48] As a member of Fagin's gang, Oliver is allowed to temporarily embrace the joys of youth (and of popular entertainment).

Naturally, this is feasible only because Bart takes numerous liberties with his source. In the original text, Fagin's gang is indeed made up of children, but these children—most notably, the Dodger—have adopted the basic cynicism and world-weariness of middle-aged men because of their lifestyle. Fagin's primary roles as corruptor and thief come together in his relationship with his charges, whom he has effectively "robbed" of their childhoods. However, Bart inverts the relationship by emphasizing the childlike qualities of Fagin, qualities that define the culture of the thieves' kitchen. Here, the "spontaneity, freedom, fancy and release" of childhood are embraced. Thus, through their infidelity to their literary forebears, Fagin and the boys paradoxically prove themselves the most Dickensian characters in the piece.

Bart's description of Fagin as a "lonely Jew" establishes a connection between the old man and the other two lead characters, Oliver and Nancy, both of whom suffer from their own sense of isolation. Bart's description likewise hints at the notion that Fagin's alienation may relate to his ethnicity, even though the adaptation never goes so far as to depict Fagin as a victim of anti-Semitism. Still, Fagin's formation of the gang suggests the desire for community, and, as noted in the Oliver section, this community is founded on ideals such as sharing, camaraderie, and playfulness. The irony lies in the fact that it is a community of thieves, and yet the moral complications raised by this reality do not negate the positive elements of the thieves' kitchen.

In analyzing Fagin's relationship with the boys, we will find it helpful to return to the character of the Artful Dodger, Fagin's closest companion and the chief representative of the ideals of the thieves' den. Dickens's depiction of the Dodger can prove somewhat startling for those who know *Oliver Twist* only through *Oliver!* (and, more specifically, through the film adaptation, which amplifies the stage character's good qualities). Although Dickens presents the Dodger as sympathetic, particularly in comparison to Fagin and Monks, he does not idealize the young criminal either. The Dodger is charismatic, friendly, and entertaining, but he is also cynical, self aggrandizing, and, of course, a thief. Kincaid is willing to overlook these flaws and links the Dodger back to Dickens's first great cockney hero, Sam Weller: like Sam, the Dodger is open, welcoming, and sardonic, and he lives his life as "a kind of brilliant parody of social convention."[49] Since the society in which the Dodger lives is corrupt, flawed, and selfish, his defiance of the law is forgivable, perhaps even estimable: "His clever refusal to take this monstrous society seriously is the best defence of the human spirit and the closest thing to a possible alternative to the system we have in this novel."[50]

However, Kincaid neglects to mention the Dodger's readiness to betray Oliver. The young pickpocket is perfectly willing to let others take the blame for his crimes, thus revealing himself to be just as self-seeking as characters like Mrs. Mann and Mr. Bumble, both of whom serve the very "system" that the Dodger is allegedly defying. Furthermore, when the Dodger is finally caught and put on trial, there is a dark subtext to his humorous swagger. His rebellious and witty repartee with the magistrate is evocative of Sam's cocky cockney interactions with Magistrate Nupkins and Sergeant Buzfuz in *The Pickwick Papers*, but it is also a disturbing indicator that the boy has been fully taken in by Fagin's romanticized view of the criminal world—he behaves exactly as Fagin predicts. His cheeky departure from the courtroom ultimately reveals that he "is Fagin's creature, a controlled role-player who revels in his own power and in the myth of criminality which he thinks will give him that power."[51] Neither the romanticized view of the thieves' den nor the parodist spirit of the Dodger's personality can save the young pickpocket from transportation.

Tellingly, the preternaturally ethical Oliver seems determined to forsake the Dodger's companionship from the moment they meet. Whereas the musical immediately emphasizes a burgeoning friendship between the Dodger and Oliver, the novel depicts Oliver as being inherently suspicious of the Dodger and his intentions so as to underscore the title character's incorruptibility: "Under this impression, he secretly resolved to cultivate the good opinion of the old gentleman as quickly as possible; and, if he found the Dodger incorrigible, as he more than half suspected he should, to decline the honour of his farther acquaintance."[52] The absence of such suspicions in the musical allows "Consider Yourself" to unfold as a purely celebratory production number.

More generally, as in the case of Fagin, Bart's Dodger is more likable and sympathetic than his novelistic predecessor, and this is partially because the ideals promoted by the two characters diverge significantly. Dickens's Dodger is a staunch proponent of criminality as a way of life, memorably lecturing Oliver on the joys of being a "prig" and eagerly striving toward the infamy of famous thieves who have been hanged or transported. Conversely, although Bart's Dodger employs a similarly parodist worldview, this parody manifests itself primarily through musical expression; "Consider Yourself" promotes community as opposed to criminality. The romantic celebration of the *Newgate Calendar* is replaced with a romantic celebration of East End culture, and the Dodger's parodist behavior in "I'd Do Anything" belies the genuine affection that he feels for Nancy and Fagin. The gentler and more affirmative values of Bart's Dodger underscore his softening of the boy's main teacher, Fagin.

The first appearance of Fagin is lifted directly from the novel, with the old man roasting sausages over the fire. In the original novel, the image of the bearded, red-haired man—described by the narrator as "a very old shrivelled Jew [with a] villainous-looking and repulsive face"[53]—standing before the flames and holding a toasting fork is obviously evocative of traditional representations of the devil, and the novel's version of the character comes close to living up to this diabolical reputation. However, Bart's version of the character will prove himself an entertaining showman and Jewish den mother, as opposed to a conniving devil and anti-Semitic stereotype. Indeed, the "maternal" element in Fagin was essential to Bart's conception of the character:

> His physical image and demeanor should be that of some kind of zany chicken, with red hair and beard sticking out spikily awry, out from his bright eyed face. [...] This chicken-like figure of a man—a mother hen protecting the little villains and pick-pockets who are his chicklets; sometimes with mock violence; sometimes with a matriarchal quality, at which moments he becomes a brooding hen.[54]

Fagin's introduction thus brings into focus what, as noted above, is arguably the most significant change that Bart made to the Dickensian source in writing *Oliver!*

Nevertheless, critics have overemphasized the contrasts between Bart's Fagin and his literary forebear, at least from a thematic standpoint. Fagin and the Artful Dodger steal every scene in the musical, and the two characters oftentimes manage to do likewise in Dickens's novel. The chapters set in Fagin's den are undoubtedly the most entertaining in the story, and the conviviality of Fagin's hideout is inestimably more alluring than the misery of the workhouse. Kinkaid writes that "[a]s it is first introduced, Fagin's world is, in almost every way, a distinctly positive contrast to the one Oliver had known. It provides a release from misery, starvation, and, most important, loneliness. [...] It is certainly better to be a thief than to be alone: the whole emotional force of the novel has made that clear."[55] In spite of (or perhaps because of) their harsh cynicism, Fagin and his followers are defined by a "vigorous and persuasive life-force."[56] Dickens captures this life force through Fagin's repeated emphasis on food and drink, his dynamic storytelling abilities, and his unwavering influence over his charges, while Bart uses music-hall songs and performance styles to convey the old man's vivacity.

Fundamentally, Dickens's Fagin possesses a captivating energy. It is his energetic personality that makes him so dangerous, however, for the criminals in his gang are all drawn to him (in spite of his physical repulsiveness). Whereas the grim certainties of the workhouse are reinforced by the tyrannical board of directors and the horrid matrons like Mrs. Corney and Mrs. Mann, Fagin injects romanticism and humor into the thieves' den, blinding his charges to the realities of their situation. Even Oliver, who is the embodiment of pure goodness, begins to fall under Fagin's spell, as he finds the old man's stories and games enthralling. Though the workhouse is permeated by a deathly sense of exhaustion and exploitation, Fagin instills the thieves' den with a hedonistic vigor that masks his own exploitative tendencies.

Bart successfully captures the dynamism of Dickens's character through music while simultaneously reducing his cunning, villainy, and wickedness to the point where they are virtually nonexistent.[57] Though purists have decried such modifications to Dickens's dark and dangerous portrait of the underworld, they have neglected the fact that the lively and celebratory elements Bart incorporates into his adaptation are actually detectable—if darkly subtle—components of Dickens's original work. Fagin's showmanship is thus in keeping with his literary predecessor, and it comes through most overtly in "Pick a Pocket or Two," which seems fitting as this Fagin number has the clearest textual basis.

Notably, every single item that Fagin places on his person is removed through some sort of visual gag: two of the boys play hopscotch to steal his spectacle case; another boy pretends to have something in his eye, and as Fagin bends down to assist him, the boy removes his watch; a group of the boys draw Fagin's attention toward something in the sky and as he looks away, one of them steals his handkerchief; the Dodger and Charley use a game of leapfrog to steal another case from his back pocket.[58] The fact that the boys use their own variations on traditional pranks and games while stealing Fagin's possessions highlights the notion that the thieves' den revolves around music and play. Equally important to the music-hall element of "Pick a Pocket or Two" is the manner that Fagin assumes when playing the game with his pupils. The prompt book notes that "Fagin straightens fingerless mittens, smoothes moustache, takes walking-stick & pushes nose in air."[59] Fagin is mockingly assuming the airs of a gentleman, and like the working-class patrons of a Victorian music hall, Fagin's boys take delight in the satirical spectacle.[60]

Though Fagin has successfully created a boisterous and vital community by imaginatively transforming his den into a makeshift music hall (complete with gin, songs, dances, and satire), he has not fully shielded the boys from the dangerous truths of their "vocation." His morbidly funny verse at the end of "I'd Do Anything" hints at the potential consequences of getting caught: the gallows. The verse is taken humorously by the boys, who unwaveringly profess that they will still "do anything" for Fagin. Then again, their willingness to assume such a risk on Fagin's behalf hints toward the potentially exploitative elements of their relationship with their mentor. In the novel, the irredeemably wicked Fagin is tickled by the fact that many of his colleagues and protégés have been sent to the gallows while he has remained safe thanks to their unwillingness to "peach" on him.

Bart's Fagin seems incapable of such callousness. His next major song, "Be Back Soon," hints at the risks that the boys will face while "on the job" but simultaneously avoids any discussion of their potentially getting caught. In "I'd Do Anything," Fagin sang of hypothetical scenarios, but now that the boys are actually setting off to "work," Fagin refuses to even consider thoughts of "the drop." Instead, he unreservedly assumes that the group will "be back soon." As in the case of its immediate predecessor, there is an underlying satirical quality to the song; yet here again the loving sentiments behind the lyrics are steeped in a genuine affection. Moreover, though Fagin and the boys sing two different melodies in counterpoint, they impressively end on the same phrase: an indication of the sense of unity and community that defines the thieves' kitchen.

Unfortunately, whatever Fagin's hopes, Oliver will *not* be back soon, though it is Fagin's behavior after the orphan's arrest that complicates the favorable portrayal of the Dickensian villain. In Act II, Fagin's determination to get Oliver back stems from self-interest. He does not want Oliver back in the gang because he thinks it the best place for the child; nor does he bother to consider that Oliver may be better off with Brownlow. Oliver's happiness never enters into Fagin's assessment of the situation, and though Oliver violates the code of the thieves' kitchen by internalizing the middle-class values of Bloomsbury, Fagin is the first to violate this code by acting in his own self-interest.[61]

Although Fagin and the Dodger's behavior throughout Act II complicates Bart's positive vision of the criminal characters, it never fully compromises this vision. In the novel, Oliver must endure physical and mental abuse from Fagin on returning to the thieves' den. The only abuse he is subjected to in this scene, as written by Bart, is verbal taunting from his peers. Moreover, Fagin's most important song, "Reviewing the Situation," is set up by the hysterical confrontation between Nancy and Sykes, a confrontation that revolves almost entirely around Oliver. Much as Oliver awakens Nancy's conscience, he seems to exert a potent effect on Fagin, for the old man is tempted to begin "reviewing the situation" only following Oliver's kidnapping and his potential mistreatment by Sykes.

Like "As Long as He Needs Me" and "Where Is Love?", "Reviewing the Situation" is a private and personal song. However, while "As Long as He Needs Me" and "Where Is Love?" both have a textual basis given Bart's insight into the motivations of Nancy and Oliver as they were written by Dickens, "Reviewing the Situation" is purely a creation for Bart's Fagin; Dickens's "merry old gentleman" would never consider leaving the criminal underworld, for Dickens's character is defined entirely by this lifestyle. Conversely, Bart's Fagin has severe misgivings about certain elements of the criminal way of life, most obviously the violence it necessitates. Fundamentally, Fagin's conflicted desires, as expressed in "Reviewing the Situation," reveal his lack of control over his own destiny, a lack of control that is analogous to Oliver's passivity and Nancy's self-deprecation. Oliver is vulnerable and lonely because of his poverty and lack of family. Nancy is vulnerable and lonely because of her masochistic love for Sykes. Fagin is just as vulnerable and lonely because of his status as "other": the Jewish motifs of the song, as described in the previous chapter, serve to underscore the notion that Fagin would be willing to live a different life, but the fact that he is a Jew would undoubtedly inhibit him from finding much support or success in most of these endeavors.

Therefore, the desire of all three of the lead characters to find love becomes more discernible. Just as Nancy is faced with the impossible choice between Sykes and Oliver, and Oliver is faced with the impossible choice between Bloomsbury and Fagin's den, Fagin is faced with the impossible choice between redemption and isolation. To redeem himself, Fagin must forsake the family he has created and renounce the thieves' kitchen. In contrast to Oliver and Nancy, however, Fagin maintains a firm commitment to the use of music-hall conventions. Whereas Nancy and Oliver both deviate from the music-hall motifs that dominate the score when singing their introspective solo numbers, Fagin continues to use music-hall standards in "Reviewing the Situation." Though it is a private number, Fagin treats it as though it were public, throwing out several rhetorical questions to the audience and justifying himself to them via comic patter. In keeping with the aforementioned emphasis on control, the song repeatedly threatens to escape Fagin's control, as his vision of a redemptive alternative becomes increasingly unfavorable and untenable while the melody accelerates.

However, the number also conveys Fagin's wiliness. In spite of the ostensible lack of control over his own destiny, it is Fagin who sets the pace for the song, as the orchestra follows his lead throughout the patter sequences. Similarly, when Fagin asks who will "change the scene" for him, the Kenny set actually transforms before the audience's eyes. Tellingly, two systems of omniscience—musical and technical—bow to Fagin's will in this song, thus hinting that the old man has more power and autonomy than he lets on. Still, his ability to transform a private reflection into a public music-hall song ensures that the audience will take his side, for he is too entertaining and endearing for us to judge him.

Bart astutely holds off on giving Fagin a truly private and reflective moment until the very end of the show, when the old man has lost everything. The breaking up of the gang in the final scene will mark an end to the merry music-hall motifs and a true moment of transition for Fagin, though sadly he has not been allowed to choose his own destiny. Rather, the choice is made for him when the gang is dissolved by outside forces. Fagin noticeably drops his music-hall persona, as his reprise of the first measures of "Reviewing the Situation" cuts off before the comical, music-hall patter begins. However, the Jewish recitative and cantorial singing remains prominent, as does the violin cadenza, which dominates in a haunting fashion.

Whatever the anti-Semitic roots of Dickens's Fagin, a reviewer at the *Jewish Chronicle* commended Bart and Moody for their reinvention of the character; notably, the critic traced various elements of their Fagin to the Yiddish theater and to Jewish musical traditions:

Introduced by Lionel Bart's heartbreaking violins in a Chassidic nigun of his own inspiration, Moody tells the audience that he has to make a living. [...] But it is in his other song, 'Reviewing the Situation,' also strongly reminiscent of the shtiebl, that the audience wildly demanded 'more.' 'Reviewing the Situation' is a long megillah in which Fagin weighs up the pros and cons of continuing his present mode of existence or turning over a new leaf. [...] This combination of Bart-and-Moody, two young men endowed with that special sweet-sour Jewish talent, is to be seen and tasted for oneself.[62]

The critic's citing of the nigun and the shtiebl reinforces the religious dimension to Fagin's songs, though given Bart's own interest in the music of the temple, and more-over, the influence of the Jewish faith and culture on both the Yiddish theater and the music hall, this is hardly surprising. Jack Gottlieb takes the matter even further, stating that "'Reviewing the Situation' [...] has its roots in a Hebrew chant. Called Havadalah (Separation), it comes from the ceremony that bids a bittersweet farewell to the Sabbath."[63] The idea of Fagin's song being tied to a bittersweet chant about separation is striking, given that the final reprise of this number at the very end of the show will indeed mark his separation from the Dodger, the boys, and the life he has lived up to this point.

Music Example 5.2 *Oliver!* musical score, 134

As noted in Chapter 2, Bart anticipated Fagin's beginning a redemptive journey, one that might very well lead him to the Holy Land. However, rather than end the play with the Jewish strains of the violin, the orchestra closes with a subtle allusion to "Who Will Buy?" (see Music Example 5.2) This succinct repetition of the "who will buy?" phrase implies a certain parallel between Fagin's fate and Oliver's fate: Oliver, now the ward in an upper-middle-class household, has embraced the philosophy of "Who Will Buy?", and if Fagin is indeed going to turn over a new leaf, it will likely mean adopting the same middle-class values as opposed to the music-hall values of "Consider Yourself" or "It's a Fine Life." As in the case of Oliver's fate, there's a sense of melancholy and loss here, for it is doubtful that Fagin's new lifestyle will embody the vitality and communal showmanship of the thieves' kitchen. On the other hand, Fagin's new journey begins just before dawn, and an optimistic sunrise awaits him. Though the unashamedly cheerful ending of the film adaptation ultimately proves more uplifting (see Chapter 7), the poignant and ambiguous ending more effectively links Fagin's journey to Oliver and Nancy's journeys, reinforcing the thematic connections between these three love stories.

THREAD 4: MR. BUMBLE AND MRS. CORNEY'S "LOVE STORY"

Mr. Bumble and Mrs. Corney are less prominent characters than the central players in the previously described love stories, though they nevertheless afford some much needed levity throughout the musical. From a thematic standpoint, their love story is the most straightforward, perhaps because neither one actually cares for the other, though before I discuss this relationship in detail it is worthwhile to address Bart's successful use of music in the comical satire of the beadle. Bumble's introduction, which instantly follows "Food, Glorious Food," is presented solely through musical underscoring, specifically through a repetition of the "Oliver" phrase on the "fat" notes of the bassoon.[64] The musical score fittingly features "pomposo" as a notation for Bumble's introduction, thus capturing the self-importance of the beadle's personality. Bumble intonates a brief and ironic blessing over the boys' dinners, a blessing analogous to the "long grace [...] said over the short commons" in Dickens's novel.[65] Notably, Bumble inverts the traditional blessing—"For what we are about to receive"—by instructing the boys to be grateful for what "you" are about to receive. The fact that Bumble puts the blessing in the second person places the prayer in an interesting context, for Bumble is not partaking in the gruel himself. Clearly, this fat beadle has been indulging in far more substantial viands. Though Bumble is instructing the boys in humility and self-denial, these are qualities that he sorely lacks. Like the "God Is Love" sign, it is a fundamentally hypocritical sentiment. Here, Bart undermines the power of the workhouse overseers by adding levity to the workhouse scenes, though unlike Dickens, who adopts a similarly satirical strategy, Bart relies on the orchestral narration as opposed to the narrator's commentary.

The most significant scene between Bumble and Mrs. Corney is the parlor scene, which sets up their main duet, "I Shall Scream." Like many similar scenes from the early Victorian adaptations of *Oliver Twist*, this courtship sequence is used for comic relief; the cynical "love song" quickly becomes a bawdy comedy sketch as Bumble forcibly gets Mrs. Corney to sit on his lap, and Mrs. Corney ends up burying Bumble's face in her "ample bosom."[66] The final thread of Bart's love theme is therefore the most comedic, and simultaneously the least loving, as Bumble and Mrs. Corney's relationship is not based on any genuine sense of affection. If Oliver's love theme revolves around the search for idyllic love, and Nancy's love theme revolves around the dangers of dependency in an abusive relationship, and Fagin's love theme revolves around the complexity of adoptive-familial love in the face of societal isolation, then Bumble and Corney's love theme is centered squarely on the comedic elements of superficial love. It is therefore unsurprising that their "love" proves the least enduring.

Whatever their lack of feeling for one another, their duet is clearly a courtship song, as a give-and-take flirtation evolves over the course of the number. Bumble moves from hand holding in verse 1 to pinching in verse 2, before finally getting Mrs. Corney to sit. Her coyness at an end, Mrs. Corney manages to gain control of the song in the middle of the second chorus, when Bumble himself takes up the "I shall scream" phrase at the prospect of Mrs. Corney sitting on his lap indefinitely. Pressing her advantage, Mrs. Corney takes the lead in the last verse. Her later dominance of her husband is appropriate, given her ability to dominate what was initially his song.

The Bumbles' brief reappearance in Act II serves a twofold purpose in supplying some humor during the more serious second act and in advancing the inheritance plot, though the latter point seems something of an afterthought; without Monks to drive this element of the story, the revelation of Oliver's birthright feels somewhat less important. Furthermore, the Bumbles are less culpable from a criminal standpoint as they do not actively participate in a conspiracy against Oliver.[67] In keeping with Bart's premise regarding the theme of the adaptation, their worst sin is not obscuring Oliver's birthright but failing to show Oliver love (as epitomized by their selling him, which is what prompts Brownlow to castigate them). The marital unhappiness of the Bumbles likewise reveals the results of their selfish kind of "love." When feelings of affection are limited to materialism and physical indulgence, there is no chance of attaining the kind of love that Oliver, Nancy, Fagin, and the boys strive toward.

CONCLUSION

Just as *Oliver Twist* is open to myriad interpretations, *Oliver!* presents many opportunities for analysis regarding the presentation of the Dickensian characters in a musical context. Such readings can likewise initiate enticing discussions about novelistic versus musical narratives and the discursive methodologies for presenting such narratives. Perhaps the greatest triumph of *Oliver!* relates directly to the culture text of *Oliver Twist*, and the fact that the show has resonated with so many people throughout the world has placed it at the forefront of *Twist*ian adaptations. The next chapter focuses on the transatlantic success of *Oliver!* while simultaneously addressing the divergent responses of American and British critics to Bart's musical. It also presents an account of the global popularity that *Oliver!* attained during its initial West End run.

CHAPTER 6

Ↄᚢↄ

Traveling Far and Wide: *Oliver!* Abroad

New York was the most obvious international market for *Oliver!*, but Donald Albery and Lionel Bart perceived that their Dickensian musical had the potential for global fame from the outset of its triumphant West End debut. However, exporting *Oliver!* was complicated by the creative team's desire to eventually produce a profitable film adaptation. Both Bart and Donmar had a significant stake in the prospect of a film version, though the success of the film would depend on a receptive global market. International productions of *Oliver!* thus required careful planning so as to avoid "tainting the waters" before the film adaptation could be realized.

"THE NEXT *MY FAIR LADY*"

Another justification for Bart and Albery's caution in exporting *Oliver!* is the sad fact that the first foreign production of *Oliver!*, a Swedish production at the magnificent Oscars Theatre in Stockholm, was an unequivocal disaster. This staging was meant to be one small part of a larger Scandinavian tour conducted by Lars Schmidt, a renowned Swedish impresario. Previously, Schmidt had achieved great success by importing *My Fair Lady*; Lerner and Loewe's musical had broken Stockholm records, playing for more than 750 performances. The idea of cultivating *Oliver!* as "the next *My Fair Lady*" extended to the casting, as renowned Swedish actor Jarl Kulle, who had played Professor Higgins in the earlier show, was set to play Fagin.[1]

Oliver! debuted in Sweden on September 13, 1961. Eight short weeks later, Schmidt wrote to Albery confirming that the Swedish production had bombed with both audiences and critics and had thus been shut down on October 22, at a significant financial loss. It had played for just forty performances.[2] From the beginning, prospects had seemed bleak. A foreign correspondent at the *Times* noted the chilly reception of the Swedish audience on opening night, writing that "the production as a whole is described as poor and unengaging by the Stockholm critics, in no way comparable with the London one."[3] In his letter to Albery, Schmidt blamed the debacle on cultural differences: "The main reason why they did not like 'Oliver' [*sic*] is that we don't have a Dickens tradition in Sweden, there are no slums, no East End, and the Cockney dialect does not mean anything to us. Of course, there were some faults in the production, but that was not the main reason. The press was very severe about the play."[4] Schmidt's determination to shift the blame from the Swedish production to the cultural issues surrounding the property seems incredibly dubious, particularly in light of the fact that these same issues had not impeded the success of *My Fair Lady*. Nevertheless, Schmidt echoed the abovementioned sentiment in a letter to Bart, explaining that "we don't know anything about the East End. Furthermore, we don't have a Cockney dialect and this sounded a bit of a construction in our language."[5] He likewise noted that the attempts to market the show around its connection to *My Fair Lady*—if any such connection actually existed—had failed, though Schmidt denied that he had purposefully tried to build the marketing campaign for *Oliver!* around its successful American predecessor: "Everybody expected another 'My Fair Lady' and although the publicity before the opening gave every indication that we were not coming in with a similar show, the critics started with the same phrase, that is to say 'this is not a new 'My Fair Lady'."[6]

Schmidt's letters reveal a curious dichotomy regarding the question of *My Fair Lady*'s relation to *Oliver!*, as his assertion that the cockney idiom and East End subject matter of *Oliver!* were incompatible with Swedish tastes belies the fact that cockney language is central to the very core of *My Fair Lady*. Still, *My Fair Lady* is less grounded in cockney culture than *Oliver!* Lerner and Loewe's score is more traditional and romantic, while the songs from *Oliver!* are fundamentally defined by the traditions of the East End. Furthermore, though *My Fair Lady*'s libretto stands among the greatest books from the golden age of Broadway, it lacks the violent and disturbing elements of *Oliver!*; ironically, by "raising the stakes" of the English musical's libretto, and thus catapulting the West End musical into the realm of the Broadway musical, Bart alienated traditionalist European audiences. The Swedish theatergoing public seemed hesitant to accept a musical that dealt with poverty, abuse, crime, and murder.

The divergent responses of the Swedish and English theatergoers who experienced *Oliver!* confirmed that several of *Oliver!*'s defining qualities, such as its working-class Englishness and its grittiness—qualities that epitomize the show's connection to the movements that defined the postwar British stage—did not necessarily transfer effectively to other cultural contexts. In the larger scheme of things, the failure of the Swedish production meant very little. A few short weeks after the Swedish premiere, another production opened in Australia to great acclaim. An undated telegram from the Australian producers boasted "Oliver [*sic*] successfully launched. Production Outstanding. Cast Splendid, Grand Reception. Excellent Press."[7] This 1961 Australian production performed admirably in both Melbourne and Sydney, and a revival in 1966 scored equally favorably with Australian critics and audiences. Nevertheless, the dichotomy between the responses to the first two foreign productions of *Oliver!* was a clear indicator to Albery that Donmar should proceed carefully, particularly in non-Anglo countries. *Oliver!* could be transported to Australia and not lose anything in "translation"—much as Dickens's Artful Dodger retained his trademark cockney cheek in the face of his own journey to Australia—but the repackaging of the show for non-British audiences was fraught with complications.

The Stockholm disaster convinced both Bart and Albery that stricter oversight of foreign productions, at both a conceptual and a production level, was a necessity. In a reply letter to Schmidt, Bart astutely noted that "we must learn from this, and have a great deal more pre-discussion when we intend to recreate a show."[8] In the same letter, Bart hinted that future attempts to produce *Oliver!* abroad might benefit from the involvement of the London creative team. Donmar eventually took a more hands-on role in the execution of foreign productions.

Albery's personal correspondence over the course of his supervision of the licensing and staging of foreign productions of *Oliver!* repeatedly displays a prudent sense of discretion. The impresario was willing to green-light foreign productions only if the producers agreed to proceed according to Donmar's standards. In many cases, this meant using some sort of variation on the Kenny set and John Wyckham's lighting scheme, as well as Coe's blocking—a difficult prospect, given the complexity of the show's scenery. As a result, Albery turned down numerous requests for foreign productions by small-scale foreign theater troupes, for many of these groups would not have been able to handle the intricate technical elements of the production. Though this technique prevented the owners from capitalizing on several foreign markets, both Albery and Bart remained focused on the overall global market for their nascent film adaptation. In a response to a letter inquiring about a Zambia production, Albery explained that "to get the production of 'Oliver!' right is a very delicate thing, so much depending upon the scenery and lighting with the kind of set used in the English production."[9] A letter to a Russian producer contains an almost identical response, as Albery maintained that Bart was equally insistent regarding the preservation of the original artistic vision for the show: "The author's view is that he only wants the play done abroad within the framework of the present production."[10] Donmar could not always commit to providing the necessary supervision for foreign productions, and many inquiries to produce *Oliver!* abroad were flatly rejected.

Initially, Bart was highly selective regarding which countries would receive permission to produce the show. Though German producers tried to acquire licensing rights for *Oliver!* soon after its West End debut—and continued to campaign for these rights in the years that followed—Bart categorically refused to approve a German production.[11] Numerous letters preserved in Albery's files reveal that Bart was resolute about this matter: "Lionel is still adamant about not presenting the show in Germany and you might tell the gentleman in question that 'no' is the answer."[12] Though none of these letters explain why the composer was so determined to prevent *Oliver!* from reaching the German stage, it seems fairly obvious that Bart was worried about the issues surrounding Fagin, particularly in light of the disastrous German release of David Lean's film adaptation (see Chapter 1). Even though Bart's version of Fagin was far-removed from Guinness's interpretation, the potential for anti-Semitic misinterpretations (or misrepresentations) of the character was high. As will be discussed later in this chapter, Bart's own frustrations with Ron Moody's portrayal of the character reinforce this point. Furthermore, there was no escaping the anti-Semitic literary roots of the character.

Bart's Jewish heritage may also have precluded his granting permission for a German production of his beloved musical. Georgia Brown later revealed that "[s]he [had] no interest in performing inside Germany 'Not after the millions of Jews....' And yet, since Lotte Lenya, it is doubtful that anyone has sung Kurt Weill in the original as effectively as Miss Brown does in her London records album."[13] Though Brown could have attained great success singing in German cabarets, and though Germany was clearly a viable market for *Oliver!*, the wounds of the Second World War were still fresh and painful. Bart's unwillingness to compromise on this matter, whether the result of personal issues or professional concerns, reflects a sense of conviction that has oftentimes been overlooked in posthumous assessments of the composer's character; one of the unfortunate by-products of the larger-than-life elements that have since been ascribed to Bart's life story is that they have obscured the genuine and very human qualities of Lionel Bart, the man.

Nevertheless, Bart became generally less cautious regarding the global productions of *Oliver!* in the years that followed, and several of his letters to Albery in 1965 reflect a growing frustration with the fact that Donmar was not taking advantage of potential foreign markets:

> Over the past couple of years we have had a number of enquires, as you know. I don't think that sufficient care or enthusiasm have been applied to these offers. I am sorry to appear to adopt such a reproving attitude, but I do feel that there is no firm organisation behind the world-wide presentation of 'Oliver!', certainly not when you compare it with the smooth manner in which 'My Fair Lady' has been handled all round.[14]

Albery was understandably annoyed and pointed out that Bart had been just as wary regarding these matters: "As far as I know, the only enquiries we have had of what I would call a substantive nature are Israel, Japan and Germany, where you refused to allow the play to be performed under any circumstances."[15] In his reply letter, Albery went on to note that the set for *Oliver!* made foreign productions of Bart's show much more complicated than global tours of *My Fair Lady*, while the tone and content of the adaptation were perhaps less "transcendent" than the defining characteristics of the Lerner and Loewe musical. "Strange as it may seem, 'My Fair Lady', albeit a large scale production is nevertheless conventional from a scenery and lighting point of view and can easily be re-created from plans," Albery explained. "'Oliver!' is a much more delicate property and is not indestructible like 'My Fair Lady.' It cannot be expected to meet with universal approval throughout the world."[16] Albery's comments comparing *Oliver!* to *My Fair Lady* in terms of its overall resonance, and more particularly his insistence that *My Fair Lady* had a greater capacity for widespread appeal, reinforce the earlier points regarding the disparate kinds of Englishness presented in the two works. Clearly, the disastrous Swedish production was still etched in Albery's memory, and he feared that similar debacles in more prominent territories would further hurt the chances of creating a successful motion picture adaptation.[17]

OLIVER! IN ISRAEL

In spite of the continuous hesitation on the part of the show's creators regarding the global tour of *Oliver!*, Donmar licensed several international productions over the course of the 1960s. Cultural differences were still an issue, however, and perhaps one of the most interesting results of sending *Oliver!* abroad involved the different cultural considerations that had to take place regarding the response to various characters or situations in the play.[18] Such considerations were fundamentally important to the staging of *Oliver!* in Israel. As early as the fall of 1960, Israeli producers expressed an interest in the property,[19] and the notion of a Hebrew production seemed natural given Bart's emphasis on Jewish musical motifs.[20] Bart was intrigued by the prospect of an Israeli production of *Oliver!*, as he had previously expressed the idea to an Israeli journalist, Raphael Bashan.[21] Still, launching the original Broadway production proved consuming, and Bart thus put off the negotiations for an official Israeli production until 1964. Bart agreed to license the production for the Habimah Theatre in Israel on the basis of the following clauses: a 6 percent royalty of the gross weekly box office receipts, first-class airfare from London to Tel Aviv (and back again) along with living expenses for a weeklong trip to Israel to see the show's debut, and a statute regarding the size of his name in comparison to the title.[22] As was the case with many of the previously licensed international productions, Albery and Bart stipulated that "[t]he production must be presented exactly the same way as it is now playing London, possibly with minor changes which might be found impossible to produce in Israel, but these must be very minor points."[23] To assist with this particular provision, Peter Coe was hired as the director.

The role of Fagin was taken up by the Polish-born Jewish actor Shraga Friedman. Understandably, Friedman chose to downplay the darker elements of the character; Moody had made Fagin sympathetic if not lovable, but Shraga took the matter even further, giving him "even more warmth and sympathy, making the rogue veritably amiable."[24] In spite of these modifications, Bart was still concerned about the ramifications of staging the adaptation in Israel. By this point, a film deal was already on the table with Romulus Films, and Bart wrote a detailed letter to Albery explaining his fears that a negative reception in Israel would invariably hurt the movie. To that end, Bart resolved that if the Israeli response to Fagin proved unfavorable, the character would have to be rewritten for the film: "I would like to confirm that the Israel opening gets as much world-wide publicity as possible, and that this should be done in conjunction with the Columbia Public Relations group. [...] If, however, the Israeli public decide to picket the play, we will just have to make FAGIN a Scotsman for the film."[25] The idea of Fagin as a Scotsman seems so absurd that one wonders if this ridiculous suggestion was simply a sardonic joke on the part of the composer, though given Bart's obsessive determination to curtail accusations of anti-Semitism, along with his increasingly erratic behavior in the buildup to the *Twang!!* debacle, it is quite possible that he was in earnest. If audiences were unable to pick up on the sympathetic qualities that defined his interpretation of the character, then Bart was willing to abandon Fagin's Jewishness entirely rather than see it misinterpreted or misappropriated with disastrous results.

Fortunately for Bart and everyone else involved, the show was not picketed in Tel-Aviv. However, it was not embraced either, and Anne Jenkins eventually concluded that the show would not prove profitable in this particular territory: "I don't think it has really been a great success there."[26] An Israeli correspondent with the *Times* asserted that

> [t]he benign portrayal of Fagin the Jew in Lionel Bart's musical *Oliver!* [...] has been sharply attacked here by critics representative of the generation of Israelis reared in a free and normal Jewish society. They conceded that enlightened European societies with guilt [sic] feelings about Christian cruelties to Jews might balk at portraying Fagin as fiendishly as Dickens had created him. But if the crook could not be portrayed faithfully, they wrote, perhaps he should not be portrayed at all.[27]

The idea of Jewish critics advocating "fidelity" to the source, in spite of the fact that the source contained gross anti-Semitic stereotypes, seems paradoxical, though it is understandable why Jewish theatergoers might balk at Bart's attempt to "whitewash" Fagin. Furthermore, the Jews who experienced *Oliver!* at Habimah were, as the newspaper noted, a "new breed of Israelis raised in the free milieu"[28] of the independent Israel. They were understandably—and justifiably—a proud people, and they resented the idea of a sympathetic Fagin for the same reason they objected to sympathetic interpretations of Shylock; such interpretations "appeared to reflect the complexes and insecurity of the persecuted Jews in European ghettos."[29] Bart's Fagin was far less anti-Semitic than Dickens's or Lean's, but the idea of depicting him as a noble yet helpless "wandering Jew" in the final moments of the play may ultimately have rendered him an even more abhorrent stereotype. In spite of these issues, the fact that the general Israeli public did not formally protest the musical was a victory in and of itself.

OLIVER! IN JAPAN

Japan was arguably the most unique destination for the touring production of *Oliver!* in the initial years of the show's existence. As early as 1964, producers in Japan were discussing the possibility of staging the show in Tokyo. In a letter to producer Michiko Serkine, Albery expressed his belief that the difficulties involved in creating a Japanese version of *Oliver!* were negotiable:

> I certainly think that the only possible solution would be to have a Japanese translation and a Japanese company but to use a reproduction of the original British scenery, costumes, and lighting and for the play to be directed by an English director with an English choreographer working in collaboration with Japanese colleagues. I also think that [...] it would be necessary to have a pproduction [sic] manager from here as well.[30]

Bart disagreed with Albery's method and felt that the best way to stage the show in Japan would be to have an English touring production travel to Tokyo instead.[31]

It was not until 1967 that a concrete plan regarding a Japanese production of *Oliver!* actually began to emerge, for Albery and Bart resolved to wait until the West End production of *Oliver!* had closed; the hope was that the original West End set could be dismantled and shipped to Tokyo's Imperial Theatre.[32] This plan ultimately proved unfeasible, however, as the wear and tear on the Kenny set precluded its being used in Japan.[33] Instead a set from one of the foreign tours made the journey east, which was beneficial in the long run given that the touring set was bigger than its West End predecessor and thus suited the large space of the Imperial Theatre. This same set eventually proved vital to the very survival of *Oliver!*, for when Cameron Mackintosh staged the all-important touring production/Albery Theatre revival in the late 1970s, he used the very same set; as he explained to the press, "it would have cost an impossible £100,000 to build [the Kenny set] from scratch."[34] Amusingly, when the production team on the 1977 revival unearthed the set in a warehouse in Leicester, "it was all wrapped in newspapers from Tokyo, 1967."[35]

Much as the Japanese set had previously "toured," it was eventually decided that a touring production of *Oliver!* made up of an international cast would travel to Tokyo.[36] One of the leading forces behind the Japanese production of *Oliver!* was Nobuko Uenishi, who would earn a prominent reputation in the Japanese theater for her skillful work in importing Western shows to Japan (and who would become Lady Albery following her marriage to Donald Albery several years later).[37] Acting under the instructions of her boss and mentor, the great Japanese impresario Kazuo Kikuta—who had a personal fondness for Dickens's novels and a personal sense of kinship with the character of Oliver Twist—Nobuko set about the arduous process of organizing the original Japanese production of *Oliver!*[38]

Though Japan was "famous for its own traditional theatre" the postwar era witnessed the country turning "more and more towards Western dramatists."[39] Furthermore, Western musicals were becoming increasingly popular in the East, as shows such as *Hello, Dolly!*, *My Fair Lady*, and *Fiddler on the Roof* opened in Tokyo in the 1960s. In spite of the cultural differences between Britain and Japan, Uenishi believed that *Oliver!* had great potential in Tokyo, in no small part because "the Japanese love Dickens."[40] Kikuta's unbridled passion for the musical, and the novel that inspired it, testified to this fact.

Casting the Japanese production proved an international experiment for Albery, who was eager to borrow cast-members from several global productions:

> We are now making some progress and have agreed to bring Robin Ramsay back from Australia to play the part of Fagin. We are also seriously considering having Maura Wedge as Nancy. [...] The reason we suggest this casting is that none of the Nancys whom Nobuko thinks were any good here are able or willing to come. We propose to engage Willoughby Goddard, an Englishman who played Bumble in New York, and I am afraid that this, at the moment, is as far as we have got.[41]

For the child parts, Albery turned his attention to America. Ultimately, two American children, Darel Glasser and John Mark, would share the title role.[42]

Among the younger cast members in the production was an American actress and singer, Linda Purl, who was living in Japan at the time and who was thus the only member of the child chorus not brought over from the USA.[43] Recalling the Japanese interest in the project, Purl reflects that "Japan has a very vibrant cultural sensibility, and vast theatergoing audience, and I think in the 60s there was a big appetite in Japan for things from the West. It was an emerging economy, much like China today. They were looking to explore everything they could from the West. So there were a lot of artists that came to perform in Japan."[44] Purl had previously starred as Helen Keller in a production of *The Miracle Worker* and was studying at the Toho Theatre Academy when she was offered the part of Bet. In spite of the fact that this production of *Oliver!* necessitated the collaboration of British, American, and Japanese creative forces, Purl fondly recalls that the process was best described as a "merging" of cultures as opposed to a "clash." Unfortunately, the fact that the adolescent cast members were all Americans meant that the older British actors were introduced to that terrifying and singularly American entity known as the "stage mother."[45]

Like many of the Western musicals that preceded it, *Oliver!* proved a hit in Tokyo. An article in the July 22, 1968, edition of *The Yomiuri*, a prominent Japanese newspaper, reported that "[t]he Imperial Theatre, which has a capacity of 1,840 was sold out for the last two weeks of the Oliver [sic]."[46] Purl speculates that the positive response to the musical reflected the general Japanese appreciation of childhood. "I think it's safe to say there's a fascination with youth in Japan," Purl claims. "It's a quality that is cherished and in that sense *Oliver!* went over extremely well in Japan. There were two young boys that performed Oliver. They alternated and they were wildly popular in Japan during the run of Oliver; they were like rock stars. [...] The children [in *Oliver!*] pull at your heartstrings so strongly, and that's something that the Japanese are willing to do, not in a public setting but certainly in the theatre."[47] As a result of the Japanese production's success, the show's international reputation was furthered significantly—a promising situation given that the film version of *Oliver!* was set to open worldwide at the end of the year. Notably, the film adaptation of *Oliver!* was an enormous hit in Japan, where it "amassed one of the biggest advance sales [...] in Tokyo's picture history."[48] In light of the cultural traits outlined by Purl, it is not surprising that Mark Lester, like the two stage Olivers who had preceded him, was embraced by the Japanese public.[49] More generally, the success of the Japanese production foreshadowed the international success of the film adaptation.

OLIVER! ON BROADWAY

Naturally, the most significant international market for *Oliver!* was the United States, and the original Broadway production of *Oliver!* would test the musical's transatlantic appeal. From early on in its development, the Broadway version of *Oliver!* was surrounded by tremendous interest and excitement. Albery's initial communications with the legendary American producer David Merrick, which actually preceded the West End debut, were indicative of his confidence in the property (see Chapter 2). It is doubtful that he would have sought out Merrick's help in finding a director if he did not believe that the show had the potential for success in both the United Kingdom and the United States.

These early communications indicate Albery's assurance that Merrick would play an instrumental role in transferring *Oliver!* to Broadway. Just two weeks into *Oliver!*'s West End run, Albery wrote to Merrick so as to tout the phenomenal success of the show:

> Everything continues apace with 'Oliver!'—business and publicity absolutely wonderful, audiences still cheering, etc. The whole thing seems quite unbelievable. The music publisher told me that they sold more copies of the sheet music of 'Oliver!' last week than all the other publishers of all the other sheet music put together. It seems quite incredible but that is what he said.[50]

If the excitement over a Broadway production of *Oliver!* was enticing to many American investors, it was equally enticing to British theater aficionados: it was the first time that an English musical was being met with such fervor from American investors. An article in the *London Evening News* boasted that "[w]hen this musical crosses the Atlantic to Broadway the money taken at the New Theatre will seem like peanuts by comparison."[51] This bold declaration was yet another crow of victory on the part of the English press, as the notion of the Broadway community taking such an active interest in an English musical was cause enough for celebration.

Albery's faith in Merrick was well placed given that Merrick had already achieved a reputation for supervising the American importation of several West End shows, and an equally prominent reputation for producing Broadway musicals.[52] Merrick was also a shrewd marketer, and some of his promotional techniques have become the stuff of Broadway legend. Granted, *Oliver!* did not need much hype to begin with. The show's reputation preceded it.

Still, not all of this interest was positive. Amongst certain factions in the American press, the fascination with *Oliver!* was roughly equivalent to the thrall that surrounds any imminent disaster. In an article for her "Voice of Broadway" column, the notorious American journalist Dorothy Kilgallen dryly opined that "[q]uite a few Americans won't understand why Mr. Merrick decided to import an anti-Semitic show in the first place."[53] An outraged Bart wrote back to Kilgallen shortly thereafter, asserting that "[a]nybody that can call my show anti-Semitic is either an idiot or a yuchner. (Yuchner is Yiddish for a muck stirrer). All the important Jewish organizations, such as the B'nai B'rith in England, California, and in fact anywhere 'OLIVER!' has appeared, have had only high praise for my treatment of the story."[54] Though Bart's Jewish/cockney cheek, as revealed in his letter, seemed the perfect means of defending his interpretation of Fagin—especially when one considers that these same elements of his own personality defined both his Fagin and his adaptation—Kilgallen was hardly the only journalist to express reservations about *Oliver!* due to the controversial history of the source. American critic Bob Thomas wrote an article whose very title posed a question that weighed heavily on both Bart and Albery: "Will U.S. Fans Cheer Dickens in Musical?" Thomas noted that although *Oliver!* had been "hailed as the best the English musical stage has had to offer since the war [...] it is still

Dickens and that means heavily-plotted, thickly accented material that may evoke American curiosity if not enthusiasm."[55] The skeptical tone of his article, in contrast to Kilgallen's, is centered less squarely around the content of the show and more on its status as an English musical, as the author inadvertently reveals the condescending attitude that defined the response of several American critics to *Oliver!* Thomas makes the snippy observation that "there is no real dancing [in *Oliver!*]"[56]—a trademark critique of English musical theater—and likewise notes that "Adam Goldberg of the Los Angeles Times cites these differences: 'The English take their tea with milk; Americans prefer lemon and sugar. Approximately, this is the difference between the English type of musical show, as exemplified in 'Oliver' [*sic*] [...] and the familiar American brand.'"[57] Goldberg's curious tea-time metaphor seems to imply that English musicals were lacking in flavor, another indication of the American skepticism toward the very notion of English musical theater.

Even British columnists who were eager to see an English musical achieve success on Broadway were uncertain as to *Oliver!*'s transatlantic appeal; they were likewise prone to using the same foreboding headlines put forth by their American counterparts, as Patricia Lewis of the *Daily Express* wrote a piece titled "I Forecast: Trouble on Broadway for 'Oliver!'" Lewis predicted that the show would "reap a wild wind of controversy" in that "Americans are more race-conscious than the British, and where the broad, heavily accented Jewish playing of Fagin here receives laughs, it may well be misconstrued as anti-Semitic on Broadway."[58] Lewis's critique highlights a unique rebuttal to the aforementioned American jingoism, as her own cultural criticism reveals the English contempt for America's juvenile "priggishness" in matters of race and culture. The idea that any American offense toward Fagin would stem from misinterpretations as opposed to genuine offense is a somewhat patronizing viewpoint. Whatever the cultural biases reflected in both of these columns, it is clear that many observers in both Britain and the United States were incredulous regarding the potential American responses to *Oliver!*

Such concerns were unfounded, as *Oliver!* proved a hit in America before it reached Broadway. Following its first tryout in Los Angeles, the show moved on to San Francisco, and then played in Detroit and Toronto before finally opening in New York the first week of 1963. By the time it reached New York, *Oliver!* had already recouped its production costs.[59] Furthermore, the reviews throughout the pre-Broadway tour were highly encouraging; Stanley Eichelbaum of the *San Francisco Examiner* noted the enthusiastic reception of the show in California, citing the "cheering, feverish excitement" of opening night and labeling the musical a "staggeringly wonderful British musical. By any standards of enjoyment, the show is a phenomenon—one that more than lives up to its advance reputation as the sensation of the London decade."[60] Paul Speegle of the *San Francisco News Call Bulletin* was equally generous with his praise, declaring the show a "smasher" and citing its unique, creative vision:

> The dark and dismal story of the boy who had the temerity to ask for more gruel has been converted into a yarn which is by turns, sprighlty [*sic*] and disarming, violent and disturbing. Under Peter Coe's bold direction and through the ingenious employment of a turntable stage designed by Sean Kenny the action is continuous. The

audience [...] doesn't have time to luxuriate in contemplation. Something is going on all the time—and all of it is wondrously theatrical.[61]

Much of this success can be attributed to the strength of the property in and of itself, though the hard work of the American production team contributed significantly to the piece's positive reception.

Nearly all of the production elements from the original West End staging, including Sean Kenny's designs and Peter Coe's blocking, were incorporated into the Broadway version. Nevertheless, Merrick would exert a definite influence on *Oliver!*, an influence that manifested itself largely through the efforts of Donald Pippin, the show's conductor and arranger. Pippin, who would go on to serve as musical director on several hit Broadway shows including *Mame* and *A Chorus Line*, had worked with Merrick previously on *Irma La Douce*.[62] Though somewhat lacking in experience, Pippin was especially eager to serve as the musical director for *Oliver!* owing to his fondness for Bart's score:

I remember very well the first time I heard *Oliver!* In those days you could only get English recordings on the black market. Therefore, somebody had brought it back from England and I heard it. I was captivated by the honesty of the music and the score and the lyrics. I'd read the story of *Oliver Twist*, and I was very familiar with the story, so to hear what they were doing with the story fascinated me.[63]

Pippin thus pursued the position despite Merrick's secretary having tried to dissuade him by pointing out that "every big name Broadway conductor was after this score. But I said, 'Get me an appointment, let me hear him say no'."[64] Pippin would later recall his intimidating interview with Merrick:

He looked like the devil without horns. [...] I said 'Mr. Merrick, I'd like to be musical director of that show.' He was so stunned, this great man. He looked up at me, amazed that this young guy—literally a nobody—would actually ask him that. He knew me because I'd been the assistant with *Irma La Douce* that he had brought over, but I was only the pianist. He said 'Why should I give the show to you?' Because I was so innocent then, I said, 'Because I love the show, I love the score, I love the music, I love everything, and nobody could do it as well as I can.' He was so taken aback by this forwardness. And he said to me, 'All right, I'll give you this show, but you'd better be as good as you think you are.' The night that I won my Tony for that show, he put his arm around my shoulder, and said 'You're as good as you thought you were!'[65]

Pippin's fondness for the property ensured that the American production of *Oliver!* would adhere closely to its West End forebear, and the young conductor was meticulous in prepping for *Oliver!*'s transatlantic journey. This prep work included visiting London to experience the show in its entirety: "I studied everything about the show, the pacing of it. The children sort of frightened me; I thought, how are we going to get kids to do that? [Still] I left feeling like I really had a good handle on it."[66] For Pippin, the show's greatest asset was its "intimacy," for in spite of the complex plot and the groundbreaking revolving set, the overall feel of the musical was personal: "It's a large story but it's told in a very intimate way."[67] Furthermore, the music-hall quality of the score necessitated an "intimate" approach to the production.

This intimacy presented certain difficulties for Pippin, however, as Merrick was eager to make the show bigger. In London, *Oliver!* had been performed with a small orchestra of only thirteen instrumentalists. However, the union contract for the Imperial Theater required the hiring of twenty-five musicians, all of whom had to be paid whether or not they performed. In his biography on Merrick, Howard Kissel, a prominent Broadway critic, dryly observes that the impresario "was not in the habit of paying anyone to do nothing,"[68] and so the show's original orchestrator, Eric Rogers, set about rewriting Bart's music for a larger ensemble. Pippin, however, was "dedicated to the smallness" of the show, and therefore decided to keep some of the instruments silent at various moments in the play before gradually bringing them in for crescendos, ultimately creating "a widening effect. During climaxes, you had the orchestra across the entire pit coming in, rather than just the thirteen pieces in the center of the orchestra."[69] Pippin thus managed to sustain a "stereophonic effect"[70] with a live orchestra.

Arranging the music for *Oliver!*'s American debut was a labor of love, but Pippin likewise had to undertake the challenging task of rehearsing the score with the child performers. "These were not professional kids," recalls Pippin. "They all had ambitious mothers who wanted them to be stars. They all had a Madame Rose. They had very short spans of concentration. They grasped the language very fast, though. We would sit and drill; we wouldn't be singing we'd just be reciting 'Food, Glorious Food,' getting a slight cockney accent on things and rounding out certain vowels."[71] Pippin maintains that even though the cockney accent came far more naturally to the West End boys, the child performers in the United States were ultimately "better actors. The kids in London sang better than ours but they didn't have the acting abilities of ours."[72] Working with the children naturally demanded patience, particularly during the rehearsal period in San Francisco as the beautiful California weather left the boys eager to get out and play. Though Pippin was willing to end rehearsals early, he found his authority challenged by a particularly rebellious young cast member who posed the age-old adolescent question that has plagued countless babysitters: "Why do we have to listen to you?" Rather than give the customary, "Because I said so" response, Pippin found an alternative means of persuasion: "I looked down at him and said, 'Because I'm bigger than you.' And it worked. We had no more trouble."[73] From that point on, Pippin bonded well with the young cast members and was somewhat awed by how quickly they took to the material, though his patient tutelage contributed to their successful retention of the words and music.

One child who benefited greatly from Pippin's guidance was Bruce Prochnik, the young English actor cast in the title role; like so many of his fellow Olivers, the thirteen-year-old faced the inevitable "puberty problem." Pippin vividly recalls that in the middle of a performance of "Where Is Love?" during the San Francisco engagement, "[Bruce's] voice cracked [...] and he was so embarrassed."[74] With the actor's father back in England, Pippin admirably sought to fill the gap during this period of

development, helping the young actor cope with the reality of his physical maturation and the more immediate issues regarding his vocal performance: "I said, 'Now,
we're going to start vocal lessons to help you lighten your voice so you don't push on
it.' I taught him how to use what would later become a falsetto voice as he became
more mature. And so, we made it to New York without a problem."[75] Pippin's tutelage
ensured that Prochnik would be able to stay on with the show.

If dealing with the children required a fair amount of patience on Pippin's part,
dealing with Merrick was, at times, equally exhausting. Like Pippin himself, Merrick
"was so in love with the show; he was nervous about it, he wanted it to be the most
successful thing that'd ever been done."[76] This desire led to micromanagement on the
part of the producer, though the promotion of *Oliver!* would test his creativity given
that New York was in the midst of a newspaper strike. Merrick thus turned to radio
and television, running on-air ads and using testimonials from preview audiences. It
was a fairly revolutionary strategy, though Merrick believed that the positive word
of mouth surrounding *Oliver!* would more than compensate for the inaccessibility of
the newspapers. Pippin recalls that, in the end,

> he was absolutely right about word of mouth selling the show. Back then, you called
> the box office direct; you didn't go through Telecharge. The box office said that after
> our second preview, the phone was ringing off the hook; they couldn't answer all the
> calls. The word of mouth was selling that show. All the pre-publicity on that show
> was fantastic, and Merrick was pretty smart to keep reports coming in before the
> strike; he fed information on what was going on on tour, the grosses it was making,
> the reviews that were happening, and so he spread a lot of information about the
> show way before we came to New York and obviously it worked.[77]

Bart was less thrilled with several of Merrick's marketing ploys, however, partially
because they fueled his own nervousness regarding the New York reception of the
property: "We sort of crept into the West End, but we came to Broadway with lots
of advance ballyhoo and I didn't feel right about it."[78] The composer was particularly
turned off by one of Merrick's craftier techniques. During the Broadway ad blitz,
Merrick appeared on WNEW radio as a "guest reviewer" and unhesitatingly labeled
Oliver! "the greatest musical of all time, a truly great classic of the theatre, transcendent, unique, incomparable, prodigious, stunning."[79] Bart was understandably embarrassed when the producer went so far as to dismiss *My Fair Lady* and *Oklahoma!*,
labeling them as inferior to *Oliver!* "It was untrue and impolite," Bart told an interviewer, "and I'm now spending a lot of time trying to undo the impression Merrick
created."[80] Still, there was no arguing with the success of Merrick's strategies, and
there is perhaps no greater indication of *Oliver!*'s revolutionary nature, nor of its phenomenal popularity, than the fact that it broke records on both sides of the Atlantic.

Oliver! formally debuted on Broadway on January 6, 1963. *Camelot* and *Carnival!*
had closed the day before, while *How to Succeed in Business Without Really Trying* was
in the middle of its impressive four-year run and *A Funny Thing Happened on the Way to
the Forum* was nearing its one-year anniversary. Fagin thus found himself flanked by
two equally conniving yet loveable American-born counterparts in J. Pierpont Finch

Figure 6.1: Broadway producer David Merrick used every marketing trick in the book to ensure *Oliver!*'s success on Broadway; he is pictured here with Bruce Prochnik, who originated the title role in New York.
Source: Photofest.

and Pseudolus. Of the two, the latter seems more analogous to Bart's Fagin given that both characters had roots in a longer literary and dramatic tradition, though Pseudolus could trace his pedigree all the way back to Ancient Rome. Moreover, the emphasis on Jewish humor in the conception of the two works and in the acting styles of the original performers was vital to the success of both productions. Several British brethren were also playing Broadway when *Oliver!* arrived, most notably the minimalist, allegorical West End musical *Stop the World—I Want to Get Off*, Robert Bolt's acclaimed drama *A Man for All Seasons*, and Dudley Moore and Peter Cook's uproarious sketch comedy show *Beyond the Fringe*.

Oliver! quickly proved to be a Broadway smash, and its popularity continued into the following year. After twenty months at the Imperial Theatre, *Oliver!* transferred to the Shubert in September 1964 and wrapped with a total of 774 Broadway performances, thus making it the longest-running English musical in the history of Broadway up to that point in time.[81] The show also received three 1963 Tony Awards: Bart won for best score, Kenny won for best set design, and Pippin won for best conducting and musical direction.

FIDELITY STRIKES BACK: *OLIVER!*'S AMERICAN RECEPTION

The response to *Oliver!* among Broadway audiences was clearly positive. However, the critical reaction in New York was less overwhelmingly affirmative than it had been in London. Indeed, the mixed feelings that some American critics had toward *Oliver!*

convey a certain protectiveness and uncertainty that stands in sharp contrast to the celebratory patriotic pride that many English theater critics took in the West End debut of *Oliver!* The fact that this uncertainty seemed to manifest itself primarily in the response to *Oliver!* as an "unfaithful" adaptation of a Dickensian novel makes the situation all the more intriguing.

Time and *Newsweek* were both especially critical of the literary facet of the musical, with the critic from *Time* asserting that Bart had "blue-penciled out the socially conscious harshness of Dickens and mauve-penciled in the timeless hokum of Showland."[82] The reviewer claims that the first sight of the workhouse orphans is misleading, for the moment they begin "Food, Glorious Food"

> the audience knows that nothing painful, nothing honest, nothing real will be inflicted upon it. In *Oliver* twisted, the Thieves' Kitchen becomes an urban Sherwood Forest, with Robin Hood Fagin teaching his pickpockets to rob from the rich and give to the deserving poor—themselves. The grim workhouses, stews and drinking dens of London become playgrounds for boys with a taste for adventure.[83]

The *Newsweek* critic was equally hostile toward the literary elements of *Twist* as reimagined in *Oliver!*, claiming that all Bart's adaptation offers is "a hurry-up plot synopsis, clashing with Dickens only in the character of Fagin. In place of the sinister old professor of pickpocketry who at the novel's end is dragged shrieking to the gallows, Bart's Fagin is a naughty old Santa Claus who slinks off, at the last curtain, vowing to turn over a new leaf."[84] Various Broadway critics followed this same trend of criticizing the musical for its divergence from the Dickensian source. John McCarten of the *New Yorker* noted that the musical "contains none of the pathos and the sad regard for humanity that the Master introduced into his novel. Instead, it seems bent on demonstrating that hunger, poverty, and oppression can be fun,"[85] while Howard Taubman of the *New York Times* lamented that "there is a deep chasm between the musical, 'Oliver,' [sic] and Charles Dicken's [sic] 'Oliver Twist.'"[86]

The fidelity criticism offered by many American critics during the initial Broadway run of *Oliver!* may have been a convenient (and diplomatic) means through which to express frustration with all of the hype surrounding *Oliver!*, an English musical that attained unparalleled success in the United States. Tellingly, those American critics who embraced *Oliver!*, like their English counterparts, chose to ignore the fidelity issue. Furthermore, many of these positive reviews expressed an appreciation for the new strides that the English were making in the realm of musical theater. The contrast between the negative, fidelity-based reviews, which seem openly hostile to *Oliver!* as both a Dickensian adaptation and, more subtly, as an English musical, and the positive, hospitable (for lack of a better word) reviews offered by other critics is striking.

The patriotic and nationalistic response of many English theater critics to *Oliver!* thus found its doppelgänger in the response of those American critics who resented the "foreign" show on principle. An article printed in the *Times* in June 1963 noted that American critics were growing wary of the "British encirclement of Broadway,"[87] a reaction matched by several actors and Broadway artists; a revue show produced at the Plaza Hotel featured a chorus sardonically singing about the desire to see *Oliver!* close and return home to England.[88] The idea of an English show becoming the hottest ticket on Broadway was clearly discomfiting to many traditionalists. In 1984, when Cameron Mackintosh attempted a Broadway revival of *Oliver!*, the *New York Times* critic Frank Rich was infinitely less diplomatic: "Until Andrew Lloyd Webber's hits started to roll off the assembly line in the 1970's, Lionel Bart's 'Oliver!' held the record as the longest-running English musical ever to play Broadway. I'm afraid that this distinction says more about the quality of other English musicals than it does about the merits of 'Oliver!' "[89] This lack of diplomacy extends to Rich's general treatment of Lloyd Webber, and Jessica Sternfeld has chronicled the "feud of a rather personal nature" that arose between the two men in the 1980s.[90] The eighties Broadway revival of *Oliver!* may have been "collateral damage" in the larger war between the New York theater critics and the English forces behind the megamusical movement.

Pippin dismissively asserts that the negative, fidelity-based critiques that greeted the original Broadway production were rooted in a certain intellectual insecurity among the New York critics. He reflects that American critics are "academic" in their basic approach: "What they're trying to prove is that 'I read Dickens, I know his book, and [*Oliver!*'s writers] didn't follow his book.' They're letting you know how brilliant they are."[91] His nonchalance is understandable given that the negative reviews did nothing to impede the show's success—another indication of *Oliver!*'s status as a forebear to the megamusical. As Sternfeld notes, "[c]ritics, in the case of the megamusical, largely ceased to matter."[92] Ironically, the very same musical movement that *Oliver!* portended would ultimately help to further weaken the significance of New York theater critics' reviews; the triumph of the English megamusical proved that a show could thrive on Broadway even in the face of bitter censure from the New York critics' circle.

THE DE-SEMITIZATION OF FAGIN ON BROADWAY

Contrasting the American and English responses to *Oliver!* reveals several interesting trends, but one of the factors complicating any such comparison is the fact that New York audiences did not experience the exact same show as London audiences. Assessing the English reaction to the Broadway production of *Oliver!* is therefore useful for providing further insights regarding the adaptation's transatlantic shifts. In the aforementioned article printed in the *Times*, the paper's New York drama critic reflected on the cultural differences between *Oliver!* in the West End and *Oliver!* on Broadway. The English critic noted that "the most tangible change is the taming of Fagin. [...] As played by Ron Moody in London, Fagin was livelier, more sinister, and slightly Jewish if mainly Cockney; in New York, Clive Revill's Fagin is milder and all Cockney."[93] Comparing the original cast recordings of the West End and Broadway productions, one can immediately detect significant divergences in the performances of the two actors. Moody's intonation conveys a decidedly Yiddish inflection pattern—most noticeably during "Pick a Pocket or Two"—to the point where the actor once joked that "it was suggested on most nights save Fridays that I might apply for a cantorial post in the local synagogue."[94] Though not as overtly ethnic as Alec Guinness's Fagin, Moody, like Guinness, pronouncedly presents Fagin's Jewishness. There is a bit of a lisp in the pronunciation of his s's, and his vowels are similarly "ethnic." In "Pick a Pocket or Two," Moody purposefully uses a nasal voice on the last repetition of the main phrase in each of the verses, making the lyrics sound something like the words to a comical Jewish folksong: "two" is pronounced "tuoy"; "pick" is pronounced "peek", etc. Revill does not incorporate any of these devices into his performance and, as the *Times* critic noted, is "all Cockney."

Though Moody had contributed heavily to the musical's success in the West End, with many critics labeling his performance as the highlight of the show, the question of his playing Fagin on Broadway proved incredibly contentious; this was due to conflicts between the actor and Lionel Bart—conflicts that had emerged long before the Broadway production took shape. Bart, who had been hesitant to cast Moody in the first place, was put off by the performer's tendency to improvise, and moreover by what he perceived to be the unruly elements of Moody's performance style. On December 13, 1960, nearly six months into *Oliver!*'s West End run, Bart wrote Albery a long letter detailing his concerns about Moody's Fagin. Part of the composer's frustration related to his contention that the actor was taking too many liberties with the character.[95] Of particular concern for Bart was the fact that several of Moody's improvisations accentuated Fagin's Jewishness.

There are no overt references to Fagin's Jewishness in Bart's libretto. Furthermore, in the absence of Dickens's narrator, who incessantly refers to Fagin as "the Jew," there is no way of knowing for certain that Fagin is Jewish. Reflecting on his original conception of the character in anticipation of the film adaptation, Bart noted that "FAGIN [. . .] should not be portrayed with anything approaching Dickens's ghetto-like image of a Jew. [. . .] He has lived in London all his life. He is therefore a Londoner. His dialect, accent and argot and language should be that of a London cockney (i.e. Stanley Holloway, Frankie Howard)."[96] Nevertheless, Bart always envisioned the character as perceptibly Jewish, as is evident from his incorporating Jewish motifs in Fagin's theme music and solo songs: "The melodies of his songs are quite sufficient to tell us the background of his heritage, without the use of any accompanying Jewish gesture, attitude or verbal inflection."[97] This somewhat "schizophrenic" interpretation of Fagin as straight-theater cockney and musical Jew can be rectified through the music-hall element that bridged the cultural gap between the two facets, and the idea of confining Fagin's Jewishness to his musical expression seemed a positive way of substituting a subtle cultural celebration for a vulgar anti-Semitic stereotype.

Though Moody was more than capable of balancing the diverse cultural traits that Bart outlined for Fagin, he was simultaneously eager to experiment with the comic facets of the Jewish character and push them beyond the scope of what Bart had intended. In his letter to Albery, Bart complained that Moody's performance would hurt the chances of the show's succeeding abroad; so strong were Bart's feelings regarding the interpretation that he went so far as to label the performance anti-Semitic despite the fact that Moody was Jewish: "Since we first opened and received all those fabulous notices, Moody's performance has become increasingly more aggressive and anti-semitic [sic]."[98] Retrospectively, Bart's case seems somewhat weakened by the fact that none of the major English newspapers that covered *Oliver!* over the course of its run commented on any anti-Semitic undertones (or overtones) within the production. Tellingly, the *Jewish Chronicle* put forth an overwhelmingly positive review in which they singled out Moody's performance as the best part of the show:

> Yet, outshining even the brilliance of the composer is the interpreter, Ron Moody, as 'Fagin.' This is a Fagin Dickens never knew, no despoiler of young boys, no evil chef concocting knavery in the thieves' kitchen, no avaricious Jew. This is Ron Moody, with Groucho Marx's loping walk, enveloped in a voluminous caftan and wearing a mad, red wig. This is the most lovable scamp of them all: not *the* Fagin, but *a* Fagin direct from the pages of Israel Zangwill or the boards of the Yiddish Theatre. [...] This is the Fagin of Ron Moody and deservedly, it stopped the show.[99]

The reviewer at the *Chronicle* appreciated Moody's ability to humanize the Dickensian character; he also appreciated the fact that Moody's performance reflected the conventions of the Yiddish Theatre (which, as noted in the previous chapters, had unique connections to English music hall). Indeed, if Moody's performance was controversial, the only person who seemed to be taking any genuine offense in Britain was Lionel Bart.[100]

This lack of indignation on the part of the English populace may have been the direct result of the stage tradition in which Moody was working, which made such characters more palatable to the English public than they would have been to theatergoers in America. Nevertheless, Bart insisted that Moody's approach to Fagin would have disastrous consequences regarding any Broadway or film productions of *Oliver!*:

> One great American director, and one equally important American actor, (both Jewish), have told me that a Jew like this has not been seen on the New York stage for 30 years—not since the days of cheap burlesque. [...] My American friends predict that his performance of Fagin will be booed off the New York stage. That is, if the present mounting word of mouth does not get the show boycotted even before it arrives on Broadway. Do not underestimate the power of New York Jews—they banned the film 'Oliver Twist.' They can do the same with 'Oliver!'[101]

Bart was somewhat mistaken in his assertion here, as New York Jewish groups did not "ban" the David Lean film adaptation, though the premiere was delayed over the controversy surrounding the movie. Nevertheless, Bart's greatest fears seemed to relate back to the continued apprehension over a global market for the musical's film adaptation, as he warned Albery that "the *general tone* of Moody's present showing [...] is quite obviously doing us so much world-wide harm."[102] Of course, one of the chief ironies of the entire conflict is that although Bart was worried about Moody's hurting the potential for a receptive international audience, Moody would eventually star in the version of the musical that would reach the widest global audience: the 1968 film adaptation (see Chapter 7).

Bart's fears about Moody playing the role in New York may or may not have been justifiable, but his larger apprehensions regarding the global repercussions of the actor's performance were clearly exaggerated. However, even though Bart's Fagin is hardly a monster, there is no escaping the text (or the legacy) from which he emerged. Numerous actors who have taken up the character since Moody have fully adopted Bart's "cockney" conception of the character, though this has served to diminish Fagin's vivacity. Cameron Mackintosh has observed that "Lionel's inherent Jewishness is what makes his take on that story work so well. [. . .] [O]ne thing that I've noticed is that when people try to go against the Jewish rhythms that are in it, it doesn't work properly."[103] Moody's approach has proved integral to his longevity in the role.

Perhaps the most incongruous element of this controversy is that by writing a show that operated in the genre of the integrated musical but that included English music-hall motifs, Bart had fully merged Jewish and cockney elements; after all, the integrated musical format was largely a product of Jewish songwriters, composers, and writers. Jack Gottlieb notes, without hyperbole, that, "[w]ere it not for compos-ers and lyricists of Jewish origin, the touchstone classics of the American musical theatre would be nonexistent."[104] Many writers have traced the early influence of Jewish culture on American musical theater, but the connection continues even to the present day. Emanuel Rubin and John H. Baron both assert that many contem-porary musicals

> [have] elements that would have been accepted on Second Avenue in the 1920s: Jewish stories, with Jewish humor and Jewish characters reflecting Jewish modes of life and Jewish daily problems, and with some elements of Jewish folk and liturgical music. To a great extent, these Jewish elements were synonymous with what American musicals had come to be through the assimilation of Jewish artists and their audiences into American life in the first half of the twentieth century.[105]

Bart's work was likewise influenced by these elements given the importance of his own Jewish heritage to his creative vision. The fact that this contribution has not been acknowledged—much as Bart's own contributions to the evolution of the English musical have not received the full credit they are due—has served to limit the full scope of the Jewish cultural contribution to the modern musical theater. Given the overall importance of *Oliver!* to the development of the postwar musical theater in the West End, one could easily defend the assertion that Jewish culture and music exerted just as profound an influence on the development of the modern English musical as it did on the development of the modern American musical. Unfortunately, the contro-versy surrounding Fagin may have indirectly impeded this realization.

The situation is fraught with an almost tragic irony, particularly when one com-pares and contrasts *Oliver!*, the most important and successful English musical of the 1960s, with *Fiddler on the Roof*, the most important and successful American musi-cal of the 1960s. *Fiddler on the Roof* epitomized the Jewish influence on American musical theater and made that influence concrete. Baron and Rubin write that "[f]or the first time on Broadway, a Jewish story by one of the greatest Jewish story tellers (Sholem Aleichem), in a Jewish setting, including Jewish jokes and Jewish prayers with Jewish music, was presented to a general American audience, and everyone loved it."[106] Even if the Jewish elements in *Oliver!* are not as pronounced, one can detect several notable similarities in the background scores to both of these musicals, and there are moments where the musical arrangements in *Oliver!* sound as though they could be seamlessly transposed into *Fiddler on the Roof*. This similarity reinforces the impact of Bart's own Jewishness, and his knowledge of Jewish music and culture, on his conception of *Oliver!*, a fact that should theoretically strengthen the notion that *Oliver!* and the modern British musical theater are rooted in the very same traditions that helped to build Broadway. However, the key differences between the two sources of these revolutionary musicals have undoubtedly prevented this notion from taking hold. *Oliver!* was not taken from "a Jewish story by one of the greatest Jewish story tellers" but rather from a Victorian novel by an English author—a novel that presents a decidedly unflattering representation of its primary Jewish character. The anti-Semitic literary roots of Fagin have distracted from the celebratory elements of Jewish cultural traditions as represented by Bart's reimagined version of the character. The natural solution in recent revivals has been to remove the Jewish element entirely, thus ensuring that there will be no controversy over the character, though this tactic has simultaneously ensured the continued disregard for the fundamental importance of Jewish music to the redefinition of the West End musical in the postwar period.

The "de-Semitization" of Fagin for the Broadway production is not particularly surprising. Undoubtedly, a British musical that featured an indelicate portrayal of a Jewish character (who was based on an anti-Semitic character from a nineteenth-century British novel no less) would have been problematic on Broadway. Though Merrick was a master of turning bad publicity into good publicity, the Fagin situation had vexed him in the year leading up to *Oliver!*'s American debut. Even so, he unhesitatingly defended *Oliver!* against those American critics who sought to play the Fagin card against it, pointing out that "Fagin is written as a sort of Pied Piper character. Some Jews are offended, I know [...] but most of them are not—it's not offensive to me at all."[107] Nevertheless, Merrick, like Bart, had been worried about what the response would be if Moody reprised the role he had made famous in the West End. Pippin addresses this issue in one of the bonus tracks on the re-issued *Oliver!* Broadway cast recording:

> Again it was Merrick, he felt that it was too ethnic; it was going to be offensive in this country. We hadn't arrived—in `62—we were not at the point of accepting ethnic things the way we do today. We have made tremendous growth in those [areas] [...] And he was afraid it just would be objectionable. So he asked Clive Revill...to find a way to not do Fagin the way Ron Moody had done it in London. [...] I really preferred Clive's performance. [...] I found him not to be so overbearing. I found he had much more charm. I found he didn't put you off as much as the other approach, which might be more authentic in terms of history.[108]

Pippin's commentary reinforces the cultural and historical divide that inevitably contributed to Merrick's desire to recast the part, though in the end this casting decision may have been inevitable, as Moody had grown fed up with the very thought of going to Broadway as a result of the incessant conflicts with Bart and the management.[109] After leaving the West End production, the actor reflected that he would not have changed the performance for New York: "Yes, I gather there is a strong feeling in New York about the character, but if I had done it I would have resisted any attempts to change the way it's played. [...] The only alternative that I can see would be to make Fagin a cockney, but then that's got nothing to do with Dickens."[110] Moody's invocation and dismissal of the "Fagin-as-a-cockney" interpretation seems a subtle refutation of Bart's written description of the character, which may give credence to the idea that Moody was determined to play Fagin his own way—the Jewish way— from the beginning.

Fortunately, the inescapable controversies that continue to emerge at the very mention of Fagin's name did not prevent *Oliver!* from becoming a global hit; nor did they sully the international waters in anticipation of the film adaptation. As Bart happily reported to Charles S. Spencer of the Anglo Jewish Association, "[t]here is no negative reaction whatsoever from the Jewish community [in New York] to my Fagin; this in spite of the fact that not one word was changed from my original English production of Oliver!"[111] He simultaneously assured Spencer that when the film adaptation reached fruition, "the finest actor in the world" would take up the part.[112] Bart's letter is ambiguous as to whether he had a specific actor in mind—he had likely set his sights on Peter Sellers by this point—or if he was simply speaking with confident hyperbole as to his hopes for the casting of the role. Still, casting aside, the global reception of *Oliver!* bore testament to the transcendent appeal of Bart's music, as well as the transcendent appeal of Dickens's story about the orphan who asked for more. The success of the film thus seemed certain. The next chapter will chronicle this subsequent phase in the legacy of *Oliver!* Sir Carol Reed's motion picture adaptation would not only immortalize *Oliver!* on film but would also serve as an important resource when the creative team sought to "reboot" Bart's stage show for a post-megamusical West End revival.

CHAPTER 7

෴

"There were scenes in the David Lean film that were simply too painful": *Oliver!* from Stage to Screen to Stage

Lionel Bart perceived cinematic potential in *Oliver!* from the very beginning of the show's development, and when the film adaptation began to take shape in the mid-1960s, Bart understandably wished to assert control over the project. In an interview with Barry Norman at the *Daily Mail*, he firmly stated that "there's the question of artistic control which I insist on retaining."[1] Bart was particularly adamant about having a say in the casting, and the *Mail* eagerly embraced the wild rumors surrounding the lead roles. These rumors included Peter O'Toole as Fagin, Elizabeth Taylor as Nancy, and Richard Burton as Sikes.[2] Besides O'Toole, Peter Sellers and Danny Kaye were high on Bart's list of potential Fagins, though Sellers eventually emerged as Bart's top choice.[3] However, Bart would soon discover that translating *Oliver!* from stage to screen was hardly as simple as assembling a "dream cast."

A CONTROVERSIAL JOURNEY FROM STAGE TO SCREEN

The central contention over the production of a film version of *Oliver!* related to Bart's 1959 contractual agreement with Donmar. A clause in the contract obligated Bart to inform Donmar if he intended to pursue an offer regarding the film rights to *Oliver!* Donmar was "entitled within ten days from the date of such notification to submit to [...] Bart either a better bona fide counter-offer to purchase the Rights by a third party or themselves to offer to purchase the Rights on the terms of the original offer."[4] Under these circumstances, Bart was required to accept the "better bona fide counter-offer" as binding. Essentially, this contract gave Donmar veto power over Bart's choice regarding the rights to the motion picture adaptation.

Brookfield Productions, a company backed by Columbia Pictures, eventually made Bart an offer of $400,000 for the film rights, and Bart was eager to accept, primarily because the studio heads were willing to guarantee Sellers for the role of Fagin. Bart's faith in the Brookfield deal may have been misplaced, for despite the promise that Sellers would play Fagin, "there was no guarantee that he would be available and so Columbia's guarantee was worthless."[5] Sellers had recently suffered a severe heart attack, and the precarious state of his health seemed a serious impediment to Brookfield's being able to ensure his involvement. Bart was nonetheless determined to pursue the deal and thus instructed his theatrical agents at Montpelier Arts & Enterprises, Ltd., to sign the contract with Brookfield.

Unfortunately for Bart, Donmar took advantage of its veto option and countered with an offer from Romulus Films, a production company operated by Sir John and James Woolf. Not only were the Woolfs willing to offer more money, but Romulus was a more reputable and established company. Consequently, Donmar presented Bart with their counteroffer: "In pursuance of the said agreement dated 13th May 1964 and the 1959 Agreement the Plaintiffs on behalf of Romulus duly submitted to the Defendant Bart by a letter dated 13th May 1964 and addressed to both Montpelier and the Defendant Bart a bona fide counter-offer which was better than the said offer by Brookfield."[6] Astonishingly, Bart was unwilling to admit that this new offer was the "better" of the two deals, despite the fact that it would have meant more money for him personally. Instead of accepting Donmar's proposal, he stubbornly pursued the Brookfield contract.

It is fitting that the situation made its way to the High Court of Chancery, for the papers associated with the lawsuit read something like the innumerable documents in the Jarndyce and Jarndyce case of *Bleak House* fame. In Bart's view, since Romulus could not guarantee Sellers, their counteroffer had failed to meet the criteria set forth in the Donmar contract. Donmar and Romulus both found Bart's objections unreasonable. The question of what constituted a "better" offer was open to some interpretation, but basing such an interpretation solely on the criterion of who would be cast in the film's lead role seemed absurd.

Albery swore out an affidavit detailing a conversation with Bart and his own thoughts regarding the contention:

> [Lionel] stated that he had no objection to Romulus Films Limited or any particular relating to the offer except that he had been told that Brookfield Productions Limited would be able to procure the services of Mr. Peter Sellers and that he regarded this as so great an advantage that he desired their offer accepted. I pointed out that nothing in their offer obliged them to procure the services of Mr. Peter Sellers nor could they have undertaken such an obligation in view of the known state of his health and that [...] Romulus Films Ltd. would willingly employ Mr. Sellers for the role if he was available and his health permitted since they had already made two films with Mr. Sellers in star parts.[7]

Still, while Romulus was willing to pursue Sellers for the role of Fagin, Sellers himself was less open to that possibility. The actor was allegedly willing to play Fagin only if Brookfield produced the film, and yet another affidavit, filed by Jules Buck of Montpelier, revealed why: Sellers was a part owner in the company.[8] This disclosure only strengthened Bart's resolve to close the deal with Brookfield.[9]

Though the question of whether or not guaranteeing Sellers constituted a "better" offer was a central source of contention in the conflict between Bart and Albery, this issue was actually just one facet of a far larger debate regarding the role that Bart would play in the development of the film. In his affidavit, Buck asserted that "to the best of my knowledge, information and belief Romulus have had no discussions with Mr. Bart about the style or character of the film, and [...] they have not in fact given it any consideration at all."[10] For Buck, and for Bart himself, this was yet another indication that the Romulus option was not a "better" offer in spite of its larger financial guarantee: Brookfield seemed willing to adopt the composer's creative vision, while the producers at Romulus were determined to do things their own way.

The issue was settled fairly quickly, as the court passed an injunction preventing Bart from distributing the film rights to Brookfield. Though Bart was heavily involved during the conceptual stage of the production process and played an important role in revising several scenes and songs, the loss of Sellers was a severe blow to his creative vision for the film.[11] Nevertheless, the positive end results of the film that was produced in the wake of such confusion and contention are undeniable.

DIRECTION AND DESIGN: THE CREATIVE VISIONS OF CAROL REED AND JOHN BOX

Since the inheritance plot to *Oliver Twist* is built almost entirely around a string of strange coincidences relating to paternal legacies, it is fitting that Carol Reed was eventually selected to direct *Oliver!* Reed was the illegitimate son of the celebrated Sir Herbert Beerbohm Tree, who had played the role of Fagin on the London stage in J. Comyns Carr's acclaimed 1905 adaptation of *Oliver Twist*. Audiences responded to the play, and, more specifically, to Tree's Fagin, with great enthusiasm; a reviewer at the *Mail* who attended the opening night performance noted that "after the fall of the last curtain, Mr. Tree announced his intention of opening his autumn season with the same piece."[12] Tree's performance resonated so strongly that the character of Fagin eventually became something of a signature role. Reed's journey toward *Oliver!* thus allowed for the realization of a previously unclaimed paternal birthright, somewhat akin to the birthright that initially eludes Dickens's orphaned protagonist because of his own illegitimacy.

Reed's experience in working with children was a significant factor in his being put at the helm of *Oliver!*, and John Woolf would later write that his primary incentive in hiring Reed was the fact that he had made a "marvellous film [...] with the little boy, *The Fallen Idol*."[13] In the souvenir booklet published for the film's release, Reed noted that,

> I enjoy working with children. Of course it can be tedious, but it can also be exhilarating. The trick is to try to start off every scene with the child. That way the little

boy gets his lines over first, and the adult actors in the scene relax knowing that the boy isn't going to spoil the scene for them. Another trick is to do a child's scene over as many times as you need to without pausing in between takes. I just keep the camera running and gently tell the child that he's doing fine but just do it once more. [...] No it's not easy directing children but when it works out it's a film director's most gratifying moment.[14]

Reed understood that the dynamic between a director and a child actor was fundamentally different from the dynamic between a director and an adult actor, and his strategy for overcoming this divergence ultimately proved successful, as in the case of his previous films. In his review of *Oliver!*, critic Felix Barker asserted that Mark Lester's moving and memorable performance as Oliver Twist was at once evocative of Bobby Henrey's performance as Phillipe in Reed's early masterpiece *The Fallen Idol*.[15]

Though Reed's previous work with children boded well for a production that would feature a large number of child actors, translating the musical to the screen meant that one of the most critically acclaimed elements of the stage production would be lost, namely, Sean Kenny's set. Kenny's brilliant revolving construction was designed for the stage, not the screen, and *Oliver!* was not going to be filmed in a theater, but rather, on a soundstage at one of Britain's greatest movie studios, Shepperton. The acclaimed

Figure 7.1: Sir Carol Reed's experience and patience working with child actors proved essential when he undertook the task of directing the film version of *Oliver!*; he is pictured here with Mark Lester.
Source: Photofest.

English production designer John Box was tasked with devising the visual dimensions of the film, and working on a massive studio lot granted Box several unique opportunities that had been denied to Kenny because of the constraints of theatrical space.

Given its formalist qualities and its ability to transform in front of the audience, the Kenny set was not defined by any tangible sense of "realism" in regard to its representation of Victorian London, whatever its Dickensian starkness. Conversely, British singer Sir Harry Secombe, who played the role of Mr. Bumble in the film, noted that "[t]o wander round the outdoor sets was to be taken back in time. The recreation of early Victorian London was authentic down to the tiniest detail. There were even real loaves of bread in the baker's shop windows."[16] Similarly, the visual splendor of Dickens's story, as told in the film version, is more detectable, for it is unburdened by the practical functionality of the Kenny set; while the Kenny set shattered the traditional illusions of the theater through this same functionality, the Box set consistently perpetuates the illusion that the story is taking place in a heavily stylized version of Dickens's London. Though there are dilapidated street corners, fully stocked merchant tables, and Victorian shopfronts as far as they eye can see, there are also merry-go-rounds, elevated locomotives, and of course, a thieves' den that is set up more like an artist's studio or music-hall stage than a criminal hideout. This combination of squalor and splendor feels inherently Dickensian, and the "storybook" qualities of the Box set emerge all the more forcefully thanks to the vibrant staging of the film's musical numbers against these backdrops. The stylized realism of the musical's narrative thus found its counterpart in the stylized realism of Box's set, which likewise captured the stylized realism of the Dickensian source.

As will be discussed later in this chapter, the hyperrealist elements of the Box set may have contributed to the perception that Reed had "Disneyfied" Dickens, creating a "theme park" version of Victorian London (complete with a working carousel and monorail). Nevertheless, Box was widely praised for his artistry and eventually won the Academy Award for Best Art Direction. Whatever his loyalties to Kenny, Bart recognized the supreme achievement of the Box set and conveyed his support and enthusiasm to the designer. In 1968, he wrote to Box to inform him "how pleased I was with your evident attempts to make the film of 'OLIVER!' something special" and he went so far as to praise Box's production design as one of the two "most rewarding" components of the film (the other being Ron Moody's performance as Fagin).[17] The inevitable trade-off was that Box's set, though visually spectacular and incredibly detailed, simultaneously "demand[ed] far less imagination from the audience than Sean Kenny's."[18] This issue of sacrificing imagination for cinematic grandeur is prophetic given the megamusical makeover that *Oliver!* would undergo twenty-six years later when it was revived at the Palladium.

CASTING THE FILM: OLD (FAGIN) MEETS NEW

Many of Reed and Woolf's casting decisions were directly responsible for the success and longevity of the motion picture. Most obvious is the casting of Ron Moody as Fagin. In this matter, audiences will continue to owe a great debt to Woolf and Reed for decades to come, for by casting Moody in this part they managed to preserve on film one of the truly great character performances in the history of the stage musical. Moody sets the pace for the film in the same way that he dominated the West End stage, though the subtle complexity that Moody brings to the role, a subtlety necessitated by the shift from a theatrical medium to a cinematic medium, creates the opportunity for an even more rich, compelling, and haunting interpretation.

Understandably, the Jewish elements from the original West End portrayal are toned down. Aside from the obvious controversy that such a depiction would have created, an over-the-top stage performance would have come out poorly onscreen. Moody later commented on the different approaches he took when performing the role, pointing out that the overtly Jewish Fagin that he had presented on stage would not have worked under the "sharp eye" of the motion picture camera:

> I played it very Jewish on the stage, but we changed it for the film. My stage Fagin caused no uproar at all, but I didn't think he was right for the film and Sir Carol Reed, the director, agreed. He's not terribly Kosher now.
>
> It is a touchy subject; mention Fagin and a lot of people erupt.
>
> That was then and this is now. Attitudes have changed. I play him kind of mockingly because I think it's healthy for us to realize that what was once anti-Semitic is now best handled by a light approach. Sort of saying to people, 'isn't it rather amusing that things were once this way but now they're changed, Thank God.'[19]

Some critics have suggested that the film version of Fagin is more analogous to Clive Revill's interpretation—as seen in the original Broadway production—and even the souvenir booklet included in the special edition copy of the Broadway cast recording claims that "Moody's film portrayal of Fagin would be much closer to Revill's than to his own stage version."[20] This is taking the matter too far, for even though Moody does not use the same mannerisms and vocal patterns that he did onstage, there is still a slightly Yiddish inflection in many of the songs, along with the cantorial style of singing that grants Fagin his Jewish dignity. More importantly, Moody's distinctive energy and vitality are still very much intact.

Perhaps even more significant is the gravitas that he incorporates into the performance. Notably, Moody's film persona seems to have been far closer to Bart's initial conception of the character than the West End performance; as noted, in the aforementioned letter to Box, Bart revealed that he found Moody's performance to be the highlight of the adaptation.[21] Given their prior conflicts over the proper way in which to play Fagin, Moody was understandably gratified to have finally won Bart over, even if the composer did not express these sentiments to him directly.[22]

There is a powerful moment in the film where Oliver, who is about to go to sleep in the thieves' den for the first time, is helped into bed by Fagin. Fagin assists the boy with taking off his shoes and the two exchange a sympathetic glance. Moody then delivers Fagin's line about Oliver going on to become "the greatest man of all time." In the novel and stage play, this line is framed sardonically, as Fagin is already trying to convert Oliver to the gang's way of life by aggrandizing the criminal lifestyle. In the film, however, Moody's delivery is marked by his gentle inflection and compassionate sincerity, as though he foresees that there is something special in this child.

His words are prophetic given the destiny that awaits Oliver at the conclusion of the film. Fagin proceeds to sing Oliver to sleep by gently reprising the chorus from "Pick a Pocket or Two."

Moody commented on the poignancy of the scene in a retrospective special on the making of the film: "There's one moment where he sings a lullaby to Oliver [...] and Oliver looks up at him like that [...] and it's what they call rachmanis, pity. Look at these kids, these poor little waifs. At least I've given them a home. They're not up the chimneys or down the mines. They're warm, they're comfortable, they're smoking fags and pipes. What more could a boy want?"[23] Notably, various film critics likewise detected the power of the lullaby scene and cited it as one of the most significant moments in the entire film; Marjorie Bilbow wrote that "[Fagin's] eyes when he watches the sleeping Oliver hold a tenderness and a tinge of remorse that amazingly do not conflict with his crafty connivings."[24] Joseph Gelmis of *Newsday* took the issue even further, describing the scene as *the* vital moment in the adaptation:

> The exact moment in 'Oliver!' at which I realized just how good a movie musical it was going to be was at the end of a long, long shot of Fagin watching his new pickpocket recruit, Oliver Twist, undress for bed. As the camera held the shot long past any functional purpose it served in the action, one began to grow uneasy with the suspicion that perhaps Fagin was a lecherous old man. Suddenly, like a revelation, the passive, thoughtful expression imperceptibly seemed to be the tender look of a man tucking his child into bed for the night. And the tone of the film was set in a poignant flash: Fagin was a father figure to this troop of little lost beggars.[25]

Moody's film version of Fagin is certainly more willing to take on paternal dimensions that are less noticeable in the original stage play, and the bond between Oliver and Fagin, which can be revealed very clearly on film thanks to Reed's ability to use close-up shots, more openly emphasizes the central theme of love. In the film, we can truly accept Bart's contention that Fagin, in his relationship with Oliver, the boys in his gang, and, most notably, the Artful Dodger, loves and desires to be loved. Bart may very well have been picturing Sellers when he assured Charles Spencer that the film would cast "the finest actor in the world" in the part of Fagin, but the plain truth is that Carol Reed found the finest Fagin in the world in Ron Moody.[26]

Whereas Moody reprised the stage role that he had made famous, newcomer Shani Wallis, who had worked mainly in cabarets and musical revues, took over the part of Nancy.[27] Wallis had recently appeared on Broadway in John Morris's underrated musical *A Time for Singing*, which closed after only forty-one performances; however, she performed the number "Let Me Love You" on the *Ed Sullivan Show*, thus drawing the attention of *Oliver!*'s producers.[28] Though the actress's talents as a vocalist were undeniable, the production team was somewhat concerned that the young, wholesome Wallis might not be able to portray the more earthy and low-class Nancy. Indeed, Wallis's clean-cut persona and youthful vibrancy may have ultimately prevented her from achieving the staying power of her stage predecessor. Several critics found her performance "tame" in comparison to Brown's, primarily because the assertiveness and world weariness that Brown brought to the role complemented the harshness of the Dickensian story (and more specifically, the Nancy-Bill subplot).[29] An anonymous reviewer at *Time and Tide London* observed that Wallis seemed "a trifle refined for Nancy as though she has to remember to drop her h's,"[30] and Eric Gillibrand summed up the feelings of several critics and viewers, noting that "Miss Wallis is a lovely young lady with a charming voice. But to me at least, she is not the passionate, lost creature created by Dickens in the novel and by Georgia Brown on the stage."[31] Nevertheless, Wallis's clean-cut qualities allowed her to bring her own distinct touches to the role by accentuating the character's youthful sensitivity and maternal devotion. Furthermore, as will be noted in detail later in this chapter, Wallis's interpretation has exerted a pronounced effect on the larger cultural perception of Dickens's character; indeed, Wallis has significantly influenced the representation of Nancy in several prominent adaptations produced in the wake of the Reed film.

Whereas Wallis received mixed reviews as Nancy, Jack Wild received near universal praise in both the United Kingdom and the United States for his turn as the Artful Dodger. Some critics went so far as to proclaim him the true star of the piece, putting him above Moody's Fagin, though it was the dynamic between the two characters (and the two performers) that truly captivated critics and audiences. Like Wallis, Wild was a big-screen neophyte. Nevertheless, he had participated in the stage version of *Oliver!*, playing in the chorus and gradually working his way up to the slightly more prominent role of Bates.[32] His performance as the Artful Dodger in the film version thus marked a culmination of sorts. It also nabbed him a well-earned Oscar nomination for Best Supporting Actor. Sadly, Wild passed away in 2006 at the age of fifty-three, having spent years battling alcoholism, and then oral cancer, which robbed him of his vocal cords. Nevertheless, Wild presented nothing but fond recollections and happy memories of his work on the motion picture in virtually every interview he gave in the decades following the film's release.[33]

Rounding out the central cast was Carol Reed's nephew Oliver Reed as Sikes, and Sir Harry Secombe as Bumble. Biographer Nicholas Wapshott writes that Reed's casting of his nephew "was far from nepotistic"[34] as Carol had tried to dissuade Oliver from pursuing acting. Nevertheless, Oliver snapped up the opportunity to work with his uncle, and spoke highly of his experience shooting the film in various retrospective interviews; at an anniversary celebration of the movie's release, the incessantly amusing yet always controversial actor delighted the audience with anecdotes regarding his antics with Butch, the bull terrier that played Bull's-Eye. As for Harry Secombe, he had already gained experience playing parts in Dickensian musicals, having originated the role of Mr. Pickwick in the Leslie Bricusse musical *Pickwick*. Secombe's charitable and kindhearted personality matched Mr. Pickwick's character far more closely than it matched the disagreeable Bumble; still, Secombe brought more to the film than his genial personality and good humor. He also brought his powerful and operatic tenor voice, which was known to audiences throughout the United Kingdom.

As for the title hero, Mark Lester had received positive reviews for his performance as Jiminee in Jack Clayton's *Our Mother's House* (1967), and though the *Lord of the Flies*-esque tone of this film seems utterly antithetical to *Oliver!* Lester won the eponymous role in the Reed adaptation. In a retrospective interview for the television special *Celebrate Oliver!*, Lester looked back on the experience of making *Oliver!* with good-humored self-deprecation: "I don't know why Carol Reed chose me as Oliver. I mean, I couldn't sing, I couldn't dance, acting [...] I don't know. I guess I must have just looked the part."[35] Certainly, a great deal of the actor's performance is based around his physical appearance. The young Lester's angelic features create a strong impression in the viewer (and the various characters, many of whom seem equally entranced by the orphan's grace), which is fitting given the importance of Oliver's fundamental handsomeness in Dickens's novel. Regarding the musical facets of the character, Lester's singing voice was dubbed, though the unearthly pitch of the replacement voice only added to the ethereal depiction of Oliver on film.[36] Although Lester epitomized the innocence and transcendence of Oliver Twist, these same qualities have often served to impede the character from capturing the imaginations of readers/viewers to the same extent as characters like the Artful Dodger. However, even if he lacked the earthy dynamism of Moody's Fagin and Wild's Dodger, Lester put forth a sincere and heartfelt performance, masterfully evoking the most important sentiments associated with the character: sympathy and compassion.

OLIVER!'S ONSCREEN EVOLUTION

Successful movie versions of stage musicals negotiate the boundaries between the stage and screen by creatively modifying the source material so that the narrative will proceed effectively on film. Less successful adaptations fall into the trap of simply transferring the work from one medium to the other. Carol Reed opted for the former approach, and though the director adhered to the basic structure of Bart's musical, the mode of storytelling allowed by cinema granted Reed the ability to include a larger number of scenes, use a wider variety of settings, and devote more time to character development. Reed thus succeeded in creating a highly entertaining and cinematic motion picture based on Bart's musical as opposed to simply creating a film version of the stage show.

In spite of the initial controversies surrounding his involvement, Bart's input was important to Reed on a conceptual level. Both men were fully convinced that the true heart of the story lay in Oliver's search for love and his interaction with the thieves. A transcribed discussion between Reed and Bart reveals their understanding of this theme:

LB. Oliver is a character looking for love and a place to belong. For the first time he feels a sense of belonging when he meets Fagin.

CR. Good to hear. So we have got to play on WHERE IS LOVE [*sic*] when we get to London for the first time. [...] [N]o one is kind to him until the wonderful time when he meets the Artful Dodger and Fagin.

LB. No Haywain [*sic*] and no lift. No fun at all until he got to London.[37]

Reed seemed to take this suggestion that there should be "no fun at all" until Oliver's arrival in London quite literally. The opening scenes of *Oliver!* are striking for their pervasively melancholy tone, and though Reed does not embrace the sheer brutality that defines the David Lean film, he nevertheless emphasizes the dismal and depressing nature of Oliver's pre-London escapades.

As noted, the basic vision of Oliver's journey (and likewise, of Dickensian London) in the film version of *Oliver!* is heavily stylized, partly because the movie musical, as a genre, invites such embellishment, but the opening scenes of the film (which are *not* set in London) contain a surprising starkness. The first thirty minutes place especial emphasis on Oliver's loneliness, degradation, and misery. Gone are the amusing comedy numbers "I Shall Scream" and "That's Your Funeral." Reed wisely excises these songs because they would detract from the depressing depiction of Oliver's life. The bleak, harsh world of the parish will later be contrasted with the vibrant, musical world of London.[38]

Reed pushes Oliver to the very depths of despair in the film's initial sequences, and the presentation of Oliver's vulnerability, loneliness, and misery from the moment he draws the long straw is heart-wrenching (the very fact that Reed includes the drawing of the lots, which is omitted from the stage musical, adds to the heavy sense of fatalism surrounding these opening scenes): when Oliver runs away from the workhouse administrators and tries crawling under a table, the other workhouse orphans kick him; during "Boy for Sale," two cruel children pelt the orphan with snowballs.[39] Reed then includes a scene of Oliver in his new job as an undertaker's mute, underscoring the procession with a reprise of the melancholy melody to "Boy for Sale." Finally, Reed reverses the order of the scenes just before Oliver sings "Where Is Love?" Oliver is humiliated by Noah and abused by Mrs. Sowerberry, Charlotte, and Bumble *before* he sings the song. "Where Is Love?" accordingly caps off the countless degradations that Oliver has been forced to endure.[40] As in the original stage play, "Consider Yourself" marks a key turning point, and the liveliness, camaraderie, and spectacle of London stands out against the backdrop of the earlier scenes set in the workhouse, though the dichotomy is even more pronounced in the film.

Throughout "Consider Yourself," Reed takes advantage of the freedoms bestowed on him by the medium of film. Whereas the stage version can only imply the size and scope of London through the comings and goings of members of the chorus, the film can actually track Oliver and the Dodger as they move across the enormous studio lot.[41] The size of the chorus adds to this sense of breadth, as the Dodger and Oliver meet dozens and dozens of extras, all of whom serve to accentuate the size and diversity of the Victorian populace. As in the play, the result is a newfound appreciation of East End community as a potential remedy for the fractured loneliness of Oliver's early life.

This sense of community is likewise enhanced by the additional settings that Reed incorporates into the motion picture. Whereas the stage play mounts four numbers in a row ("Pick a Pocket or Two," "It's a Fine Life," "I'd Do Anything," and "Be Back Soon") in Fagin's den, Reed is able to transition to a different setting and add a diverse group of characters into the chorus as Nancy sings "It's a Fine Life" with the barflies, prostitutes, and scoundrels who occupy the Three Cripples.[42] This revision expands the scope of the criminals' community beyond Fagin and his pupils while accentuating the camaraderie and conviviality of the underworld as established in the den. Once again, the viewer must consider that although Oliver's life with the criminal class is neither luxurious nor honest, this collection of individuals seems happier, livelier, and more congenial than virtually any other group of characters in the film.

SIKES, OLIVER, AND NANCY ONSCREEN

In the same scene, Reed takes advantage of the opportunity to introduce Sikes, illustrating one of the most fundamental improvements to the source. By shifting the action from Fagin's den to the Three Cripples much earlier, the director is able to establish Sikes's role far sooner. In the film, a brief scene in which Sikes turns over his stolen booty to Fagin is beautifully underscored by the melody to "My Name," which is not actually sung in the film. The tradeoff here is understandable. Whereas Bart's Sikes, who is not introduced until the second act, must make a dramatic entrance and sing an intense song so as to quickly establish himself as the heavy, Reed's Sikes, introduced far earlier, can operate at a more leisurely pace. In spite of his intimidating looks, the audience is not quite sure what to feel toward Sikes until about halfway through the film. Furthermore, by not having Sikes sing, Reed manages to set the housebreaker in contrast to the other thieves and scoundrels, all of whom express themselves through music. Sikes is fundamentally a loner, even within the community of his fellow thieves. In *Enchanted Evenings*, Geoffrey Block scrutinizes "the premise that a musical comedy character will be denied three-dimensionality or identity if he or she is not allowed to sing."[43] It is somewhat paradoxical that the non-singing cinematic Sikes is ultimately a more complex and three-dimensional character than his stage predecessor.

Here it is worth mentioning Oliver Reed's performance as Sikes, for the added profundity that the younger Reed brought to a seemingly one-dimensional character reinforces the depth of the controversial actor's talents. In describing his approach to Sikes, Oliver Reed reflected that his performance was fundamentally modern:

> [T]he problem became: how do you play a nineteenth-century thug. I play him in a contemporary way to relate the violence in him to the violence people who see the movie understand from their own lives. The original Sikes would have pushed his way in and taken what he wanted. He didn't talk about it. He didn't think. He didn't argue. But today he's more self-conscious about what he's doing. He'll make some attempt to discuss things first.[44]

This self-consciousness is perhaps the defining characteristic of Oliver Reed's performance, though his mention of the character "discussing things first" belies the fact that there is a sullen quietness to his Sikes.[45] He exchanges no words with Fagin during their first encounter; furthermore, Sikes virtually ignores Nancy during her singing of "It's a Fine Life," despite her flirting with him. Her final verse, in which she pines for the creation of a "happy home, happy husband, happy wife" is particularly moving as the person she is singing about has already been presented onscreen and demonstrated that he takes her for granted.

Nevertheless, Sikes is not inhuman. He shows mild affection toward Bull's-Eye during Nancy's song, and, after the number concludes, he allows Nancy to walk alongside him as they depart the Three Cripples. Whereas the Sikes in the stage musical must be presented solely in his capacity as a brute, Oliver Reed is able to convey to the audience that Sikes truly has feelings for Nancy but is incapable of expressing them properly. These new facets of Sikes are perhaps best presented in a scene written for the motion picture. As Sikes tries to sleep, Nancy noisily cooks his breakfast in a saucepan; annoyed, he orders her to go and procure money from Fagin. Before she leaves, she asks if he loves her. The frustrated Sikes exclaims: "Oh, course I do, I live with you, don't I?" There is genuine conviction in his voice, but he never actually tells her that he loves her. Here it is almost possible to pity Sikes for his inability to convey his feelings for Nancy. However, as the film progresses and Nancy's loyalties shift from Sikes to Oliver, the housebreaker becomes more violent toward her and any sympathy that we might have developed for the character is lost. Even before he beats her to death, however, Sikes seems burdened by the way he treats her. In John Glavin's outstanding collection of essays on Dickensian film adaptations, John Romano states that he found Robert Newton, who portrayed Sikes in Lean's 1948 classic, "wooden compared to Oliver Reed [...] who always carries, from the beginning, this anxiety."[46] Romano's reference to "anxiety" seems a perfect parallel to Oliver Reed's own emphasis on the "self-consciousness" that defined his performance. Oliver Reed's conflicted portrayal of Sikes stands out as a uniquely multifaceted interpretation of a flat character, and the tragedy of the Nancy-Sikes relationship is heightened by the added depth given to the housebreaker.

Along with the extra depth granted to Sikes, Carol Reed added significant depth to the relationship between Nancy and Oliver, though as in the case of Sikes credit for this element of the film must also go to the performers: Shani Wallis and Mark Lester display a palpable chemistry in their respective roles, and Reed capitalized on this chemistry while shooting the musical. In the film, when the other boys in Fagin's gang taunt Oliver for his good manners, Nancy immediately takes his side. The stage version of "I'd Do Anything" is built around Dodger's interactions with Nancy and Oliver's interactions with Bet, but the film version focuses primarily on the Nancy-Oliver relationship, and Reed repeatedly incorporates medium and close-up shots of the two simply smiling at one another, thus heightening the connection between the characters. By accentuating Nancy's maternal devotion to Oliver from early on, Reed is able to make her character even more sympathetic; he is likewise able to more effectively justify her later actions.

In the stage play, Nancy's refusal to help Sikes abduct Oliver is based on her desire to keep herself safe. Conversely, the film makes it clear that she is adamant about preserving Oliver's chance for happiness as she pleads with Sikes on the orphan's behalf: "Why can't you leave the boy alone? He won't do you no harm. Why can't you leave him where he is, where he'll have the chance of a decent life?"[47] Bart's stage musical emphasizes Nancy's determination to make Oliver part of a community, but Reed fully embraces the idea that Nancy is a surrogate mother figure for Oliver. Like Oliver's mother, she makes great sacrifices and endures much pain so as to protect and preserve the child she loves. Furthermore, just as Oliver lost his mother, he is doomed to lose Nancy.

FINDING A SUITABLE ENDING

The climax of the film reinforces the influence of the David Lean adaptation on Bart's creative vision, and Reed's virtual duplication of the Lean rooftop sequence will be discussed in detail shortly.[48] However, the final scenes featuring Fagin diverge significantly from both the stage play and the Lean film. While Fagin and the boys escape the den through a back exit, Fagin accidentally drops his treasure chest into a deep pool of mud and is unable to recover his prized possessions. Broke and alone, Fagin reprises "Reviewing the Situation" and prepares to face a new day as a reformed man. However, while the play ends here, the film features a joyful reunion between Fagin and the Artful Dodger who happily reprise another verse of "Reviewing the Situation" together before skipping off merrily while the sun rises before them.

This unambiguous and upbeat ending is perhaps the most significant alteration to the stage source, though there is evidence that Bart himself helped conceive this alternative conclusion (in spite of his taking a somewhat negative view of it in later years).[49] As noted in Chapter 2, Bart had initially campaigned for a purely happy ending in contrast to Peter Coe's darker vision. Thankfully, Bart did not revive the "Fagin becomes a beadle/Dodger becomes a footman" scenario in his pitch to Reed, though he nevertheless sent the director an outline for a more joyous finale: "Fagin left alone; decides to 'turn over a new leaf' sings –SHORT REPRISE—VERSE—'REVIEWING THE SITUATION'. End of reprise. Dodger approaches, holding aloft two slimy jewels he had 'rescued'. Fagin and Dodger 'pal up'. REPRISE (As duet) –verse and chorus 'REVIEWING THE SITUATION'."[50] Though the final scene in the film proceeds somewhat differently—the Dodger presents Fagin with a recently lifted wallet as opposed to recovered jewels—the layout of the scenes is identical. Moody and Wild would touchingly recreate the final shots of their two characters dancing off into the sunrise for the *After They Were Famous* reunion special, and their restaging of the scene has become all the more poignant since Wild's passing.

As for the title character's happy ending, Reed simply shows a weary Oliver returning home with Brownlow and embracing Mrs. Bedwin. Reed's decision to keep the finale subdued and silent reinforces the lack of music in the middle-class environment and accentuates the musicality of Fagin's world. Fittingly, Fagin and the Dodger are the last characters to sing. The finale likewise hints at Reed's own contention that Oliver may have been better off with Fagin and the Dodger than with Brownlow. In an interview with Allen Wright, Reed explained that he "enjoyed bringing out the difference between Fagin's disreputable den and the charming crescent where Mr. Brownlow lives, and Sir Carol's sympathies lie with the former. 'If I were a child', he says, 'I would prefer the thieves' kitchen to that awful man and his pretty house'."[51] On film, Fagin and the Dodger's ending is infinitely more celebratory and uplifting than Oliver's.

*OLIVER!'*S RECEPTION AND LEGACY

Carol Reed was able to create not only an excellent film adaptation of Lionel Bart's *Oliver!* but an excellent film adaptation of *Oliver Twist*. The positive reception of the piece by both critics and audiences is a testament to this success. Additionally, the film allowed the global market of the property to expand even further, as territories that had been excluded from the early international tours received their first true introduction to Bart's vision of Dickens's novel. Perhaps the most noteworthy of these territories was the USSR, as *Oliver!* was screened during the 1969 Moscow Film Festival. Andrew Filson happily informed Carol Reed that "the audience broke into spontaneous applause repeatedly during the performance and at the end there was a long period of rhythmic clapping, which is the highest accolade they give. The Festival cinema, which has 6,000 seats, has been in operation for three Festivals and I was told that no film had ever had such a warm welcome."[52] The film received a Gold Medal from the festival board despite the fact "that *Pravda* was not entirely satisfied with the attitude of the film to the question of crime or to the happiness of the oppressed poor."[53] Bart, Moody, and John Box were also honored with awards, and the idea of *Oliver!* receiving such a favorable response in Soviet Russia is yet another testament to the transcendent appeal of Reed's film, Bart's musical, and Dickens's story.

Even if the film version of *Oliver!* did not present the same sense of originality that defined the stage version, the very fact that the most successful film musicals had all been produced in Hollywood up to that point in time meant that the Englishness of the project would once again assert itself as an innovative triumph: *Oliver!* had been produced by English producers, directed by an English director, and filmed at an English movie studio. The same sense of nationalism that had defined the West End response thus reemerged. Film critic Felix Barker proudly boasted that *Oliver!* was the "biggest, best, and, oh yes, probably the most expensive musical ever made in a British studio,"[54] while Arthur Steele celebrated the fact that the British "not only have a first-class musical made in Britain, but [. . .] a particularly British musical."[55] The write-up most evocative of the earlier West End reviews came from Marjorie Bilbow, who labeled *Oliver!* "[a] musical that we can all be proud of for the killing blow it gives to the old adage about our inability to produce a musical with all the vigour and vitality that has for so long been the trademark only of the best American products."[56] Perhaps even more impressive was the fact that film critics in the United States, unlike their Broadway counterparts, were just as generous with their praise. In fact, the film would go on to receive its greatest accolades in the United States.

After generating a great deal of "Oscar buzz," *Oliver!* went on to win five Academy Awards, including Best Picture, Best Director, Best Art Direction, Best Score, and Best Sound. Moreover, acclaimed choreographer Onna White received a special Oscar for Outstanding Choreography Achievement for her brilliant staging of the film's musical numbers. However, the individual who had garnered the most significant build-up regarding Academy Award recognition, Ron Moody, went home empty-handed. Moody seemed a lock for Best Actor, but he was up against two other gifted British actors in Alan Bates and Peter O'Toole. The three English performers may have split the vote, allowing dark horse Cliff Roberts to win. Nevertheless, Moody received several accolades for his performance, including the Golden Globe for Best Actor in a Musical or Comedy. Surprisingly, the American Academy was more generous toward *Oliver!* than the British Academy, which did not bestow a single award on Reed's musical.[57] Still, the lack of British recognition made the American reception of *Oliver!* all the more significant, and *Oliver!* stood out as a major example of British domination of the 1969 Oscars.

Winning both the Oscar and Golden Globe for Best Picture was an impressive feat, but perhaps the adaptation's greatest achievement was winning over the intractable Pauline Kael of the *New Yorker*. Kael, who had penned scathing reviews of other Oscar-winning sixties musical films such as *West Side Story* and *The Sound of Music*, offered *Oliver!* nothing but the highest praise in her article "The Concealed Art of Carol Reed." Kael's admiration for the movie was directed largely toward Reed himself, who had succeeded in creating an unpretentious, nostalgic film in an era where most filmmakers were self-consciously focused on innovation.[58] This issue of "old-fashioned" entertainment is an interesting one to consider given that *Oliver!* was produced when the film musical was on its way out of fashion. The end of the 1960s was about to give way to the brutal cynicism of the 1970s. *Oliver!* may have dominated the 1969 Oscars, but the decidedly *un*-musical *Midnight Cowboy* was named "Best Picture" at the Forty-Second Academy Awards ceremony the following year.[59] That *Oliver!* found such success in an increasingly "inharmonious" era highlights what Kael found to be one of the most appealing qualities of Reed's film: its escapism.

The most striking moment in Kael's review is a paragraph comparing the film version of *Oliver!* to the original stage musical:

> No one who sees this movie is likely to say, 'But you should have seen *Oliver!* on the stage!' On the stage it was the kind of undistinguished musical that people took their children to, dutifully. Though not on a level with *The Sound of Music*, it had that detestable kind of mediocre respectability; it was an English version of Broadway Americana, and I walked out on it.[60]

The contrast between Kael's reaction to the stage and film versions of *Oliver!* is arresting, though the main reasons for her appreciation of the film reinforce the freedom granted to Reed by the medium of the motion picture, and likewise, the creativity of the director in exploring the narrative possibilities of that medium. In a sense, the film is more Dickensian than its stage source, for the large-scale portrayal of London, along with the stylized artistry behind the settings and locations, immediately evokes the popular image of Dickens's concept of the great metropolis. As Kael put it, "[t]he stylization encourages us to notice the conventions of the story as we are enjoying the story. It seems to put quotation marks around everything Dickensian, yet not in a cloying way—rather, in a way that makes us more aware of some of the qualities of Dickens' art."[61] Whereas the Lean film played up the starkness of the Dickensian source, Reed's film gravitates more naturally toward the novel's allegorical romanticism, which is fitting given the genre in which he was working.

Notably, toward the end of her article, Kael compared *Oliver!* to the Lean adaptation, concluding that the Reed film is "much easier to take [...] I don't think the softening of this particular material is to be lamented. There were scenes in the David Lean film that were simply too painful."[62] Kael's comparisons between the unyieldingly dark film directed by Lean and the bright, lively musical directed by Reed can serve as a useful starting point for one of the more controversial critical debates associated with *Oliver!*

REED VS. LEAN IN THE BATTLE FOR THE *TWIST* CULTURE TEXT

The widespread popularity of the film, which stretched even further than the popularity of the original stage show, meant that *Oliver!* would now exert a stronger influence on the culture text of *Oliver Twist* than ever before, a fact that simultaneously made it a bigger target for Dickensian purists. In the archival text *Charles Dickens on the Screen*, Michael Pointer presents a particularly stinging criticism of *Oliver!*:

> But for all its popularity and success, it was not a good Dickens film. The jollification of Dickens, long the cinema's way of moderating the difficult parts of the stories, swamped the subject, and fundamental changes were made to nearly all the principal characters. Soft-faced Mark Lester was clearly the opposite of a workhouse boy. Apple-cheeked Jack Wild as the Artful Dodger had obviously never roughed it for years. Fat, jovial Harry Secombe was the antithesis of the oily Bumble, and Shani Wallis as Nancy looked more like the girl next door than an ill-used whore. The despicable Fagin was turned into a picaresque old rogue who was allowed to escape to further villainy, scampering off down the road at the end in a Chaplinesque image of which director Carol Reed should have been ashamed.[63]

Pointer's criticisms are limited entirely to the issue of fidelity to the Dickensian source, and most of his complaints are sophomoric as he resorts to judging the characters by the appearances of the actors cast in the roles as opposed to truly analyzing the idea of *Oliver!* as an "adaptation" of the Dickens novel. Furthermore, Pointer repeatedly displays a lack of familiarity with the stage source: "Reed should also have been ashamed of the unacknowledged borrowings from David Lean's *Oliver Twist* in story line and appearance. The similarities are too many to be coincidental. *Oliver!* is much closer to the David Lean film than to the Charles Dickens novel or Lionel Bart's stage musical."[64] Pointer—an adamant supporter of Lean's Dickensian adaptations—repeatedly expresses righteous indignation regarding Reed's "unacknowledged borrowing" from the Lean version. However, Bart himself had acknowledged that the Lean film played a role in his conception of *Oliver!*; to say that Reed's film is closer to the Lean film than to its stage source is somewhat absurd because the narrative of the stage source was influenced by the narrative of the Lean film.

Nevertheless, Lean was apparently agitated by the similarities between his film and Reed's adaptation. In his biography on the famed director, Stephen Silverman prefigures many of Pointer's criticisms: "Indeed, though ostensibly based on the 1960 London stage musical by Lionel Bart, the movie version [...] is more of an uncredited adaptation of the Lean film in story line and look than of either the Dickens novel or the Bart stage show."[65] Silverman goes on to note that Lean found *Oliver!* "very difficult to talk about,"[66] thus implying that he too felt as if Reed had stolen from his movie. It is striking that Lean continues to hold something of a monopoly on adaptations of *Oliver Twist* given that the 1948 film was just one (albeit outstanding) adaptation in a long series of adaptations of the story, though there are numerous factors that contribute to this issue of Lean's *Twist* vs. Reed's *Oliver!*, not the least of which relate to the genial rivalry that existed between the two filmmakers.

Granted, there are certain shots and sequences in the Reed film that indubitably borrow from the Lean version. The most obvious example is the rooftop climax, where Sikes tries to escape the police while holding Oliver hostage. As noted in Chapter 1, Lean's revised ending is even more suspenseful than Dickens's original treatment of Sikes's flight given the fact that Oliver's safety is still not ensured, and Reed seems to be channeling Lean in his direction of the climactic chase that results in Sikes's death. The final moments of the two films are also identical, as both adaptations end with Oliver being embraced by Mrs. Bedwin following his return to Mr. Brownlow's house. Interestingly, the screenplay indicates even more parallels between the two adaptations, as the Reed film was supposed to open with Oliver's mother limping to the workhouse, giving birth to her son, and dying immediately after kissing him; this is the exact sequence of events with which Lean begins his adaptation. This scene was apparently filmed but cut from the final version of the picture.[67]

As Pointer indicates, these similarities are probably not coincidental, though the elements of Reed's film taken from the Lean piece are not simple instances of "plagiarizing" from another movie, but rather an intertextual engagement with the cinematic perception of the *Twist* narrative as it had been shaped by Lean. The basic fact that Bart's musical had been translated to a cinematic narrative was problematic for some critics, however. Several journalists who penned unfavorable reviews of the Reed film framed their critiques in the context of the Lean adaptation, though they were not necessarily comparing and contrasting the two works in and of themselves so much as they were comparing and contrasting the *visions* of the two works as necessitated by the mediums. John Russell Taylor of the *Times* wrote one of the most noteworthy negative reviews of the film in which he criticized Reed's vision because it felt incongruous to merge the realism and detail of the Lean film with the imagination and fantasy of a stage musical:

> On stage, Lionel Bart's musical was a graceful, determinedly non-realistic charade, achieving all in its best effects by sophisticated play with theatrical conventions. Sir Carol Reed's new film falls disastrously between the two stools, by trying to drop the numbers from the stage musical into the generally realistic context of the earlier film [directed by David Lean].[68]

Similarly, Patrick Fleet of the *Bristol Evening Post* felt that there was an incongruity between cinematic realism and theatrical escapism that made it difficult for him to accept the characters' bursting into song and dance: "Unluckily, [Reed] has chosen every now and then to break into big, set-piece musical routines, seemingly lifted straight off some enormous stage, with milkmaids tripping down the footlights and soldiers marching off into the wings. This so fatally affects the film that it seems to break in two."[69] Though such criticisms raise intriguing questions about the influence of mediums on the success of adaptations, as well as the relationships between musical and nonmusical film interpretations of literary sources, Taylor and Fleet's critiques belie the fact that the film version of *Oliver!* eventually exerted just as wide-reaching an effect on the cinematic perceptions of *Twist* as its 1940s predecessor.

The direct impact of *Oliver!* on the culture text of *Twist* can be detected in the family-oriented approach taken by numerous directors and screenwriters who have adapted Dickens's novel for film and television in the decades following the Reed film. Reed's influence is perhaps most noticeable in subsequent treatments of Fagin. With the exception of Eric Porter's depiction of the character in the utterly lugubrious 1985 BBC adaptation—an adaptation that is even starker than the Lean film, albeit far less impressive—virtually every major adaptation of *Oliver Twist* produced since 1968 has featured a somewhat sympathetic interpretation of Fagin prefigured to some degree by the Reed film. The 1982 Clive Donner telefilm, featuring George C. Scott as Fagin, plays up the paternal side of the character, as Scott's Fagin is incredibly kind to Oliver and perfectly willing to let the child go and live with Brownlow. Other examples of Fagins influenced to varying degrees by the Reed adaptation can be found in the 1997 Disney Channel adaptation starring Richard Dreyfus, the 1999 ITV adaptation with Robert Lindsay, the 2005 Polanski film with Ben Kingsley, and the 2007 BBC version featuring Timothy Spall. Dreyfus's Fagin repeatedly and exaggeratingly dotes on the boys like a proud father, presenting the same sort of comical thoughtfulness embodied by Moody in his performance of numbers like "Be Back Soon." Here, as in the Reed film, the children in Fagin's gang are allowed to act like children thanks to the equally childish personality of Fagin, and in certain scenes the cavorting within the thieves' den virtually duplicates the choreography of "I'd Do Anything." Lindsay's interpretation is one of the more unique incarnations of the character in the years since the Reed film, though even Lindsay's Fagin seems more evocative of Moody than of Guinness, given the theatricality associated with this version of the old man; here, Fagin is the consummate showman, repeatedly using magic tricks, dances, and music so as to keep his audience, namely the gang, enthralled.[70] Though the Polanski film borrows heavily from the Lean film, basically duplicating Lean's climax, Polanski's adaptation also presents an ambiguously sympathetic and genuinely paternal Fagin whose parental affection is evocative of the compassion that Moody shows toward Oliver in the Reed film. Finally, Spall's Fagin is defined by his otherness rather than his wickedness and embodies the fragile weariness of Moody's Fagin.

There are countless other examples of the Reed film's influence on these family-oriented adaptations of *Twist*. The Disney Channel version places heavy emphasis on the friendship between Oliver and the Artful Dodger, while the 1999 miniseries features Nancy singing tavern songs at the Three Cripples. The Donner film and the 2007 serial stress Nancy's maternal devotion to Oliver, as she provides physical care for him in the former and emotional support for him in the latter. Indeed, all five of the aforementioned film adaptations accentuate this quality of Nancy's character, a quality that heavily characterizes Reed's *Oliver!* and that virtually defines Wallis's Nancy. The cultural perception of the relationship between Nancy and Oliver has been heavily influenced by the Reed adaptation; in fact, this element may be the film's most enduring contribution to the culture text. Though Kay Walsh emphasizes the character's fundamental strength in the Lean film, there is an abrasiveness to her Nancy that, even if true to the book, prevents her from overtly displaying love for Oliver. The maternal version of Nancy—frequently clad in red in what may be a direct homage to Wallis's iconic costume—that now dominates our collective perception of the character can be traced back to the Reed adaptation.

OLIVER! AND THE DISNEYFICATION OF DICKENS

This influence reinforces the tendency of adaptors to work from previous adaptations as opposed to returning to the original source,[71] and here again it is possible to bridge the gap between the culture text and the world of advertising, as the aforementioned examples of *Oliver!*'s influence on the depiction of characters in subsequent adaptations alludes to Mary Cross's description of the "new attachments" created through marketing: "This public sign system, in making meaning for products, has created a new world view, offering utopia in a narrative of going out to buy, a simulacrum of the world that drives us to products as substitutes for experience."[72] In a sense, the film versions of Dickens's characters, with their long "shelf-life," have created a "new world view" of the original Dickensian texts, and a "simulacrum" of the text that substitutes for the actual experience of reading the novel; when we hear the names of Fagin, Oliver Twist, Nancy, the Artful Dodger, Bill Sikes, and Mr. Bumble, the images (and sounds) that immediately spring to mind come from the Carol Reed film, and the directors and screenwriters of subsequent adaptations seem keenly aware of that fact.

In light of this link between the adaptation and advertising, it is not surprising that the release of the film saw the Dickensian merchandising phenomenon reach new heights just in time for the 1968 Christmas season. Perhaps the most noteworthy and ironic craze initiated by *Oliver!* was the one that ran through the British fashion industry, as the film's enormously popular child characters, Oliver Twist and the Artful Dodger, inspired various designers to pattern items of clothing based on the costumes seen in the film. The *Scottish Daily Express* reported that Edward Mann and Paul Blanche actually designed ladies' hats in the Victorian style of the film, including a modified topper with white crepe based on Oliver's uniform whilst working for Sowerberry and a fashionable orphan's cap (which, in and of itself, seems to be something of a paradox): "Oliver [sic] as a film has earned the praise it deserved—it has also produced some delightful fashions for today."[73] There is something ironic about the exploitation of *Oliver!* given that the exploitation of Oliver Twist in Dickens's own novel is meant to inspire righteous indignation in the reader. The loss of the darker, polemical elements of Dickens's text meant the loss of the social consciousness that defined Dickens's vision, which may account for why Reed's *Oliver!* continues to offend the sensibilities of Dickens purists.

Oliver Twist, as it was written by Dickens, hardly fits the traditional definition of "family entertainment," and yet *Oliver!*, along with most of the adaptations of *Twist* that followed, could clearly be categorized as such. The widespread appeal of Reed's *Oliver!*, along with the global marketing campaign behind it, meant that *Oliver!* was now capable of usurping the meaning of Dickens's original novel entirely. Several of the critics who reviewed the film not only anticipated such a usurpation but seemed to delight in the prospect; Felix Barker humorously described the characters in the film as "Bartian," claiming that the term now carried greater weight than the term "Dickensian," while an anonymous reviewer with *Time* magazine asserted that "Dickens was dead to begin with [. . .] as dead as Jacob Marley."[74]

The two aforementioned tendencies of the Reed film, mass marketing and cultural usurpation, seem at once evocative of the trend that has come to be known as "Disneyfying," and given *Oliver!*'s emphasis on a sentimental and marketable retelling of a darker and more complex story, the Disney label certainly seems to apply.[75] The main objection to Disneyfication on the part of most critics and academics is that Disney seizes total control over the popular representation of the original property, thus allowing the Disney version to become the only relevant version. Today, the very mention of Winnie-the-Pooh calls to mind Disney's ubiquitous cartoon version of the character as opposed to A. A. Milne's stories. The same can be said of characters from Carroll's *Alice* books and Grahame's *Wind in the Willows*, as well as characters from Kipling's *Jungle Book*s. This tendency is more than apparent in the case of the Reed film.

Nevertheless, the Disney-like usurpation of *Oliver Twist* on the part of the Reed adaptation may simply be a unique manifestation of "Theme Park Victoriana." In his essay of the same name, John Gardiner examines the current trends in studying the Victorians, most of which present "a view of history in museums, visitor attractions and shops that foregrounds the interactive and the commercial."[76] Gardiner's assessment underscores the perception of Victorian culture in a postmodern world. Furthermore, Reed's vision of Dickensian London, with its overwhelming visual and auditory spectacle, exemplifies a "theme park" vision of Victorian England. Disney has long held a monopoly on our perception of what a theme park can (and should) be, and the issues of Disneyfying Dickens and "theme park Victoriana" seem to be variations on the same theme. The opening of the Dickens World theme park is perhaps the ultimate example of this merger, though these same tendencies, specifically in regard to Dickens, have been supplemented thanks to the enduring popularity of adaptations such as *Oliver!*—adaptations that kept the author's characters embedded in our popular culture by exploring their vibrancy while exploiting their commercial potential.

Umberto Eco and Jean Baudrillard famously cited Disney when defining hyperrealism and simulacra, labeling Disneyland as the epitome of postmodern ad culture, and Eco's statements regarding the power of the "fake" to take the place of the "real" and ultimately be accepted as the "real" reinforces the previous statements about the power of the culture text, and of adaptations like *Oliver!*, to define *Oliver Twist* in the minds and hearts of the general populace.[77] However, Baudrillard poignantly concluded that the concept of marketing Disneyland as a fantasy world was flawed since "all of Los Angeles and the America surrounding it are no longer real, but of the order of the hyperreal and of simulation. It is no longer a question of false representation of reality (ideology), but of concealing the fact that the real is no longer real, and thus of saving the reality principle."[78] Although the theme park vision of Victoriana (and of Dickensian London) presented in the Reed film is an example of simulacra,

Baudrillard's statement about the "real" no longer being "real" resonates even more strongly in the context of Gardiner's arguments; it seems impossible to critique Reed's *Oliver!* for its Disneyfied take on *Oliver Twist* given that the Disneyfication of Dickens and the Victorian era in the popular consciousness had already taken place.

Furthermore, the contemporary perception of Victoriana, a perception rooted in the popularity of Dickens and his characters, has rendered the issues of "reality" and "authenticity" even more questionable. Building on Gardiner's theories, Ann Heilmann and Mark Llewellyn have noted the "long-standing trope that Dickens equates to the Victorian and that much of the mainstream public perception of the nineteenth century is, in fact, rooted in a Dickensian sense of the period."[79] Essentially, the popular influence of Dickens's "romantic realism" has colored the postmodern perception of the Victorian age, much as the popular influence of Carol Reed's *Oliver!* has colored the postmodern perception of Dickens and *Oliver Twist*. As Heilmann and Llewellyn observe, "if what most of us imagine as the authentic representation of the Victorians is derived from our knowledge of the Dickensian adaptation on our TV and film screens, then Dickens World becomes a magnified and multiplied imitation of an imitation."[80] As in the case of hyperrealism, however, the "imitation" quickly becomes accepted as "real." If, as Baudrillard has stated, there is no separating Disneyland from the "real" America, then there is no separating Carol Reed's film version of *Oliver!* from the "real" *Oliver Twist*.

A MEGAMUSICAL JOURNEY FROM SCREEN TO STAGE

In light of the enduring popularity and attractiveness of the Reed film, it is likely that *Oliver!* will continue to define the cultural perception of what Dickens's *Oliver Twist* could (and should) be. The film has also come to define what stage versions of *Oliver!* could (and should) be. When Cameron Mackintosh, Sam Mendes, and Lionel Bart revised *Oliver!* in 1994 for the all-important Palladium Theatre revival, the film served as the inspiration for several noteworthy changes to the libretto. The overall scale of the show likewise changed significantly. The creative vision of the Sean Kenny set alternated between two extremes of Wagnerian unity and Brechtian displacement, but the new set was defined entirely by cinematic hyperrealism, which served to create and sustain the theatrical illusions Kenny had shattered.

Mackintosh's involvement with *Oliver!* dated back to the 1965 touring production. The irony of *Oliver!*'s parading through Manchester while Bart's disastrous Robin Hood musical *Twang!!* was limping along in the same location in anticipation of its West End debut is undeniable; however, perhaps the greatest irony in relation to this production was that Mackintosh, then an eager young assistant stage manager, would eventually shape *Oliver!*'s destiny. As Sheridan Morley put it, *Oliver!* has, in many ways, proved to be the "key musical" of Mackintosh's career.[81] In 1994, with the debut of the Palladium version, Mackintosh granted *Oliver!* a paradoxical evolution; Bart's musical, which had helped to prefigure the megamusicals of the Lloyd Webber era, would now stand alongside these descendants in terms of its scale and visual grandness.

Though Mackintosh had always held Sean Kenny's creations in the highest esteem, the central disadvantage to the Kenny set was that virtually every production that used this scenery had to duplicate Coe's staging.[82] Mackintosh noted that the Kenny set "was [...] keeping the show imprisoned in its old production. Unless I took the gamble to change the set, I would never get a talented director to give the show a fresh look."[83] Thus, when Mackintosh revived *Oliver!* in 1994, the production would prove to be more than a simple restaging. Instead, Mackintosh presented a total "reboot" shaped heavily by the Reed adaptation.

One of the most significant contrasts between this new vision for the piece and Kenny's vision was the idea of naturalism. The Kenny set had been highly abstract, but production designer Anthony Ward's new scenery would, like Box's before him, prove far more "tangible" in its depiction of the various locations. Ward notes that "we didn't want the audience to wonder where they were at any point."[84] The Kenny set, through its reuse of the staircases and trucks, required that the audience fill in some of the contrasting visual details of the various locations; Ward's set took care of these details through its cinematic sumptuousness. Ward would notably cite both the film version of *Oliver!* and the Lean adaptation as the chief inspirations for his design.[85]

The sheer geographic breadth of the Palladium adaptation is at once evocative of the Reed adaptation. To fully convey the scope of London as it is portrayed in "Consider Yourself," Ward designed two different views of the dome to St. Paul's Cathedral: a small one, intended mainly for background views, and a larger version, intended for close-up appearances. By alternating between the two sets as the Dodger sings his number, Ward creates the illusion that the young pickpocket is navigating through the enormous metropolis and continuously moving toward the East End. Whereas Kenny's set was not designed to simulate such an effect, Ward's set attempts to achieve the stylized yet detailed hyperrealism that defined Box's scenery.

With Ward's set and costume designs helping to visually distinguish the show from its previous incarnations, Mackintosh sought out other gifted artists to assist in the reinvention of *Oliver!*, including director Sam Mendes, choreographer Matthew Bourne, sound designers Paul Groothuis and Mike Walker, and lighting designer David Hersey. The producer later noted that with a few exceptions, "none of the production team [...] had even been born when Lionel's masterpiece was first written."[86] The new creative team instinctively consulted the film for inspiration regarding the new vision, as Mendes's first encounter with *Oliver!* had been through the Reed adaptation. His additions to the libretto, including the appearance of the parish board during "Oliver," the early introduction of Sykes following "Pick a Pocket or Two," and the expanded development of the Nancy-Oliver relationship, were all inspired by the Reed adaptation. Significantly, as in the case of Ward's set designs, Mendes likewise turned to the Lean adaptation as a source. The director includes an orchestral prelude featuring Agnes, clearly on the verge of giving birth, limping her way across the moors toward the workhouse. Mendes's writing of the scene is a virtual duplication of Lean's opening scene:

> The curtain rises on a windswept moor. There is a storm and in the near darkness we
> begin to make out the figure of a woman, dressed in rags, slowly but purposefully

heading towards us. The storm rages and grows stronger, flashes of lightning briefly illuminating her agonised face. As she arrives downstage a huge clap of thunder and flash of lightning light up a set of enormous wrought iron gates which read 'Workhouse' (in reverse). As she collapses, a little old serving maid rushes to her aid. As the wind blows, she is dragged inside and the music of the storm grows calmer. In the darkness the cry of a little baby is heard.[87]

For the first time in the musical's history, Agnes appears as a character—another indication of the sweeping, cinematic tenor of the revival.

Oliver! debuted at the Palladium on December 8, 1994; the opening night performance brought things full-circle, as the response of the crowd was virtually identical to the response of those theatergoers who had first experienced *Oliver!* on its opening night in 1960.[88] There was also a similar sense of victory within the English press; Rebecca Fowler wrote an article for the *Times* on the recent string of phenomenally successful British megamusicals that had dominated both the West End and Broadway. Fowler triumphantly notes that the arrival of the megamusical meant that "the British [had] [...] beat the Americans at their own game," and the wildly successful relaunch of *Oliver!* was simply further proof of the British domination of this genre that had once been so fundamentally American.[89]

The revival could not fully duplicate the critical response of its forebear, however, and several critics took exception to the changes that had been made to *Oliver!*, viewing them as representative of the excessiveness of the post-1980s theater. Julie Burchill of the *Sunday Times* commented on the intimidating dominance of the scenery, claiming that "[t]he stars of this revival—and this is always depressing to write—are the sets. My tot, a veteran of hi-tech special effects, was gasping: 'Are those clouds real?' 'No, baby, they're painted'. 'No, they're real. They've opened the roof up'. You've heard of actors eating the scenery—well, you find yourself wishing that this scenery would eat the actors."[90] It is the standard argument made against megamusicals that the scenery dominates the show, though ironically, the same criticism had been directed toward Sean Kenny's sets in the 1960s. Unfortunately, though Mackintosh's personal touch had helped take *Oliver!* into a new decade, Bart's musical would now be subject to the same criticism that many traditionalists automatically leveled toward megamusicals.

Interestingly, some of the critics who complained about the new production drew attention to the musical's lack of social outrage. Though Anna Lee of *West End Extra* praised *Oliver!* as an excellent musical, she complained that the Palladium revival had imprudently placed visual grandeur over narrative/theme and had thus failed to explore the adaptation's potential for genuine social criticism: "This is a musical of our time. Bart's adaptation of *Oliver Twist* is a searing indictment of poverty, and how it is a one-way street to crime. The whole essence of *Oliver!* is that society is to blame."[91] Paul Taylor similarly criticized the "dogged sanitization" of the Dickens text and felt that the musical failed to live up to its polemical possibilities: "The opening bodes well for those craving a darker, more David Lean-like vision. Pitiless weather: thunder, lightning; a pregnant girl collapsing before the workhouse gates silhouetted on the scrim. But there's so little real darkness in what follows that, by the time [...] Oliver launched into 'Where is Love' [*sic*], you wonder what he's whingeing about."[92] Perhaps such criticisms were inevitable given that the Palladium *Oliver!* had to face a more cynical press and a less idealistic populace. Another *Sunday Times* reviewer noted that "'Oliver!' is a 1960s musical. Does anybody remember the 1960s? Bliss was it in that dawn to be alive, working class, cocky and swaggering; and Bart's musical, cheerful, cheeky and basically optimistic, paid homage to a culture that was emerging from being mere local colour to being a part of life."[93] Though the show remained enjoyable and relevant for this critic, it was, in many ways, reflective of a far less scornful, jaded, and skeptical time period, whatever the contemporary tendency to "look back in anger."[94]

Still, the unenthusiastic reviews did little to dissuade audiences from coming out in droves; the revival ran for a remarkable 1,352 performances and launched a successful tour of the United Kingdom and Canada. By the time *Oliver!* closed, it had broken Palladium records.[95] *Oliver!* was thus established as "the most successfully revived of all home-grown British musicals since the war."[96] It was through the Palladium adaptation that Cameron Mackintosh accomplished his goal of securing *Oliver!*'s future. The musical that had helped to start his career now owed him a distinct debt of gratitude for the almost paternal care that he had shown toward it. In a strange way, Mackintosh had become *Oliver!*'s Mr. Brownlow.

He would outdo himself more than ten years later when he revived the show again, this time at the Theatre Royal, Drury Lane. While the Palladium version had come close to his ideal vision of what *Oliver!* could be, Drury Lane offered a unique opportunity to see this ideal reach fruition, primarily owing to the structural differences between the two theaters:

> The only problem with the Palladium is that although it is a huge theatre, it's not a very deep stage. So we did end up with it being slightly too Cinemascope, and what we have at Drury Lane now is the basis of the same set but with the wonderful depth and imagination that Sean Kenny had originally, so it's the best of both worlds. The show works infinitely better at Drury Lane than it ever did at the Palladium; it was enjoyable at the Palladium, but it's a true grand melodrama now at Drury Lane on a scale that no one will ever see again.[97]

If the Palladium version had embraced the notion of a "cinematic" staging, the Drury Lane revival took this concept to the next level. The new production so dwarfed its 1960 forebear that it almost seemed a stage adaptation of the Reed film as opposed to a revival of the stage production.

The casting of the beloved comic actor Rowan Atkinson in the part of Fagin contributed to the hype surrounding the revival. Furthering the buzz was *I'd Do Anything*, a highly publicized TV talent competition to cast a pair of unknowns in the roles of Oliver and Nancy. Though Dickens created many adventures for young Oliver, the journey from literary hero to reality television star is perhaps even more fascinating than anything the Inimitable Boz could have conjured up for his titular character. In the end, Laurence Jeffcoate, Gwion Jones, and Harry Stott were all chosen to share the lead role while fan-favorite Jodie Prenger won the part of Nancy. Between the

Figure 7.2: The spectacular staging of *Oliver!* at Drury Lane is more reminiscent of the Reed film adaptation than the original stage property.
Source: "Who Will Buy?" from *Oliver!* at Theatre Royal, Drury Lane. Photograph by Catherine Ashmore. Copyright Oliver Productions Ltd. & Oliver Promotions Ltd.

publicity surrounding the casting of Atkinson in the role of Fagin and the exposure of *I'd Do Anything*, it is understandable why the Drury Lane revival went on to break the record for the largest advance ticket sales in the history of the West End. Before it had formally premiered at Drury Lane on January 14, 2009, *Oliver!* had banked £15 million.[98]

As Mackintosh predicted, the show dwarfed its Palladium predecessor in virtually every sense, and the overall critical reaction was more enthusiastic. Reviewers embraced the sentimentality, optimism, and basic exuberance of Bart's revised Dickensian vision, citing it as the perfect remedy for the economic woes that were plaguing the United Kingdom at the time of its premiere. In the face of "hard times," an appealing and energetic take on the dark and gothic world of Dickens resonated strongly. Mark Shenton praised the show for its "unremorseful spectacle and happy-go-lucky tone," claiming that these qualities

> are extremely helpful in alleviating some of the doldrums of the period. With the credit crunching in every retail and leisure sector at the moment, theatre producers are cautious about the future. Nevertheless, Cameron Mackintosh is clearly determined to buck the naysayers and has paradoxically spared no expense in bringing back to the West End one of the shows with which he began his career. [...] It's exactly the overwhelming vote of confidence that we need right now and this may be just the show we need, too: *Oliver!* is set against even harsher times but puts such a silver lining in them that it ultimately inspires love, affection and hope.[99]

Quentin Letts reinforced this sentiment, stating that "[a]nyone who needs cheering up—and after recent job news, heaven knows, that probably means most of us— should get along to Drury Lane sharpish and catch this humdinger of a night."[100] Charles Spencer likewise invoked the specter of the credit crisis, and noted that in the face of such trying circumstances it is beneficial to hone in on the lighter, more hopeful side of Dickens:

> And once you have bought into Bart's shameless sentimentality, you remember that Dickens could be shamelessly sentimental too on occasion, and settle down to wallow in a superbly melodic musical that presses all the emotional buttons while seeming especially apt and uplifting in hard times. How we all long for a kindly Mr. Brownlow to rescue us from the credit crunch just as he rescues Oliver from Fagin. Somehow our own Mr. Brown doesn't quite fit the bill.[101]

If the 1994 reviews displayed the inhospitable cynicism of a people who had little use for the working-class optimism of the fifties and sixties, the Drury Lane reviews reflect the weary hopefulness of a people trying to cling to a sentimental, romantic tradition (as epitomized by both Dickens *and* Bart) in the face of uncertainty. This dichotomy reinforces the significance of *Twist* as a constantly evolving culture text, one shaped by the cultural perceptions of those who adopt, adapt, and embrace the story.

Mackintosh lived his own *Twist*ian Cinderella-story through his journey from stage-hand to impresario, and his custodianship of *Oliver!*, the musical, is indeed evocative of Mr. Brownlow's sponsorship of Oliver, the character. Of course, if Mackintosh is to *Oliver!* what Brownlow is to Oliver Twist, one must return to the question posed by Carol Reed: was Oliver better off with Fagin? That is to say, was *Oliver!* better off in its original form, with its ramshackle, music-hall staging, as opposed to its post-Palladium form, with its luxurious, cinematic, megamusical makeover? Perhaps the greatest loss in this evolution was not the Kenny set itself, but rather the interactive intimacy that the Kenny set promoted. In reviewing the film adaptation of *Oliver!*, critic Derek Allwright noted, "[i]f I have any doubts at all they are only those that relate to the original play, in which the stylised [sic] set of Sean Kenny gave the musical just the right dream-like quality. The translation onto film has not only made the sets very realistic but has necessitated stretching some of the numbers out to a point where they begin to pall a little."[102] Bart's "dreamlike" vision of Dickensian London as a fantasy world was epitomized by the plainness of the Kenny set, which required a healthy dose of imagination on the part of the audience in order to function properly. The Reed film, with its stylized realism, was far less exacting in terms of audience creativity, and the megamusical incarnation of *Oliver!* likewise precludes such an investment.

EPILOGUE

Less than ten years into its existence, *Oliver!* had broken performance records in England and America, spawned an Oscar-winning film adaptation, and changed the face of English musical theater. Despite its relative infancy, the legacy of *Oliver!* already seemed ensured. If *Oliver!* was thriving, however, its creator was floundering. The late sixties and seventies witnessed the fall of Lionel Bart, which, much like his meteoric rise, has entered into the realm of popular lore. Stories of his spending sprees, his binges, and his material pleasures—including the toilet bowl that played Handel's water music when it was flushed—have become part of the "legend" of Lionel Bart. However exaggerated these stories may be, Bart's post-*Oliver!* decline seems symptomatic of the "nouveau riche" phenomenon that devastated the lives and careers of countless artists.

Bart's tendencies toward materialism and profligacy may have been manifestations of deeper personal demons, as several of his friends and collaborators reflect that the composer's self-destructive habits were indicative of his numerous internal struggles. "I think Lionel was always haunted about going back to those days of poverty, so it must have been something ticking in the psyche," speculates Jack Grossman, who views Bart's reckless spending sprees in his post-*Oliver!* years as manifestations of an overwhelming determination to erase the memories of his impoverished East End upbringing.[1] This fear of being forever tainted by past poverty is yet another link between Bart and Dickens, though Bart's spending habits set him in sharp contrast to Dickens, who, despite achieving tremendous financial success as an author, publisher, and public speaker, exhibited an almost perpetual anxiety about money throughout his life. Whereas Dickens's early financial hardships left him dreading the specter of penury well into his adult years, Bart's journey from rags to riches and back again reflected a disturbing lack of financial prudence in spite of the deprivation that he had endured growing up in the East End.

Unfortunately, the fame and fortune inspired by *Oliver!* had instilled Bart with a false confidence in the sustainability of his wealth. In the *Celebrate Oliver!* television special, one of the composer's nephews reflected that Bart had labored under the delusion that so long as one was continuously earning a substantial amount of money from royalties, one could uninhibitedly spend a significant percentage of that income and still never have to worry about one's finances.[2] This almost Micawber-esque sentiment seems eerily fitting given the Dickensian elements running throughout Bart's life and work. Bart sadly never reached Mr. Micawber's renowned conclusion, however: "Annual income twenty pounds, annual expenditure nineteen nineteen and six, result happiness. Annual income twenty pounds, annual expenditure twenty pounds ought and six, result misery."[3]

Like Grossman, Donald Pippin attributes Bart's behavior to an indistinct insecurity, noting that the composer "seemed so uncomfortable being this important writer; he felt like he had to show you his success with his clothes, and his car, and his telephone, and his apartment."[4] Pippin reflects that "my observation would be that he was a very neglected person and his emotional needs were very vast."[5] Although this emotional neediness may have been rooted in the difficulties of his own childhood, as the young Bart was forced to cope with being the youngest child in what was already a large and overburdened family, it is likely that these issues stemmed from a variety of sources, including his anxieties about his attractiveness and his insecurities regarding his homosexuality.[6] Bart's dependence on the companionship and approval of others inevitably contributed to his haphazard spending, as he lavished expensive gifts on the hangers-on who made up his circle.

STURM UND *TWANG!!*

This same lack of control came to define the behind-the-scenes process on his subsequent musicals. Though *Blitz!* and *Maggie May* enjoyed respectable runs, the former was an unquestionable disappointment in the wake of *Oliver!*'s stunning success; today, it is most remembered for Sean Kenny's incredibly elaborate set and for Noël Coward's immortal quip that it was louder and longer than the titular historical event. The limitations of *Blitz!* were partly the result of Bart's breaking from the production process that had defined his previous theatrical successes. Whereas *Fings, Lock Up Your Daughters,* and *Oliver!* had developed as collaborative efforts, *Blitz!* became something of a pet project for Bart, and his micromanagement of the musical created numerous difficulties. Reflecting on Bart's methodology, Cameron Mackintosh asserts that "when [Lionel] was really in charge of everything, like with *Blitz!*, it was a bit of a shambles. There were marvelous ingredients but no outside eye: no producer to stand outside. He basically staged it all; it was his complete vision and nobody said 'no' to him."[7] Bart's newfound creative freedom and authorial power, as defined by the success of *Oliver!*, proved to be a hindrance instead of a help; Mackintosh reaffirms that "he needed a really strong producer, as well as working with a really strong director, and he ended up doing it all, basically producing the shows and directing them, and therefore nobody could focus him."[8]

The disastrous Robin Hood musical *Twang!!* is almost universally regarded as the turning point in Bart's career and fortunes. Nevertheless, this is another example of the hyperbole surrounding Bart's life story. Certainly, *Twang!!* was a debacle, but every writer, producer, and composer must deal with the occasional flop; to label *Twang!!* as a true "crossroads" in Bart's life is to assign it far greater significance than it deserves. *Twang!!* can be read as the *symbol*—and not the source—of Bart's ruin, for it signified that his excesses, both personal and professional, had irreversibly halted the momentum of his early career.

There were myriad reasons for *Twang!!*'s failure, though many stemmed from the overarching issues as defined by Mackintosh. Although Bart was working closely with one of his greatest inspirations and collaborators, Joan Littlewood, their new partnership proved disastrous. Bart's increasingly erratic behavior invariably hurt the production process, while Littlewood's improvisational approach to directing was inappropriate for staging a large-scale, big-budget musical. Her difficulties managing the scope of the musical only fueled Bart's desire to assert himself and wrest control of the project away from his director: "Littlewood accused [Harvey] Orkin, Bart and [Oliver] Messel of incompetence and obstinacy. When Bart fought back, she told him he had never known his own limitations. The exchange of insults continued for nearly thirty minutes."[9] Littlewood quit the production that same day.

Bart may have been in the right in trying to depose Littlewood, whose relationship with the cast had become toxic.[10] Still, Alastair Davidson concurs with Mackintosh's analysis of the problem, pointing out that "[Lionel] wanted more and more control of his shows. And this was the big problem with both *Blitz!* and *Maggie May*. Then he completely went off on his own and conceived the disastrous *Twang!!* [...] At that point, he was doing everything on his own. He was producing and directing, and he wasn't a director."[11] Ironically, Bart's overestimation of his own directorial abilities may have been the inevitable result of his earlier collaborations with Littlewood, as Derek Paget recalls that Littlewood's relationship with Bart seemed to epitomize some of the more ominous qualities of her collaborative approach to the theatrical production process: "I'll just tell you this one story about Joan, because this is illustrative of what she was like in some ways. You'll often hear, other people tell similar sorts of stories, she would build people up quite a lot, and she would either build them up to a place which they couldn't sustain or she would build them up in order to knock them down."[12] Though Paget acknowledges that Littlewood "loved Lionel dearly,"[13] it seemed as though she had inadvertently "created a monster" in her flattering of Bart during the early stages of his career (though the success of *Oliver!* was equally culpable in this regard).

As discussed in Chapter 1, the full blame for the *Twang!!* debacle cannot be placed on Littlewood's shoulders, nor on Bart's, though just as he was haphazardly spending money on frivolities outside of the theater, he simultaneously allowed the budget for *Twang!!* to spiral out of control. Initially budgeted at a staggering £85,000 (nearly six times the budget of *Oliver!* and almost £1.4 million in today's currency), *Twang!!* allegedly cost over £100,000.[14] Coupled with the financial catastrophe was an even more alarming decline in Bart's creative output. His musical version of Fellini's *La Strada* ran for only one night on Broadway in 1969, and his adaptation of Hugo's *Notre Dame de Paris*, a musical that he called *Quasimodo*, never reached the stage despite having been in development since the early sixties.[15] Following these unsuccessful efforts, Bart almost faded into obscurity. In his own text on the history of musical theater, the great Alan Jay Lerner reflected that "[i]t is difficult to believe that talent such as Lionel Bart's could simply disappear,"[16] and yet this is seemingly what happened. Though it is clichéd to describe Bart as a "victim of his own success," as in the case of most clichés there is truth to the assertion.

In spite of his having created one of the greatest musicals of all time in *Oliver!*, Bart himself felt a certain sense of frustration regarding the all-encompassing power of his magnum opus, even early on in its existence. In 1966, in the wake of the *Twang!!* disaster, Bart expressed his aggravation with the fact that *Oliver!* was being used as a measuring stick for all of his other works, and noted that the success of his masterpiece was suffocating and restrictive:

> I would like you all to know that at this point I am very much involved in trying to forget that I was ever responsible for [*Oliver!*]. I like to think that I am a person of the present, and it's diffiult [sic] to sit on laurels and stay 'with it', let alone get ahead of 'it'. That is why I avoid walking or driving down Saint Martin's Lane in London where the posters outside the New Theatre say 'OLIVER! LONGEST RUNNING MUSICAL IN HISTORY'. Who wants to feel eighty-four when you're only thirty-six? And who wants to be pigeon-holed as a successful pro.[sic] And give up the free-dom of having the right to sometimes fail at what your [sic] trying to communicate, because you're still an amateur and you know it.[17]

Bart's letter reveals the inevitable frustrations that the composer had to endure in the wake of *Oliver!*'s astonishing triumph, for the very idea of "topping" *Oliver!* became virtually unfathomable and thus cast a certain cloud over all of his future projects—which inevitably supplemented the "elderly" feelings that characterized Bart's per-ception of himself even at this early stage in his life and career. The missive likewise displays a certain authorial humility that seems to contradict the previous assertions that Bart had allowed his ego to get the best of him in the post-*Oliver!* years and was thus left with an overinflated sense of his own capabilities. Indeed, Bart's desire to be granted the "right" to fail casts the *Twang!!* debacle in a new light, as though the disas-ter was less the result of self-destructive arrogance and more the result of unsuccess-ful experimentation on the part of a composer who was desperately trying to escape the shadow of his previous works. Granted, the two factors inevitably supplemented one another, though the letter seems to hint toward the notion that Bart's eventual retreat from show business had less to do with his failures, as epitomized by *Twang!!*, and more to do with a general sense of frustration and weariness brought on by the hopeless struggle to live up to the expectations of *Oliver!*[18]

It is, of course, wildly paradoxical to cast *Oliver!* in such a pessimistic light and hail *Twang!!* as a sympathetic underdog that embodied Bart's shattered dreams in the years following his greatest success. As noted in the previous chapter, Bart was faced with an ironic juxtaposing when the 1965 touring production of *Oliver!* came through Manchester; while *Oliver!* opened to rave reviews at the Manchester Opera House, *Twang!!* was falling apart at the Palace Theatre. Undaunted, the composer again expressed a desire to emerge from the shadow of *Oliver!*, explaining to the press, "[t]hey cook the same dish every day in Oliver's workhouse. If I dished up exactly the same show every time—well I think the audiences would start to stay away. I'm still confident that in time I'm going to hear the same kind of applause for

'Twang!!' that I heard for 'Oliver!' tonight."[19] Nevertheless, as the *Twang!!* catastrophe consumed his life in the mid-1960s, *Oliver!*'s continued success and perpetual popularity provided a certain cold comfort for the weary composer. In a *Daily Mail* article, Douglas Marlborough noted that *Oliver!* broke the record for longest-running West End musical of all time on November 20, 1965, around the very same time Bart was dealing with the frustrations of the *Twang!!* crisis in Manchester. "But yesterday was a day for jollity," notes Marlborough. "Led by the band of the Irish Guards and a float carrying children from the *Oliver!* cast, 100 children from homes around London marched from the Old Curiosity Shop, near Kingsway, London along the Strand to the New Theatre."[20] Tellingly, "[t]he only time Mr. Bart's smile vanished was when someone brought up *Twang!!*"[21]

Lionel Bart's inability to duplicate the magic of *Oliver!* is both utterly disheartening and completely understandable; he was neither the first nor the last musical theater composer to face an unhappy realization regarding the inability to top himself. Even toward the end of his life, Bart seemed somewhat frustrated by this reality. Though Mackintosh proved a generous friend and supporter throughout the composer's final years, Bart lamented that Mackintosh's method for producing shows precluded their experimenting on new musical projects as opposed to returning to *Oliver!*: "Cameron said, 'Oh, we've got to have a script on the table.' I said, 'But with that formula you'd have turned down *Oliver!*' "[22] Whatever his frustrations, Bart later confided to Brenda Evans that he considered Mackintosh to be "a righteous man."[23] It was only the second time Evans had ever heard Bart use the word "righteous" in describing a friend or acquaintance, and unlike the fair-weather friends of the 1960s, Mackintosh proved himself worthy of the distinctive designation. By heavily involving Bart in the 1994 Palladium revival, by granting him a percentage of the revenues, and, perhaps most importantly by promoting the composer's involvement as part of the musical's "rebirth," Mackintosh helped to ensure that Bart's name would forever be spoken in conjunction with his creation. The composer likewise had the joy of witnessing his musical's enduring popularity, as the opening night celebrations surrounding *Oliver!*'s return to the West End transported him back in time to the night of *Oliver!*'s 1960 premiere: "As the curtain fell [. . .] the audience rose to its feet and roared for so long the bewildered cast ran out of encores. Impresarios dream of such moments."[24] Following the show's debut at the Palladium, an emotional Bart noted that "[i]t was a wonderful evening."[25] In reflecting on the final years of Bart's life, Evans recalls that "[Lionel] was far happier in later life, when he had nothing."[26] One hopes that if Bart did indeed find peace in privation following years of excess, he likewise made peace with *Oliver!*'s dominant hold over his musical and theatrical legacy.

OLIVER!'S DICKENSIAN PROGENY

Though the 1994 Palladium revival proved the perpetual popularity of *Oliver!*, the piece had already established itself as more than a 1960s fad. More immediate revivals, including the 1977 West End revival at the Albery Theatre (its original home),

Figure E.1: The enduring power of Lionel Bart's musical genius is bound up with the enduring power of his Dickensian musical masterpiece.
Source: Used by permission of the Lionel Bart estate.

were welcomed by critics with both a warm sense of nostalgia and a new appreciation for what this show had achieved.[27] Irving Wardle wrote that it was

> [s]ad to think that [*Oliver!*] first appeared 17 years ago, since when there has hardly been a single British musical worth remembering. As Bart's own subsequent work proved, the success of this piece cannot be reduced to formula. But there it stands, as a lasting demonstration that a virile dramatic form can be built out of the old music-hall tradition, and that the stage can popularize classics without betraying them.[28]

As noted in Chapter 4, it was left up to Lloyd Webber to capitalize on the global English musical theater revival that Bart had initiated nearly twenty years earlier.

Still, even though the megamusicals of the Lloyd Webber era are arguably *Oliver!*'s most noteworthy progeny, Bart's musical initiated another intriguing (if somewhat less prolific) musical legacy by sparking a Dickensian craze. In the fifty years since *Oliver!*'s debut, stage and film musical adaptations of *The Pickwick Papers*, *Nicholas Nickleby*, *The Old Curiosity Shop*, *A Christmas Carol*, *David Copperfield*, *Hard Times*, *A Tale of Two Cities*, *Great Expectations*, and *The Mystery of Edwin Drood* have followed.

The results have been decidedly mixed, and the obscurity of several of these adaptations is a testament to their lack of success, but it is doubtful that many of these musicals would have reached fruition had it not been for *Oliver!*'s popularity.

The most immediate successor to *Oliver!* was Cyril Ornadel and Leslie Bricusse's *Pickwick*, a 1963 West End musical based on Dickens's first novel. This musical, most remembered for its signature song "If I Ruled the World" (which conveys Mr. Pickwick's naïve yet benevolent worldview), effectively capitalized on the buzz surrounding its Dickensian predecessor and proved a success in its own right in the West End before a disastrous Broadway transfer.[29] Directed by Peter Coe and designed by Sean Kenny, *Pickwick* adopted the *Oliver!* formula of using music-hall-style songs to preserve a sense of Englishness while employing the narrative techniques of the integrated musical. The prominence of music-hall motifs in *Pickwick* is fitting given the importance of Sam Weller's cockney wit to the adaptation (and to the original text). However, perhaps the most admirable quality of *Pickwick* is Wolf Mankowitz's libretto, which effectively transforms Dickens's peripatetic miscellany into a linear and coherent story told through music. Whatever its discrepancies, *Oliver Twist* remains an inherently more consistent novel than *The Pickwick Papers*, and the creative team behind *Oliver!* had the benefit of using the Lean film as a model while writing the libretto. Mankowitz had far less guidance in this regard, and the coherence of *Pickwick* is striking considering its source. Nevertheless, the very notion of integration feels somehow antithetical to the wildly disjointed yet infinitely amusing narrative of the original text. A more purposefully nonintegrated music-hall adaptation, one that emphasized comic scenes and musical turns as opposed to narrative coherence and integrated numbers, would more accurately capture the rollicking spirit of the Dickensian source.

Ironically, such a technique proved vital to a musical adaptation of Dickens's final novel, *The Mystery of Edwin Drood*. Rupert Holmes's adaptation of this text remains the most successful Dickensian stage musical produced in the wake of *Oliver!* Holmes memorably takes the music-hall concept of *Oliver!* and *Pickwick* to its natural conclusion by crafting a music-hall revue built around a unique Dickensian narrative. Here, a troupe of Victorian music-hall performers eagerly put forth their own boisterous adaptation of *The Mystery of Edwin Drood*, Dickens's unfinished murder mystery. Some of the songs are "integrated" into the *Drood* narrative, but there is a diegetic quality to every single number in the show, and the actors/characters are always conscious of the transition from speech to song. Although this highly experimental adaptation purposefully deemphasizes the Dickensian source—Holmes memorably described the adaptation as a "springboard for a series of theatrical moments and events, using a literary curiosity as a trampoline"[30]—the piece nevertheless reveals the possibilities of using nonintegrated models when adapting literary texts for the musical stage. Furthermore, whatever its infidelities to Dickens, Holmes's adaptation insightfully explores the connections between Dickens and music hall, specifically the shared sense of community through audience involvement. The audience is a vital participant in shaping the narrative of Holmes's musical, just as they were vital participants in shaping Dickens's approach to serialization and in shaping music-hall performers' approach to singing.[31]

The Royal Shakespeare Company's groundbreaking adaptation of *Nicholas Nickleby*, though not a musical, included a great deal of stage music as written by the late Stephen Oliver; more significantly, it employed this music in a wide variety of forms and contexts, occasionally alternating between Wagnerian unity (e.g., setting Dickens's narrative prose to music as Nicholas and Smike journey toward Portsmouth) and Brechtian irony (e.g., the singing of an uplifting carol while the spotlight shines down on Nicholas holding the body of an impoverished orphan boy). The less ambitious rock musical *Smike*, originally broadcast by the BBC and then adapted for the stage, presents a more traditional "show within a show" musical narrative about a group of schoolboys enacting a musical interpretation of the Dotheboys Hall chapters from Dickens's third novel.

Unsurprisingly, musical adaptations of *A Christmas Carol* have proved quite common and will likely continue to do so, but then, *A Christmas Carol* has always been an entity unto itself. Like *Oliver!*, Leslie Bricusse's film *Scrooge* (later adapted for the stage) uses a traditional book-musical narrative, while Alan Menken's *A Christmas Carol: The Musical* is virtually sung through and thus seems more Wagnerian. Nevertheless, both adaptations effectively explore the musical highpoints of Dickens's novella and hone in on the most "musical" moments in the story; the numbers in *Scrooge* frequently overlap with the shift from speech or recitative to song in *A Christmas Carol: The Musical*. Like *Oliver!*, both adaptations grant younger viewers an entryway into Dickens's text. Brian Henson's *The Muppet Christmas Carol* takes this concept one step further, as the sprightly yet sincere musical adaptation, featuring an incredibly effective score by songwriter Paul Williams, actually concludes with the Great Gonzo recommending that younger viewers take up the book. As noted, the Disneyfication of Dickens by Bart helped pave the way for many of these family musicals.

Fittingly, the most Disneyfied Dickensian musical of all time was a musical adaptation of *Oliver Twist* produced by Walt Disney Studios: *Oliver & Company*. Set in 1988 New York City, this animated film recasts several of the Dickens characters as animals: Oliver is an orphaned kitten taken under paw by Dodger, a streetwise mutt. Fagin is the dog's master, a destitute scrap dealer who is in debt to the brutal gangster Sykes. The film closely follows the narrative of *Oliver!*, from the initial encounter between Dodger and Oliver through Oliver's becoming part of the gang and being cared for by Fagin, to the botched robbery for which he is "caught" and subsequently exonerated/adopted (here he is taken in by a rich little girl), to his abduction by the gang, through a final confrontation with Sykes and a happy ending that sees the orphan permanently adopted by the rich family. As in *Oliver!*, Fagin is reinvented as a sympathetic co-protagonist, and the design and function of Fagin in the animated film seems consciously evocative of Bart's vision of the character (minus his trademark beard): as in the film version of *Oliver!*, Fagin is gangly and ragged, has matted red hair, wears a long green coat with absurdly deep pockets, and sports brown fingerless gloves. Furthermore, he is portrayed as the gang's caretaker and benevolent provider, and the presentation of the gang is almost uniformly positive. Although the film boasts a creative premise and provides another key example of the intertextuality promoted by the *Twist* culture text (ironically, it can be read as a Disney adaptation of Reed's film adaptation of *Oliver!*), its score is composed almost entirely of pop music. The result is that the songs are neither particularly memorable nor particularly relevant to the Dickensian storyline, and the adaptation suffers as a result.[32]

Though hardly a Disney classic, *Oliver & Company* found some success on its release and has gradually gained a following among Disney fans. Other Disneyfied Dickensian musicals have fared poorly in comparison. Many of these musicals have purposefully modeled themselves on *Oliver!* in the hope of capturing the spark of Bart's adaptation, but this technique has frequently resulted in the works' being unfavorably compared to their all-important predecessor. Anthony Newley virtually duplicated the *Oliver!* formula for his ambitious but ill-conceived 1975 family-film musical *Mr. Quilp*; here, Newley portrays Little Nell's tormentor (and the most despicable character in the entire Dickens canon), Daniel Quilp, as a lovable rascal in the vein of Bart's Fagin. However, by reducing Quilp's villainy to roguishness, Newley and the creative team likewise reduce the dramatic conflict of Dickens's narrative, and the film suffers as a result. Similarly, when Al Kasha and Joel Hirschorn adapted *David Copperfield* into the Broadway musical *Copperfield*, their musical came across as a derivative attempt to capitalize on *Oliver!*'s legacy: here was another Dickensian musical featuring a downtrodden orphan protagonist trying to make his fortune while surrounded by a wide array of lively musical characters. Just as *Mr. Quilp* bombed at the box office, *Copperfield* closed after thirteen Broadway performances.

Jill Santoriello's more recent Dickensian musical, an adaptation of *A Tale of Two Cities*, was also dismissed as derivative, though critics found it imitative of *Les Misérables* as opposed to *Oliver!* It seems unfair to fault the creative team for adopting several of Boublil and Schönberg's megamusical conventions in the conception and execution of the adaptation, especially given the similar characteristics of the two novelistic sources (not to mention the overlapping subject matter); however, the failure of *A Tale of Two Cities* reinforces the fact that the era of the eighties megamusical has passed. Unfortunately, this reality may bode ill for future Dickensian musicals. The possibility of musical adaptations of previously unexplored novels like *Martin Chuzzlewit*, *Dombey and Son*, *Bleak House*, *Little Dorrit*, and *Our Mutual Friend* is enticing, but it seems as though following the *Les Misérables* model would be the only viable means of successfully preserving the complicated plots to these sprawling nineteenth-century novels, and finding a way of "topping" *Les Misérables* would be an arduous task to say the least.

WHAT HAPPENS WHEN *OLIVER!* IS SEVENTY?

The results of the Dickensian musical craze have been inconsistent, but *Oliver!*'s significance in encouraging composers to explore the musical potential of Dickens is undeniable. Given the enduring power of *Oliver!*, the potential for future musical adaptations of Dickens will always be tenable. However, in a post-megamusical era, the question of just how to adapt Dickens's more complicated works successfully to the musical stage is not easily answered. The question of what form later revivals of *Oliver!* will take is similarly unclear, for the Drury Lane revival pushed the potential of the musical's cinematic grandeur to the limit. Would an old-school revival using the Kenny set capture the nostalgic appeal of the musical and the "simpler" time that it once represented? Would a revised libretto that incorporated some of the scenes and characters who failed to make the final cut help to expand the scope of the musical's narrative and the "where is love?" theme? Would a complete revision to the very form of the musical—one that dismissed the integrated narrative in exchange for an experimental, music-hall framework à la Holmes's *Drood*—breathe new life into the musical while simultaneously preserving its timeless songs? Or should an ambitious young composer take the piece in the opposite direction and fully convert it into a megamusical by exchanging the dialogue for operatic recitative, expanding the scope of the musical score, and advancing the Dickensian narrative beyond the novel's first sixteen chapters?

Sadly, we cannot turn to the musical's creator for guidance. When Lionel Bart passed away in 1999, the world lost one of the great talents in the history of musical theater—a man whose contributions to the English musical were central to its evolution. Dickensians everywhere should likewise mourn the loss, for *Oliver!* helped to take the culture text of *Oliver Twist* in a unique and fascinating direction, a direction that ultimately helped to introduce Dickens's beloved characters to a new generation of followers and that continues to provide a unique entryway into the world of Dickensiana. If "Where Is Love?" is indeed the central unifying thread to *Oliver!*, then the title question has already been answered in the public's love for this treasure of the musical stage.

NOTES

INTRODUCTION

1. Sheridan Morley and Ruth Leon, *Hey, Mr. Producer! The Musical World of Cameron Mackintosh* (New York: Back Stage Books, 1998), 10.
2. Sheridan Morley, *Spread a Little Happiness: The First Hundred Years of the British Musical* (London: Thames and Hudson, 1987), 7.
3. Malcolm Andrews, *Dickens on England and the English* (Sussex: Harvester Press, 1979), xv–xvi.
4. Charles Dickens, "Address in the First Number of 'Household Words'," in *The Centenary Edition of the Works of Charles Dickens, Miscellaneous Papers*, vol. 1 (New York: Scribner's, 1911), 181.
5. Juliet John, *Dickens and Mass Culture* (Oxford: Oxford University Press, 2010), 15.
6. Ibid., 5.
7. Benedict Anderson, *Imagined Communities*, rev. ed. (New York: Verso, 1991), 7.
8. Ibid., 6.
9. Peter Bailey, "Introduction: Making Sense of Music Hall," in *Music Hall: The Business of Pleasure*, ed. Peter Bailey (Philadelphia: Open University Press, 1986), viii.
10. John, *Dickens and Mass Culture*, 77.
11. Sabine Clemm, *Dickens, Journalism, and Nationhood: Mapping the World in* Household Words (New York: Routledge, 2009), 4.
12. Anthony Easthope, *Englishness and National Culture* (New York: Routledge, 1999), 12.
13. John, *Dickens and Mass Culture*, 62–63.
14. Ibid., 18–20.
15. Scott Miller, *Strike up the Band: A New History of Musical Theatre* (Portsmouth: Heinemann, 2007), 81.
16. As Jessica Sternfeld notes in her exemplary text on the megamusical, "the word may sound funny, but it is probably the most accurate term [...] [to describe] a kind of musical theater that rose to prominence in the 1970s and 1980s and that remains a dominant force on Broadway today." Sternfeld attributes the term to the *New York Times* and mentions that it has become something of an umbrella term for blockbuster musicals. Most megamusicals share several dominant traits, many of which are implied by their designation: the stories are somehow epic, the music is usually continuous, and the staging, sets, properties, and effects are always visually spectacular. Sternfeld, *The Megamusical* (Bloomington: Indiana University Press, 2006), 1.
17. Jay Clayton, *Charles Dickens in Cyberspace* (New York: Oxford University Press, 2003), 152.
18. Ibid.
19. The question (and timetable) of *Oliver!*'s development became a legal issue when Lionel Bart's music label, Peter Maurice, Ltd., sued over the rights to the musical's

songs (see Chapter 2). Donald Albery was adamantly against the notion of Bart's tes-
tifying on the subject of *Oliver!*'s conception, warning that "[i]t would always be a
different story. [Lionel] is capable of inventing anything." Transcribed conversation
between Donald Albery of Donmar Productions and Davenport Lyons, solicitor to
Jock Jacobsen, May 25, 1961, 1. Sir Donald Albery Collection, DAT 194.003. Harry
Ransom Center, University of Texas at Austin.

CHAPTER 1

1. Juliet John, *Charles Dickens's* Oliver Twist: *A Sourcebook*, ed. Juliet John (New York:
Routledge, 2006), 1.
2. Paul Davis, *The Lives and Times of Ebenezer Scrooge* (New Haven: Yale University Press,
1990), 3.
3. Paul Schlicke, ed., *The Oxford Reader's Companion to Dickens* (New York: Oxford
University Press, 1999), 437.
4. Mary Cross, "Introduction" in *Advertising and Culture: Theoretical Perspectives*, ed.
Mary Cross (Westport: Praeger, 1996), xi.
5. Ibid.
6. Adaptation theorist Linda Hutcheon notes that oftentimes "the audience will recognize that a work is an adaptation of more than one specific text. For instance, when
later writers reworked—for radio, stage, and even screen—John Buchan's 1914 novel,
the *Thirty-Nine Steps*, they often adapted Alfred Hitchcock's dark and cynical 1935 film
adaptation along with the novel (Glancy 2003: 99–100). And films about *Dracula* today
are as often seen as adaptations of other earlier films as they are of Bram Stoker's novel."
Linda Hutcheon, *A Theory of Adaptation* (New York: Routledge, 2006), 21.
7. Malcolm Morley recounts the disastrous results of this first recorded adaptation of
Oliver Twist, quoting the reviews from three Victorian journals that labeled the piece
"'a very meager and dull affair and the sooner taken from the bills the better'; [...] 'a
thing more unfit for any stage, except that of a Penny Theatre, we never saw'; [...] 'It
was consigned by the audience to the lower depths of Tartarus'." There have been several debates regarding the identity of the author of this adaptation. F. Dubrez Fawcett
asserts that it was written by J. S. Coyne, "a fertile writer of farces, and one of the found-
ers, in 1847, of *Punch*." Conversely, Richard P. Fulkerson insists that the first adaptation was written by Gilbert A. a`Beckett. The card catalogue for the Lord Chamberlain's
manuscripts collection at the British Library also lists a`Beckett as the author.
    Malcolm Morley, "Early Dramas of *Oliver Twist*," *The Dickensian* 43 (1947): 75.
    F. Dubrez Fawcett, *Dickens the Dramatist* (London: W. H. Allen, 1952), 54.
    Richard P. Fulkerson, "The Dickens Novel on the Victorian Stage" (Ph.D. diss.,
Ohio State University, 1970), 93.
8. Some of these episodes listed in the table do not correspond precisely to their novelistic counterparts; for example, in the Searle adaptation, the botched robbery takes
place at Brownlow's house as opposed to the Maylie house. Nevertheless, the chart
is meant to signify approximately what points in the plot were presented on the
Victorian stage, even if they were not presented "to the letter" of the novel.
9. "The Screen: A Packed House for a Poor House," *New York Times*, October 30, 1922, 19.
10. John, *Sourcebook*, 106–7.
11. Martin Green, "Some Versions of the Pastoral: Myth in Advertising; Advertising as
Myth," in *Advertising and Culture: Theoretical Perspectives*, ed. Mary Cross (Westport:
Praeger, 1996), 45.
12. Paul P. Kennedy, "British Cameras Grind out *Oliver Twist*," *New York Times*, November
9, 1947, X5.
13. Quoted in ibid.

14. Amusingly, a film critic at *The Sketch* failed to anticipate just how important these innovations would be in the larger legacy of *Oliver Twist*, dryly noting that Lean had "invented two extra refinements of torture: an opening scene in which Oliver's mother is seen struggling towards the workhouse in the last agonies of travail, and a climax in which Oliver is forced to scramble over the rooftops and fix the rope that hangs Bill Sikes. The first of these innovations, I admit, is very effectively done; the second seems to me both savage and silly." Lean's "savage and silly" conclusion became the standard ending for several prominent adaptations of *Oliver Twist*, and Carol Reed's virtual duplication of this climax in the film version of *Oliver!* has reinforced the enduring power of Lean's vision. Review of David Lean's *Oliver Twist, The Sketch*, July 21, 1948, 44.

15. John, *Sourcebook*, 100.

16. Joss Marsh, "Dickens and Film," in *The Cambridge Companion to Charles Dickens*, ed. John O. Jordan (Cambridge: Cambridge University Press, 2001), 218.

17. There were larger political issues behind the protest, as several British films were being protested by Jewish groups at the time.

   Kevin Brownlow, *David Lean: A Biography* (New York: St. Martin's Press, 1996), 246.

18. "Baton Charge on Berlin *Oliver Twist* Objectors," *The Daily Telegraph and Morning Post*, February 22, 1949, 1.

19. Cyril Connolly, "Comment," *Horizon* 15, no. 87 (April 1947): 151.

20. Peter Mandler, *The English National Character: The History of an Idea from Edmund Burke to Tony Blair* (New Haven: Yale University Press, 2006), 196.

21. Mark Donnelly, *Sixties Britain: Culture, Society, and Politics* (New York: Pearson Longman, 2005), 16.

22. Mandler, *English National Character*, 196.

23. Ibid., 4.

24. Dominic Sandbrook, *Never Had It So Good: A History of Britain from Suez to the Beatles* (London: Little Brown, 2005), 44.

25. Ibid., 174.

26. Alan Sinfield, "The Theatre and Its Audience," in *Society and Literature, 1945–1970*, ed. Alan Sinfield (New York: Holmes & Meier, 1983), 178.

27. Though *Look Back in Anger* was hailed as revolutionary, it was simultaneously quite conventional in regard to its form. Nadine Holdsworth notes that *Look Back in Anger* was "widely credited with revolutionizing the content, if not the form, of British theatre," while Frances Gray notes that Osborne "failed to challenge the accepted idea of what theatre really *is*."

   Nadine Holdsworth, *Joan Littlewood* (New York: Routledge, 2006), 25. Frances Gray, *John Arden* (New York: Grove Press, 1983), 3 (Gray's emphases).

28. John Osborne, *Look Back in Anger* (New York: S. G. Phillips, 1957), 17.

29. Ibid., 84.

30. Ibid.

31. Colin MacInnes, "Pop Songs and Teenagers" in *England, Half English* by Colin MacInnes (London: MacGibbon & Kee, 1961), 56.

32. David Ian Rabey, *English Drama Since 1940* (New York: Longman, 2003), 30.

33. It is important to note that Macmillan's words have consistently been taken out of context; Macmillan was not celebrating the smug sense of economic supremacy that defined the late 1950s, but rather warning *against* the complacent materialism that characterized the period.

   Robert Hewison, *Too Much: Art and Society in the Sixties, 1960–75* (New York: Oxford University Press, 1987), 5–6.

34. Arnold Wesker, *The Kitchen* (London: Jonathan Cape, 1966), 58.

35. Ibid., 79.
36. Arnold Wesker, *Chicken Soup with Barley*, in *The Wesker Trilogy* (Random House: New York, 1960), 77.
37. Alan Sinfield, "Queen's English" in *The Revision of Englishness*, eds. David Rogers and John McLeod (Manchester: Manchester University Press, 2004), 31.
38. Cameron Mackintosh, interview by author, July 12, 2010.
39. Ibid.
40. Caryl Brahms, "The Dickens and the Don," *John O'London's Weekly*, July 14, 1960, 3.
41. Osborne, *Look Back in Anger*, 63.
42. Bart was six years old when the Battle of Cable Street took place, though he later maintained that he was "very aware, of that sort of persecution [even then]." His older brother Sam, whom he idolized, helped to inspire his leftist political views, for Sam was "very left wing" and participated in the anti-Mosley protests in the East End before going to fight Franco in the Spanish Civil War.
    Lionel Bart, *South Bank Show*, Transcript, Roll 3, 6–8, Lionel Bart Foundation Archive.
43. Quoted in Michael Billington, "Arnold Wesker: Food for Thought," *The Guardian*, May 21, 2012, http://www.theguardian.com/stage/2012/may/21/arnold-wesker-food-for-thought.
44. Ibid.
45. Rabey, *English Drama*, 39.
46. Quoted in Dominic Shellard, *British Theatre Since the War* (New Haven: Yale University Press, 1999), 70. (Reading's emphases)
47. Rabey acknowledges the centrality of "Kenneth Tynan's famously significant and commercially crucial review of *Look Back*" to the play's success, while Dominic Shellard takes the matter even further, noting that the coining of the term "angry young men" at Royal Court translated into an incredibly effective marketing campaign in spite of the artificiality of the group label.
    Rabey, *English Drama*, 31. Shellard, *British Theatre*, 56.
48. Rabey, *English Drama*, 31.
49. Kenneth Tynan, "The Voice of the Young," *The Observer*, May 13, 1956, 11.
50. Martin Esslin, "Foreword," in *Playwrights' Theatre* by Terry W. Browne (London: Pitman, 1975), iv.
51. Shellard, *British Theatre*, 56.
52. Sandbrook, *Never Had It So Good*, 27.
53. E. Ellis Cashmore, *No Future: Youth and Society* (London: Heinemann, 1984), 9.
54. Bill Osgerby, *Youth in Britain Since 1945* (Oxford: Blackwell, 1998), 5.
55. Colin MacInnes, "Young England, Half English," in *England, Half English* (London: MacGibbon & Kee, 1961), 11.
56. Osgerby, *Youth in Britain*, 26.
57. Sandbrook, *Never Had It So Good*, 414.
58. Ibid., 434.
59. Paul Ward, *Britishness Since 1870* (New York: Routledge, 2004), 90–91.
60. MacInnes, "Young England, Half English," 13.
61. Ibid., 13–14.
62. Ibid., 14.
63. Ibid., 15.
64. Ibid.
65. Ibid.
66. Gordon Thompson, *Please Please Me: Sixties British Pop, Inside Out* (Oxford: Oxford University Press, 2008), 4.

67. In *Enchanted Evenings*, Geoffrey Block traces the American musical tradition back to *H.M.S. Pinafore*, and Raymond Knapp likewise emphasizes this comic opera's importance while simultaneously noting the tendency of American performers and producers to play up the effeminacy of the English characters for satirical purposes.

    Geoffrey Block, *Enchanted Evenings: The Broadway Musical from* Show Boat *to Sondheim* (New York: Oxford University Press, 1997), 4.

    Raymond Knapp, *The American Musical and the Formation of National Identity* (Princeton: Princeton University Press, 2005), 34–39, 45.

68. Kurt Ganzl, *The Musical: A Concise History* (Boston: Northeastern University Press, 1997), 194.

69. Sheridan Morley, *Spread a Little Happiness: The First Hundred Years of the British Musical* (London: Thames and Hudson, 1987), 29.

70. Ibid., 103.

71. Shellard, *British Theatre*, 23.

72. For an excellent summary of the characteristics of the integrated musical, see Geoffrey Block's essay "Integration" in the *Oxford Handbook of the American Musical*.

73. Scott McMillin sums up Rodgers and Hammerstein's own "endorsement" of the integrated formula in chapter 1 of *The Musical as Drama*.

    Scott McMillin, *The Musical as Drama* (Princeton: Princeton University Press, 2006), 1–2.

74. Block cites "*Show Boat*'s unprecedented integration of music and drama, its three-dimensional characters, and its bold and serious subject matter, including miscegenation and unhappy marriages."

Block, *Enchanted Evenings*, 20–21.

75. Geoffrey Block, "Integration" in *Oxford Handbook of the American Musical*, eds. Raymond Knapp, Mitchell Morris, Stacy Wolf (New York: Oxford University Press, 2011), 108.

    Mark N. Grant, *The Rise and Fall of the Broadway Musical* (Boston: Northeastern University Press, 2004), 88.

76. McMillin, *Musical as Drama*, 5, 156–57.

77. Ibid.

78. Ibid., 103. (McMillin's emphases)

79. Ibid., 15, 19.

80. Lehman Engel, *Words with Music: The Broadway Musical Libretto* (New York: Schirmer, 1981), 246.

81. McMillin, *Musical as Drama*, 21.

82. As McMillin puts it, "Jud is capable of rape if Laurey does go out with him, capable of arson if she doesn't."

    Ibid., 51.

83. John Snelson, " 'We said we wouldn't look back': British Musical Theatre, 1935–1960," in *The Cambridge Companion to the Musical*, eds. William A. Everett and Paul R. Laird (Cambridge: Cambridge University Press, 2002), 115.

84. Cecil Smith, "Clap Hands! It's a British Musical," *Daily Express*, August 6, 1954.

As far as *The Boy Friend* was concerned, however, Wilson denied this claim, and in the author's note preceding the libretto he explicitly states, "I would like to make it clear, here and now, that this show was never intended as a 'reply to *Oklahoma!*' or indeed to any of the very successful and essentially modern American musicals. I feel that the English Theatre has very far to go before it can rival Broadway in this field." Wilson's reference to the "modern" quality of American musicals indicates that his own piece was tied heavily to the conventions of the past.

    Sandy Wilson, *The Boy Friend* (New York: Dutton, 1955), 20.

85. In the title of his review of *Salad Days*, Smith encouraged readers to "Clap Hands! It's a British Musical," and he praised the fact that "Not a joke, or a rhyming lyric sounds like *Kiss Me Kate* or *Guys and Dolls*. Not a member of the cast tries to behave as though he has grown up on Broadway."
Smith, "Clap Hands."
86. Snelson, "'We said we wouldn't look back'," 116.
87. Anthony Cookman, "At the Theatre," *The Tatler*, January 27, 1954, 132.
88. Review of *Salad Days*, *The Sketch*, August 25, 1954.
89. Snelson, "'We said we wouldn't look back'," 115.
90. Ibid., 116.
91. McMillin, *Musical as Drama*, 21.
92. In the Dickens text, the housebreaker's name is spelled S-i-k-e-s. Various adaptations, including the Lean film, have spelled it with a "y" instead. The surviving *Oliver!* draft materials alternate between the two forms, though in the official script, score, and program for the original production it is spelled S-y-k-e-s. Later revivals, and the Carol Reed film adaptation, restored Dickens's spelling. For clarity, all references to the housebreaker as he is depicted in the stage version of *Oliver!* will be spelled S-y-k-e-s.
93. Ivor Novello, *Gay's the Word* (New York: Samuel French, 1951), I-1-1.
94. Dors had an indirect connection to *Oliver!*, as she played the decidedly unglamorous role of Charlotte in Lean's *Oliver Twist*.
95. Of the British musicals listed above, only *The Boy Friend* achieved true transatlantic success, however. The initial Broadway production ran an impressive 485 performances, though the overall tone of the show was modified heavily for the American audiences. As Ganzl writes "the feeling and the mood were gone. Broadway's *Boy Friend* was no more the new 1920s musical it had been created to be. It was the burlesque everyone at the Players' had wished to avoid."
Kurt Ganzl, *British Musical Theatre, Vol. II, 1915–1984* (New York: Oxford University Press, 1986), 646.
96. Kenneth Tynan, "The Broadway Package," *The Observer*, May 4, 1958, 15.
97. Ibid.
98. Anthony Cookman of the *Tatler* similarly observed that "the really vital thing [...] is that we never feel that [Shaw's] dialogue is being interrupted for song and dance or that song and dance are reluctantly making way for the resumption of the dialogue. One melts into the other with a sort of magic fluidity."
Anthony Cookman, "Moments I Shall Remember," *The Tatler*, May 14, 1958, 370.
99. Morley, *Spread a Little Happiness*, 8.
100. David Walsh and Len Platt, *Musical Theatre and American Culture* (Westport: Praeger, 2003), 113.
101. As Walsh and Platt note, "it is because Eliza becomes the power that she and Higgins can marry. Her transformation allows Higgins to reform himself by recognizing his need for her [...] and so establishes a love relationship between them, and not just one of master and servant."
Ibid., 113–14.
102. Bart claimed to have adopted the name while passing St. Bartholomew's Hospital during his trips between the East End and the West End when he began studying at the St. Martin's School of Art, and although this is the version of the story that is widely circulated, his friend and archivist Brenda Evans flatly denies it by pointing out discrepancies in the time frame of the two occurrences; instead, she cites an article in a 1966 issue of *London Life* stating that Begleiter adopted the

name after mistakenly being addressed as "Mr. Bart" by a patron at his printing business.

Brenda Evans, interview by author, July 6, 2010.

"Consider Yourself 'In' with a Lionel Bart Poster," *London Life*, August 27, 1966.

103. Brenda Evans, letter to author, October 13, 2010.
104. Ron Moody, "Reviewing the Situation," *Jewish Chronicle*, April 9, 1999.
105. Cameron Mackintosh, interview by author.
106. Moody, "Reviewing the Situation."
107. Bart's informal methodology for writing music presents an additional correlation with his heritage; just as Bart composed music in his head rather than on paper, early Jewish music existed solely in an oral tradition as opposed to its being documented in musical notation. Jack Gottlieb writes that Jews traditionally "sustained their musical heritage more through oral communication than by written form"; this was due primarily to the rabbinical suspicion toward formal documentation.

Jack Gottlieb, *Funny, It Doesn't Sound Jewish* (Albany: State University of New York Press, 2004), 13.
108. Quoted in Paul Hamer, "Bart: Bentleys to Bankruptcy and Back," *TV Times*, 87, no. 14, March 31, 1977: 16.
109. Lionel Bart, *South Bank Show*, Transcript, Roll 3, 17–18, Lionel Bart Foundation Archive.
110. Dennis Barker, "Fings Ain't Wot They Used T'Be," *The Guardian*, April 5, 1999, 12.
111. Quoted in "The Man Who Asked for More," *Times*, December 10, 1994, 33.
112. Lionel Bart, *South Bank Show*, Transcript, Roll 3, 2, Lionel Bart Foundation Archive.
113. John Gorman, *Knocking Down Ginger* (London: Caliban Books, 1995), 136–37.
114. Ibid., 138.
115. Evans confirms that aside from its narrative influence on *Oliver!* the Lean film was one of Bart's favorite movies. Bart later praised the film as "superb" in an unpublished autobiographical reflection.

Brenda Evans, interview by author. Lionel Bart, Personal Reflection on *Oliver!* #2, 2/9. Lionel Bart Foundation Archive.
116. Gorman, *Knocking Down Ginger*, 153–54.
117. Michael Freedland, "'Unity Was My Turning Point,'" *Belfast News-Letter*, April 17, 1964. Gorman, *Knocking Down Ginger*, 175.
118. Jack Grossman, interview by author, July 15, 2010.
119. Colin Chambers, *The Story of Unity Theatre* (New York: St. Martin's Press, 1989), 18.
120. Quoted in Malcolm Hulke, ed., "Here Is Drama: Behind the Scenes at Unity Theatre, London" (England: Unity Theatre Society, 1963), 3.
121. Heinz Lowenstein, "Contributions to a Discussion on the Production of Plays at Unity Theatre," 5. Unity Theatre: theatre company records. Victoria and Albert Museum Theatre Collections.
122. Jack Grossman, interview by author.
123. Ibid.
124. Ibid.

At Unity, Bart found a noteworthy mentor in the beloved comic actor Alfie Bass, who directed *Turn It Up!* one of Bart's most prominent Unity projects. It is understandable that Bart and Bass would gravitate to one another given their mutual Jewish-cockney background and their shared fondness for music-hall songs.

Cathryn Rose, "How Alfie Got into the Singing Game," *Leicester Evening Mail*, July 4, 1958, 5.
125. See Grand Palais file at the Victoria and Albert Museum Theatre Collections.
126. Gorman, *Knocking Down Ginger*, 175.

127. Harry Landis, interview by author, July 28, 2010.
128. Chambers, *Story of Unity Theatre*, 331.
129. Jack Grossman, interview by author.
130. Ibid.
131. Quoted in Robert Chalmers, "Out But Not Down," *Daily Telegraph*, January 17, 1992, 14.
132. Chambers, *Story of Unity Theatre*, 351.
133. Ibid.
134. Julian Glover, interview by author, July 15, 2010.
135. Harry Landis, interview by author.
136. Quoted in Freedland, " 'Unity Was My Turning Point.' "
137. Quoted in ibid.
138. Jack Grossman, interview by author.
139. "Lionel Bart," *The South Bank Show*, ITV (UK), December 11, 1994, television.
140. Jack Grossman, interview by author.
141. Jock Jacobsen, letter to Bernard Heinz, May 23, 1958. Unity Theatre: theatre company records, THM/9/2/1/15. Victoria and Albert Museum Theatre Collections.
142. Bernard Heinz, letter to Jock Jacobsen, May 30, 1958. Unity Theatre: theatre company records, THM/9/2/1/15. Victoria and Albert Museum Theatre Collections.
143. Ibid.
144. The very concept of "plagiarism" is somewhat problematic in this context as Bart's method of writing music did not involve formal annotation. Thus, he certainly did not "copy" the musical notes from the Grossman songs; what is more likely is that he pulled the melodies from his memory and adapted them to suit his needs. During my interview with Grossman and Julian Glover, they sang a few bars of the two songs, and the similarities between the corresponding songs from *Oliver!* exist on a basic, melodic level.
    Jack Grossman, interview by author. Julian Glover, interview by author.
145. Jack Grossman, interview by author.
146. Cameron Mackintosh, interview by author.
147. Quoted in Freedland, "Unity Was My Turning Point."
148. Nevertheless, several of his Unity colleagues noted that he was inevitably drawn to the glitz of the popular music scene. "He just loved the pop scene," notes Grossman, and Landis agrees that "Lionel was interested in fame. So he adapted himself into the pop world." Recalling his friend and one-time partner's entry into the "pop world," Gorman, in an ominous and prophetic metaphor, notes that "[f]ame can be as a drug, and Lionel, who had an obsession to become famous, was hooked." Jack Grossman, interview by author.
    Harry Landis, interview by author.
    Gorman, *Knocking Down Ginger*, 193.
149. For many people in Britain, the coffee-bar craze was another example of the unhealthy trend toward Americanization.
    Michael Brocken, *The British Folk Revival, 1944–2002* (Burlington: Ashgate, 2003), 75.
150. Gorman, *Knocking Down Ginger*, 192.
151. Tommy Steele, *Bermondsey Boy: Memories of a Forgotten World* (London: Michael Joseph, 2006), 240–41.
152. MacInnes, "Young England, Half English," 13.
153. Humorously, just as Bart would cite his joining Unity Theatre as the turning point of his life, a 1959 interview with the *Leicester Evening Mail* bestowed the same label on his first meeting with Tommy Steele, reinforcing the tension between these two separate elements of his career.

Jenny Firth, "Meeting Tommy Was the Turning Point," *Leicester Evening Mail*, March 26, 1959.

154. Cameron Mackintosh, interview by author.

155. Robert Leach, *Theatre Workshop: Joan Littlewood and the Making of Modern British Theatre* (Exeter: University of Exeter Press, 2006), 138.

156. Holdsworth, *Joan Littlewood*, 31.

157. Leach, *Theatre Workshop*, 139.
    Oliver! a London musical that embraced a similar cockney energy, opened just a few short months after the Littlewood project that marked the culmination of this postwar Workshop movement, *Sparrers Can't Sing*.

158. Ibid., 141.

159. Ossia Trilling, "The New English Realism," *The Tulane Drama Review*, 7, no. 2 (Winter 1962): 187.

160. Ibid., 188.

161. Gordon M. Wickstrom, "The Heroic Dimension in Brendan Behan's 'The Hostage'," *Educational Theatre Journal*, 22, no. 4 (December 1970): 407.

162. Margaret Eddershaw, *Performing Brecht: Forty Years of British Performances* (New York: Routledge, 1996), 45.

163. Leach, *Theatre Workshop*, 111.

164. Because of conflicts between Littlewood and Brecht's assistant Karl Weber, and Littlewood's having to direct herself in the role of Mother Courage (as demanded by Brecht himself), the production was a chaotic disaster.
    Leach, *Theatre Workshop*, 112.
    Eddershaw, *Performing Brecht*, 46.
    Howard Goorney, *The Theatre Workshop Story* (London: Methuen, 1981), 102.

165. Martin Esslin, "Brecht and the English Theatre," in *Brecht Sourcebook*, eds. Carol Martin and Henry Bial (London: Routledge, 2000), 151.

166. Ibid., 149.

167. Kurt Weill, "Note by Kurt Weill," in *The Threepenny Opera*, by Bertolt Brecht (New York: Arcade, 1994), 98.

168. Lionel Bart, *South Bank Show*, Transcript, Roll 5, 6, Lionel Bart Foundation Archive.

169. Quoted in Frank Norman, *Why Fings Went West* (London: Lemon Tree Press, 1975), 46.

170. Ibid. 46–50.

171. Eric Johns, "Fings Is Buzzin' at the Garrick in Soho Saga," *The Stage*, February 18, 1960, 17.

172. Quoted in Joan Littlewood, *Joan's Book: The Autobiography of Joan Littlewood* (London: Methuen, 2003), 540.
    Leach asserts that there are many untruths or half-truths in Littlewood's autobiography, claiming that "I have been warned by several of her closest associates from Theatre Workshop to treat its contents with extreme caution." Whether or not Bart's involvement with *Fings* emerged exactly as Littlewood recounts, it is undeniable that she had a great fondness for the composer, and simultaneously, that he was particularly interested in the project. Leach, *Theatre Workshop*, x.

173. Joan Littlewood, Introduction, in *Fings Ain't Wot They Used T'Be* by Frank Norman (New York: Grove Press, 1962), 5.

174. Ibid.

175. "Theatre Worker," *The Observer*, March 15, 1959, 11.

176. "Lionel Bart," *The South Bank Show*.

177. Scott Miller, *Strike Up the Band: A New History of Musical Theatre* (Portsmouth: Heinemann, 2007), 81.

178. Barry J. Faulk, *Music Hall and Modernity: The Victorian Discovery of Popular Culture* (Athens: Ohio University Press, 2004), 24.

179. Ibid., 43.

180. Connecting the Brechtian *Fings* to the American "concept musical" is admittedly problematic given that the latter is so thoroughly associated with Stephen Sondheim, who has openly spoken of his distaste for Brecht's plays. Still, Foster Hirsch has noted that in spite of this antipathy, Sondheim's musicals are strongly evocative of Brecht and Weill's collaborations.

   Thomas R. Nadar, "Brecht and His Musical Collaborators," in *A Bertolt Brecht Reference Companion*, ed. Siegfried Mews (Westport: Greenwood Press, 1997), 267.

   Foster Hirsch, *Harold Prince and the American Musical Theater* (Cambridge: Cambridge University Press, 1989) 15-17.

181. Lionel Bart, *South Bank Show*, Transcript, Roll 5, 14. Lionel Bart Foundation Archive.

182. Bertolt Brecht, *Brecht on Theatre: The Development of an Aesthetic* (London: Methuen, 1964), 85.

183. McMillin notes that although Brecht rejected integration (and, perhaps even more significantly, capitalism), he was nevertheless fond of American musical theater. Brecht himself would describe the American musical as an "authentic expression of all that is American," and though he was giving a backhanded compliment, he nevertheless appreciated the American model and rejected the notion of its Wagnerian qualities. Weill likewise asserted that American musical comedy was fundamentally different from Wagner's concept of opera.
McMillin, *Musical as Drama*, 26.

   Bertolt Brecht, "How *The Duchess of Malfi* Ought to be Performed," in *Bertolt Brecht: Collected Plays*, vol. 7, eds. Ralph Manheim and John Willett (New York: Random House, 1974), 422.

   Warren Storey Smith, "Musik von Kurt Weill wird als ungewöhnlich bezeichnet," in *Kurt Weill Musik und Theater* by Kurt Weill (Berlin: Henschelverlag Kunst und Gesellschaft, 1990), 338.

184. Morley, *Spread a Little Happiness*, 153.

185. Ibid.

186. Arthur Jackson, *The Best Musicals from Show Boat to A Chorus Line: Broadway, Off Broadway, London* (New York: Crown, 1977), 102.

187. Bart humorously reminisced that "people called it Guys and Dolls [*sic*] with their flies undone, and [...]we were largely responsible for the censorship of the theatre, [*sic*] the Lord Chamberlain would send a scout around to see the show. And it there [*sic*] was reams of notes." Lionel Bart, *South Bank Show*, Transcript, Roll 5, 13–14. Lionel Bart Foundation Archive.

   For further information about the censoring of the show, see Norman's *Why Fings Went West*, pp. 65–68, and Goorney's *The Theatre Workshop Story*, pp. 118–20.

188. Although Bart was rapidly emerging as a dominant force in the English theater, Miles would later reminisce that he was still "just a simple working lad keen as mustard to get his feet on to the ladder of stardom."

   Bernard Miles, *Lock Up Your Daughters* (New York: Samuel French, 1967), iii.

189. Tsai Chin, interview by author, October 17, 2010.

190. Peter Coe biographical abstract. Sir Donald Albery Collection, DAT 114.001, Folder 1. Harry Ransom Center, University of Texas at Austin.

191. Tsai Chin, interview by author.

192. The full scope of Coe's contributions to *Lock Up Your Daughters* remains unknown, as he undertook the task of revising Miles's libretto. Actor Trevor Ray, who played Quill in the original production and who would go on to originate the role of Noah Claypole in *Oliver!* asserts that Coe "literally [took] the script and reconstructed it completely from the eighteenth-century original. [...] And because it was Bernard Miles who'd built the theatre and was opening it and funded it [...] [Miles] got the credit for the book." As will be discussed in the next chapter, the extent of Coe's contributions to the *Oliver!* libretto remains similarly undocumented, although as in the case of *Lock Up Your Daughters* Coe was determined to return to the source text.
      Trevor Ray, interview by author, June 26, 2010.
193. "Who's Who: Sean Kenny's." *The Observer.* July 31, 1960, 19.
194. Quoted in Carol Wright, "A Tough Line with Fantasy," *Times*, September 22, 1967, 11.
195. Quoted in Stanley Eichelbaum, "Sean Kenny Sets the Stage," *Theatre Arts Magazine*, Dec. 1962, 20.
196. Quoted in Dusty Vineberg, "Theatre Designer Encourages Innovation," Misc. Publicity Scrapbook, Sean Kenny Papers. Box 2. Victoria and Albert Museum Theatre Collections.
197. Ibid.
198. Irving Wardle, "A View of the Stage," *New Society*, July 13, 1976, 56.
199. Early on in *Oliver!*'s run, Peter Coe, like Lionel Bart, would find himself in a situation where "he had three hits running simultaneously in London's West End—'The Miracle Worker,' 'The World of Suzie Wong' and 'Oliver!'" Herbert Mitgang, "Peter Coe, Theatre Director; Staged 'Oliver' [*sic*] on Broadway," *New York Times*, June 3, 1987.

CHAPTER 2

1. Lionel Bart, "One of the Worldwide Family," in *Oliver!: The London Palladium Souvenir Program* (London: Dewynters, 1994).
2. John Harvey, *Victorian Novelists and Their Illustrators* (London: Sidgwick & Jackson, 1970), 8–9.
3. Dickens proposed alternate titles for the anthology, including *Sketches by Boz and Cuts by Cruikshank* or *Etchings by Boz and Wood Cuts by Cruikshank*.
      Jane R. Cohen, *Charles Dickens and His Original Illustrators* (Columbus: Ohio State University Press, 1980), 16.
4. Jay Clayton, *Charles Dickens in Cyberspace* (New York: Oxford University Press, 2003), 3–4.
5. Similarly, the film *Anna and the King of Siam* (1946) gave Rodgers and Hammerstein a narrative outline from which they could develop a successful musical adaptation of the 1944 novel of the same name.
6. Lionel Bart, *South Bank Show*, Transcript, Roll 5, 17. Lionel Bart Foundation Archive.
7. Lionel Bart, draft of letter to Tams-Witmark, 1966. Lionel Bart Foundation Archive.
8. Quoted in Jenny Firth, "Meeting Tommy Was the Turning Point," *Leicester Evening Mail*, March 26, 1959.
9. Quoted in ibid.
10. Lionel Bart, letter to Patricia McCarthy, November, 22 1979, 1-2. Lionel Bart Foundation Archive.
11. Transcribed conversation between Donald Albery of Donmar Productions and Davenport Lyons, solicitor to Jock Jacobsen, May 25, 1961, 1. Sir Donald Albery Collection, 194.003. Harry Ransom Center, University of Texas at Austin.

12. "Lionel Bart Was Told 'Forget Stage'," *Evening Standard*, June 9, 1961.

13. "Lionel Bart Wins 'Oliver!' Fight," *Daily Herald*, June 10, 1961.

14. In an unpublished autobiographical fragment, Bart reflected on his fears that his *Oliver Twist* musical project would not be taken seriously due to his status as a writer of pop songs: "I suppose I looked like an upstart to the protectors of the great literary heritage, some of whom were already asking whether this was going to be 'Rockin Round the Gruel Bowl.'"

    Lionel Bart, Personal Reflection on *Oliver!* #2, 2/9. Lionel Bart Foundation Archive.

15. Bart, "One of the Worldwide Family."

16. W. A. Darlington, "No Business Like Musical Business," *Daily Telegraph*, April 26, 1958.

17. As Peter Roberts later wrote in a review for *Plays and Players*, "[o]ne would hardly have thought that the appalling brutality, ugliness, and poverty of the Victorian Workhouse would have been quite the thing for a jolly musical romp."

    Peter Roberts, Review of *Oliver! Plays and Players* (August 1960): 17.

18. "Sir Donald Albery: Theatre Impresario of Catholic Tastes," *Times*, September 15, 1988, 14.

19. "Sir Donald Albery," *The Independent*, September 16, 1988.

20. "Sir Donald Albery: Theatre Impresario of Catholic Tastes," 14.

21. Ibid.

22. "A Shrewd Arty-Crafty Fellow is Mr. Albery," *Evening Standard*, January, 17 1964, 8.

23. In spite of his support, "Littlewood was always very quick to condemn Albery and other traditional producers for depleting her company, conveniently overlooking the fact that without their investment, it would have been very difficult to nurture the actors and writers that she did."

    Kate Dorney, *The Changing Language of Modern English Drama, 1945–2005* (New York: Palgrave Macmillan, 2009),122.

24. Quoted in "Theatrical Manager with an Open Mind," *Times*, March 20, 1961, 3.

25. Kurt Ganzl, *British Musical Theatre, Vol. II 1915–1984* (New York: Oxford University Press, 1986), 770.

    In their biography on Lionel Bart, David and Caroline Stafford note that Bart's nieces and nephews contributed to the recording by singing the child parts.

    David and Caroline Stafford, *Fings Ain't Wot They Used T'Be: The Lionel Bart Story* (London: Omnibus Press, 2011), 59.

26. Anne Jenkins, letter to Jock Jacobsen, May 9, 1959. Sir Donald Albery Collection, DAT 114.001, Folder 2. Harry Ransom Center, University of Texas at Austin.

27. Jock Jacobsen, letter to Anne Jenkins, May 6, 1959. Sir Donald Albery Collection, DAT 114.001, Folder 2. Harry Ransom Center, University of Texas at Austin.

28. Anne Jenkins, undated memo to Donald Albery on Donmar's funding of *Oliver!* Sir Donald Albery Collection, DAT 114.003. Harry Ransom Center, University of Texas at Austin.

29. Emile Littler, letter to Donald Albery, May 9, 1960. Sir Donald Albery Collection, DAT 114.003. Harry Ransom Center, University of Texas at Austin.

30. Ibid.

31. Littler was known for taking a confrontational approach to the production process; fellow British impresario Peter Saunders touches on Littler's "many lawsuits" in a section of his biography where he chronicles the endeavors of various British producers in the 1950s and 1960s.

    Peter Saunders, *The Mousetrap Man* (London: Collins, 1972), 236.

Subsequent to *Oliver!*'s success, Littler sued Albery over a dispute regarding the distribution of the show's profits. In Albery's summation, Littler's complaints related to:

"(1) Hire charges made by Donmar productions to the production;
(2) Charges made in respect of the services of the employees of Donmar Productions Ltd. in connection with the production and
(3) Christmas bonuses and gifts paid to the staff of the theatre"

Donald Albery, letter to Margot Fonteyn de Arias, January 30, 1964. Sir Donald Albery Collection, DAT 114.003. Harry Ransom Center, University of Texas at Austin.

Albery sent Littler a letter on November 17, 1964. The missive contained revealing data regarding just how much profit Littler had made off his investments with Donmar: "I thought you would like to have the enclosed statement of profits and losses up to April 1964, which the Accountants have just prepared for all our investors. As you will see in your case it shows losses of £10,334 and profits of £91,228, making you a net profit of £80,894 at that date."

Donald Albery, letter to Emile Littler, November 17, 1964. Sir Donald Albery Collection, DAT 114.003. Harry Ransom Center, University of Texas at Austin.

Littler was unimpressed, and in a follow-up reply he unhesitatingly affirmed that the issue transcended such questions of losses and gains: "[I]t makes no difference to a principle."

Emile Littler, letter to Donald Albery, November 18, 1964. Sir Donald Albery Collection, DAT 114.003. Harry Ransom Center, University of Texas at Austin.

32. Jenkins, undated memo to Donald Albery.
33. Donald Albery, telegram to David Merrick, June 26, 1959. Sir Donald Albery Collection, DAT 114.001, Folder 2. Harry Ransom Center, University of Texas at Austin.
34. David Merrick, telegram to Donald Albery, July 3, 1959. Sir Donald Albery Collection, DAT 114.001, Folder 2. Harry Ransom Center, University of Texas at Austin.
35. Howard Goorney, *The Theatre Workshop Story* (London: Methuen, 1981), 110, 205–6.
36. Theatre Workshop, *Oh What a Lovely War* (London: Methuen, 2000), ix.
37. Ibid., xi.
38. Vera Stegmann, "Brecht Contra Wagner: The Evolution of the Epic Music Theater," in *A Bertolt Brecht Reference Companion*, ed. Siegfried Mews (Westport: Greenwood Press, 1997), 251.
39. Lionel Bart, letter to Donald Albery, August 10, 1959. Sir Donald Albery Collection, DAT 114.001, Folder 2. Harry Ransom Center, University of Texas at Austin.
40. Ibid.
41. Donald Albery, letter to Lionel Bart, December 4, 1959. Sir Donald Albery Collection, DAT 114.001, Folder 2. Harry Ransom Center, University of Texas at Austin.
42. Coe's marriage to the talented Chinese actress Tsai Chin ultimately helped to shape his career; Chin had casually mentioned to Albery that her husband was the director of *Lock Up Your Daughters* and Albery immediately asked her if she would like for Coe to direct her in *Suzie Wong*, an invitation to which the delighted Chin responded affirmatively.
Tsai Chin, interview by author, October 17, 2010.
43. Donald Albery, letter to Milton Goldman, March 28, 1960. Sir Donald Albery Collection, DAT 114.001, Folder 2. Harry Ransom Center, University of Texas at Austin.
44. Alastair Davidson, interview by author, September 5, 2010.

45. As a Unity Theatre alumnus, Maitland strongly believed in the importance of granting young people opportunities to produce theater. Actress Carmen Munroe recalls
that Maitland was a dedicated supporter of the West Indian Students Union, teaching
drama to the various students who chose to participate in the organization's activities. "She was easy to make friends with," Munroe recollects. "Wonderful, open sort of
person. She wasn't there to convert people: 'you must do this, you must do that'. She
was at ease with people who were different; she held the classes and I used to go there
after work. And we had drama classes there in Earls Court." Eventually, she began
staging classic British and American dramas with all black casts. Munroe herself was
involved in Maitland's all-black production of Eugene O'Neill's *Anna Christie:*

> "There was, at the time, a drama competition amongst the county councils in
> London [...] and we were rehearsing and playing, doing the play, *Anna Christie*—
> all black cast. And I loved it. I absolutely, absolutely loved it. This was the first time
> I was going to be really working in theatre. And Joan put us through this thing, and
> she entered our group. We did a scene, the scene on the wharf, and we won. And
> one of the things we won was to be able to do the play at Unity Theatre, which must
> have been because of her association with Unity. And that was my introduction to
> Unity. [...] I got stuck in there and I thought, 'I love this place, and I love all the
> people there.' It was just like hundreds of Joans."

    Carmen Munroe, interview by author, December 27, 2010.
46. In an undated letter kept in the Lionel Bart Foundation Archive, Maitland expressed
her gratitude to Bart for his having helped her to "[develop] a real talent as a lyric
writer." Maitland later collaborated with famed British songwriter Richard Kerr on
several noteworthy pop songs in the 1960s and 1970s.
    Joan Maitland, letter to Lionel Bart, Lionel Bart Foundation Archive.
47. In a letter to Maitland, Bart noted that "[y]ou are the same as myself, when it comes
to living above your income. I'm sure we'll both catch up with ourselves one day soon."
Several of Maitland's letters to Bart convey the notion that she found herself in dire
financial straits in the 1960s. Lionel Bart, letter to Joan Maitland, February 14, 1964.
Lionel Bart Foundation Archive.
48. Stephen Komlosy, letter to Ira Tulipan, October 1, 1968. Lionel Bart Archive
200102/0063, University of Bristol Theatre Collection.
49. Harry Landis, interview by author, July 28, 2010.
50. Lionel Bart, *South Bank Show*, Transcript, Roll 5, 19. Lionel Bart Foundation Archive.
51. "Generous Bart," *Daily Mail*, March 1961 (1961 Scrapbook—Lionel Bart Foundation
Archive).
52. Winifred Carr, "Vivid reminder of twenty-two short years ago," *Daily Telegraph*, May
7, 1962.
53. Joan Maitland, letter to Lionel Bart, March 30, 1965. Lionel Bart Foundation Archive.
54. History would repeat itself a few years later when Bart began work on a coffee-table
book inspired by *Oliver!*—one that would feature color photographs from the film
adaptation. Though Maitland was initially involved in the project, Bart was eager to
maintain creative control: "I am very much desirous of carrying out the entire operation—compiling, etcetera, myself personally [*sic*]. This may seem unjust to Joan
Maitland, but for a number of reasons [...] I wish to deserve the credit for this book's
contents. Such inner reward can only come from the knowledge that I have carried
out the major portion of the work involved."
    Lionel Bart, letter to Leslie Frewin, February 16, 1967. Lionel Bart Foundation
Archive.

55. Harry Landis, interview by author.
56. Ironically, these royalties left her in a more secure financial position than Lionel Bart himself. Landis claims that

> "[Lionel] threw money about like there was no tomorrow, and of course, that was when he found himself with no money and he had to sell the rights to his music in order to get some capital. And Joan of course had to have a percentage of what he sold it for because she was involved in his finances that way due to his agreement over *Oliver!* When these people bought—and I remember her showing me the deal—when these people bought the rights to his music, and all his future music, she still had to get her percentage of what she had been involved with."

> Harry Landis, interview by author.
> Even as *Oliver!* slipped away from Bart himself, Maitland maintained control over her percentage of the rights. When the film version of *Oliver!* debuted, Maitland received 8.2 percent of Bart's 3.75 percent of the gross. The idea of Maitland earning a small percentage of a small percentage may seem trivial, but when one considers the millions of pounds generated by *Oliver!* in all of its various incarnations, the sums immediately multiply in terms of their overall significance.
> Wendy Read, letter to Jeffrey Green, August 20, 1969. Lionel Bart Archive 200102/0063, University of Bristol Theatre Collection.

57. In 1968, Maitland exchanged letters with Stephen Komlosy and alluded to the fact that she would be willing to "sell" her credit for *Blitz!* if Bart was interested in receiving sole authorship credit on a potential film version of the show:

> "As you probably know, I was co-Author with Lionel of the book of [*Blitz!*], and have always been very interested in the further exploitation of it, and on various occasions Lionel and I have had discussions concerning possible re-writes. For a number of reasons, however, we have always both been too involved in other things to work together on it, and since Lionel tells me that he is interested in making it into a film himself, I suggested to him that he might like to buy out my copyright, in order to have an unencumbered free hand."

> Joan Maitland, letter to Stephen Komlosy, September 11, 1968. Lionel Bart Archive 200102/0063, University of Bristol Theatre Collection.

58. Jim Lovensheimer, "Texts and Authors" in *Oxford Handbook of the American Musical*, eds. Raymond Knapp, Mitchell Morris, and Stacy Wolf (New York: Oxford University Press, 2011), 20.
59. Mark N. Grant, *The Rise and Fall of the Broadway Musical* (Boston: Northeastern University Press, 2004), 53.
60. Raymond Knapp, *The American Musical and the Formation of National Identity* (Princeton: Princeton University Press, 2006), 3–4.
61. Roland Barthes, "The Death of the Author" in *Image, Music, Text* (New York: Hill and Wang, 1977), 147.
62. "Lionel Bart on an 'Epic' Musical," *Times*, March 22, 1962, 16.
63. Bart considered other titles, one of the more ridiculous being *Who Loves Oliver?* which sounds as if it should be the title of a sitcom as opposed to a musical. Still, this title reinforces the centrality of "Where Is Love?" to the narrative, as conceived by Bart.
    Lionel Bart, letter to Donald Albery, August 10, 1959.
64. The edition of the novel that Bart used as his primary source is not indicated in the table.

65. Lionel Bart, *Oliver Twist*, early outline. Lionel Bart Foundation Archive.
66. Whereas "Consider Yourself" focuses on the burgeoning friendship between the Dodger and Oliver, "I'm Going to Seek My Fortune" is ostensibly built around the contrasts between the two characters, as Bart notes that the song should initially be sung by Oliver and then reprised by Dodger "with Double meanings"; these "double meanings" would likely have revealed the divergence between Oliver's innocent worldview and Dodger's more cynical interpretation of what it means to "seek one's fortune" (a contrast firmly rooted in the original text).
    Ibid.
67. This early list of songs both reinforces and contradicts Bart's own reflections on the initial stages of the musical score; Bart recalled that he began the show with six songs: "Food, Glorious Food," "I'd Do Anything," "Reviewing the Situation," "Consider Yourself," "Who Will Buy?" and "As Long As He Needs Me," and that most of the other numbers were written in the latter part of the rehearsal period. As noted above, all of these songs, with the exception of "Consider Yourself," existed on a basic, conceptual level from early on in the production process, though it is highly unlikely that they were all complete in the earliest stages of *Oliver!*'s development; similarly, the score was in a state of flux for months before the rehearsal period began, as it was constantly adapting to fit the ever-changing narrative. Sadly, the Bart/Maitland recording has been lost, and there is no way to confirm which songs (or, more specifically, which versions of which songs) existed at the time that Bart pitched the concept to Donald Albery.
    Bart, Personal Reflection on *Oliver!* #2, 2/9.
68. This attempt to connect the Brownlow and Maylie storylines by merging the two families was a common plot device in several early stage adaptations of the play, and also in the Cowen film.
69. Bart, *Oliver Twist*, early outline.
70. Bart was not the first playwright to consider combining the two scenes. In Arthur Williams's adaptation, first produced in 1912, the adaptor used the same device and included Dodger as a witness in Magistrate Fang's court, mainly as a way of including dialogue from the humorous trial scene in Dickens's original novel.
71. This plot development is yet another fairly common modification to the story in film and stage adaptations, as it permits the preservation of the robbery scene without having to include the Maylie family. Of course, the idea of Sikes using Oliver to rob the house of a man whom Oliver has come to love and respect makes this device somewhat illogical. Still, the plot modification dates back to the very first adaptation of *Oliver Twist*: the 1838 "burletta in two acts."
72. This coincidence is actually one of the less outrageous twists of fate in Dickens's novel. The Artful Dodger just happens to pick the pocket of Mr. Brownlow, who just happens to be an old friend of Oliver's father, Edwin; Sikes just happens to rob a countryside house, which just happens to be the home of Rose Maylie, who just happens to be Oliver's aunt.
73. Numerous adaptors have overcome this issue by simply using the Dodger as Fagin's spy. This modification appears in several prominent adaptations, including the Lean film, the 1999 ITV miniseries, and the Polanski film.
74. Bart, *Oliver Twist*, early outline.
75. Ibid.
76. Bart, letter to Patricia McCarthy, 3.
77. Ibid.
78. Lionel Bart, *Oh, Oliver!* libretto fragment, 13. Lionel Bart Foundation Archive.

79. Lionel Bart, unlabeled libretto fragment, 1.4.15-1.4.15A. Lionel Bart Foundation Archive.

80. The origins of "Consider Yourself" are ambiguous. David and Caroline Stafford cite Tommy Steele's comments that Bart had originally conceived certain elements of "Consider Yourself" for an unproduced musical that he called *Petticoat Lane*. However, they later quote Bart's own written reflections on the number, which paint a vivid and ostentatious picture of a moment of spontaneous creation that saw the composer finally conceptualizing the perfect song for the Artful Dodger and "testing it out" via an improvised session of street-singing.
    Stafford, *Fings Ain't Wot They Used T'Be*, 59, 99.

81. A subsequent outline for the musical adaptation that was actually entitled *Oliver* reinserts "I'm Going to Seek My Fortune," thus indicating that Bart had not truly discarded the number, but rather was still considering it as a possibility for the Dodger-Oliver scene. Lionel Bart, "Oliver" outline. Lionel Bart Foundation Archive.

82. Bart, *Oh, Oliver!* libretto fragment, 20.

83. Ibid., 23.

84. Other songs were still being added or discarded at this point. Curiously, the spiral lists a number that is not mentioned in any other surviving draft materials titled "How Low Can You Get?"

85. Lionel Bart, *Oliver* spiral notebook. Lionel Bart Foundation Archive.

86. Lionel Bart, Suggested New Version. Lionel Bart Foundation Archive.

87. Ibid.

88. Ibid.

89. Lionel Bart, *Oliver* spiral.

90. Ibid.

91. Bart, unlabeled libretto fragment, 3.4.79–3.4.80.

92. Several handwritten annotations from an unknown writer indicate that the creative team likewise perceived the need to remove the discussion of Bet's situation and focus the scene squarely on Nancy and Oliver; the annotated version of the scene reads as follows (italics signify added words/sentences):

> NANCY: ~~Can you guess who you are going to meet tonight, Oliver, in this dark place?~~
>
> OLIVER: ~~It is dark. Why couldn't you tell me before, and why did we have to come all the way here?~~
>
> NANCY: ~~It's a gentleman who was very good to you and his daughter, and I wish to heaven I'd never taken you from them!~~
>
> OLIVER: ~~Rose! Rose and Mr. Brownlow.~~ Oh, Nancy, ~~are they~~ *is Rose* really coming here?
>
> NANCY: Yes and ~~they're~~ *she's* coming to take you home again ~~with them~~, Oliver, and away from Fagin's and all of us.
>
> OLIVER: ~~Home! To that lovely house again! I can't believe it Nancy. But how did you...?~~
>
> NANCY: I put a sleeping draught in the drink tonight, so that I could get you out without Bill or anyone knowing....
>
> OLIVER: ~~But what will they do to you,~~ *Will he hurt you,* Nancy, when ~~they~~ *he* finds out?
>
> NANCY: ~~There's time enough to think about that.~~ *Never mind about that.*
>
> OLIVER: ~~(thinking for a while)~~
>   ~~Then let's go back and get Bet.~~

NANCY: ~~We can't Oliver. I belong there, and so does Bet – besides it's too late now.~~
OLIVER: ~~Then I can't go. I can't go and leave Bet there.~~
NANCY: ~~Don't you want to go back to those kind people, that will love you and give you a home?~~ I'll tell you something but it's a great secret, because I think they would like to tell you themselves. They are your very own family, Oliver. Rose's sister was...your mother.
OLIVER: My mother! My family! ~~You mean I really belong somewhere?! I knew I did.~~ Oh, Nancy. ~~Thank you for telling me. But I still can't go – I couldn't leave Bet like that. Unless she can come too, I can't go.~~
NANCY: ~~Don't worry about Bet, Oliver. She's used to that life. Besides I'll look after her.~~ Shh. They'll be here soon.

93. Like Lean, Bart seems to have envisioned Brownlow in this role from the very beginning, as the early outlines indicate that the woman in the portrait would ultimately be revealed as his daughter.
94. Bart, unlabeled libretto fragment, 3.3.76.
95. Charles Dickens, *Oliver Twist* (Oxford: Oxford University Press, 1999), 327.
96. Bart, unlabeled libretto fragment, 3.4.79.
97. The scrap from the draft script that included the scene between Rose and Nancy features a line from Brittles; however, his name is crossed out and Mrs. Bedwin's name has been written in its place, thus indicating that Mrs. Bedwin may have been a replacement for Brittles as opposed to a replacement for Rose, though it is likely that all three of these characters were featured in one of the midpoint versions of the libretto.
    Ibid., 3.3.76.
98. Bart, Suggested New Version.
    The absence of these two songs is intriguing given that both of these numbers would be cut from the film version of *Oliver!* so as to downplay any sort of humor in the early workhouse scenes and transition to the London scenes more quickly (see Chapter 7).
99. New Songs/Re-writes summary. Lionel Bart Foundation Archive.
    Though this note page provides vital clues as to how the show was developing, it is undated and its author is unknown. It is likely that Peter Coe produced the page; the notes included on the page "Make Bet affection a little more *implicit*" and "Play Bet down a little" seem to coincide with Coe's overall focus on reducing Bet's role in the piece.
100. One might assume that Brittles was eventually discarded in favor of Grimwig, for Grimwig is not mentioned in any of the previously discussed outlines or tables; nevertheless, the annotations to the draft script containing the Nancy-Rose confrontation include a brief allusion to Grimwig by Mr. Brownlow, which seems to imply that Grimwig and Brittles were both included in the script.
101. Bart, Suggested New Version.
102. Lionel Bart, Notes on paste-up by Peter Coe, February 4, 1960, 2. Lionel Bart Foundation Archive.
103. Lionel Bart, Oliver—Peter's Version. Lionel Bart Foundation Archive.
104. The separate notes page maintains that the script should "Plot one of gang [*sic*] spying on Nancy" and "Make clearer how Sykes was tipped off."
    New Songs/Re-writes summary.

A compromise may have been contemplated, as the scraps of the unlabeled libretto indicate that Rose and Nancy are being spied on by a character called "Barney," apparently one of Sykes's fellow housebreakers as opposed to a member of Fagin's gang. The name is likely derived from the Jewish criminal of the same name in the original text.

Bart, unlabeled libretto fragment, 3.4.79–80.

105. Nevertheless, the scene was eventually scripted, as the fragments from the draft containing the Rose-Nancy confrontation include references to this conclusion: "Enter DODGER, resplendent in the ex-beadle's rather voluminous outfit, complete with mace in one hand, and toasting-fork in the other. He is followed by a second ASSISTANT who is bearing an enormous dish of sizzling sausages." Annotations to the scene seem to indicate that whoever was reviewing the script knew that this plot twist would be cut, as most of the scene is crossed out.

Lionel Bart, unlabeled libretto fragment, 3.6.86.

106. Bart, Notes on paste-up by Peter Coe, 2.

107. New Songs/Re-writes summary.

The inclusion of this sentimental ending would seem to contradict my earlier assumption that Coe typed up these notes, as this conclusion is not in keeping with his general vision of the musical. Still, perhaps Coe viewed it as a compromise between his own stark vision and Bart's sentimental vision of either Fagin or the Dodger as the new beadle.

108. Lionel Bart, Suggested New Breakdown (B), Lionel Bart Foundation Archive.

109. Ibid.

110. Bart, Notes on paste-up by Peter Coe, 2.

111. New Songs/Re-writes summary.

112. Bart, Notes on paste-up by Peter Coe, 2.

113. Martin Esslin asserts that "Brechtian theatre is a theatre designed to arouse indignation in the audience, dissatisfaction, a realization of contradictions. [...] That is why [...] the good characters are invariably crushed and defeated. Brecht believed that the audience's indignation with the existing order would necessarily and automatically lead them to support the Marxist alternative."

Martin Esslin, *Brecht: The Man and His Work*, New, Revised Edition (Garden City: Anchor Books, 1971),150–51.

114. Nevertheless, several critics in Britain could perceive Brechtian implications lurking beneath the surface of the seemingly blithe musical; an anonymous critic at the *Times* argued that "one could connect *Oliver!* with the more serious new plays; it was possible to see this musical as one more expression of an anti-social rebellion against the ruling class. The true values of the play were embodied in the outlaws, Fagin and Nancy." These abstractions would have been rendered concrete had Bart opted to send Fagin to his death.

"British Encirclement of Broadway," *Times*, June 26, 1963, 15.

115. Bart, Notes on paste-up by Peter Coe, 2.

116. It is difficult to determine the precise origins of "It's a Fine Life." In the years following *Oliver!*'s premiere, Bart claimed that he had written the song after having been inspired by Georgia Brown's performance as Nancy: "I grew the song 'It's a Fine Life' during the rehearsals, as a direct result of the dimension that Georgia had added to the part."

Lionel Bart, Reflection on Georgia Brown, Lionel Bart Foundation Archive.

However, his enthusiasm seems to contradict the general reservations that Bart expressed to Coe regarding this number. Furthermore, the Coe "paste-up" memo is dated as having been written in early February, which means that the composition of "It's a Fine Life" preceded the actual rehearsal process by several months. Most likely, this is another example of Bart's tendency to improve on the truth. Nevertheless, it is highly likely that Brown's lustful and passionate performance as Nancy granted Bart new insights into the number's potential, and that the composer developed it based on her portrayal.

117. In his summation of Coe's libretto, Bart noted that Coe's reduction of Bet's role included the virtual elimination of her "love story" with Oliver; here, Oliver is "utterly happy" with Brownlow and has "no regret[s]."

　　　Bart, Oliver—Peter's Version.

118. Bart, Notes on paste-up by Peter Coe, 1.

119. Bart's memo praises Coe for his conception of the finale to Act I, as the singing of "Be Back Soon" (still titled "We'll Be Back") initiated a brisk journey from the thieves' kitchen to the robbery scene, and finally to "the ballet chase ending in Oliver's capture." It was also Coe's idea to transition straight from "Oom Pah Pah" to Sykes's "My Name."

　　　Bart, Notes on paste-up by Peter Coe, 1–2.

120. Lionel Bart, General overall comment, in Notes on paste-up by Peter Coe. Lionel Bart Foundation Archive.

121. Ibid.

122. John Higgins, "How Peter Coe Comprehends the Twentieth Century," *Times*, March 13, 1980, 11.

123. Alastair Davidson, interview by author.

　　　The Bart memo reinforces this fact, as the composer notes several changes that Coe made to the script, many of which were clearly rooted in Dickens's dialogue.

　　　Bart, Notes on paste-up by Peter Coe, 1–2.

124. Cameron Mackintosh, interview by author, July 12, 2010.

125. Curiously, the table lists "Oliver" as a reprise, though this song does not exist earlier in the outline; in its place is "Oliver Twist Has Asked for More." The earlier listing may be a typo, for the red spiral notebook indicates that around this time Bart had already renamed the workhouse punishment song for the title character.

126. This song is also listed as a "reprise" despite there being no predecessor in the table.

127. The omission of "Boy for Sale" here may be an error on Bart's part, as this song was part of the show from the beginning and it is unlikely that Coe ever proposed cutting it.

CHAPTER 3

1. Lionel Bart, draft of letter to Tams-Witmark, 1966. Lionel Bart Foundation Archive.

2. Sean Kenny, "Designing 'Oliver'[sic]," *TABS* 18, no. 2 (September 1960): 7, 10.

3. Quoted in Stanley Eichelbaum, "Sean Kenny Sets the Stage," *Theatre Arts Magazine*, (December 1962), 20.

4. Kenny, "Designing 'Oliver'[sic]," 10.

5. Ibid.

6. Ibid.

7. Ibid., 11.

　　　Though Kenny designed the *Oliver!* set on the basis of the perspective and movement of the title character, the first location that he actually sketched was the thieves' kitchen, which he felt "had to give the feeling of the play, of the music, of the people, and so on." This fact is yet another indication of the centrality of Fagin's gang to the general creative vision behind the adaptation.

　　　Ibid. 7–8.

8. Quoted in Vivien Hislop, "In a setting by Sean... for Kenny," *Daily Mail*, February 12, 1968, 9.

9. Carol Wright, "A Tough Line with Fantasy," *Times*, September 22, 1967, 11.

10. "The Stage Designer Who Makes One Sit Up," *Times*, January 24, 1966, 14.

11. Robert Leach, *Theatre Workshop: Joan Littlewood and the Making of Modern British Theatre* (Exeter: University of Exeter Press, 2006), 194.

12. Irving Wardle, "A View of the Stage," *New Society*, July 13, 1967, 56.

13. Quoted in Dusty Vineberg, "Theatre Designer Encourages Innovation." Sean Kenny Misc. Publicity Scrapbook, Box 2. Sean Kenny Archive. Victoria and Albert Museum Theatre Collections.

14. Kenneth Tynan, "New Amalgam," *The Observer*, October 19, 1958, 19.

15. Kenneth Tynan, "The Under-Belly of Laughter," *The Observer*, July 3, 1960, 25.

16. Ibid.

17. Quoted in Vineberg, "Theatre Designer Encourages Innovation."
Kenny might have taken Tynan's fears as a compliment, for he admitted that the *Blitz!* scenery and effects were *meant* to intimidate the audience: "It is in the finale that Kenny's handiwork makes off with the show: a bomb explodes onstage and one of the three-story buildings collapses in the direction of the audience. 'A great many people are simply terrified', he remarked, with apparent satisfaction." Eichelbaum, "Sean Kenny Sets the Stage," 20.

18. Kenneth Tynan, *A View of the English Stage 1944–1963* (London: Davis-Poynter, 1975), 342–343.

19. Peter Denton, "The Quiet Genius of a Man Behind the Scenes," *Epsom and Ewell Herald*, June 21, 1963.

20. Quoted in John Goodwin, ed., *British Theatre Design: The Modern Age* (New York: St. Martin's Press, 1989), 151.

21. Scott McMillin, *The Musical as Drama* (Princeton: Princeton University Press, 2006), 155.

22. Ibid.

23. Ibid., 156.

24. Ibid., 160. (McMillin's emphases)

25. Ibid., 156–57.

26. Kenny, "Designing 'Oliver'[sic]," 7.

27. Ibid.

28. Kenny viewed his set as cinematic, at least in terms of its functionality and its ability to condense and accelerate the narrative; he noted that *"Oliver* [sic] had to run like a film because the choreography and movement had to run easily on the stage. My sets must help the flow of the play."
Kenny, "Designing 'Oliver'[sic]," 7.

29. Lionel Bart, letter to Patricia McCarthy, November 22, 1979, 3. Lionel Bart Foundation Archive.

30. Cameron Mackintosh, interview by author, July 12, 2010.

31. Kenny designed the set and lighting for Unity's production of *Bloomsday*; he was friends with the show's writer and director, Allan McClelland. Just as he would later paint the skyline of Dickensian London on the wall of the New Theatre, "Kenny painted Dublin on Unity's back wall" to complete the look for *Bloomsday*.
Colin Chambers, *The Story of Unity Theatre* (New York: St. Martin's Press, 1989), 352.

32. Sean Kenny, "An address by Sean Kenny to the Lighting Equipment Manufacturers Association," 8. Annual Luncheon at the Chateau Champlain Hotel. Montreal. June, 22 1967. Sean Kenny Archive. Victoria and Albert Museum Theatre Collections.

33. Wright, "A Tough Line with Fantasy," 11.
34. The latter might very well have been his greatest achievement, though notably it was a piece grounded in the principle of movement, much like its predecessor, the *Oliver!* set. The $300,000 stage he designed for Las Vegas consisted of disc-shaped platforms and stairways that could be raised, lowered, and repositioned at the push of a button. An article in the *L.A. Times* stated that the stage was "dubbed 'Octuramic', because it does somehow resemble an octopus with its many moving platforms that lift, drop and revolve, while carrying, naturally, beauteous damsels in various stages of undress as well as other performers."

   John L. Scott, "On Electronic Stage," *L.A. Times*, January 7, 1964, 6.
35. Ronald Bryden, "A Gulliver Landmark," *The Observer*, December 29, 1968, 20.
36. Cameron Mackintosh, interview by author.
37. Bart, letter to Tams-Witmark.
38. Brenda Evans, interview by author, July 6, 2010.
39. Surviving records of this project can be found in the University of Bristol Theatre Collection. These records include a cable from Lionel Bart to David Picker: "Kenny and myself more than desirous to present Tolkien as Herb Jaffe may have indicated. Thought it to start in theatre medium involving back projection animation live actors and pre-screened action also involving lazer beam device amongst others. Fortunately we have London venues and much equipment at our disposal for early 1970."

   Lionel Bart, cable to David Picker, September 26, 1969. Lionel Bart Archive 200102/0063, University of Bristol Theatre Collection. Picker sent a reply a few days later claiming that he was willing to discuss the project, "[though] our inclinations are that *Lord of the Rings* should be a feature motion picture and not a stage musical." Both telegrams seem somehow prophetic, as *Lord of the Rings* would indeed be adapted into a feature motion picture and a stage musical, albeit with widely divergent outcomes.

   David Picker, letter to Lionel Bart, September 30, 1969. Lionel Bart Archive 200102/0063, University of Bristol Theatre Collection.
40. Throughout her autobiography, *Loving Peter*, Cook recounts Kenny's ever-increasing instability due to his dependence on drugs and alcohol.

   Judy Cook, *Loving Peter: My Life with Peter Cook and Dudley Moore* (London: Platkus, 2008), 81–85; 88–89.
41. Brenda Evans, interview by author.
42. The use of Brechtian conventions in the design and function of *Oliver!*'s scenery would prove inspirational in the development of yet another revolutionary Dickensian stage adaptation: the Royal Shakespeare Company's epic version of *The Life and Adventures of Nicholas Nickleby*.

   David Edgar, "An Evening with David Edgar," October 8, 2009, lecture delivered at Playmakers Repertory Theatre, University of North Carolina at Chapel Hill.
43. Martin Esslin, "Brecht and the English Theatre," in *Brecht Source Book*, eds. Carol Martin and Henry Bial (London: Routledge, 2000), 149. (Esslin's emphases)
44. Ibid.

   Though Esslin regarded *Oliver!* as a "thoroughly mediocre musical," he praised Sean Kenny's designs as a masterful endorsement of Brechtian staging techniques.
45. Roger Hardwick, interview by author, July 8, 2010.
46. Quoted in Peter Denton, "The Quiet Genius of a Man Behind the Scenes."
47. Roger Hardwick, interview by author.

   In his reflections on the postwar trends in British set design, Roy Strong notes that "The theatre ceased to be an escape from the dreariness of post-war Britain into a magic world; rather, in the 1960s and 1970s, it was theatre which reminded its audiences [...] that an unpleasant real world still existed. Black and grey predominated and whole theatres and sets became monuments to a Stygian gloom." While Strong's assessment conflicts with the generally celebratory elements of Bart's adaptation, not to mention the "magic" of the Kenny set (as described above by Alastair Davidson), his analysis of the drabness and gloom that characterized the color schemes of the 1960s and 1970s British theatre is certainly relevant to Kenny's vision.

Roy Strong, "The Years Before" in *British Theatre Design: The Modern Age*, ed. John Goodwin (New York: St. Martin's Press, 1989), 19.

48. Alastair Davidson, interview by author, September 5, 2010.
49. Ibid.
50. Ibid.
51. Quoted in "The Stage Designer Who Makes One Sit Up," 14.
52. Alastair Davidson, interview by author.
53. Lisa Gordon-Smith, "Designed for Export: New Techniques Will Make Touring Easier—Ian Albery," *The Stage*, July 5, 1962, 15.
54. Ian Albery, "Planning of the 'Oliver!' National Tour," *TABS*, 24, no. 1 (March 1966): 6.
55. Roger Hardwick, interview by author.
56. Quoted in Peter Denton, "The Quiet Genius of a Man Behind the Scenes."
57. Alastair Davidson, interview by author.
58. Quoted in "The Stage Designer Who Makes One Sit Up," 14.
59. Quoted in Fred Norris, "Experiment in Touring Theatre—It's Just Like Going to the Circus," *Birmingham Mail*, January 21, 1961.
60. Bernard Miles, letter to Donald Albery. January 14, 1960. Sir Donald Albery Theatre Collection, 114.001, Folder 2. Harry Ransom Center, University of Texas at Austin.
61. Anne Jenkins, undated memo to Donald Albery, Sir Donald Albery Theatre Collection, 114.001, Folder 2. Harry Ransom Center, University of Texas at Austin.
62. *Oliver!* audition schedule, December 23, 1959. Lionel Bart Foundation Archive.
63. Anne Jenkins, memo to Monty Berman, July 10, 1961. Sir Donald Albery Theatre Collection. Harry Ransom Center, University of Texas at Austin.
64. Trevor Ray, interview by author, June 26, 2010.
65. In a 1965 interview, Donald Albery stated that "[m]ore than 700 boys" had performed in *Oliver!* up to that point. Though this is likely an inflated estimate, the licensing issue, coupled with Bart and Albery's determination to make sure that the child chorus included talented singers, meant that children were constantly being cycled in and out.

Quoted in "'Oliver!' in it's [sic] Sixth year," *The Stage*, December 9, 1965, 15.

66. Donald Albery, letter to Lionel Bart, January 24, 1961. Sir Donald Albery Theatre Collection, 114.001, Folder 1. Harry Ransom Center, University of Texas at Austin.
67. Report of the Departmental Committee on the Employment of Children as Film Actors, in Theatrical Work and in Ballet, Home Department (London: His Majesty's Stationery Office, 1950), 13.
68. Ibid.
69. Ibid., 14.
70. Ibid., 37.
71. Ibid.
72. Anne Jenkins, letter to Messrs. Tughan and Walmsley, December 3, 1965. Sir Donald Albery Theatre Collection, 196.003. Harry Ransom Center, University of Texas at Austin.

In another letter, Jenkins elaborated on Donmar's policy regarding the child actors, noting that the boys were "given licenses for 3 lots of 13 weeks, making 39 weeks in all and a good many of the children have been able to come back for a second lot of 39 weeks."

    Anne Jenkins, letter to Ivor Brown. Sir Donald Albery Theatre Collection, 196.003. Harry Ransom Center, University of Texas at Austin.

73. Edna Doré, interview by author, July 3, 2010.
74. Ibid.
75. Report of the Departmental Committee on the Employment of Children as Film Actors, in Theatrical Work and in Ballet, 21.
76. Ibid., 23.
77. Charles Dickens, *Oliver Twist* (Oxford: Oxford University Press, 1999), 4.
78. Cyril Gibbins, letter to Anne Jenkins, July 4, 1960. Sir Donald Albery Theatre Collection, 114.001, Folder 1. Harry Ransom Center, University of Texas at Austin.
79. Dickens, *Oliver Twist*, 4.
80. Tony Robinson, interview by author, July 24, 2010.
    Robinson also understudied the role of the Artful Dodger and played this part several times over the course of his run.
81. Ibid.
82. Ibid.
83. Ibid.
84. Ibid.
85. That same sense of playfulness would contribute heavily to Moody's tendency to improvise, a tendency that would eventually bring him into conflict with Bart (see Chapter 6).
86. Tony Robinson, interview by author.
87. Ibid.
88. A similar situation would unfold during the production of the film adaptation, as the teenaged members of Fagin's gang found themselves distracted by Shani Wallis's low-cut dress.
    "Oliver!" After They Were Famous, January 1, 2005, Tyne Tees Television, Television.
89. Joseph Wershba, "Sweet Georgia Brown," *New York Post Magazine*, May 5, 1963, 2.
90. Lionel Bart, reflection on Georgia Brown. Lionel Bart Foundation Archive.
91. Ibid.
92. Wershba, "Sweet Georgia Brown," 2.
93. Trevor Ray, interview by author.
    Alastair Davidson, interview by author.
94. Bart, reflection on Georgia Brown.
95. As noted in Chapter 1, Brown appeared on the program on February 9, 1964; this particular episode would also mark the first American appearance of the Beatles. Ironically, Shani Wallis, who would replace Brown in the film adaptation, was first noticed by the film's producers while singing on *Sullivan* (see Chapter 7).
96. Sheridan Morley, "Archetype of the Genuine English Classic Musical," *Times*, December 14, 1983, 9.
97. "A Handful of Songs: The Lionel Bart Story—Part 2," August 19, 2005, BBC Radio 2.
98. Radio interview, 199?, audio cassette. Lionel Bart Foundation Archive.
99. Kurt Ganzl, *British Musical Theatre*, Volume II (New York: Oxford University Press, 1986), 770.
    Ganzl claims that this issue actually brought the pre-production process to a halt. The chronology here is somewhat confusing, however, as Albery offered Australian actor Cyril Ritchard the role of Fagin in the late spring of 1960, just a few months before the play was set to open. Ganzl's text states that it took a full nine months for

Bart to concede to casting Moody as Fagin, and Moody did indeed audition for the
show as early as December 1959, as his name appears on a surviving casting sheet.
Nevertheless, the delay in the production from December 1959 to June 1960 was
likely due to myriad issues regarding the continued evolution of the show's form and
narrative as opposed to simply being due to the question of who would ultimately
play Fagin.

 Donald Albery, letter to Milton Goldman, March 28, 1960. Sir Donald Albery
Theatre Collection, 114.001, Folder 2. Harry Ransom Center, University of Texas at
Austin.

 Oliver! Audition Schedule.
100. Quoted in Morley, "Archetype of the Genuine English Classic Musical," 9.
101. Ibid.
102. Quoted in Ben Silverstone, "The Exclamation Factor," *Jewish Chronicle*, November 18,
2005, 23.
103. Quoted in ibid.
104. Ron Moody, interview with Ann McFerran, *Sunday Times*, June 12, 2005.
  http://www.timesonline.co.uk/tol/life_and_style/article529091.ece
105. Quoted in Ben Silverstone, "The Exclamation Factor," 23.
106. Sheridan Morley, *Spread a Little Happiness: The First Hundred Years of the British
Musical* (London: Thames and Hudson, 1987), 154.
107. Lionel Bart, *Oliver!* musical score (London: Lakeview Music, 1960), 112–13.
108. Alastair Davidson, interview by author.

 Tsai Chin reinforces this assertion, noting that "Peter was extremely intelligent
and very intuitive about the theatre. [...] Improvisation became extremely important
[to him]. He would improvise with the cast before anybody knew their lines."

 Tsai Chin, interview by author, October 17, 2010.
109. Radio interview, 199?, audio cassette. Lionel Bart Foundation Archive.
110. Among the lost treasures from the rehearsal period was a new song in which Fagin
would teach the Artful Dodger how to speak Yiddish; ironically, in spite of the numerous Jewish touches that Moody added to the part, he disliked the idea and persuaded
Bart to drop the number: "[Bart] wanted to do a number where I was going to teach
Dodger—Martin Horsey—Yiddish. [...] He didn't do it, maybe he was just talking,
because he was buzzing with ideas all the time."

 Radio interview, 199?, audio cassette. Lionel Bart Foundation Archive.
111. Radio interview, 1992, audio cassette. Lionel Bart Foundation Archive.
112. Alastair Davidson, interview by author.
113. Ibid.
114. Cameron Mackintosh, interview by author, July 12, 2010.
115. The basic issue of dance proved something of a stumbling block for the British from
a macro perspective regarding modern musical theater, as musicals from the fifties
could not match the dynamic forms of dance that defined various American musicals
from the postwar period, including *Oklahoma!* and *West Side Story*. Indeed, as is clear
from the lack of formal choreography in *Oliver!* dance remained somewhat incompatible with the British musical stage even as the British musical began to modernize. In
1963, a columnist for *Plays and Players* wrote:

"Since *Oklahoma* [sic] serious American choreographers like Martha Grahame,
Jerome Robbins and Michael Kidd have choreographed a musical as carefully as a
ballet. In the dance sequences of *West Side Story* musical comedy and pure ballet
merged irrevocably. It was not a case of the cast singing, as one critic wrote of *Salad*

Days, 'Oh, look at me. Oh, look at me I'm *almost* dancing'—the cast of an American musical could really dance."

"Lilly White Boy," *Plays and Players* (May 1963): 20.

116. Alastair Davidson, interview by author.
117. Ibid.
118. Ibid.
119. Lionel Bart, *Oliver!* musical score (London: Lakeview Music, 1960), 119.
120. Bart clearly had bigger ambitions for the song, "Who Will Buy?" as the audience is not simply presented with the milkmaid, strawberry seller, rose seller, and knife grinder. Instead, the song includes verses from a chair-mender, a mackerel-woman, and a chimney sweep.

    Lionel Bart, *Oliver!* Wimbledon libretto, II-2-13. Lord Chamberlain's Plays Collection, Manuscripts, British Library.
121. Lionel Bart, "One of the Worldwide Family," in Oliver!: *The London Palladium Souvenir Program* (London: Dewynters PLC, 1994).

    While part of the original West End cast, Humphries understudied the part of Fagin. Humphries would later joke in the *Celebrate Oliver!* retrospective that it was frustrating being Ron Moody's understudy as Moody was "always on" and never ill; thus, Humphries would be kept waiting in the wings, wishing whatever kinds of harm he could upon Moody in hopes that he would eventually get his chance to replace the lead actor as Fagin. In the same special, Moody jokingly retorted that one of the joys of being a lead actor is that it gives one the chance to torment understudies. Still, Humphries would go on to play Fagin in the West End return engagement, and during the Palladium revival in the 1990s; finally, he served as a judge on *I'd Do Anything*, helping to pick the performer who would take on the role of Nancy in the Drury Lane revival.

    Celebrate Oliver! December 26, 2005, BBC, Television.
122. Lionel Bart, "One of the Worldwide Family."
123. Radio interview, 199?, audio cassette. Lionel Bart Foundation Archive.
124. Bart, draft of letter to Tams-Witmark.
125. Donald Albery, letter to Joan Littlewood and Gerry MacColl, June 14, 1960. Sir Donald Albery Theatre Collection, DAT 114.001, Folder 2. Harry Ransom Center, University of Texas at Austin.
126. Ibid.

CHAPTER 4

1. Quoted in "'Oliver!' in it's [sic] Sixth year," *The Stage*, December 9, 1965, 15.
2. Alastair Davidson, interview by author, September 5, 2010.
3. Ibid.
4. "'Oliver!' in it's [sic] Sixth year," 15.
5. Alastair Davidson, interview by author.
6. Ibid.
7. Lionel Bart, "One of the Worldwide Family," in *Oliver!: The London Palladium Souvenir Program* (London: Dewynters, 1994).

    The traditional belief is that Bart exited the theater because of a problem with the revolve; he was convinced that the show would be a disaster due to this malfunction. Bart recounts this version of the story in the Palladium souvenir brochure. Alastair Davidson refutes this account, however, and insists that the opening night performance "was a perfect show; we had absolutely no problems whatsoever." Davidson concedes that from where Bart was sitting, it may have seemed as if the revolve had stuck, but "I can assure you that it was a perfect show. We had no technical problems of any sort that evening."

Alistair Davidson, interview by author.

8. "A Handful of Songs: The Lionel Bart Story—Part 2," August 19, 2005, BBC Radio 2.

9. A retrospective article in the *Guardian* notes that the show received twenty-three curtain calls on opening night.

"Curtain Up," *The Guardian*, June 18, 2003, A11.

10. Donald Albery, letter to Roger Stevens, July 2, 1960. Sir Donald Albery Theatre Collection, DAT 114.001, Folder 1. Harry Ransom Center, University of Texas at Austin.

11. "Dickens—to Music," *Yorkshire Evening Post* (Leeds), July 9, 1960.

12. Tony Robinson, interview by author, July 24, 2010.

13. Radio interview, 199?, audio cassette. Lionel Bart Foundation Archive.

14. Flash photography warning to be inserted in program, Sir Donald Albery Theatre Collection, DAT 114.001, Folder 1. Harry Ransom Center, University of Texas at Austin.

15. Donald Albery, letter to Franklin Weaver, January 2, 1962. Sir Donald Albery Theatre Collection, DAT 195.003. Harry Ransom Center, University of Texas at Austin.

16. The Lionel Bart archival folder at the University of Bristol contains a 1968 log documenting all of the pop recordings of songs from *Oliver!* These include recordings of "As Long as He Needs Me" by Shirley Bassey, Anita Bryant, Judy Garland, and Doris Day; a recording of "Consider Yourself" by Ray Charles; recordings of "Where is Love?" by Sammy Davis, Jr., Johnny Mathis, and Shani Wallis; and recordings of "Who Will Buy?" by Barbara Streisand and Nancy Sinatra.

Lionel Bart Archive 200102/0063, University of Bristol Theatre Collection.

17. J. Clarke, letter to Duncan Melvin, August 15, 1961. Sir Donald Albery Theatre Collection, DAT 196.002. Harry Ransom Center, University of Texas at Austin.

18. Glyn Mills & Co advertisement, *Oliver!* program (1963), Windham Theatres, printed by John Waddington Ltd., London.

19. North Thames Gas advertisement, *Oliver!* program (1960), Windham Theatres, printed by John Waddington Ltd., London.

20. Bernard Levin, "Bold and Bright and It Made Me Whistle," *Daily Express*, July 1, 1960. (emphases added)

21. Robert Muller, "Everyone Will Ask for More," *Daily Mail*, July 1, 1960.

22. Harold Conway, "It's Such a Good Twist," *Daily Sketch*, July 1, 1960.

23. Milton Shulman, "This One Could Start an Avalanche," *Evening Standard*, July 1, 1960.

24. "Lionel Bart's 'Oliver!' Tops The Thousandth Performance." Press Release from Duncan Melvin. October 27, 1962. Lionel Bart Foundation Archives.

25. David Ian Rabey, *English Drama Since 1940* (New York: Longman, 2003), 31.

26. Dominic Shellard, *British Theatre Since the War* (New Haven: Yale University Press, 1999), 57.

27. Kenneth Tynan, "The Voice of the Young," *The Observer*, May 13, 1956, 11.

28. T. C. Worsley, "Oliver," [*sic*], *London Financial Times*, July 1, 1960.

29. Tony Robinson, interview by author.

30. As Rabey points out, television contributed immeasurably to the excitement surrounding *Look Back in Anger*, though Royal Court was in effect using television to promote a play "which attacks the vicariousness of English life." Similarly, postwar prosperity and materialism (so anathema to Jimmy Porter's worldview) were essential to the ascent of television in the 1950s.

Rabey, *English Drama Since 1940*, 29.

31. Ibid., 32.

32. Muller, "Everyone Will Ask for More."

33. Allan Hale, "Musical Hit . . . and Made in Britain," *Manchester Evening News*, September 23, 1960.

34. Roy Shepherd, "Musical 'Oliver Twist' Spins to Success," *Sheffield Star*, September 3, 1960.

35. "A Battle Is on for 'Oliver!' " *London Evening News*, July 8, 1960.

36. C. B. Mortlock, "We Can Do This as Well as Americans," *City Press* (London), July 8, 1960.

37. Andrew Gamble and Tony Wright, "Introduction: The Britishness Question," in *Britishness: Perspectives on the Britishness Question*, eds. Andrew Gamble and Tony Wright (Malden, MA: Wiley-Blackwell, 2009), 4.

38. John Osborne, *Look Back in Anger* (New York: S. G. Phillips, 1957), 17.

39. Richard Hayton, Richard English, and Michael Kenny, "Englishness in Contemporary British Politics" in *Britishness: Perspectives on the Britishness Question*, eds. Andrew Gamble and Tony Wright (Malden, MA: Wiley-Blackwell, 2009), 127.

40. Antony Easthope, *Englishness and National Culture* (New York: Routledge, 1999), 10.

41. Ibid. Although nostalgia and sentiment may seem antithetical to looking back in anger, Osborne, through his celebration of music hall, embraces the sentimental ideal of a community (and a performance style) that is "immediate, vital, and direct."
    John Osborne, *The Entertainer* (New York: Criterion Books, 1958), 7.

42. G. H. Mair, "The Music-Hall," *English Review* (August 1911), 123.

43. Ibid.

44. Ibid., 124.

45. Osborne, *The Entertainer*, 7.

46. Paul Schlicke, ed., *The Oxford Reader's Companion to Dickens* (New York: Oxford University Press, 1999), 395.

47. Charles Dickens, *Oliver Twist* (Oxford: Oxford University Press, 1999), 198–99.

48. The narrator's emphasis on the degradation of women seems to foreshadow Dickens's fixation on fallen women in later novels such as *David Copperfield*, though Nancy was the first (and perhaps the foremost) of these characters.

49. Schlicke, ed., *The Oxford Reader's Companion to Dickens*, 395–96.

50. Charles Dickens, "The Amusements of the People (II)," in *The Amusements of the People and Other Papers: Reports, Essays and Reviews, 1834–1851*, ed. Michael Slater (Columbus: Ohio University Press, 1996), 196.

51. Ibid., 198 (Dickens's emphases).

52. "Music-Halls," *All The Year Round*, 25.619 (October 9, 1880), 520.
    This ambiguous critique of the music hall was something of a hallmark of the middle-class response to the institution. Rudolf Dircks put forth a similarly backhanded compliment in an 1892 article printed in *The Theatre*:
    "Let me say at once that, on one score, I take no objection to a music-hall performance. Let it be granted that its popularity justifies its existence; that it provides, for the most part, harmless amusement for a class of persons whose small share of taste it is not likely to corrupt."
    Rudolf Dircks, "The Apotheosis of the Music Hall," *The Theatre* (Nov. 1892), 193.
    F. Anstey offered a similar critique in *Harper's Monthly*, writing that "those who assert that the London poor are a joyless class, incapable of merriment, should see this crowd when genuinely amused, and consider whether there is not some exaggeration in descriptions of their hopeless gloom. True, the farce that provokes their

risibility is not a masterpiece of refined humor, but there is real humor of a rough and primitive kind in it nevertheless."

F. Anstey, "London Music Halls," *Harper's Monthly*, (January 1891), 196.

53. "Music-Halls," 522.

54. Peter Bailey, *Popular Culture and Performance in the Victorian City* (Cambridge: Cambridge University Press, 1998), 99.

55. Lionel Bart, *South Bank Show*, Transcript, Roll 3, 9. Lionel Bart Foundation Archive.

56. Peter Gammond, ed., *Music Hall Songbook* (Vermont: David & Charles/EMI, 1975), 7.

57. Raymond Knapp and Mitchell Morris, "Tin Pan Alley Songs on Stage and Screen Before World War II," in *Oxford Handbook of the American Musical*, eds. Raymond Knapp, Mitchell Morris, and Stacy Wolf (New York: Oxford University Press, 2011), 88.

58. Raymond Knapp, *The American Musical and the Formation of National Identity* (Princeton: Princeton University Press, 2005), 78.

59. Ibid., 77–79.

60. Christopher Pulling, *They Were Singing and What They Sang About* (London: George G. Harrap, 1952), 123 (Pulling's emphases).

61. Peter Davison, "Afterword," *Theatre and Song* (Teaneck: Somerset House, 1978), 190/8.

62. Peter Gammond, ed., *Best Music Hall and Variety Songs* (London: Wolfe, 1972), 61.

63. Peter Davison, *Songs of the British Music Hall* (New York: Oak, 1971), 184.

64. Ibid., 187.

65. Deborah Vlock, *Dickens, Novel Reading, and the Victorian Popular Theatre* (New York: Cambridge University Press, 1998), 125.

66. "Music Hall," 523.

67. Ibid.

68. David Mazower, *Yiddish Theatre in London* (London: Jewish Museum, 1996), 11.

69. Quoted in Anna Tzelniker, *Three for the Price of One* (London: Spiro Institute, 1991), 9.

70. Marsha Bryan Edelman, *Discovering Jewish Music* (Philadelphia: Jewish Publication Society, 2003), 39.

71. Radio interview, 199?, audio cassette. Lionel Bart Foundation Archive.

72. "Night at the Grand Palais," *Times*, June 11, 1957, 3.

73. Ibid.

74. Ibid.

75. Mazower, *Yiddish Theatre*, 23.

76. Jack Gottlieb, *Funny, It Doesn't Sound Jewish* (Albany: State University of New York Press, 2004), 12.

77. Edelman, *Discovering Jewish Music*, 40.

78. "Lionel Bart," *The South Bank Show*, ITV (UK), December 11, 1994, Television.

79. Ibid.

80. Ronald Pearsall, *Victorian Popular Music* (Detroit: Gale Research, 1973), 47.

81. Max Beerbohm, "Dan Leno," in *A Selection from Around Theatres* (Garden City: Doubleday, 1960), 201.

82. "Lionel Bart," *The South Bank Show*.

83. Tony Robinson, interview by author.

84. Osborne, *Look Back in Anger*, 81–82.

85. Barry Faulk, *Music Hall and Modernity: The Victorian Discovery of Popular Culture* (Athens: Ohio University Press, 2004), 41.

86. G. J. Mellor, *Northern Music Hall* (Newcastle: Graham, 1970), 117.

87. Roger Wilmut, *Kindly Leave the Stage!: The Story of Variety, 1919–1960* (London: Methuen, 1985), 16 (Wilmut's emphases).

In an article for the *Observer Magazine*, John Osborne likewise noted that "[m]ost academics would argue that the golden age of the music hall flowered about 1912, the year of the first Royal Command Performance, and from then on the rot set in."

John Osborne, "The Nation's Theatre," *Observer Magazine* (April 20, 1975): 22.

88. T. S. Eliot, "Marie Lloyd," in *Selected Prose of T. S. Eliot*, ed. Frank Kermode (New York: Harcourt Brace Jovanovich, 1975), 173.

89. Ibid., 174.

90. Faulk, *Music Hall and Modernity*, 26.

91. Peter Bailey, "Custom, Capital and Culture in the Victorian Music Hall," in *Popular Culture and Custom in Nineteenth-Century England*, ed. Robert D. Storch (New York: St. Martin's Press, 1982), 187–89.

Peter Bailey, "Introduction: Making Sense of Music Hall" in *Music Hall: The Business of Pleasure* (Philadelphia: Open University Press, 1986), xv.

92. Bailey, "Introduction," xv.

93. Bailey's arguments build off socialist theories of popular culture, as Peter Burke has analyzed "the distinction between the culture which comes *from* ordinary people [. . .] and the culture which is provided *for* ordinary people by someone else."

Peter Burke, "The 'Discovery' of Popular Culture," in *People's History and Socialist Theory*, ed. Raphael Samuel (Boston: Routledge & Kegan Paul, 1981), 218 (Burke's emphases).

Burke also notes the ease with which "folk culture" is adapted into popular culture by means of capitalist exploitation:

"Popular culture grows out of the local way of life, and necessarily changes with it. The spread of literacy, the growing power of the nation-state and the rise of commercial capitalism were bound to transform both the oral traditions and the material culture of different regions. Some of the 'primitive' traditions discovered by folklorists in the nineteenth century may not have gone back more than a generation or two."

Burke, "The 'Discovery' of Popular Culture," 217.

94. Jeffrey Richards, *Imperialism and Music: Britain, 1876–1953* (New York: Manchester University Press, 2001), 324.

95. Bailey, "Custom, Capital, and Culture," 198.

96. Even Joan Littlewood, who so thoroughly embraced working-class culture and working-class musical traditions in her plays, struggled with this issue; Kate Dorney states that in spite of Littlewood's attempt to present a truthful representation of working-class culture in her 1950s plays, her "'authentic' Cockneys were beginning to look very similar to the stereotypical cockney she had [initially] set out to challenge."

Kate Dorney, *The Changing Language of Modern English Drama, 1945–2005* (New York: Palgrave Macmillan, 2009), 121.

97. Ernest Walter, "London's Noisy Music Halls Embodied the Cockney Spirit," *Vancouver Daily Province*, September 26, 1942, 3.

98. Faulk, *Music Hall and Modernity*, 48.

99. Ibid.

It is important to note that music-hall songs were oftentimes quite patriotic, and perhaps even nationalistic or jingoistic, particularly in times of war; Jeffrey Richards traces the rise of patriotic music-hall songs from the Boer War up through World War I, though "by the time the Great War ended the heyday of music hall and music-hall patriotism had passed and music hall was transmuting into variety." Osborne alludes to this fact in *The Entertainer*, though Archie's chauvinistic music-hall songs are meant to serve as ironic and pathetic reminders of a lost empire in the wake of the Suez Crisis. Richards, *Imperialism and Music*, 337.

100. Raymond Knapp, "Performance, Authenticity, and the Reflexive Idealism of the American Musical," in *Oxford Handbook of the American Musical*, eds. Raymond Knapp, Mitchell Morris, and Stacy Wolf (New York: Oxford University Press, 2011), 408.

101. Ibid., 409.

102. Bailey maintains that in spite of the proliferation of prewar music-hall laments, music hall did not officially die out until the 1950s with the rise of television.
        Bailey, "Introduction," xiii.

103. Raymond Knapp, *The American Musical and the Formation of National Identity* (Princeton: Princeton University Press, 2005), 119.

104. Ibid., 122.

105. McMillin and Steyn echo several of these points, noting the American musical's fixation on community.
        Scott McMillin, *The Musical as Drama* (Princeton: Princeton University Press, 2006), 83.
        Mark Steyn, *Broadway Babies Say Goodnight: Musicals Then and Now* (New York: Routledge, 2000), 97.

106. Donald Pippin, interview by author, October 26, 2010.

107. "Novel into Musical," *Times,* September 8, 1962, 9.

108. "New Records: Dickens with Music," *Plays and Players* (October 1960).

109. "Lionel Bart on an 'Epic' Musical," *Times*, March 22, 1962, 16.

110. Quoted in Ibid.

111. Quoted in Ibid.

112. Bart's comments throughout this article are directed primarily toward *Blitz!*, though he links *Blitz!* to *Oliver!* on the basis of his own approach to (and philosophy of) musical theater.

113. "Lionel Bart on an 'Epic' Musical," 16.

114. Ibid.

115. Conway, "It's Such a Good Twist."

116. Muller, "Everyone Will Ask for More."

117. Brian McFarlane notes that the "true to the spirit" argument is actually just another form of fidelity criticism, one stressing fidelity to an abstract element of the text as opposed to the concrete, narrative fidelity stressed in traditional fidelity criticism.
        Brian McFarlane, *Novel to Film: An Introduction to the Theory of Adaptation* (Oxford: Oxford University Press, 1996), 9.

118. J. C. Trewin, "What the Dickens!" *Birmingham Post*, July 6, 1960.

119. Ibid.

120. J. C. Trewin, "Thomas, Oliver, and Eugene," *Illustrated London News,* July 16, 1960.

121. Ibid.

122. Pulling, *They Were Singing*, 20.

123. Walter, "London's Noisy Music Halls Embodied the Cockney Spirit," 3.

124. Davison, *Songs of the British Music Hall*, 230.

125. Ibid., 231.

126. J. Greaves, letter to Lionel Bart, October 23, 1960. Lionel Bart Foundation Archive.

127. Lionel Bart, letter to J. Greaves, November 2, 1960. Lionel Bart Foundation Archive.

128. Muller, "Everyone Will Ask for More."

129. J. C. Trewin, "Thomas, Oliver, and Eugene."

130. Peter Mandler, *The English National Character: The History of an Idea from Edmund Burke to Tony Blair* (New Haven: Yale University Press, 2006), 26.

131. Thomas Leitch, *Film Adaptation and its Discontents* (Baltimore: Johns Hopkins University Press, 2007), 16.

132. "A Dickens musical," *Liverpool Post*, July 1, 1960, 5.

133. Frederic Jameson, *Postmodernism, or the Cultural Logic of Late Capitalism* (Durham: Duke University Press, 1991), 19.

134. Juliet John, *Dickens and Mass Culture* (Oxford: Oxford University Press, 2010), 124.

135. Richards, *Imperialism and Music*, 324–25.

136. Sheridan Morley, *Spread a Little Happiness: The First Hundred Years of the British Musical* (London: Thames and Hudson, 1987), 154.

137. Cameron Mackintosh, interview by author, July 12, 2010.

138. Steyn, *Broadway Babies*, 163.

139. Quoted in "Lionel Bart on an 'Epic' Musical," 16.

140. Ron Moody, *A Still Untitled (Not Quite) Autobiography* (London: JR Books, 2010), 158.

141. Henry Hewes, "Britain's Unruly Waifs," *Saturday Review*, January, 19 1963, 26 (Hewes's emphases).

142. Lionel Bart, interview with Anthony Brown (transcript), "For Art's Sake," Southampton Television, April 29, 1964, 3. Lionel Bart Foundation Archive.

143. Ibid.

144. Ibid.

145. Denny Flinn uses the term disparagingly when describing Lloyd Webber's works in his text on the history of musical theater:

"Poperetta fits neatly into Andrew Lloyd Webber's desire for continuous musical events. The strength of this concept is that the division between the reality of book scenes and the more theatrical level of song and dance do not conflict. There's no need to craft the transitions. [...] The danger is that the bookless musical fails to use dialogue and dance to further ideas they could better communicate. [...] Sung-through shows lack the integration that makes the American musical the great and original art form that it is. Artists like Lloyd Webber and [Harold] Prince attempt to make the musical all music, harking back to an older, simpler form of theatre that lacked integration."

Denny Martin Flinn, *Musical!: A Grand Tour* (New York: Schirmer, 1997), 475.
Though Flinn's criticism about the lack of transitions within mega-musicals seems valid, the notion that these musicals are not "integrated" is curious given that music, lyrics, dialogue, and plot are all combined into a single entity in the "sung-through" formula. As noted in Chapter 1, several scholars of American musical theatre view mega-musicals as *excessively* integrated.

146. Jessica Sternfeld, *The Megamusical* (Bloomington: Indiana University Press, 2006), 86.

147. Trevor Ray, interview by author, June 26, 2010.

148. Sternfeld, *The Megamusical*, 87.

149. Ibid. 80.

150. Roger Hardwick, interview by author, July 8, 2010.

151. Quoted in Barry Singer, *Ever After* (New York: Applause, 2004), 42.
The *Les Miz/Oliver!* connection continues to run deep to this day, and the character of Gavroche remains a prominent link in this regard; Daniel Huttlestone, who played the role of Fagin's scene-stealing youngest charge Nipper in the Drury Lane revival, went on to play Gavroche in the West End and eventually in Tom Hooper's film adaptation.

152. Cameron Mackintosh, interview by author.

153. Sternfeld, *The Megamusical*, 77.

154. Ibid.

155. Steyn, *Broadway Babies*, 171.

156. Ibid.

157. Edna Doré, interview by author, July 3, 2010.

158. Tony Robinson, interview by author.

159. Bart, "One of the Worldwide Family."

CHAPTER 5

1. Following *Oliver!*'s triumphant debut, Bart wrote to Rogers thanking him for his work and praising him as having "a greater sense of theatre than any other musician I know in England."

   Lionel Bart, letter to Eric Rogers, August 23, 1960. Lionel Bart Foundation Archive.

2. Jonathan Culler, *The Pursuit of Signs* (London: Routledge, 1981), 170.

3. Roland Barthes, "The Death of the Author," in *Image, Music, Text* (New York: Hill and Wang, 1977), 146.

4. Gérard Genette, *Paratexts* (New York: Cambridge University Press, 1997), 76.

5. Bart used the same titling technique for several of his other musicals, including *Blitz!* and the ill-fated *Twang!!*

6. Lionel Bart, letter to Ron Moody, December 15, 1960. Lionel Bart Foundation Archive.

7. "Lionel Bart," *The South Bank Show*, ITV (UK), December 11, 1994, television.

8. Scott McMillin, *The Musical as Drama* (Princeton: Princeton University Press, 2006), 41–42.

9. Ibid., 127.

10. George J. Worth, *Dickensian Melodrama* (Lawrence: University of Kansas Press, 1978), 41.

11. Karin Lesnik-Oberstein, "*Oliver Twist*: The Narrator's Tale," *Textual Practice* 15, no. 1 (2001): 87.

12. Ibid. (Lesnik-Oberstein's emphases).

13. Ibid., 87–88.

14. Lesnik-Oberstein links this disparity to "a problem of language," which she finds essential to the overall meaning of the narrator's role in the novel and to the overarching emphasis on Oliver's incorruptibility. The narrator repeatedly reveals the inherent dishonesty of the novel's "storytellers," including Mrs. Mann, Mr. Bumble, Mrs. Corney, Fagin, etcetera. However, the narrator himself adopts a similarly dishonest linguistic strategy; thus, Oliver's lack of verbal expressiveness is a sign of his transcendent morality. Lesnik-Oberstein's interpretation is particularly intriguing in relation to *Oliver!*, for here the narrator does *not* use words. In this context, the orchestra achieves a level of integrity that Dickens's narrator lacks, which seems fitting given that the orchestra's music oftentimes sets up moments of honest revelation for the musical's characters through song. Ibid., 88.

15. In his essay on the conventions of musical theater songs, Paul Laird describes the "I want" number as a song that "takes place early in a show and discloses a main character's primary motivation."

   Paul R. Laird, "Musical Styles and Song Conventions" in *Oxford Handbook of the American Musical*, eds. Raymond Knapp, Mitchell Morris, and Stacy Wolf (New York: Oxford University Press, 2011), 34.

16. *Oliver!* original London production prompt book, 3. Cameron Mackintosh Ltd. Cameron Mackintosh Archive.

17. Charles Dickens, *Oliver Twist* (Oxford: Oxford University Press, 1999), 16.

18. Richard Hanneford, "The Fairy World of *Oliver Twist*," *Dickens Studies Newsletter* 8 (1977): 34.

19. Lionel Bart, *Oliver!* musical score (London: Lakeview Music, 1960), 12.

20. *Oliver!* original London production prompt book, 7. Cameron Mackintosh Ltd. Cameron Mackintosh Archive.

21. Dickens, *Oliver Twist*, 34.

22. James R. Kincaid, *Dickens and the Rhetoric of Laughter*, Oxford: Clarendon Press, 1971), 50–51.

23. Dickens, *Oliver Twist*, 26.

24. Kincaid, *Dickens and the Rhetoric of Laughter*, 51.

25. McMillin proposes that reflective solos need not be read solely as a "deepening of a psychological entity"; they can likewise be understood as a "change of mode in the characterization itself."

     McMillin, *Musical as Drama*, 43.

26. Ibid., 47.

27. In emphasizing the connection between Oliver's asking for more and his singing "Where Is Love?" I am deviating somewhat from McMillin, who stresses the "split" that exists within musical characters when they transition from "book time" to "number time."

     McMillin, *Musical as Drama*, 43.

28. Dickens, *Oliver Twist*, 84.

29. Bart, *Oliver!* musical score, 38.

30. *Oliver!* original London production prompt book, 47. Cameron Mackintosh Ltd. Cameron Mackintosh Archive.

31. This misperception is largely a result of the enormous popularity of the film version of the musical, which has had significant repercussions on the structure of the adaptation, and, more specifically, on the tenor of the Oliver-Nancy relationship (see Chapter 7).

32. Lionel Bart, *Oliver!* (libretto; New York: Tams-Witmark, 1960), 52.

33. In the same scene, Oliver's humorous observation that it might be preferable to be a book seller (as opposed to a book writer) underscores the capitalist sensibilities that he seems to have inherited as part of his secret, middle-class birthright. The statement is also a subtle gibe at Dickens's publisher, Richard Bentley.

34. Mr. Brownlow's charitable nature seemingly contradicts this point, but the revelation of Oliver's pedigree negates this notion; Mr. Brownlow is ultimately looking out for the needs of his grandson as opposed to showing charity toward a stranger.

35. The prompt book accentuates the young pickpocket's newfound disregard for Oliver, and the two characters almost come to blows as a result of the Dodger's taunting. *Oliver!* original London production prompt book, 70. Cameron Mackintosh Ltd. Cameron Mackintosh Archive.

36. Bart, *Oliver!* libretto, 2.

37. J. S. Bratton, "Jenny Hill: Sex and Sexism in the Victorian Music Hall," in *Music Hall: Performance and Style*, ed. J. S. Bratton (Philadelphia: Open University Press, 1986), 93. Though Bratton expresses skepticism toward this phenomenon, he nevertheless acknowledges the power of this and other "myths" of the Victorian music hall.

38. Dagmar Kift, *The Victorian Music Hall: Culture, Class, and Conflict* (Cambridge: Cambridge University Press, 1996), 136.

     Given these assumptions, it was oftentimes the policy of London magistrates to consider unaccompanied women in the halls as prostitutes. Most proprietors had little choice but to put up signs prohibiting women unaccompanied by gentlemen, for many middle-class critics of the music hall automatically assumed that the proprietors were actively promoting prostitution; Bailey points out that many prostitutes managed to avoid being banned, however, by assuming respectable disguises and conducting their business transactions surreptitiously.

Peter Bailey, *Popular Culture and Performance in the Victorian City* (Cambridge: Cambridge University Press, 1998), 145.

39. Kift, *Victorian Music Hall*, 137.
40. Ibid., 138.
41. In his instructional text on writing musicals, Stephen Citron notes that "[w]hen critics zero in for the kill on a musical, they usually attack the second act."
Stephen Citron, *The Musical from the Inside Out* (Chicago: Ivan D. Ree, 1992), 148.
42. Carol Reed would rectify this matter in his film adaptation (see Chapter 7).
43. Given the breadth of the story that remains to be told, it is somewhat surprising that Bart chooses to open Act II with "Oom Pah Pah," which, though a lively and engaging number, has absolutely nothing to do with the narrative. Still, "Oom Pah Pah" seems a fitting place to begin since the second half of the show will focus heavily on Nancy; this particular number reinforces the reckless yet joyful hedonism that defines her way of life, but the negative consequences of that recklessness will manifest themselves shortly.
44. Dickens, *Oliver Twist*, 95.
45. *Oliver!* original London production prompt book, 57. Cameron Mackintosh Ltd. Cameron Mackintosh Archive.
46. Robert R. Garnett, "*Oliver Twist*'s Nancy: The Angel in Chains," *Religion and the Arts* 4, no. 4 (2000): 506.
In the same passage, Garnett likewise alludes to Sikes's inability to seek redemption: "Hoping that Sikes will renounce his brutish existence for a life of abstinence and prayer is not only futile, however, but even paradoxical, for he is the embodiment of matter devoid of soul; without his brutishness, Sikes would not exist at all."
47. Considering his letter's context, it is entirely possible that Bart purposefully devalued the centrality of Fagin and his pupils to the musical's narrative. Bart's primary goal in writing this letter was to express his displeasure at Moody's continued improvising (see Chapter 6). He thus sternly informed the actor that the show was not meant to revolve around Fagin: "During our last argument you claimed 'OLIVER!' was your show and the proof was there nightly in the laughter and tumultuous applause that you personally receive. I must disagree with you. 'OLIVER!' is not your show." Bart, letter to Ron Moody, December 15, 1960.
48. Paul Schlicke, *Dickens and Popular Entertainment* (London: Unwin Hyman, 1988), 14.
49. Kincaid, *Dickens and the Rhetoric of Laughter*, 69.
50. Ibid.
51. Juliet John, *Charles Dickens's Oliver Twist: A Sourcebook*, ed. Juliet John (New York: Routledge, 2006), 165.
52. Dickens, *Oliver Twist*, 59.
53. Ibid., 63.
54. Lionel Bart, "Thoughts on Fagin," January 23, 1967. Lionel Bart Foundation Archive.
55. Kincaid, *Dickens and the Rhetoric of Laughter*, 72.
56. Ibid., 73.
57. Fagin's threatening of Oliver following the child's inadvertent spying on his treasure hoard is the only moment in the show where Bart comes close to depicting the old man as monstrous, and the blocking for the scene in the original prompt book shows an uncharacteristic burst of violence from this tamer version of the character: "Fagin drags Oliver over to L. & throws him on the floor D/S." *Oliver!* original London production prompt book, 41. Cameron Mackintosh Ltd. Cameron Mackintosh Archive.
58. Bart, *Oliver!* musical score, 52–55.
59. *Oliver!* original London production prompt book, 35. Cameron Mackintosh Ltd. Cameron Mackintosh Archive.

60. Furthering the music-hall format of the number is the depiction of Fagin as a magician of sorts, as is made evident by the trick string of handkerchiefs that he employs when playing the pickpocket game with Oliver. Robert Lindsay would explore this element of Fagin's personality in even greater depth in the 1999 ITV adaptation of *Oliver Twist*.

61. One could argue that Fagin's hoarding of his personal treasures also runs contrary to the philosophy of the thieves' den. This miserly component of Fagin's personality is indeed a contrast to the Dodger's philosophy of communal sharing, though it does not prevent Fagin from sharing other goods with the boys and providing for their needs. Fagin's collection is presented as a guilty pleasure; Fagin never actually profits from the materials contained in his chest, nor does he gloat about the joys of sending people to the gallows so as to secure his fortune. Nevertheless, its very presence reinforces the stereotypical foundations on which the literary character was built. In the recent West End revivals, as a means of counteracting (or, at the very least, distracting the audience from) the distasteful stereotype of the "covetous Jew," actors have exploited the comic potential within the scene and turned Fagin into a Victorian era "prop comic" who makes a humorous joke about virtually every piece of treasure in his chest.

62. "This Fagin Is Unique," *Jewish Chronicle*, July 8, 1960, 26.

63. Jack Gottlieb, *Funny, It Doesn't Sound Jewish* (Albany: State University of New York Press, 2004), 149.

64. Bart would later explain that this phrase was meant to embody the waddling arrogance of Mr. Bumble's gait, another indication of the composer's talent for writing character-based songs/music. Mark Steyn, *Broadway Babies Say Goodnight: Musicals Then and Now* (New York: Routledge, 2000), 173.

65. Dickens, *Oliver Twist*, 12.

66. Bart, *Oliver!* musical score, 19.

67. Bart's "tacking on" the death of Old Sally and the revelation of the locket seems ironically evocative of Dickens's own haphazard "retconning" of Agnes's death scene by reinventing Mrs. Thingummy as Old Sally and having her speak of the theft of the locket (see Appendix B).

CHAPTER 6

1. "Oliver! Disappoints the Swedes," *Times*, September 21, 1961, 16.

2. Lars Schmidt, letter to Donald Albery, November 8, 1961. Sir Donald Albery Collection, DAT 195.001. Harry Ransom Center, University of Texas at Austin.

3. "Oliver! Disappoints the Swedes," 16.

4. Schmidt, letter to Donald Albery.

5. Lars Schmidt, letter to Lionel Bart, November 7, 1961. Lionel Bart Foundation Archive.

6. Ibid.

7. Anonymous telegram on *Oliver!*'s debut in Australia. Sir Donald Albery Collection, DAT 204.002. Harry Ransom Center, University of Texas at Austin.

8. Lionel Bart, letter to Lars Schmidt, November 15, 1961. Lionel Bart Foundation Archive.

9. Donald Albery, letter to K. Bentham, January 15, 1965. Sir Donald Albery Collection, DAT 195.001. Harry Ransom Center, University of Texas at Austin.

10. Donald Albery, letter to De. E. Ingram, October 25, 1965. Sir Donald Albery Collection, 196.003. Harry Ransom Center, University of Texas at Austin.

11. Even in other cases, where Bart was more accommodating regarding the continental production rights, he maintained that Donmar should remain actively involved in the process: "Lionel [...] generally insists that each production is supervised by us."
    Donald Albery, letter to P. McNaughton, October 25, 1965. Sir Donald Albery Collection, DAT 196.003. Harry Ransom Center, University of Texas at Austin.
12. Jules Buck, letter to Donald Albery, May 4, 1964. Sir Donald Albery Collection, DAT 195.001. Harry Ransom Center, University of Texas at Austin.
13. Joseph Wershba, "Sweet Georgia Brown," *New York Post Magazine*, May 5, 1963, 2.
14. Lionel Bart, letter to Donald Albery, February 11, 1965. Sir Donald Albery Collection, DAT 195.001. Harry Ransom Center, University of Texas at Austin.
15. Donald Albery, letter to Lionel Bart, February 12, 1965. Sir Donald Albery Collection, DAT 195.001. Harry Ransom Center, University of Texas at Austin.
16. Ibid.
17. Ibid.
18. Albery's administrative assistant, Anne Jenkins, sent a wry note to her employer about a request from the producers in Holland, noting that "Fiz rang to say she had a successful trip but there was one scene the Dutch wanted to alter in the script—the Old Sally dying scene—instead of seeing her dying they would like M rs [*sic*] Bumble to report her death to Bumble and exhibit the locket—apparently the good bourgeois Dutch would have their enjoyment daunted by this scene."
    Anne Jenkins, memo to Donald Albery, July 15, 1963. Sir Donald Albery Collection, DAT 203.001. Harry Ransom Center, University of Texas at Austin.
19. In his 1961 letter imploring Bart to license the show for an Israeli production, Israeli producer Ori Levy stated that "It has been almost a year since my first letter to you. My enthusiasm for 'Oliver' [*sic*] is still strong, and I will not be satisfied until it is shown here."
    Ori Levy, letter to Lionel Bart, October 15, 1961. Lionel Bart Foundation Archive.
20. Raphael Bashan, letter to Lionel Bart, October 20, 1961. Lionel Bart Foundation Archive.
21. Ibid.
22. Lionel Bart, letter to Donald Albery, April 2, 1965. Sir Donald Albery Collection, DAT 203.003. Harry Ransom Center, University of Texas at Austin.
23. Jock Jacobsen, letter to Donald Albery, November, 18 1964. Sir Donald Albery Collection, DAT 203.003. Harry Ransom Center, University of Texas at Austin.
24. "Sympathetic Fagin Shocks Jews," *Times*, March 4, 1966, 15.
25. Lionel Bart, letter to Donald Albery, August 20, 1965. Sir Donald Albery Collection, DAT 203.003. Harry Ransom Center, University of Texas at Austin.
26. Anne Jenkins, letter to Joan Maitland, May 9, 1966. Sir Donald Albery Collection, DAT 203.003. Harry Ransom Center, University of Texas at Austin.
27. "Sympathetic Fagin Shocks Jews," 15.
28. Ibid.
29. Ibid.
30. Donald Albery, letter to Michiko Serkine, June 19, 1964. Sir Donald Albery Collection, DAT 195.001. Harry Ransom Center, University of Texas at Austin.
31. Larry Parnes, letter to Donald Albery, April 15, 1966. Sir Donald Albery Collection, DAT 196.003. Harry Ransom Center, University of Texas at Austin.
32. William Hickey, "She's over Here to Take 'Oliver!' to Tokyo," *Daily Express*, August 11, 1967.
33. "Under Wraps," *Daily Telegraph*, December 29, 1977.
34. Quoted in Ibid.
35. Roger Hardwick, interview by author, July 8, 2010.

36. A full-scale Japanese production of the show with a Japanese cast would take shape almost ten years later.

    Ibid.

37. William Hickey's article on the Tokyo production of *Oliver!* seemed to foreshadow the romantic involvement between the two, as Albery sang Uenishi's praises on both a professional and personal level: "'She is one of the most incredible people I have ever met,' said Mr. Albery, who is helping her choose a new English cast for the Tokyo version. 'She is an excellent businesswoman and exquisitely beautiful.'"

    Hickey, "She's over Here to Take 'Oliver!' to Tokyo."

38. Lady Nobuko Albery, email to author, August 6, 2013.

39. Hickey, "She's over Here to Take 'Oliver!' to Tokyo."

40. Quoted in ibid.

41. Donald Albery, letter to Kazuo Kikuta, October 12, 1967. Sir Donald Albery Collection, DAT 200.003. Harry Ransom Center, University of Texas at Austin.

42. Sir Donald Albery Collection, DAT 201.001. Harry Ransom Center, University of Texas at Austin.

43. Linda Purl, interview by author, November 17, 2010.

44. Ibid.

45. Ibid.

46. Review of *Oliver!* in Toho, *The Yomiuri*, July 22, 1968. (translation)

47. Ibid.

48. "Tokyo Has a Yen for 'Oliver!'" *Daily Cinema*, October 1, 1968.

49. Sometimes, this embrace could prove suffocating. Joey Koehm, one of the American chorus boys, recalled that the show attracted many "fan girls" in Japan, several of whom "pulled my sweater almost off me." Quoted in Barbara Carlson, "Young Stars Nonplussed," *Hartford Courant*, July 25, 1968.

50. Donald Albery, letter to David Merrick, July 14, 1960. Sir Donald Albery, 202.001. Harry Ransom Center, University of Texas at Austin.

51. "A Battle Is on for 'Oliver!'" *London Evening News*, July 8, 1960.

52. Merrick had previously imported several major English postwar dramas, such as *Look Back in Anger* (1958), *The Entertainer* (1958), and *A Taste of Honey* (1960). Just prior to the Broadway debut of *Oliver!*, Merrick produced Leslie Bricusse and Anthony Newley's *Stop the World—I Want to Get Off*; the minimalist musical ran an impressive 556 Broadway performances, thus surpassing its original West End production.

    Howard Kissel, *David Merrick: The Abominable Showman* (New York: Applause, 1993), 513–35.

53. Dorothy Kilgallen, "The Voice of Broadway," *New York Journal American*, September 14, 1962, 15.

54. Lionel Bart, letter to Dorothy Kilgallen, September 1962. Lionel Bart Foundation Archive.

55. Bob Thomas, "Will U.S. Fans Cheer Dickens in Musical?" *Traveler* (Boston), August 9, 1962.

56. Ibid.

57. Ibid.

58. Patricia Lewis, "I Forecast: Trouble on Broadway for 'Oliver!'" *Daily Express*, September 28, 1961.

59. Donald Pippin, interview by author, October 26, 2010.

    According to Howard Kissel, "the long pre-Broadway tour allowed the show to repay its investments well before it reached the New York critics."

    Kissel, *David Merrick*, 248.

60. Stanley Eichelbaum, "'Oliver!' Is a Staggering, Wonderful Show," *San Francisco Examiner*, September 26, 1962, 5C2H.

61. Paul Speegle, "'Oliver!' Is a Smasher," *San Francisco News Call Bulletin*, September 26, 1962.

62. Donald Pippin, interview by author.

63. Ibid.

64. Ibid.

65. Ibid.

66. Ibid.

During his time in London, Pippin also met Lionel Bart and immediately perceived the dichotomy between the man's talent and his destructive indulgences: "He was very charming. [But] I could tell right away that he was already a victim of the nouveau riche mentality."

67. Ibid.

68. Kissel, *David Merrick*, 250.

69. Donald Pippin, interview by author.

70. Ibid.

71. Ibid.

72. Ibid.

73. Ibid.

74. Ibid.

75. Ibid.

76. Ibid.

77. Ibid.

78. Quoted in Joyce Egginton, "Too Much Ballyhoo," *Scene*, 17, January 26, 1963, 14.

79. Quoted in Barbara Lee Horn, *David Merrick: A Bio-bibliography* (New York: Greenwood, 1992), 135.

80. Quoted in Egginton, "Too Much Ballyhoo," 14.

81. *Oliver!* revisited Broadway the following year for a brief return engagement at the Martin Beck Theatre.

82. "Oliver Twisted," *Time*, January 11, 1963, 52.

83. Ibid.

84. "New Twist," *Newsweek*, January, 14, 1963, 65.

85. John McCarten, "No Social Significance," *New Yorker*, January19, 1963, 60.

86. Howard Taubman, "'Oliver Twist' as a Musical," *New York Times,* January 8, 1963, 5.

87. "British Encirclement of Broadway," *Times*, June 26, 1963, 15.

88. Ibid.

89. Frank Rich, "Mood in 'Oliver' [*sic*] Revival," *New York Times*, April 30, 1984, C11. The failure of the 1984 Broadway revival, which closed after just thirteen previews and seventeen performances, may be an indication that *Oliver!* maintained a greater cultural appeal in its native England, though Cameron Mackintosh, who produced the revival, blamed Rich's *New York Times* review. Cameron Mackintosh, "Reviewing the Situation," in *Oliver!* London Palladium Souvenir Program (London: Dewynters, 1994).

90. Jessica Sternfeld, *The Megamusical*, (Bloomington: Indiana University Press, 2006), 74.

91. Donald Pippin, interview by author.

92. Sternfeld, *The Megamusical*, 4. Nevertheless, the more general response among New York reviewers was largely positive, and the reviews of the "hospitable" critics mirrored those of their West End counterparts in several respects. John McClain of the

New York Journal American unhesitatingly labeled *Oliver!* "a breakthrough for the British in a field which has so long been dominated by Americans," while John Chapman of *New York Daily News* happily welcomed *Oliver!* to Broadway by labeling it "one of the most impressive British products to be imported here since the first Rolls Royce."

    John McClain, review of original Broadway production of *Oliver! New York Theatre Critics' Reviews* 24, no. 22 (1963): 397.

    John Chapman, review of original Broadway production of *Oliver! New York Theatre Critics' Reviews* 24, no. 22 (1963): 399.

93. "British Encirclement of Broadway," 15.
94. Ron Moody, *A Still Untitled (Not Quite) Autobiography* (London: JR Books, 2010), 168.
95. Moody would later reflect that "[f]or me, making the show work was getting belly laughs—like most variety artists. But the straight actor believes you fix the performance in rehearsal and that's it. My portrayal of Fagin was all to do with my experience in comedy and revue."

    Ron Moody, interview with Ann McFerran, *Sunday Times*, June 12, 2005.
    http://www.timesonline.co.uk/tol/life_and_style/article529091.ece

96. Lionel Bart, "Thoughts on Fagin," January 23, 1967. Lionel Bart Foundation Archive.
97. Ibid.
98. Lionel Bart, letter to Donald Albery, December 6, 1960, 1. Sir Donald Albery Theatre Collection, 196.001. Harry Ransom Center, University of Texas at Austin.
99. "This Fagin Is Unique," *Jewish Chronicle*, July 8, 1960, 26.
100. Peter Coe understandably found Bart's increasingly public objections to Moody's West End performance counterproductive, for by drawing attention to the potentially anti-Semitic elements of Moody's interpretation, Bart was effectively creating negative buzz around the actor and the show. By January 1961, Coe was so offended by Bart's "slander" of Moody that he wrote to Albery on the subject, informing the producer:

    "I have received telephone calls from the press concerning Lionel Bart's admission to several people outside our immediate circle in this country & abroad that he is dissatisfied with Ron Moody's performance in Oliver [*sic*], that the performance is anti-Semitic, & that *he* would not consider lettering [*sic*] Ron play the part in New York. This is not only disloyal conduct affecting the whole company it is utterly without scruples and vaguely slanderous towards Ron."

    Peter Coe, letter to Donald Albery, January 26, 1961. Sir Donald Albery Theatre Collection, 196.001. Harry Ransom Center, University of Texas at Austin.
101. Bart, letter to Donald Albery, December 6 1960, 3–4. Sir Donald Albery Theatre Collection, 196.001. Harry Ransom Center, University of Texas at Austin.
102. Ibid., 6. (Bart's emphases)
103. "A Handful of Songs: The Lionel Bart Story—Part 2," August 19, 2005, BBC Radio 2.
104. Jack Gottlieb, *Funny, It Doesn't Sound Jewish* (Albany: State University of New York Press, 2004), 1.
105. Emanuel Rubin and John H. Baron, *Music in Jewish History and Culture* (Sterling Heights: Harmonie Park Press, 2006), 195.
106. Ibid., 274.
107. Quoted in Lewis, "I Forecast: Trouble on Broadway for 'Oliver!'"
108. Donald Pippin, "Differences Between the London and New York Productions," commentary track, *Oliver! Broadway Deluxe Collector's Edition* (RCA Victor Broadway, 2003).
109. Moody, *Autobiography*, 206.

110. Quoted in Lewis, "I Forecast: Trouble on Broadway for 'Oliver!'"

111. Lionel Bart, letter to Charles S. Spencer, December 6, 1963. Lionel Bart Foundation Archive.

112. Ibid.

CHAPTER 7

1. Quoted in Barry Norman, "Danny Kaye Here to Talk About Fagin," *Daily Mail*, January 19, 1961.

2. David Lewin, "Now a Film: *Oliver!*" *Daily Mail*, July 6, 1963.

   As noted in Chapter 1, the creative team restored Dickens's spelling of the housebreaker's surname for the film adaptation. Any reference to the film version's Sikes will be spelled S-i-k-e-s.

3. Kaye and Bart reportedly met to discuss the role while the American actor was visiting London in 1961, which would seem to indicate that Kaye may have been an early favorite for the role before Bart shifted his attention to Sellers.

   Norman, "Danny Kaye Here to Talk About Fagin."

4. Writ between Donmar Productions Limited (Plaintiff) and Lionel Bart, Montpelier Arts and Enterprises Limited, Brookfield Productions Limited, Lionel Bart Limited, and Oliver Promotions Limited (Defendants), May 21, 1964, 2. Sir Donald Albery Collection, DAT 194.003. Harry Ransom Center, University of Texas at Austin.

5. "The Copyright in 'Oliver'[*sic*]," *Times*, Law Report, June 4, 1964, 17.

6. Writ, 5.

7. Donald Albery, Affidavit in Donmar vs. Lionel Bart, May 21, 1964, 6–7. Sir Donald Albery Collection, DAT 194.003. Harry Ransom Center, University of Texas at Austin.

8. Jules Buck, Affidavit in Donmar vs. Lionel Bart, May 1964, 10. Sir Donald Albery Collection, DAT 194.003. Harry Ransom Center, University of Texas at Austin.

9. Ironically, Brookfield and Sellers would eventually become associated with Lionel Bart's greatest failure as opposed to his greatest success; Brookfield helped to back the Manchester production of *Twang!!*

   Benedict Nightingale, "Farewell to 'Twang!!' at last," *The Guardian*, November 27, 1965, 3.

10. Buck, Affidavit, 10.

11. Adding insult to injury was a clause included in the contract between the two parties stating that Romulus would exert full control regarding whether or not *Oliver!* would be referred to as "Lionel Bart's *Oliver!*" in the opening credits. The issue of whether Bart's name would precede the title card seems to have been yet another contentious issue, one that was dragged out by Bart's agents until the very end of the production process (see letters between Bart's agent Stephen Komlosy and John Woolf, Lionel Bart Archive 200102/0063, University of Bristol Theatre Collection).

    Writ, Annexus 3 (added May 13, 1964).

12. "Review of *Oliver Twist*," *Daily Mail*, July 11, 1905.

13. Quoted in Morris Bright, *Shepperton Studios: A Visual Celebration* (London: Southbank, 2005), 206.

14. "Carol Reed," *Oliver!* souvenir booklet (Columbia Pictures, 1968), 34.

15. Felix Barker, "'Oliver!' Leaves Us All Begging for More," *Evening News*, September 26, 1968, G9.

16. Quoted in Bright, *Shepperton Studios*, 206.

17. Lionel Bart, letter to John Box, March 26, 1968. Lionel Bart Foundation Archive.

18. Ian Sainsbury, "*Oliver!*—A Face from the Crowd," *Morning Telegraph* (Sheffield, Yorkshire), December 1967.

19. Quoted in A. L. Zambrano, *Dickens and Film* (New York: Gordon Press, 1977), 333.

20. *Oliver! Broadway Deluxe Collector's Edition* booklet (RCA Victor Broadway, 2003), 12.

    Carol Reed linked the film version to Revill's performance, not in terms of the Jewish element but in terms of the overall harshness of the character's personality. Reed noted that "I didn't see who did it here in New York—Clive Revill, wasn't it?—but I understand it was smoothed down for Broadway as well." Still, this same quotation reveals that Reed did not direct Moody with Revill's interpretation in mind. Quoted in Leo Mishkin, "Sir Carol Reed 'Still Learning,'" *Morning Telegraph*, December 20, 1968, 3.

21. Bart, letter to John Box.

22. Ron Moody, *A Still Untitled (Not Quite) Autobiography* (London: JR Books, 2010), 257.

23. *"Oliver!" After They Were Famous*, January 1, 2005, Tyne Tees Television, television.

24. Marjorie Bilbow, Review of *Oliver!*, *Daily Cinema*, September 30, 1968.

25. Joseph Gelmis, "'Oliver!' Rich in Fun and Poignancy," *Newsday*, December 12, 1968, 22A.

26. Lionel Bart, letter to Charles S. Spencer, December 6, 1963. Lionel Bart Foundation Archive.

27. It is incorrect to assume that the conflicts between Georgia Brown and Moody during the initial run of *Oliver!* contributed to the recasting of the part; not only is there no evidence to support this claim, but Moody notes that given his own precarious position on the list of potential Fagins, the idea of his having had influence over the casting of Nancy is illogical.

    Ron Moody, interview with Ann McFerran, *Sunday Times*, June 12, 2005.

    http://www.timesonline.co.uk/tol/life_and_style/article529091.ece

28. *"Oliver!" After They Were Famous*.

29. John Mahoney wrote that "Shani Wallis's Nancy is vocally perfect but dramatically wan, lacking the bawdy and bruised toughness the role demands," and Derek Allwright agreed that Wallis "looks too nice for the part" and lacked the "gustiness" of Georgia Brown.

    John Mahoney, "Columbia's 'Oliver' [sic] Is Timeless and Vivid, Joyous Entertainment," *Hollywood Reporter*, September 30, 1968, 3.

    Derek Allwright, "Pace, Flair and Style," *Where To Go*, October 3, 1968, 27.

30. Review of *Oliver! Time and Tide, London*, October 9, 1968.

31. Eric Gillibrand, "Wonderful 'Oliver!' You Couldn't Ask for More," *Manchester Evening News*, December 21, 1968.

32. Wild's older brother Arthur had actually played the title role in *Oliver!* in the West End prior to Jack's work on the film. The brothers broke into show business through their friendship with the young Phil Collins, who also played in *Oliver!* as the Artful Dodger during the initial West End run.

    Harry Weaver, "The *Newest* Artful Dodger," *Scottish Daily Mail*, September 20, 1968.

33. *Celebrate Oliver!* December 26, 2005, BBC, television.

34. Nicholas Wapshott, *Carol Reed: A Biography* (New York: Knopf, 1994), 321.

35. *Celebrate Oliver!*

36. Lester's vocals were dubbed by Kathe Green, the daughter of John Green, the film's musical director. Green did not receive credit for her vocals, as the producers "thought it would kill the picture if anybody knew it was not Mark's voice." Green graciously kept this secret well into her adult years. She likewise reflected that, whatever his vocal limitations, Lester was the true star of the piece: "I fell in love with him singing for him on that screen...How could you not? He was gorgeous. Columbia loved him

too." Quoted in Fiona Whitty, "The Girl on a Motorbike Who Sang all Oliver's Songs," *The Mail on Sunday*, December 19, 2004, 29.

37. Transcribed conversation between Lionel Bart and Carol Reed, January 18, 1967, 1. Lionel Bart Foundation Archive.

38. The transcribed conversation between Reed and Bart reveals that Bart was more than willing to part with "That's Your Funeral," as he agreed with Reed's assertion that it would not fit the tenor of the early scenes; Bart noted that "[t]he theatrical reasons for having 'THAT'S YOUR FUNERAL' was that we felt a need of comedy. But I wouldn't regret losing song [*sic*] at all." The situation regarding "I Shall Scream" is less clear, as Reed alludes to his hopes of placing the song *after* "Boy for Sale"; Bart seems to have been resistant to this modification as he felt that "Boy for Sale" was the natural follow-up to "I Shall Scream." Still, Bart's own description of the number as showcasing "[a] touch of slapstick" may have convinced Reed that the number, as a whole, was unsuitable for the stark opening scenes of the film. The earliest surviving draft of the screenplay indicates that the number had already been cut by March 1967.
    Ibid., 1, 2.

39. The shots of Oliver being led through the snow by Bumble further the bleak and melancholy imagery of the opening scenes, though they also lead to one of the biggest bloopers in the film. The opening scenes suggest that it is winter time, but when Oliver arrives in London, it is clearly summer.

40. Tom Hooper made a similar and equally effective choice in the film version of *Les Misérables* by reversing the order of "I Dreamed a Dream" and "Lovely Ladies."

41. In spite of the musical and stylistic flourishes that dominate the song, there is a striking realism to the number regarding the geographical topography of the set; Bart astutely noted that "'Consider Yourself' dances its way through the various London markets—Covent Garden, Billingsgate, and Spitalfields—in the correct geographical sequence, along the route that people would take towards the East End." Quoted in Will Adams and Tricia Adams, *London: A Nostalgic Look at the Capital Since 1945* (Wadenhoe: Past & Present, 1997), 8.

42. A 1967 draft of the screenplay follows the stage version more closely, as "It's a Fine Life" is sung as a duet between Nancy and Bet as they journey to Fagin's den to visit with the boys. Notably, this early script includes several notes containing Bart's own reflections on this number: "The main purpose of this song is to establish NANCY's relationship with BET and the 16-year-old's idolatry of her living patron-saint. In fact, NANCY's marvellous [*sic*] knock-about, slapstick, unpatronising attitude to kids in general should be underlined wherever possible." Vernon Harris, *Oliver!* draft screenplay, March 10, 1967, 58. BFI Archives.

43. Geoffrey Block, *Enchanted Evenings: The Broadway Musical from* Show Boat *to Sondheim* (New York: Oxford University Press, 1997), 51.

44. Quoted in Edwin Miller, "A Real Modern Artist of Our Time," *Seventeen* (December 1968), 99.

45. In the same interview, Reed reflected that his quiet, perhaps even soft-spoken approach to acting was what made him seem distinct, for it flew in the face of what the audience expected from him and from his characters: "The thing I've learned—the only thing I've learned is to speak softly. To play against the way I look. That creates tension, interest, excitement. A lot of the talk about acting is bull. The main thing is to look real, to bring something that holds the audience's attention." Quoted in ibid., 98–99.

46. John Romano, "Dickens, Psychoanalysis and Film: A Roundtable," in *Dickens on Screen*, ed. John Glavin (Cambridge: Cambridge University Press, 2003), 13.
47. Reed likewise takes the estimable qualities of the thieves further. The friendship between the Dodger and Oliver is more significant in the film than in the original play, with the Dodger helping to shield Oliver from Sikes's wrath, just as the paternal relationship between Fagin and his charges (specifically Oliver and the Dodger) is more pronounced.
48. Reed's buildup to the rooftop climax includes a clever reimagining of "Oom Pah Pah." Nancy performs the song so as to create a diversion, which allows her to sneak Oliver out of the Three Cripples and over to London Bridge. The result is that the number retains its diegetic function while simultaneously serving a narrative purpose; more generally, the lighthearted song becomes infinitely more suspenseful and adds a level of paradox to the heavy tone of the scene.
49. As discussed in this chapter, Bart and Sam Mendes incorporated many elements of the Reed film into the Palladium revival, but rather than include the film's happy ending, they preserved the bittersweet ending from the original West End production:

> "Lionel was not keen on the film ending. He thought it was too lighthearted. The Palladium ending is what Lionel wanted and reverts back to his original book of the show. Cameron said that for Lionel, being a Jewish East Ender himself, the Palladium ending is also about the dignity of the Jewish race pulling themselves together and facing life again."

Given the hardships that Bart himself had endured, his appreciation for Fagin's determination to try to carve out a new life for himself in the face of adversity seems even more understandable.

Rosy Runciman, email to author, June 14, 2008.
50. Lionel Bart, *Oliver!* film suggested story outline. Lionel Bart Foundation Archive.
51. Allen Wright, "'Oliver' [*sic*] First Musical by Thrills Expert." *Scotsman*, December 9, 1968.

Reed's comments belie the fact that Joseph O'Connor gives an outstanding and passionate performance as Brownlow, admirably overcoming many of the role's limitations.
52. Andrew Filson, letter to Carol Reed, July 31, 1969. *Oliver!* files, BFI Archives.
53. Ibid.
54. Barker, "'Oliver!' Leaves Us All Begging for More," G9.
55. Arthur Steele, "'Oliver,'[*sic*] the Mach 1 Musical," 3.
56. Bilbow, Review of *Oliver!*
57. John Woolf attributed the discrepancy to the divergences in the voting processes and screening procedures used by the two organizations.

"How They Made the Choice," *Daily Cinema*, April 19, 1969.
58. Pauline Kael, "The Concealed Art of Carol Reed," *New Yorker*, December 14, 1968, 193.
59. Several movie musical masterpieces, including *Fiddler on the Roof* and *Cabaret*, were still on the horizon; even so, *Oliver!* was the last movie musical to win the Oscar for Best Picture until *Chicago* in 2002.
60. Kael, "The Concealed Art of Carol Reed," 193.
61. Ibid.
62. Ibid., 195.
63. Michael Pointer, *Charles Dickens on the Screen* (London: Scarecrow Press, 1996), 85.
64. Ibid., 86.
65. Stephen M. Silverman, *David Lean* (New York: Abrams, 1989), 79.
66. Quoted in ibid.

67. The evidence for this assertion lies in promotional shots released by the studio, and in two picture-book adaptations of the film both of which include photographs of the deathbed scene. Bart seems to have been wary of incorporating this scene into the film, as the transcribed conversation between Bart and Reed reveals the composer's conviction that the film should forgo depicting Oliver's birth; still, Bart was open to the possibility of starting the film with a birth scene so long as the scene remained silent (as in the Lean film): "The first spoken word in the film—without music—should be Oliver saying 'Please sir can I have some more food?' [sic]."
Bart, conversation with Carol Reed transcript, 1.

68. John Russell Taylor, "Dickens Musical Makes a Disappointing Film," *Times*, September 26, 1968, 15.

69. Patrick Fleet, "Split-Level Spectacular," *Bristol Evening Post*, May 3, 1969.

70. Notably, Lindsay had previously portrayed the character in the Palladium revival of *Oliver!* and won an Olivier Award for his performance.

71. In their text on neo-Victorianism, Mark Llewellyn and Ann Heilmann write that "Andrew Davies, the most significant adaptor of nineteenth-century literature from the 1990s to the present comments on his awareness of previous adaptations: 'I make myself watch the old adaptations, so at least if I plagiarize them I'm doing it consciously.' This internalization of the nature of adaptation, whereby adaptations speak to themselves and one another rather than only to the precursor text, has led to a paradigmatic shift in the nature of adaptation itself."
Ann Heilmann and Mark Llewellyn, *Neo-Victorianism: The Victorians in the Twenty-first Century, 1999–2009*. New York: Palgrave Macmillan, 2010), 212.

72. Mary Cross, "Reading Television Texts: The Postmodern Language of Advertising," in *Advertising and Culture: Theoretical Perspectives*, ed. Mary Cross (Westport: Praeger, 1996), 2.

73. "Oliver's All of an Eye-catcher." *Scottish Daily Express*, January, 17, 1969.

74. "New Movies," *Time*, December 13, 1968, 36.

75. *Oliver Twist* was officially Disneyfied in 1988 with the release of the animated film *Oliver & Company* (see Epilogue).

76. John Gardiner, "Theme-park Victoriana," in *The Victorians Since 1901*, eds. Miles Taylor and Michael Wolff (Manchester: Manchester University Press, 2004), 167.

77. Umberto Eco, "Travels in Hyperreality," in *Travels in Hyper Reality* (New York: Harcourt Brace Jovanovich, 1983), 43.

78. Jean Baudrillard, "Simulacra and Simulations," in *Selected Writings* (Stanford: Stanford University Press, 1988), 172.

79. Heilmann and Llewellyn, *Neo-Victorianism*, 214.

80. Ibid.

81. Sheridan Morley and Ruth Leon, *Hey, Mr. Producer! The Musical World of Cameron Mackintosh* (New York: Back Stage Books, 1998), 20.

82. Ibid., 160.

83. Cameron Mackintosh, "Reviewing the Situation," in *Oliver!: The London Palladium Souvenir Program* (London: Dewynters, 1994).

84. Quoted in "The Design Challenge," in *Oliver!: The London Palladium Souvenir Program* (London: Dewynters, 1994).

85. Ibid.

86. Mackintosh, "Reviewing the Situation."

87. Lionel Bart and Sam Mendes, *Oliver!* Palladium draft (1994), v. Cameron Mackintosh Ltd. Cameron Mackintosh Archive.

88. Rebecca Fowler, "Begging for More," *Sunday Times*, December 11, 1994, 14.

89. Ibid.

90. Julie Burchill, "Great Sets, But a Small Show," *Sunday Times*, December 11, 1994, 14.

91. Anna Lee, Review of *Oliver!, West End Extra*, December 16, 1994.

92. Paul Taylor, "Hard Day at the Workhouse," *The Independent*, December 10, 1994, 28.

93. "Theatre Check," *Sunday Times*, December 18, 1994, 8–46.

94. Blaming the nineties context of the Palladium revival may be erroneous given that just three short years prior to the Palladium staging, a revival at Sadler's Wells had met with tremendous acclaim. Notably, many of the critics who embraced this earlier revival of Bart's show touted the musical's enduring power. Alastair Macauly wrote that *Oliver!* "stands up remarkably well," and Melanie McDonagh added that the show was "still fresh" even thirty-one years after its debut. It is hard to believe that the world could have changed so much in three years that critics who had embraced *Oliver!* as timeless in 1991 suddenly found it to be dated in 1994. Rather, it seems that most of the critics who objected to the 1994 revival objected to it on principle because of its new status as a megamusical. Tellingly, John Gross's favorable review of the Sadler's Wells production hinted that *Oliver!*'s best qualities were anathema to the megamusical movement: "[*Oliver!* is a] contrast with the big musicals of recent years. Faced with their pretensions on the one hand and their general lack of good tunes on the other, it is easy to forget that the requisite of a successful musical used to be a few hummable hit numbers."

      Alastair Macauly, Review of *Oliver!, London Financial Times*, January 17, 1991.

      Melanie McDonagh, "Victorian Vigour," *Evening Standard*, January 16, 1991.

      John Gross, Review of *Oliver!, Sunday Telegraph*, January 20, 1991.

95. Morley and Leon, *Hey, Mr. Producer!*, 164.

96. Ibid.

97. Cameron Mackintosh, interview by author, July12, 2010.

98. Ben Hoyle and Jack Malvern, "Give Us More: *Oliver!* Pulls in £15m Before It Even Opens," *Times*, January 15, 2009, 4.

99. Mark Shenton, "You Will Be Wanting More," *Sunday Express*, January 18, 2009, 64.

100. Quentin Letts, "Consider Yourself a Musical Star, Mr. Bean," *Daily Mail*, January 16, 2009, 60.

101. Charles Spencer, "A Travesty of Dickens, and Fantastic Showbiz," *Daily Telegraph*, January 15, 2009, 3.

102. Allwright, "Pace, Flair and Style," 27.

EPILOGUE

1. Jack Grossman, interview by author, July 15, 2010.

2. *Celebrate Oliver!* December 26, 2005, BBC, television.

3. Charles Dickens, *David Copperfield* (New York: Oxford University Press, 1999), 197.

4. Donald Pippin, interview by author, October 26, 2010.

5. Ibid.

6. In regard to the former issue, Harry Landis remembers that "[Lionel] had three nose jobs until it was perfect for him. He felt he was ugly, and I think that played on his mind." Landis also perceived Bart's fears and apprehensions regarding his homosexuality: "I remember him saying to me one day, 'Harry, I think I'm queer'."

      Harry Landis, interview by author, July 28, 2010.

7. Cameron Mackintosh, interview by author, July 12, 2010.

8. "Lionel Bart," *The South Bank Show*, ITV (UK), December 11, 1994, television.

9. Jon Bradshaw, "Down in the Forest Someone Stirred," *Queen*, January 19, 1966, 57.

10. Ibid., 58.

11. Alastair Davidson, interview by author, September 5, 2010.
12. Derek Paget, interview by Hannah Dodd, *British Library: Theatre Archive Project*, December 4, 2007.
13. Ibid.
14. Douglas Marlborough, "Twang!! Goes on at Record Cost," *Daily Mail*, November 22, 1965.
15. There are allusions to *Quasimodo* in countless Bart interviews from the 1960s, and Bart continued to mention the project well into the 1990s, constantly expressing his hope that it would eventually reach the stage.
16. Alan Jay Lerner, *The Musical Theatre: A Celebration* (New York: Da Capo, 1989), 221.
17. Lionel Bart, draft of letter to Tams-Witmark, 1966. Lionel Bart Foundation Archive.
18. As hinted in Chapter 3, this retreat was likewise the result of the pervasive sense of loss that surrounded Bart in the years following his success, and the sudden and premature deaths of many of the individuals who helped create *Oliver!* is one of the more tragic elements of the musical's biography. The death of Sean Kenny in 1973 shattered Bart, and the unexpected death of Georgia Brown in 1992 was equally devastating.
    Brenda Evans, interview by author, July 6, 2010.
    In 1987, Peter Coe died in a car accident, marking the loss of one of the guiding forces behind *Oliver!*'s success and behind Bart's early theatrical career.
    Herbert Mitgang, "Peter Coe, Theatre Director; Staged 'Oliver' [*sic*] on Broadway," *New York Times*, June 3, 1987.
19. Quoted in John Stevenson, "The Sound of Success Comes Back to Bart," *Daily Mail: Manchester Edition*, November 23, 1965.
20. Douglas Marlborough, "Bang!!" *Daily Mail*, November 29, 1965.
21. Ibid.
22. Quoted in Mark Steyn, *Broadway Babies Say Goodnight* (New York: Routledge, 1999), 176.
23. Brenda Evans, interview by author.
24. Rebecca Fowler, "Begging for More," *Sunday Times*, December 11, 1994, 14.
25. Quoted in David Lister, "Classic Revival Is Sure to Pick a Pocket or Two," *The Independent*, December 9, 1994.
26. Brenda Evans, interview by author.
27. This revival was the culmination of a touring production organized by Cameron Mackintosh.
28. Irving Wardle, "*Oliver!*, Albery," *Times*, December 29, 1977, 5.
29. Steven Suskin devotes an entire chapter to the Broadway failure of *Pickwick* in his text *Second Act Trouble*, which chronicles some of the most infamous bombs in the history of the Broadway musical.
30. Rupert Holmes, *The Mystery of Edwin Drood* (New York: Nelson Doubleday, 1986), v.
31. Christopher Tookey's creative but less successful adaptation of *Hard Times* takes a similar narrative approach through a clever framing device that sees Dickens himself visiting a circus and participating in a music-hall style dramatization of his novel.
32. Though Howard Ashman wrote the film's opening number, one wishes he and Alan Menken had written the entire score, given their unparalleled success at writing songs for Broadway-like Disney musicals such as *The Little Mermaid* and *Beauty and the Beast*.

BIBLIOGRAPHY

Adams, Will, and Tricia Adams. *London: A Nostalgic Look at the Capital Since 1945.* Wadenhoe: Past & Present, 1997.

Albery, Donald. Affidavit in Donmar vs. Lionel Bart, May 21, 1964. Sir Donald Albery Collection, 194.003. Harry Ransom Center, University of Texas at Austin.[1]

Albery, Donald. Letter to David Merrick, July 14, 1960. Sir Donald Albery, 202.001. Harry Ransom Center, University of Texas at Austin.

Albery, Donald. Letter to De. E. Ingram, October 25, 1965. Sir Donald Albery Collection, DAT 196.003. Harry Ransom Center, University of Texas at Austin.

Albery, Donald. Letter to Emile Littler, November 17, 1964. Sir Donald Albery Collection, DAT 114.003. Harry Ransom Center, University of Texas at Austin.

Albery, Donald. Letter to Franklin Weaver, January 2, 1962. Sir Donald Albery Collection, DAT 195.003. Harry Ransom Center, University of Texas at Austin.

Albery, Donald. Letter to Joan Littlewood and Gerry MacColl, June 14, 1960. Sir Donald Albery Collection, DAT 114.001, Folder 2. Harry Ransom Center, University of Texas at Austin.

Albery, Donald. Letter to K. Bentham, January 15, 1965. Sir Donald Albery Collection, DAT 195.001. Harry Ransom Center, University of Texas at Austin.

Albery, Donald. Letter to Kazuo Kikuta, October 12, 1967. Sir Donald Albery Collection, DAT 200.003. Harry Ransom Center, University of Texas at Austin.

Albery, Donald. Letter to Lionel Bart, December 4, 1959. Sir Donald Albery Collection, DAT 114.001, Folder 2. Harry Ransom Center, University of Texas at Austin.

Albery, Donald. Letter to Lionel Bart, January 24, 1961. Sir Donald Albery Collection, DAT 114.001, Folder 1. Harry Ransom Center, University of Texas at Austin.

Albery, Donald. Letter to Lionel Bart, February 12, 1965. Sir Donald Albery Collection, DAT 195.001. Harry Ransom Center, University of Texas at Austin.

Albery, Donald. Letter to Margot Fonteyn de Arias, January 30, 1964. Sir Donald Albery Collection, DAT 114.003. Harry Ransom Center, University of Texas at Austin.

Albery, Donald. Letter to Michiko Serkine, June 19, 1964. Sir Donald Albery Collection, DAT 195.001. Harry Ransom Center, University of Texas at Austin.

Albery, Donald. Letter to Milton Goldman, March 28, 1960. Sir Donald Albery Theatre Collection, DAT 114.001, Folder 2. Harry Ransom Center, University of Texas at Austin.

Albery, Donald. Letter to P. McNaughton, October 25, 1965. Sir Donald Albery Collection, DAT 196.003. Harry Ransom Center, University of Texas at Austin.

Albery, Donald. Letter to Peter Coe, June 12, 1961. Sir Donald Albery Collection, DAT 196.001. Harry Ransom Center, University of Texas at Austin.

---

[1]Copyright for materials in the Donald Albery Theatre Collection belongs to Lady Nobuko Albery.

Albery, Donald. Letter to Roger Stevens, July 2, 1960. Sir Donald Albery Collection, DAT 114.001, Folder 1. Harry Ransom Center, University of Texas at Austin.

Albery, Donald. Letter to Ron Moody, April 7, 1961. Sir Donald Albery Collection, DAT 196.001. Harry Ransom Center, University of Texas at Austin.

Albery, Donald. Letter to Ron Moody, April 14, 1961. Sir Donald Albery Collection, DAT 196.001. Harry Ransom Center, University of Texas at Austin.

Albery, Donald. Letter to Ron Moody, April 17, 1961. Sir Donald Albery Collection, DAT 196.001. Harry Ransom Center, University of Texas at Austin.

Albery, Donald. Telegram to David Merrick, June 26, 1959. Donald Albery Collection, DAT 114.001, Folder 2. Harry Ransom Center, University of Texas at Austin.

Albery, Ian. "Planning of the 'Oliver!' National Tour." *TABS*, 24, no. 1 (March 1966): 4–13.

Albery, Lady Nobuko. Email to author, August 6, 2013.

Allwright, Derek. "Pace, Flair and Style." *Where To Go*. October 3, 1968: 27–28.

Anderson, Benedict. *Imagined Communities*, Revised Edition. New York: Verso, 1991.

Andrews, Malcolm. *Dickens on England and the English*. Sussex: Harvester Press, 1979.

Anonymous telegram on *Oliver!*'s debut in Australia. Sir Donald Albery Collection, DAT 204.002. Harry Ransom Center, University of Texas at Austin.

Anstey, F. "London Music Halls." *Harper's Monthly*. (January 1891): 189–202.

Bailey, Peter. "Custom, Capital and Culture in the Victorian Music Hall." In *Popular Culture and Custom in Nineteenth-Century England*, ed. Robert D. Storch, 180–208. New York: St. Martin's Press, 1982.

Bailey, Peter. "Introduction: Making Sense of Music Hall." In *Music Hall: The Business of Pleasure*, ed. Peter Bailey, viii–xxiii. Philadelphia: Open University Press, 1986.

Bailey, Peter. *Popular Culture and Performance in the Victorian City*. Cambridge: Cambridge University Press, 1998.

Barker, Dennis. "Fings Ain't Wot They Used T'Be." *The Guardian*, April 5, 1999: 12–13.

Barker, Felix. " 'Oliver!' Leaves Us All Begging for More." *Evening News*, September 26, 1968: G9.

Bart, Lionel. Cable to David Picker, September, 26 1969. Lionel Bart Archive 200102/0063, University of Bristol Theatre Collection.

Bart, Lionel. Draft of letter to Tams-Witmark, 1966. Lionel Bart Foundation Archive.

Bart, Lionel. General overall comment in Notes on paste-up by Peter Coe. Lionel Bart Foundation Archive.

Bart, Lionel. Interview with Anthony Brown (transcript). "For Art's Sake." Southampton Television Ltd., April 29, 1964. Lionel Bart Foundation Archive.

Bart, Lionel. Letter to Charles S. Spencer, December 6, 1963. Lionel Bart Foundation Archive.

Bart, Lionel. Letter to Donald Albery, April 2, 1965. Sir Donald Albery Collection, DAT 203.003. Harry Ransom Center, University of Texas at Austin.

Bart, Lionel. Letter to Donald Albery, August 10, 1959. Sir Donald Albery Collection, DAT 114.001, Folder 2. Harry Ransom Center, University of Texas at Austin.

Bart, Lionel. Letter to Donald Albery, August 20, 1965. Sir Donald Albery Collection, DAT 203.003. Harry Ransom Center, The University of Texas at Austin.

Bart, Lionel. Letter to Donald Albery, December 6, 1960. Sir Donald Albery Theatre Collection, 196.001. Harry Ransom Center, University of Texas at Austin.

Bart, Lionel. Letter to Donald Albery, February 11, 1965. Sir Donald Albery Collection, DAT 195.001. Harry Ransom Center, University of Texas at Austin.

Bart, Lionel. Letter to Dorothy Kilgallen, September 1962. Lionel Bart Foundation Archive.

Bart, Lionel. Letter to Eric Rogers, August 23, 1960. Lionel Bart Foundation Archive.

Bart, Lionel. Letter to J. Greaves, November 2, 1960. Lionel Bart Foundation Archive.

Bart, Lionel. Letter to Joan Maitland, February 14, 1964. Lionel Bart Foundation Archive.

Bart, Lionel. Letter to John Box, March 26, 1968. Lionel Bart Foundation Archive.

Bart, Lionel. Letter to Lars Schmidt, November 15, 1961. Lionel Bart Foundation Archive.

Bart, Lionel. Letter to Leslie Frewin, February 16, 1967. Lionel Bart Foundation Archive.

Bart, Lionel. Letter to Patricia McCarthy, November 22, 1979. Lionel Bart Foundation Archive.

Bart, Lionel. Letter to Ron Moody, December 15, 1960. Lionel Bart Foundation Archive.

Bart, Lionel. Notes on paste-up by Peter Coe, February 4, 1960. Lionel Bart Foundation Archive.

Bart, Lionel. *Oh, Oliver!* libretto fragment. Lionel Bart Foundation Archive.

Bart, Lionel. *Oliver!* film suggested story outline. Lionel Bart Foundation Archive.

Bart, Lionel. *Oliver!* (libretto). New York: Tams-Witmark, 1960.

Bart, Lionel. *Oliver!* (musical score). London: Lakview Music, 1960.

Bart, Lionel. Oliver—Peter's Version outline. Lionel Bart Foundation Archive.

Bart, Lionel. *Oliver* spiral notebook. Lionel Bart Foundation Archive.

Bart, Lionel. *Oliver!* Wimbledon libretto, II-2-13. Lord Chamberlain's Plays Collection, Manuscripts, British Library.

Bart, Lionel. *Oliver Twist* (early outline). Lionel Bart Foundation Archive.

Bart, Lionel. "One of the Worldwide Family." In *Oliver!: The London Palladium Souvenir Program*. London: Dewynters, 1994.

Bart, Lionel. Personal Reflection on *Oliver!* #2. Lionel Bart Foundation Archive.

Bart, Lionel. Reflection on Georgia Brown. Lionel Bart Foundation Archive.

Bart, Lionel. *South Bank Show*, Transcript, Roll 3. Lionel Bart Foundation Archive.

Bart, Lionel. *South Bank Show*, Transcript, Roll 5. Lionel Bart Foundation Archive.

Bart, Lionel. Suggested New Breakdown (B). Lionel Bart Foundation Archive.

Bart, Lionel. Suggested New Version. Lionel Bart Foundation Archive.

Bart, Lionel. "Thoughts on Fagin." January 23, 1967. Lionel Bart Foundation Archive.

Bart, Lionel. Unlabeled libretto fragment. Lionel Bart Foundation Archive.

Bart, Lionel, and Sam Mendes, *Oliver!* Palladium libretto draft. 1994. Cameron Mackintosh Ltd. Cameron Mackintosh Archive.

Barthes, Roland. "The Death of the Author." In *Image, Music, Text* by Roland Barthes, 142–48. New York: Hill and Wang, 1977.

Bashan, Raphael. Letter to Lionel Bart, October 20, 1961. Lionel Bart Foundation Archive.

"Baton Charge on Berlin Oliver Twist Objectors." *The Daily Telegraph and Morning Post*, February 22, 1949: 1.

"A Battle Is on for 'Oliver!'" *London Evening News*, July 8, 1960.

Baudrillard, Jean. "Simulacra and Simulations." In *Selected Writings* by Jean Baudrillard, 166–84. Stanford: Stanford University Press, 1988.

Beerbohm, Max. "Dan Leno." In *A Selection from Around Theatres* by Max Beerbohm, 200–204. Garden City: Doubleday, 1960.

Bilbow, Marjorie. Review of Carol Reed's *Oliver! Daily Cinema*, September 30, 1968.

Billington, Michael. "Arnold Wesker: Food for Thought." *The Guardian*, May 21, 2012, http://www.theguardian.com/stage/2012/may/21/arnold-wesker-food-for-thought.

Block, Geoffrey. *Enchanted Evenings: The Broadway Musical from Show Boat to Sondheim*. New York: Oxford University Press, 1997.

Block, Geoffrey "Integration." In *Oxford Handbook of the American Musical*, eds. Raymond Knapp, Mitchell Morris, and Stacy Wolf, 97-110. New York: Oxford University Press, 2011.

Bradshaw, Jon. "Down in the Forest Someone Stirred." *Queen*, January 19, 1966: 53–60.

Brahms, Caryl. "The Dickens and the Don." *John O'London's Weekly*, July 14, 1960: 3.

Bratton, J. S. "Jenny Hill: Sex and Sexism in the Victorian Music Hall." In *Music Hall: Performance and Style*, ed. J. S. Bratton, 92–110. Philadelphia: Open University Press, 1986.

Brecht, Bertolt. *Brecht on Theatre: The Development of an Aesthetic*. London: Methuen, 1964.

Brecht, Bertolt. "How The Duchess of Malfi Ought to Be Performed." In *Bertolt Brecht: Collected Plays*, Vol. 7, eds. Ralph Manheim and John Willett, 422–23. New York: Random House, 1974.

Bright, Morris. *Shepperton Studios: A Visual Celebration*. London: Southbank, 2005.

"British Encirclement of Broadway." *Times*, June 26, 1963: 15.

Brocken, Michael. *The British Folk Revival, 1944–2002*. Burlington: Ashgate, 2003.

Brownlow, Kevin. *David Lean: A Biography*. New York: St. Martin's Press, 1996.

Bryden, Ronald. "A Gulliver landmark." *The Observer*, December 29, 1968: 20.

Buck, Jules. Affidavit in Donmar vs. Lionel Bart. May 1964. Sir Donald Albery Collection, 194.003. Harry Ransom Center, University of Texas at Austin.

Buck, Jules. Letter to Donald Albery, May 4, 1964. Sir Donald Albery Collection, DAT 195.001. Harry Ransom Center, University of Texas at Austin.

Burchill, Julie. "Great Sets, But a Small Show." *Sunday Times*, December 11, 1994: 14.

Burke, Peter. "The 'Discovery' of Popular Culture." In *People's History and Socialist Theory*, ed. Raphael Samuel, 216–26. Boston: Routledge & Kegan Paul, 1981.

Carlson, Barbara. "Young Stars Nonplussed." *Hartford Courant*, July 25, 1968.

"Carol Reed." *Oliver!* souvenir booklet. Columbia Pictures, 1968.

Carr, Winifred. "Vivid reminder of twenty-two short years ago." *Daily Telegraph*, May 7, 1962.

Cashmore, E. Ellis. *No Future: Youth and Society*. London: Heinemann, 1984.

Celebrate Oliver! December 26, 2005, BBC (UK), television.

Chalmers, Robert. "Out but Not Down." *Daily Telegraph*, January 17, 1992.

Chambers, Colin. *The Story of Unity Theatre*. New York: St. Martin's Press, 1989.

Chapman, John. Review of original Broadway production of *Oliver! New York Theatre Critics' Reviews* 24.22 (1963), 399.

Chin, Tsai. Interview by author, October 17, 2010.

Citron, Stephen. *The Musical from the Inside Out*. Chicago: Ivan D. Ree, 1992.

Clarke, J. Letter to Duncan Melvin, August 15, 1961. Sir Donald Albery Collection, DAT 196.002. Harry Ransom Center, University of Texas at Austin.

Clayton, Jay. *Charles Dickens in Cyberspace*. New York: Oxford University Press, 2003.

Clemm, Sabine. *Dickens, Journalism, and Nationhood: Mapping the World in* Household Words. New York: Routledge, 2009.

Coe, Peter. Letter to Donald Albery, January 26, 1961. Sir Donald Albery Collection, 196.001.

Cohen, Jane R. *Charles Dickens and His Original Illustrators*. Columbus: Ohio State University Press, 1980. Harry Ransom Center, University of Texas at Austin.

Connolly, Cyril. "Comment." *Horizon* 15, no. 87 (April 1947): 151–54.

"Consider Yourself 'In' with a Lionel Bart Poster." *London Life*, August 27, 1966.

Conway, Harold. "It's Such a Good Twist." *Daily Sketch*, July 1, 1960.

Cook, Judy. *Loving Peter: My Life with Peter Cook and Dudley Moore*. London: Platkus, 2008.

Cookman, Anthony. "At the Theatre." *The Tatler*, January 27, 1954: 132.

Cookman, Anthony. "Moments I Shall Remember." *The Tatler*, May 14, 1958: 370.

"The Copyright in 'Oliver'[sic]," *Times*, Law Report, June 4, 1964: 17.

Cross, Mary. "Introduction" in *Advertising and Culture: Theoretical Perspectives*, ed. Mary Cross, xi–xiii. Westport: Praeger, 1996.

Cross, Mary. "Reading Television Texts: The Postmodern Language of Advertising." In *Advertising and Culture: Theoretical Perspectives*, ed. Mary Cross, 1–10. Westport: Praeger, 1996.

Culler, Jonathan. *The Pursuit of Signs*. London: Routledge, 1981.

"Curtain Up." *The Guardian*. June 18, 2003: A11.

Darlington, W. A. "No Business Like Musical Business." *Daily Telegraph*, April 26, 1958.

Davidson, Alastair. Interview by author, September 5, 2010.

Davis, Paul. *The Lives and Times of Ebenezer Scrooge*. New Haven: Yale University Press,1990.

Davison, Peter. "Afterword." In *Theatre and Song*, 8/187–8/195. Teaneck: Somerset House, 1978.

Davison, Peter. *Songs of the British Music Hall*. New York: Oak, 1971.

Denton, Peter. "The Quiet Genius of a Man Behind the Scenes." *Epsom and Ewell Herald*, June 21, 1963.

"The Design Challenge." In *Oliver!: The London Palladium Souvenir Program*. London: Dewynters, 1994.

Dickens, Charles. "Address in the First Number of *Household Words*." In *The Centenary Edition of the Works of Charles Dickens, Miscellaneous Papers*, Vol. 1, 181–83. New York: Charles Scribner's Sons, 1911.

Dickens, Charles. "The Amusements of the People (II)." In *The Amusements of the People and Other Papers: Reports, Essays and Reviews, 1834–1851*, ed. Michael Slater, 193–201. Columbus: Ohio University Press, 1996.

Dickens, Charles. *David Copperfield*. New York: Oxford University Press, 1999.

Dickens, Charles. *Oliver Twist*. New York: Oxford University Press, 1999.

"A Dickens Musical." *Liverpool Post*, July 1, 1960: 5.

"Dickens—to Music." *Yorkshire Evening Post* (Leeds), July 9, 1960.

Dircks, Rudolf. "The Apotheosis of the Music Hall." *The Theatre* (November 1892): 193–97.

Donnelly, Mark. *Sixties Britain: Culture, Society, and Politics*. New York: Pearson Longman, 2005.

Doré, Edna. Interview by author, July 3, 2010.

Dorney, Kate. *The Changing Language of Modern English Drama, 1945–2005*. New York: Palgrave Macmillan, 2009.

"Early Dramas of *Oliver Twist*." *The Dickensian* 43 (1947): 74–79.

Easthope, Anthony. *Englishness and National Culture*. New York: Routledge, 1999.

Eco, Umberto. "Travels in Hyperreality." In *Travels in Hyperreality* by Umberto Eco, 1–58. New York: Harcourt Brace Jovanovich, 1983.

Eddershaw, Margaret. *Performing Brecht: Forty Years of British Performances*. New York: Routledge, 1996.

Edelman, Marsha Bryan. *Discovering Jewish Music*. Philadelphia: Jewish Publication Society, 2003.

Edgar, David. "An Evening with David Edgar." October 8, 2009. Lecture delivered at Playmakers Repertory Theatre, University of North Carolina at Chapel Hill.

Egginton, Joyce. "Too Much Ballyhoo." *Scene* 17, January 26, 1963: 14.

Eichelbaum, Stanley. " 'Oliver!' Is a Staggering, Wonderful Show." *San Francisco Examiner*, September 26, 1962: 5C2H.

Eichelbaum, Stanley. "Sean Kenny Sets the Stage." *Theatre Arts Magazine* (Dec. 1962): 20.

Eliot, T. S. "Marie Lloyd." In *Selected Prose of T. S. Eliot*, ed. Frank Kermode, 172–74. New York: Harcourt Brace Jovanovich, 1975.

Engel, Lehman. *Words with Music: The Broadway Musical Libretto*. New York: Schirmer, 1981.

Esslin, Martin. "Brecht and the English Theatre." In *Brecht Sourcebook*, eds. Carol Martin and Henry Bial, 147–55. London: Routledge, 2000.

Esslin, Martin. *Brecht: The Man and His Work*, New, Revised Edition. Garden City: Anchor Books, 1971.

Esslin, Martin. Foreword. In *Playwrights' Theatre*, by Terry W. Browne, iii–v. London: Pitman, 1975.

Evans, Brenda. Interview by author, July 6, 2010.

Evans, Brenda. Letter to author, October 13, 2010.

"Fagin Quits Oliver!" *Daily Mail*, July 17, 1961.

Faulk, Barry J. *Music Hall and Modernity: The Victorian Discovery of Popular Culture*. Athens: Ohio University Press, 2004.

Fawcett, F. Dubrez. *Dickens the Dramatist*. London: Allen, 1952.

Filson, Andrew. Letter to Carol Reed, July 31, 1969. *Oliver!* files. BFI Archives.

Firth, Jenny. "Meeting Tommy Was the Turning Point." *Leicester Evening Mail*, March 26, 1959.

Flash photography warning to be inserted in program. Sir Donald Albery Collection, DAT 114.001, Folder 1. Harry Ransom Center, University of Texas at Austin.

Fleet, Patrick. "Split-level Spectacular." *Bristol Evening Post*, May 3, 1969.

Flinn, Denny Martin. *Musical!: A Grand Tour*. New York: Schirmer, 1997.

Fowler, Rebecca. "Begging for More." *Sunday Times*, December 11, 1994: 14.

Freedland, Martin. "Fings Look Up for Lionel Bart." *Daily Telegraph*, December 9, 1994.

Freedland, Michael. "'Unity Was My Turning Point'." *Belfast News-Letter*, April 17, 1964.

Fulkerson, Richard P. "The Dickens Novel on the Victorian Stage." Ph.D. diss., Ohio State University, 1970.

Gamble, Andrew, and Tony Wright. "Introduction: The Britishness Question." In *Britishness: Perspectives on the Britishness Question*, eds. Andrew Gamble and Tony Wright, 1–9. Malden, MA: Wiley-Blackwell, 2009.

Gammond, Peter, ed. *Best Music Hall and Variety Songs*. London: Wolfe, 1972.

Gammond, Peter, ed. *Music Hall Songbook*. Vermont: David & Charles/EMI, 1975.

Ganzl, Kurt. *British Musical Theatre, Vol. II 1915–1984*. New York: Oxford University Press, 1986.

Ganzl, Kurt. *The Musical: A Concise History*. Boston: Northeastern University Press, 1997.

Gardiner, John. "Theme-park Victoriana." In *The Victorians Since 1901*, eds. Miles Taylor and Michael Wolff, 167–80. Manchester: Manchester University Press, 2004.

Garnett, Robert R. "*Oliver Twist*'s Nancy: The Angel in Chains." *Religion and the Arts* 4, no. 4 (2000): 491–516.

Gelmis, Joseph. "'Oliver!' Rich in Fun and Poignancy." *Newsday*, December 12, 1968: 22A.

"Generous Bart," *Daily Mail*, March 1961. 1961 Scrapbook, Lionel Bart Foundation Archive.

Genette, Gérard. *Paratexts*. New York: Cambridge University Press, 1997.

Gibbins, Cyril. Letter to Anne Jenkins, July 4, 1960. Sir Donald Albery Collection, DAT 114.001, Folder 1. Harry Ransom Center, University of Texas at Austin.

Gillibrand, Eric. "Wonderful 'Oliver!' You Couldn't Ask for More." *Manchester Evening News*, December 21, 1968.

Glover, Julian. Interview by author. July 15, 2010.

Glyn Mills & Co advertisement, *Oliver!* program (1963). Windham Theatres Ltd., printed by John Waddington Ltd., London.

Goodwin, John, ed. *British Theatre Design: The Modern Age*. New York: St. Martin's Press, 1989.

Goorney, Howard. *The Theatre Workshop Story*. London: Methuen, 1981.

Gordon-Smith, Lisa. "Designed for Export: New Techniques Will Make Touring Easier—Ian Albery." *The Stage*, July 5, 1962: 15.

Gorman, John. *Knocking Down Ginger*. London: Caliban Books, 1995.

Gottlieb, Jack. *Funny, It Doesn't Sound Jewish*. Albany: State University of New York Press, 2004.

Grant, Mark N. *The Rise and Fall of the Broadway Musical*. Boston: Northeastern University Press, 2004.

Gray, Frances. *John Arden*. New York: Grove Press, 1983.

Greaves, J. Letter to Lionel Bart, October 23, 1960. Lionel Bart Foundation Archive.

Green, Martin. "Some Versions of the Pastoral: Myth in Advertising; Advertising as Myth." In *Advertising and Culture: Theoretical Perspectives*, ed. Mary Cross, 29–47. Westport: Praeger, 1996.

Gross, John. Review of *Oliver!* at Sadler's Wells. *Sunday Telegraph*, January 20, 1991.

Grossman, Jack. Interview by author. July 15, 2010.

Hale, Allan. "Musical Hit...and Made in Britain." *Manchester Evening News*, September 23, 1960.

Hamer, Paul. "Bart: Bentleys to Bankruptcy and Back." *TV Times* 87, no. 14. March 31, 1977: 14–16.

"A Handful of Songs: The Lionel Bart Story—Part 2." Presented by Matt Lucas and Barbara Windsor. Produced by Elliot Davis. August 19, 2005. BBC Radio 2.

Hanneford, Richard. "The Fairy World of *Oliver Twist*." *Dickens Studies Newsletter* 8 (1977): 33–36.

Hardwick, Roger. Interview by author, July 8, 2010.

Harris, Vernon. *Oliver!* draft screenplay. March 10, 1967. *Oliver!* files. BFI Archives.

Harvey, John. *Victorian Novelists and Their Illustrators*. London: Sidgwick & Jackson, 1970.

Hayman, Ronald. *British Theatre Since 1955: A Reassessment*. Oxford: Oxford University Press, 1979.

Hayton, Richard, Richard English, and Michael Kenny. "Englishness in Contemporary British Politics." In *Britishness: Perspectives on the Britishness Question*, eds. Andrew Gamble and Tony Wright, 122–35. Malden, MA: Wiley-Blackwell, 2009.

Heilmann, Ann, and Mark Llewellyn. *Neo-Victorianism: The Victorians in the Twenty-First Century*, 1999–2009. New York: Palgrave Macmillan, 2010.

Heinz, Bernard. Letter to Jock Jacobsen, May 30, 1958. Unity Theatre: theatre company records, THM/9/2/1/15. Victoria and Albert Museum Theatre Collections.

Hewes, Henry. "Britain's Unruly Waifs." *Saturday Review*, January, 19 1963: 26.

Hewison, Robert. *Too Much: Art and Society in the Sixties, 1960–75*. New York: Oxford University Press, 1987.

Hickey, William. "She's Over Here to Take 'Oliver!' to Tokyo." *Daily Express*, August 11, 1967.

Higgins, John. "How Peter Coe Comprehends the Twentieth Century." *Times*, March 13, 1980: 11.

Hirsch, Foster. *Harold Prince and the American Musical Theater*. Cambridge: Cambridge University Press, 1989.

Hislop, Vivien. "In a Setting by Sean...for Kenny." *Daily Mail*, February 12, 1968: 9.

Holdsworth, Nadine. *Joan Littlewood*. New York: Routledge, 2006.

Holmes, Rupert. *The Mystery of Edwin Drood*. New York: Nelson Doubleday, 1986.

Horn, Barbara Lee. *David Merrick: A Bio-Bibliography*. New York: Greenwood, 1992.

"How They Made the Choice," *Daily Cinema*, April 19, 1969.

Hoyle, Ben, and Jack Malvern. "Give Us More: *Oliver!* Pulls in £15m Before It Even Opens." *Times*, January 15, 2009: 4.

Hulke, Malcolm (ed.). "Here Is Drama: Behind the Scenes at Unity Theatre, London." England: Unity Theatre Society, 1963.

Hutcheon, Linda. *A Theory of Adaptation*. New York: Routledge, 2006.

Jackson, Arthur. *The Best Musicals from* Show Boat *to* A Chorus Line: *Broadway, Off Broadway, London*. New York: Crown, 1977.

Jacobsen, Jock. Letter to Anne Jenkins, May 6, 1959. Sir Donald Albery Collection, DAT 114.001, Folder 2. Harry Ransom Center, University of Texas at Austin.

Jacobsen, Jock. Letter to Bernard Heinz, May 23, 1958. Unity Theatre: theatre company records, THM/9/2/1/15. Victoria and Albert Museum Theatre Collections.

Jacobsen, Jock. Letter to Donald Albery, November, 18 1964. Sir Donald Albery Collection, DAT 203.003. Harry Ransom Center, University of Texas at Austin.

Jameson, Frederic. *Postmodernism, or the Cultural Logic of Late Capitalism*. Durham: Duke University Press, 1991.

Jenkins, Anne. Letter to Ivor Brown. Sir Donald Albery Collection, DAT 196.003. Harry Ransom Center, University of Texas at Austin.

Jenkins, Anne. Letter to Joan Maitland, May 9, 1966. Sir Donald Albery Collection, DAT 203.003. Harry Ransom Center, University of Texas at Austin.

Jenkins, Anne. Letter to Jock Jacobsen, May 9, 1959. Sir Donald Albery Collection, DAT 114.001, Folder 2. Harry Ransom Center, University of Texas at Austin.

Jenkins, Anne. Letter to Messrs. Tughan and Walmsley, December 3, 1965. Sir Donald Albery Collection, 196.003. Harry Ransom Center, University of Texas at Austin.

Jenkins, Anne. Memo to Donald Albery, July 15, 1963. Sir Donald Albery Collection, DAT 203.001. Harry Ransom Center, University of Texas at Austin.

Jenkins Anne. Memo to Monty Berman, July 10, 1961. Sir Donald Albery Collection. Harry Ransom Center, University of Texas at Austin.

Jenkins, Anne. Undated memo to Donald Albery. Sir Donald Albery Collection, DAT 114.001, Folder 2. Harry Ransom Center, University of Texas at Austin.

Jenkins, Anne. Undated memo to Donald Albery. Sir Donald Albery Collection, DAT 114.003. Harry Ransom Center, University of Texas at Austin.

Jinks, John. "Oliver No. 9: Heading for the Pint-Sized Record." *Daily Mail*, February 9, 1965.

John, Juliet. *Charles Dickens's* Oliver Twist: *A Sourcebook*, ed. Juliet John. New York: Routledge, 2006.

John, Juliet. *Dickens and Mass Culture*. Oxford: Oxford University Press, 2010.

Johns, Eric. "Fings Is Buzzin' at the Garrick in Soho Saga." *The Stage*, February 18, 1960: 17.

Junkin, John. Radio interview, 1992, audio cassette. Lionel Bart Foundation Archive.

Kael, Pauline. "The Concealed Art of Carol Reed." *New Yorker*. December 14, 1968: 193–96.

Kennedy, Paul P. "British Cameras Grind out *Oliver Twist*." *New York Times*, November 9, 1947: X5.

Kenny, Sean. "An Address by Sean Kenny to the Lighting Equipment Manufacturers Association," 8. Annual Luncheon at the Chateau Champlain Hotel. Montreal. June, 22 1967. Sean Kenny Archives. Victoria and Albert Museum Theatre Collections.

Kenny, Sean. "Designing 'Oliver'[sic]." *TABS* 18, no. 2 (September 1960): 7–12.

Kift, Dagmar. *The Victorian Music Hall: Culture, Class, and Conflict*. Cambridge: Cambridge University Press, 1996.

Kilgallen, Dorothy. "The Voice of Broadway." *New York Journal American*, September 14, 1962: 15.

Kincaid, James R. *Dickens and the Rhetoric of Laughter*. Oxford: Clarendon Press, 1971.

Kissel, Howard. *David Merrick: The Abominable Showman*. New York: Applause, 1993.

Knapp, Raymond. *The American Musical and the Formation of National Identity*. Princeton: Princeton University Press, 2005.

Knapp, Raymond. "Performance, Authenticity, and the Reflexive Idealism of the American Musical." In *Oxford Handbook of the American Musical*, eds. Raymond Knapp, Mitchell Morris, and Stacy Wolf, 408–21. New York: Oxford University Press, 2011.

Knapp Raymond, and Mitchell Morris. "Tin Pan Alley Songs on Stage and Screen Before World War II." In *Oxford Handbook of the American Musical*, ed, Raymond Knapp, Mitchell Morris, and Stacy Wolf, 81–96. New York: Oxford University Press, 2011.

Komlosy, Stephen. Letter to Ira Tulipan, October 1, 1968. Lionel Bart Archive 200102/0063, University of Bristol Theatre Collection.

Laird, Paul R. "Musical Styles and Song Conventions." In *Oxford Handbook of the American Musical*, eds. Raymond Knapp, Mitchell Morris, and Stacy Wolf, 33–44. New York: Oxford University Press, 2011.

Landis, Harry. Interview by author. July 28, 2010.

Leach, Robert. *Theatre Workshop: Joan Littlewood and the Making of Modern British Theatre*. Exeter: University of Exeter Press, 2006.

Lee, Anna. Review of *Oliver!* at the Palladium. *West End Extra*, December 16, 1994.

Leitch, Thomas. *Film Adaptation and Its Discontents*. Baltimore: Johns Hopkins University Press, 2007.

Lerner, Alan Jay. *The Musical Theatre: A Celebration*. New York: Da Capo, 1989.

Lesnik-Oberstein, Karin. "*Oliver Twist*: The Narrator's Tale." *Textual Practice* 15, no. 1 (2001), 87–100.

Letts, Quentin. "Consider Yourself a Musical Star, Mr. Bean." *Daily Mail*. January16, 2009: 60.

Levin, Bernard. "Bold and Bright and It Made Me Whistle." *Daily Express*, July 1, 1960.

Levy, Ori. Letter to Lionel Bart, October 15, 1961. Lionel Bart Foundation Archive.

Lewin, David. "Now a Film: *Oliver!*" *Daily Mail*, July 6, 1963.

Lewis, Patricia. "I Forecast: Trouble on Broadway for 'Oliver!'" *Daily Express*, September 28, 1961.

"Lilly White Boy." *Plays and Players* (May 1963): 20.

Lionel Bart Radio interview, 199?, audio cassette. Lionel Bart Foundation Archive.

"Lionel Bart," *The South Bank Show*, ITV (UK), December, 11 1994, television.

"Lionel Bart on an 'Epic' Musical." *Times*, March 22, 1962: 16.

"Lionel Bart Was Told 'Forget Stage'." *Evening Standard*, June 9, 1961.

"Lionel Bart Wins 'Oliver!' Fight," *Daily Herald*, June 10, 1961.

"Lionel Bart's 'Oliver!' Tops The Thousandth Performance." Press Release from Duncan Melvin. October 27, 1962. Lionel Bart Foundation Archives.

Lister, David. "Classic Revival Is Sure to Pick a Pocket or Two." *The Independent*, December 9, 1994.

Littler, Emile. Letter to Donald Albery, May 9, 1960. Sir Donald Albery Collection, DAT 114.003. Harry Ransom Center, University of Texas at Austin.

Littler, Emile. Letter to Donald Albery, November 18, 1964. Sir Donald Albery Collection, DAT 114.003. Harry Ransom Center, University of Texas at Austin.

Littlewood, Joan. Foreword. In *Fings Ain't Wot They Used T'Be*, by Frank Norman, 5. New York: Grove Press, 1962.

Littlewood, Joan. *Joan's Book: The Autobiography of Joan Littlewood*. London: Methuen, 2003.

Lovensheimer, Jim. "Texts and Authors." In *Oxford Handbook of the American Musical*, eds. Raymond Knapp, Mitchell Morris, and Stacy Wolf, 20–32. New York: Oxford University Press, 2011.

Lowenstein, Heinz. Contributions to a Discussion on the Production of Plays at Unity Theatre. Unity Theatre: theatre company records. Victoria and Albert Museum Theatre Collections.

Macauly, Alastair. Review of *Oliver!* at Sadler's Wells. *London Financial Times*, January 17, 1991.

MacColl, Ewan. "Grass Roots of Theatre Workshop." *Theatre Quarterly*. (January-March 1973): 58–68.

MacInnes, Colin. "Pop Songs and Teenagers." In *England, Half English*, by Colin MacInnes, 45–60. London: MacGibbon & Kee, 1961.

MacInnes, Colin. "Young England, Half English." In *England, Half English*, by Colin MacInnes, 11–19. London: MacGibbon & Kee, 1961.

Mackintosh, Cameron. Interview by author. July 12, 2010.

Mackintosh, Cameron. "Reviewing the Situation." In Oliver!: *The London Palladium Souvenir Program*. London: Dewynters, 1994.

Mahoney, John. "Columbia's 'Oliver' [sic] Is Timeless and Vivid, Joyous Entertainment." *Hollywood Reporter*, September 30, 1968: 3.

Mair, G. H. "The Music-Hall." *English Review* (August 1911): 122–29.

Maitland, Joan. Letter to Lionel Bart, March 30, 1965. Lionel Bart Foundation Archive.

Maitland, Joan. Letter to Lionel Bart, undated. Lionel Bart Foundation Archive.

Maitland, Joan. Letter to Stephen Komlosy, September 11, 1968. Lionel Bart Archive 200102/0063, University of Bristol Theatre Collection.

"The Man Who Asked for More." *Times*. December 10, 1994: 29–35.

Mander, Raymond, and Joe Mitchenson. *British Music Hall: A Story in Pictures*. New York: London House and Maxwell, 1965.

Mandler, Peter. *The English National Character: The History of an Idea from Edmund Burke to Tony Blair*. New Haven: Yale University Press, 2006.

Marlborough, Douglas. "Bang!!" *Daily Mail*, November 29, 1965.

Marlborough, Douglas. "Twang!! Goes on at Record Cost." *Daily Mail*, November 22, 1965.

Marsh, Joss. "Dickens and Film." In *The Cambridge Companion to Charles Dickens*, ed. John O. Jordan, 204–23. Cambridge: Cambridge University Press, 2001.

Mazower, David. *Yiddish Theatre in London*. London: Jewish Museum, 1996.

McCarten, John. "No Social Significance." *New Yorker*, January19, 1963: 60.

McClain, John. Review of original Broadway production of *Oliver! New York Theatre Critics' Reviews* 24.22 (1963), 397.

McDonagh, Melanie. "Victorian Vigour." *Evening Standard,* January 16, 1991.

McFarlane, Brian. *Novel to Film: An Introduction to the Theory of Adaptation*. Oxford: Oxford University Press, 1996.

McMillin, Scott. *The Musical as Drama*. Princeton: Princeton University Press, 2006.

Mellor, G. J. *Northern Music Hall*. Newcastle: Graham, 1970.

Merrick, David. Telegram to Donald Albery, July 3, 1959. Donald Albery Collection, DAT 114.001, Folder 2. Harry Ransom Center, University of Texas at Austin.

Miles, Bernard. Letter to Donald Albery. January 14, 1960. Sir Donald Albery Theatre Collection, 114.001, Folder 2. Harry Ransom Center, University of Texas at Austin.

Miles, Bernard. *Lock Up Your Daughters*. New York: Samuel French, 1967.

Miller, Edwin. "A Real Modern Artist of Our Time." *Seventeen* (December 1968): 98–100; 161.

Miller, Scott. *Strike Up the Band: A New History of Musical Theatre*. Portsmouth: Heinemann, 2007.

Mishkin, Leo. "Sir Carol Reed 'Still Learning'." *Morning Telegraph*, December 20, 1968: 3.

Mitgang, Herbert. "Peter Coe, Theatre Director; Staged 'Oliver' [sic] on Broadway." *New York Times*, June 3, 1987.

Moody, Ron. Interview with Ann McFerran. *Sunday Times*, June 12, 2005. http://www. timesonline.co.uk/tol/life_and_style/article529091.ece

Moody, Ron. Letter to Donald Albery, April 12, 1961. Sir Donald Albery Collection, DAT 196.001. Harry Ransom Center, University of Texas at Austin.

Moody, Ron. Radio interview, 199?, audio cassette. Lionel Bart Foundation Archive.

Moody, Ron. "Reviewing the Situation." *Jewish Chronicle*, April 9, 1999.

Moody, Ron. *A Still Untitled (Not Quite) Autobiography*. London: JR Books, 2010.

Morley, Malcolm. "Early Dramas of *Oliver Twist*." *The Dickensian* 43 (1947): 74–79.

Morley, Sheridan. "Archetype of the Genuine English Classic Musical." *Times*, December 14, 1983: 9.

Morley, Sheridan. *Spread a Little Happiness*. London: Thames and Hudson, 1987.

Morley, Sheridan, and Ruth Leon. *Hey, Mr. Producer!* New York: Back Stage Books, 1998.

Mortlock, C. B. "We Can do This as Well as Americans." *City Press*, July 8, 1960.

Muller, Robert. "Everyone Will Ask for More." *Daily Mail*, July 1, 1960.

Munroe, Carmen. Interview by author, December 27, 2010.

"Music-Halls." *All the Year Round*. 25, no. 619 (October 9, 1880): 520–24.

Nadar, Thomas R. "Brecht and His Musical Collaborators." In *A Bertolt Brecht Reference Companion*, ed. Siegfried Mews, 261-78. Westport: Greenwood Press, 1997.

"New Movies." *Time*, December 13, 1968: 36.

"New Records: Dickens with Music." *Plays and Players* (October 1960).

New Songs/Re-writes summary. Lionel Bart Foundation Archive.

"New Twist." *Newsweek*, January, 14, 1963: 65.

"Night at the Grand Palais." *Times*, June 11, 1957: 3.

Nightingale, Benedict. "Farewell to 'Twang!!' at last." *The Guardian*, November 27, 1965: 3.

Norman, Barry. "Danny Kaye Here to Talk About Fagin." *Daily Mail*, January 19, 1961.

Norman, Frank. *Why Fings Went West*. London: Lemon Tree Press, 1975.

Norris, Fred. "Experiment in Touring Theatre—It's Just Like Going to the Circus." *Birmingham Mail*, January 21, 1961.

"Novel into Musical." *Times*, September 8, 1962: 9.

Novello, Ivor. *Gay's the Word*. New York: Samuel French, 1951.

"*Oliver!*" *After They Were Famous*. January 1, 2005, Tyne Tees Television (UK), Television.

Oliver! Film. Directed by Carol Reed. London: Columbia, 1968.

"'Oliver!' in It's [*sic*] Sixth Year." *Stage and Television Today*, December 9, 1965: 15.

"Oliver's All of an Eye-Catcher." *Scottish Daily Express*, January, 17, 1969.

Oliver! audition schedule, December 23, 1959. Lionel Bart Foundation Archive.

Oliver! Broadway Deluxe Collector's Edition booklet (RCA Victor Broadway, 2003), 12.

Oliver! budget. Sir Donald Albery Collection, DAT 194.002. Harry Ransom Center, University of Texas at Austin.

"Oliver! Disappoints the Swedes," *Times*, September 21, 1961: 16.

Oliver! original London production prompt book. Cameron Mackintosh Ltd. Cameron Mackintosh Archive.

Oliver! Sean Kenny set rotation chart. Cameron Mackintosh Ltd. Cameron Mackintosh Archive.

Oliver Twist: A Burletta in Two Acts. 1838. Plays from the Lord Chamberlain's Office, Volume LXXXI, 404–821. Lord Chamberlain's Plays Collection, Manuscripts, British Library.

"Oliver Twisted." *Time*, January 11, 1963: 52.

Osborne, John. *The Entertainer*. New York: Criterion Books, 1958.

Osborne, John. *Look Back in Anger*. New York: S. G. Phillips, 1957.

Osborne, John. "The Nation's Theatre." *Observer Magazine* (April 20, 1975): 20–24.

Osgerby, Bill. *Youth in Britain Since 1945*. Oxford: Blackwell, 1998.

"A Packed House for a Poor House." *New York Times*, October 30, 1922: 19.

Paget, Derek. Interview by Hannah Dodd, *British Library: Theatre Archive Project*, December 4, 2007.

Parnes, Larry. Letter to Donald Albery, April 15, 1966. Sir Donald Albery Collection, DAT 196.003. Harry Ransom Center, University of Texas at Austin.

Pearsall, Ronald. *Victorian Popular Music*. Detroit: Gale Research, 1973.

Peter Coe biographical abstract. Sir Donald Albery Collection, DAT 114.001, Folder 1. Harry Ransom Center, University of Texas at Austin.

Picker, David. Letter to Lionel Bart, September 30, 1969. Lionel Bart Archive 200102/0063, University of Bristol Theatre Collection.

Pippin, Donald. "Differences Between the London and New York Productions" (commentary track). *Oliver! Broadway Deluxe Collector's Edition*. RCA Victor Broadway, 2003.

Pippin, Donald. Interview by author, October 26, 2010.

Pointer, Michael. *Charles Dickens on the Screen*. London: Scarecrow Press, 1996.

Pulling, Christopher. *They Were Singing and What They Sang About*. London: George G. Harrap & Co., 1952.

Purl, Linda. Interview by author, November 17, 2010.

Rabey, David Ian. *English Drama Since 1940*. New York: Longman, 2003.

Ray, Trevor. Interview by author, June 26, 2010.

Read, Wendy. Letter to Jeffrey Green, August 20, 1969. Lionel Bart Archive 200102/0063, University of Bristol Theatre Collection.

Report of the Departmental Committee on the Employment of Children as Film Actors, in Theatrical Work and in Ballet, Home Department, Presented to Parliament by the Secretary of State for the Home Department by Command of His Majesty—August 1950 London: His Majesty's Stationery Office, 1950.

Review of David Lean's *Oliver Twist*. *The Sketch*, July 21, 1948: 44.

Review of J. Cormyns Carr's *Oliver Twist*. *Daily Mail*, July 11, 1905.

Review of *Oliver! Time and Tide*, London, October 9, 1968.

Review of *Oliver!* in Toho. *The Yomiuri*, July 22, 1968. Sir Donald Albery Collection, DAT 201.001. Harry Ransom Center, University of Texas at Austin.

Review of *Salad Days*, *The Sketch*, August 25, 1954.

Rich, Frank. "Mood in 'Oliver' [*sic*] Revival." *New York Times*, April 30, 1984: C11.

Richards, Jeffrey. *Imperialism and Music: Britain, 1876–1953*. New York: Manchester University Press, 2001.

Roberts, Peter. Review of *Oliver! Plays and Players* (August 1960): 17.

Robinson, Tony. Interview by author, July 24, 2010.

Romano, John. "Dickens, Psychoanalysis and Film: A Roundtable." In *Dickens on Screen*, ed. John Glavin, 11–26. Cambridge: Cambridge University Press, 2003.

Ron Moody/Georgia Brown "Contract." Sir Donald Albery Collection, DAT 196.001. Harry Ransom Center, University of Texas at Austin.

Rose, Cathryn. "How Alfie Got into the Singing Game." *Leicester Evening Mail*, July 4, 1958: 5.

Rubin, Emanuel, and John H. Baron. *Music in Jewish History and Culture*. Sterling Heights: Harmonie Park Press, 2006.

Runciman, Rosy. Email to author. June 14, 2008.

Sainsbury, Ian. "*Oliver!*—A Face from the Crowd." *Morning Telegraph* (Sheffield, Yorkshire), December 1967.

Sandbrook, Dominic. *Never Had It So Good: A History of Britain from Suez to the Beatles*. London: Little Brown, 2005.

Saunders, Peter. *The Mousetrap Man*. London: Collins, 1972.

Schlicke, Paul. *Dickens and Popular Entertainment*. London: Unwin Hyman, 1988.

Schlicke, Paul (ed.). *The Oxford Reader's Companion to Dickens*. New York: Oxford University Press, 1999.

Schmidt, Lars. Letter to Donald Albery, November 8, 1961. Sir Donald Albery Collection, DAT 195.001. Harry Ransom Center, University of Texas at Austin.

Schmidt, Lars. Letter to Lionel Bart, November 7, 1961. Lionel Bart Foundation Archive.

Scott, John L. "On Electronic Stage." *L.A. Times*, January 7, 1964: 6.

"The Screen: A Packed House for a Poor House." *New York Times*, October 30, 1922: 19.

Shellard, Dominic. *British Theatre Since the War*. New Haven: Yale University Press, 1999.

Shenton, Mark. "You Will Be Wanting More." *Sunday Express*, January 18, 2009: 64.

Shepherd, Roy. "Musical 'Oliver Twist' Spins to Success." *Sheffield Star*, September 3, 1960.

"A Shrewd Arty-Crafty Fellow Is Mr. Albery." *Evening Standard*, January, 17 1964: 8.

Shulman, Milton. "This One Could Start an Avalanche." *Evening Standard*, July 1, 1960.

Silverman, Stephen. *David Lean*. New York: H. N. Abrams, 1989.

Silverstone, Ben. "The Exclamation Factor." *Jewish Chronicle*, November 18, 2005: 23.

Sinfield, Alan. "Queen's English." In *The Revision of Englishness*, eds. David Rogers and John McLeod, 30–39. Manchester: Manchester University Press, 2004.

Sinfield, Alan. "The Theatre and Its Audience." In *Society and Literature, 1945–1970*, ed. Alan Sinfield, 173–98. New York: Holmes & Meier, 1983.

Singer, Barry. *Ever After*. New York: Applause, 2004.

"Sir Donald Albery." *The Independent*, September 16, 1988.

"Sir Donald Albery: Theatre Impresario of Catholic Tastes." *Times*, September 15, 1988: 14.

Smith, Cecil. "Clap Hands! It's a British Musical." *Daily Express*, August 6, 1954.

Snelson, John. " 'We Said We Wouldn't Look Back': British Musical Theatre, 1935–1960." In *The Cambridge Companion to the Musical*, eds. William A. Everett and Paul R. Laird, 101–19. Cambridge: Cambridge University Press, 2002.

Speegle, Paul. " 'Oliver!' Is a Smasher." *San Francisco News Call Bulletin*, September 26, 1962.

Spencer, Charles. "A Travesty of Dickens, and Fantastic Showbiz." *Daily Telegraph*, January 15, 2009: 3.

Stafford, David and Caroline Stafford, *Fings Ain't Wot They Used T'Be: The Lionel Bart Story*. London: Omnibus Press, 2011.

"The Stage Designer Who Makes One Sit Up." *Times*, January 24, 1966: 14.

Stage Manager's report on Moody-Brown feud, April 6, 1961. Sir Donald Albery Theatre Collection, DAT 196.001. Harry Ransom Center, University of Texas at Austin.

Steele, Arthur. " 'Oliver,' [*sic*] the Mach 1 Musical," 3. *Oliver!* clippings. BFI Archive.

Steele, Tommy. *Bermondsey Boy: Memories of a Forgotten World*. London: Michael Joseph, 2006.

Stegmann, Vera. "Brecht Contra Wagner: The Evolution of the Epic Music Theater." In *A Bertolt Brecht Reference Companion*, edited by Siegfried Mews, 238–60. Westport: Greenwood Press, 1997.

Sternfeld, Jessica. *The Megamusical*. Bloomington: Indiana University Press, 2006.

Stevenson, John. "The Sound of Success Comes Back to Bart." *Daily Mail: Manchester Edition*, November 23, 1965.

Steyn, Mark. *Broadway Babies Say Goodnight: Musicals Then and Now*. New York: Routledge, 2000.

Storey Smith, Warren. "Musik von Kurt Weill wird als ungewöhnlich bezeichnet." In *Kurt Weill Musik und Theater* by Kurt Weill, 338–39. Berlin: Henschelverlag Kunst und Gesellschaft, 1990.

Strong, Roy. "The Years Before." In *British Theatre Design: The Modern Age*, ed. John Goodwin, 17–21. New York: St. Martin's Press, 1989.

"Sympathetic Fagin Shocks Jews." *Times*, March 4, 1966: 15.

Taubman, Howard. " 'Oliver Twist' as a Musical." *New York Times*, January 8, 1963: 5.

Taylor, John Russell. "Dickens Musical Makes a Disappointing Film." *Times*. September 26, 1968: 15.

Taylor, Paul. "Hard Day at the Workhouse." *The Independent*. December 10, 1994: 28.

"Theatre Check." *Times*, December 18, 1994: 8.46.

"Theatre Worker." *The Observer*, March 15, 1959: 11.

Theatre Workshop. *Oh What a Lovely War*. London: Methuen, 2000.

"Theatrical Manager with an Open Mind." *Times*, March 20, 1961: 3.

"This Fagin Is Unique." *Jewish Chronicle*, July 8, 1960: 26.

Thomas, Bob. "Will U.S. Fans Cheer Dickens in Musical?" *Traveler* (Boston), August 9, 1962.

Thompson, Gordon. *Please Please Me: Sixties British Pop, Inside Out*. Oxford: Oxford University Press, 2008.

"Tokyo Has a Yen for 'Oliver!'" *Daily Cinema*, October 1, 1968.

Transcribed conversation between Donald Albery of Donmar Productions and Davenport Lyons, solicitor to Jock Jacobsen, May 25, 1961. Sir Donald Albery Collection, DAT 194.003. Harry Ransom Center, University of Texas at Austin.

Transcribed conversation between Lionel Bart and Carol Reed, January 18, 1967. Lionel Bart Foundation Archive.

Trilling, Ossa. "The New English Realism." *Tulane Drama Review*, 7, no. 2 (Winter 1962): 184–93.

Trewin, J. C. "Thomas, Oliver, and Eugene." *Illustrated London News*, July 16, 1960.

Trewin, J. C. "What the Dickens!" *Birmingham Post*, July 6, 1960.

Tynan, Kenneth. "The Broadway Package." *The Observer*, May 4, 1958: 15.

Tynan, Kenneth. "New Amalgam." *The Observer*, October 19, 1958: 19.

Tynan, Kenneth. "The Under-Belly of Laughter." *The Observer*, July 3, 1960: 25.

Tynan, Kenneth. *A View of the English Stage 1944–1963*. London: Davis-Poynter, 1975.

Tynan, Kenneth. "The Voice of the Young." *The Observer*, May 13, 1956: 11.

Tzelniker, Anna. *Three for the Price of One*. London: Spiro Institute, 1991.

"Under Wraps," *Daily Telegraph*, December 29, 1977.

Vineberg, Dusty. "Theatre Designer Encourages Innovation." Misc. Publicity Scrapbook, Sean Kenny Archive, Box 2. Victoria and Albert Museum Theatre Collections.

Vlock, Deborah. *Dickens, Novel Reading, and the Victorian Popular Theatre*. New York: Cambridge University Press, 1998.

Walsh, David, and Len Platt. *Musical Theatre and American Culture*. Westport: Praeger, 2003.

Walter, Ernest. "London's Noisy Music Halls Embodied the Cockney Spirit." *Vancouver Daily Province*, September 26, 1942: 3.

Wapshott, Nicholas. *Carol Reed: A Biography*. New York: Knopf, 1994.

Ward, Paul. *Britishness Since 1870*. New York: Routledge, 2004.

Wardle, Irving. "*Oliver!* Albery." *Times*. December 29, 1977: 5.

Wardle, Irving. "A View of the Stage." *New Society*, July 13, 1976: 56.

Weaver, Harry. "The *Newest* Artful Dodger." *Scottish Daily Mail*, September 20, 1968.

Weill, Kurt. "Note by Kurt Weill." In *The Threepenny Opera*, by Bertolt Brecht, 98–99. New York: Arcade, 1994.

Wershba, Joseph. "Sweet Georgia Brown." *New York Post Magazine*, May 5, 1963: 2.

Wesker, Arnold. *Chicken Soup with Barley*. In *The Wesker Trilogy*, by Arnold Wesker, 9–77. Random House: New York, 1960.

Wesker, Arnold. *The Kitchen*. London: Jonathan Cape, 1966.

Whitty, Fiona. "The Girl on a Motorbike Who Sang All Oliver's Songs." *The Mail on Sunday*, December 19, 2004: 29.

"Who's Who: Sean Kenny's." *The Observer*. July 31, 1960: 19.

Wickstrom, Gordon M. "The Heroic Dimension in Brendan Behan's 'The Hostage'." *Educational Theatre Journal*, 22, no. 4 (December 1970): 406–11.

Wilmut, Roger. *Kindly Leave the Stage! The Story of Variety, 1919–1960*. London: Methuen, 1985.

Wilson, Sandy. *The Boy Friend*. New York: Dutton, 1955.

Worsley, T. C. "Oliver," [*sic*]. *London Financial Times*, July 1, 1960.

Worth, George J. *Dickensian Melodrama*. Lawrence: University of Kansas Press, 1978.

Wright, Allen. "'Oliver' [*sic*] First Musical by Thrills Expert." *Scotsman*, December 9, 1968.

Wright, Carol. "A Tough Line with Fantasy." *Times*, September 22, 1967: 11.

Writ between Donmar Productions Limited (Plaintiff) and Lionel Bart, Montpelier Arts and Enterprises Limited, Brookfield Productions Limited, Lionel Bart Limited, and Oliver Promotions Limited (Defendants), May 21, 1964. Sir Donald Albery Collection, DAT 194.003. Harry Ransom Center, University of Texas at Austin.

Zambrano, A.L. *Dickens and Film*. New York: Gordon Press, 1977.

INDEX

adaptation, theories of, 2, 10–11, 126, 134–135, 189, 200–201, 218n6, 261n71
See also fidelity criticism
Albery, Donald, 8, 50–51, 55, 91, 92, 97, 99, 104, 105, 217–218n19, 253n37
  conflicts over film adaptation of *Oliver!*, 181–183
  and international productions of *Oliver!*, 160–161, 162–168, 252n11
  investment in *Oliver!*, 51–52, 53 table 2.1, 228–229n31
  and Joan Littlewood, 51, 52, 55, 102–103, 228n23
Albery, Ian, 50, 51, 87
American musical,
  American traits, 1, 25, 26, 30, 122, 174–175, 221n67, 226n183
  compared with English musical, 25, 26–29, 30, 43, 49–50, 124, 148, 169, 241n115
  dominance in postwar England, 4, 25–26, 29, 108–109, 221n84
  influence on Lionel Bart, 2, 41, 43, 49, 54–55, 123–124, 148
  and integration, 26–27, 41, 49–50, 54, 114, 129, 134, 135, 136, 221nn72–74
  See also English musical
  See also megamusical
Anderson, Benedict, 3, 110
angry young men,
  and Englishness, 20, 107–108, 110–111, 121
  influence in the postwar theatre, 21–22, 33, 107
  as marketing device, 22, 107–108, 220n47
  values, 19–20, 23, 108, 111

  See also Osborne, John
  See also Wesker, Arnold
anti-Semitism, 31, 75, 152, 156, 162, 176, 179, 186, 220n42
  accusations against *Oliver!*, 165, 168, 169, 176–177, 256n100
  in David Lean's *Oliver Twist*, 15, 17, 97, 162
  See also Fagin
Artful Dodger, 77, 104, 153, 188, 259n47
  characterization in Dickens's novel, 151, 152–153, 232n66
  deleted scenes and songs, 60, 61–62, 66, 69, 74, 232n66, 241n110
  and Fagin, 152–154, 155, 187, 193, 241n110, 251–252n61
  fate, 72, 74, 75, 193, 235n105
  working-class ethos, 113, 114–115, 143, 146
  See also Wild, Jack
"As Long as He Needs Me", 60, 71, 124, 149–151
  See also Nancy
authorship, concepts of, 37–38, 56–59, 134–135

Bailey, Peter, 4, 113, 120, 246n93, 246n102, 250n38
Bart, Lionel, 30–32, 48–49, 105, 123–124, 129, 132 fig. 4.1, 132–133, 212 fig. E1, 222–223n102, 242n7
  approach to Dickens's *Oliver Twist*, 49, 55, 63, 65, 124–126, 127, 134–135, 189
  and the Artful Dodger, 72, 74, 113, 151–153, 155, 193
  as author of *Oliver!*, 56–59,
  and cockney language/culture, 28, 31, 39, 40, 43, 223n124